CONSTITUTIONAL SEPARATION OF POWERS: CASES & COMMENTARY

CONSTITUTIONAL SEPARATION OF POWERS: CASES & COMMENTARY

By

Thomas M. Beck

VANDEPLAS PUBLISHING

UNITED STATES OF AMERICA

Constitutional separation of powers: cases & commentary

Beck, Thomas M.

Published by:

Vandeplas Publishing - December 2010

801 International Parkway, 5th Floor
Lake Mary, FL. 32746
USA

www.vandeplaspublishing.com

ISBN: 978-1-60042-132-7

For Amanda, World's Greatest Wife.

Table Of Contents

About The Author

After graduating from the University of Virginia School of Law in 1992, Thomas Beck spent the next 16 years in private practice with the global law firm Jones Day, during which time he represented clients in federal and state courts across the United States. In 2008, after being nominated by President George W. Bush and unanimously confirmed by the United States Senate, he became Chairman of the Federal Labor Relations Authority (FLRA), an independent, quasi-judicial federal agency. Mr. Beck is currently a Member of the FLRA, in which capacity he has impartially adjudicated, and participated in published decisions resolving, nearly 500 legal disputes. He has taught courses on separation of powers and the legislative process at the George Mason University School of Law. As this book goes to print, he has been nominated by President Barack Obama to be a Member of the National Mediation Board and his nomination is pending in the Senate.

Author's Note

Several years ago, when the George Mason University School of Law first invited me to teach a course as an adjunct professor, I said that I would enjoy doing so if they would allow me to teach a subject that was not within my regular area of practice, which consisted primarily of representing large companies in civil litigation. The law school's administration agreed. So, for the next two years, I taught a semester-long course on the legislative process. Before I could instruct bright and eager law students on this subject, I first had to teach it to myself. In the process of doing so, and in discussing the subject with my students, I learned much that I had not previously known about the processes of the Congress in particular and the workings of the federal government in general.

At that point, the Bush Administration's War on Terror was in full swing and the Supreme Court was rendering decisions that -- in ways unexpected by many observers -- sharply limited the power of the commander in chief. These are the decisions discussed at the end of this book.

As a result of both studying the role of the Legislative Branch and watching the interplay of the President, the Congress, and the Supreme Court in the War on Terror, I developed a strong interest in the separation of powers principles that are built into our constitutional form of government. Consequently, I put aside the course on legislative process, outlined a new course on separation of powers, and taught this new course for the next two years.

This book is a direct result of my experience teaching separation of powers. After studying the subject myself and then teaching the course twice, I felt I had the makings of a decent casebook. As is probably obvious from its length, this book is not intended to be a comprehensive treatment of all possible aspects of separation of powers law and principles; such a work would require several volumes and thousands of pages. Rather, this single volume is intended to offer a useful overview of what I consider to be the most important and interesting issues within the study of separation of powers. It is also designed to be a casebook from which an informative and interesting semester-long course on the subject can be taught.

The reader can, of course, judge whether I have achieved what I intended.

Thomas M. Beck
November 2010

CHAPTER ONE:
HISTORICAL BACKGROUND OF
GOVERNMENTAL SEPARATION OF POWERS

THE HISTORICAL ANTECEDENTS

The government of the United States is characterized by the "separation of powers" among its three principal components, the Legislative Branch, the Executive Branch, and the Judicial Branch. The phrase "separation of powers" has become a shorthand way of acknowledging that each branch has its own sphere of responsibility and authority and that, in general, these respective spheres do not -- and should not -- interfere with one another. But, while the government of the United States is renowned for the separation of powers among its three co-equal branches, it is hardly the first or only government to have governing authority distributed among different governmental components.

More than 2000 years ago, the governmental authority of the Roman Republic was shared among various bodies and officials, such as the Senate, legislative assemblies, and magistrates. The Roman Senate was a deliberative body that controlled fiscal matters and foreign policy and was, therefore, the predominant political force during most of the nearly five centuries of the Republic. Two consuls were selected from among the senators to wield executive power, principally in the form of managing military affairs. The consuls (acting jointly -- one could veto the decisions of the other) were the closest thing to a chief executive in ancient Rome. Other domestic executive functions were performed by a variety of magistrates elected by legislative assemblies of the people. As the name suggests, legislative assemblies also enacted laws that governed everyday life in the Republic. The assemblies were not representative bodies; rather, like the democratic assemblies of ancient Athens, they were venues for direct participation and voting by all citizens. Membership in such assemblies was organized according to social status -- that is, plebeian or patrician; by geography; and by a citizen's status as a civilian or a member of the military. Other officials, called "tribunes," provided a further check on the exercise of governmental power against plebeians. By bodily interposing themselves (or "interceding") against the actions of magistrates, tribunes could effectively veto perceived abuses against the plebeians.

Two millennia later, political theorist John Locke wrote about separate legislative and executive powers in his *Second Treatise on Civil Government*, published in 1690. Although Locke's writings were known to and inspired some of the American Framers, he did not envision the three co-equal branches of government reflected in the Constitution. Locke viewed the Legislative Branch as the "supreme power" or "supreme authority." He explained (in Chapter 13, Section 15) that "the legislative must needs be the supreme, and all other powers . . . derived from and subordinate to it." Because the legislature best reflects the collective will of the people and is responsible for policy-making, it should be the predominant force within the government. Although the legislature was supreme in Locke's governmental scheme, he also understood that there must be an executive who is responsible for enforcing the laws and protecting the people, because the legislature cannot be assembled at all times. Locke did not see the judiciary playing a substantial role in governing.

A few decades later, the French political philosopher Montesquieu proposed both a distinct separation of power between the legislature and the executive, and a significant role for a separate and independent judiciary. In his *The Spirit of the Laws*, published in 1748, he explains (in Book 11):

> When the legislative and executive powers are united in the same person, or in the same body of magistrates, there can be no liberty; because apprehensions may arise, lest the same monarch or senate should enact tyrannical laws, to execute them in a tyrannical manner.
>
> Again, there is no liberty, if the judiciary power be not separated from the legislative and executive. Were it joined with the legislative, the life and liberty of the subject would be exposed to arbitrary control; for the judge would be then the legislator. Were it joined to the executive power, the judge might behave with violence and oppression.

Roughly 40 years after *The Spirit of the Laws* was published, the most vocal proponents of the United States Constitution credited Montesquieu with the concept of constitutional separation of powers among three branches. In Federalist No. 47, Montesquieu is referred to as "the oracle who is always consulted and cited on this subject."

CONTRAST TO PARLIAMENTARY SYSTEMS

Notwithstanding Montesquieu's vision of three roughly co-equal branches, it is remarkable that the Framers crafted the constitutional structure as they did, given that the system of representative government with which they were most familiar was the parliamentary system of Great Britain. The three-branch system of the

United States is quite different from the typical parliamentary form of government found in other representative democracies around the world.

In a parliamentary system, the legislature is supreme, as Locke advocated. Generally, there is no separate executive with real power to check the actions of the Legislative Branch. There may be a head of state, such as a benign monarch or a president, but these officials have no power (or only nominal power) to veto legislation, make appointments to senior positions, or otherwise exercise the sort of executive power that the President of the United States routinely exercises. In the parliamentary system, the head of government (as opposed to the symbolic head of state) is a member of the legislature, drawn from that body to act as prime minister. Other senior officials, such as cabinet secretaries, are also drawn from the parliamentary body to take on executive responsibilities. Thus, there is no executive who is separately elected by the people and independent of the legislature. Further, in most parliamentary systems, there is no judicial review -- and occasional invalidation -- of legislative enactments.

Although parliamentary systems lack the checks on legislative power that are represented in the United States by an independent and powerful executive and judiciary, there are other checks inherent in these systems. Parliamentary governments are often coalition governments in which no single party or interest enjoys overwhelming influence. Further, if the majority coalition or party takes steps that alienate a substantial number of members, it risks a no-confidence vote and possible loss of power. Also, parliamentary systems often feature bicameralism (two differently composed chambers must agree before the parliamentary body can take action) and federalism (governmental authority is divided between a federal government and provincial or other regional governments).

THE FAILED ARTICLES OF CONFEDERATION

The Framers eschewed the parliamentary system with which they were most familiar, but in doing so, they did not initially settle on the federal governmental structure reflected in the Constitution. Their first effort at a governing structure for the new nation took form in the Articles of Confederation, which was in place from 1781 to 1788.

Because of the deep skepticism with which the Framers viewed governmental power, the Articles government was not a strong central government that effectively unified the former colonies that created it. The basic premise of the Articles government was that it would enable the former colonies to present a unified front when dealing with the rest of the world, but domestically, the most important aspects of governing were left to the individual states. The central government was empowered to carry out military action on behalf of the member states, and to negotiate treaties on behalf of the states as a group. However, the Articles government had little power to act domestically. For example, it could not regulate commerce among the states. Further, it was not authorized to levy direct taxes; for revenue, it relied on essentially voluntary payments from the states. Because the states were hobbled by debts they had contracted during the Revolutionary War, payments to the federal government were not forthcoming with the frequency or in the amounts necessary for the government to function effectively.

The weakness of the central government under the Articles manifested itself in specific ways that aroused dissatisfaction among many. It was unable to enforce elements of the Treaty of Paris that formally ended the Revolutionary War, such as returning to former British loyalists lands that had been confiscated by the states, or ending British occupation of the Northwest Territory. It was unable to prevent Spanish interference with free navigation of the Mississippi River.

Ultimately, the glaring ineffectiveness of the central government was demonstrated by its non-responsiveness to Shays' Rebellion in Massachusetts. With states and individuals laboring under heavy debts from the war, over several months in 1786 and 1787, farmers in Massachusetts protested against foreclosures and confiscations of their property. Receiving little relief from the legislature or the courts, the protesters, led by farmer and Revolutionary War veteran Daniel Shays, moved to seize weapons from the Springfield Armory. The local militia commander responsible for responding to the uprising sought permission to use the weapons contained in the armory. His request was denied by Secretary of War Henry Knox, who believed that approval from Congress was required, but Congress was not in session and was therefore unable to grant such approval. Under the Articles, there was no president or similar executive who could act to enforce laws or maintain security in the absence of Congress. Acting on his own initiative, the militia commander accessed the armory's weapons and dispersed the protesters; however, the point was made that the central government was little help in maintaining domestic security.

There were other complaints about the Articles government that went beyond its military weakness. Commercial interests wanted regular, enforceable tariffs on imports, and a single, reliable currency. Others wanted the central government to assume the war debts of the several states. Still others wanted a more active and more inward-looking central government that would facilitate westward expansion.

THE PUSH FOR A NEW CONSTITUTION: THE FEDERALIST PAPERS

The various grievances against the Articles government motivated some to advocate for a stronger central government -- but one still restrained by internal checks and balances. The first step toward a new constitution occurred when delegates from several states met in Annapolis, Maryland in 1786 in an effort to regularize and facilitate trade among the states. Too few states were represented at this Annapolis Convention to modify the Articles, but they produced a report -- sent to the Congress and the legislatures of all states -- recommending that a broader convention be held to address the infirmities of the Articles. The result was the Constitutional Convention, which gathered in Philadelphia in 1787.

Although the very purpose of the Convention was to address the weaknesses that had been observed in the Articles of Confederation, there were those among the Convention's delegates who were skeptical of -- and who ultimately opposed -- the vision of a more muscular federal government that evolved during the Convention's debates. These Anti-Federalists, led by Patrick Henry, preferred the regime under the Articles, which left supremacy on domestic matters to the individual states. They also feared that a separate and perpetual executive would eventually become a monarch. Once the new Constitution was finalized by the Convention and presented to the states for ratification, the same fundamental debate that had consumed the Philadelphia Convention -- whether to create a more powerful federal government -- began in the states.

In late 1787 and early 1788, several state legislatures voted by large margins to ratify the new Constitution; however, anti-federalism remained particularly strong in New York, where the governor and much of the legislature opposed the new Constitution. In response, supporters of the Constitution, known as Federalists, argued vigorously for ratification. Under the pen name Publius, three Federalist leaders, James Madison (principal author of the Constitution and fourth President of the United States), Alexander Hamilton (first Secretary of the Treasury), and John Jay (first Chief Justice of the United States), published a series of articles in New York newspapers arguing for ratification. These Federalist Papers are by far the most extensive and authoritative contemporaneous commentary on the Constitution and the sort of government that its proponents envisioned. Among other things, they explained the need for, and the workings of, the critical checks and balances among the three branches of the new government.

Federalist 48

In Federalist 48, Madison remarks that the Legislative, Executive and Judicial Branches, although separate, are to some degree "connected and blended as to give to each a constitutional control over the others." Consistent with Locke's notions of legislative supremacy, Madison also explains that experience has demonstrated:

> The legislative department is everywhere extending the sphere of its activity, and drawing all power into its impetuous vortex . . . It's constitutional powers being at once more extensive, and less susceptible of precise limits, it can, with the greater facility, mask, under complicated and indirect measures, the encroachments which it makes on the co-ordinate departments.

Thus, Federalist 48 focuses on concerns about abuse of power by the legislature. Madison goes on to offer specific examples, drawn from the experiences of Virginia and Pennsylvania, of legislatures exceeding their proper authority because they controlled the budgets of the other departments and because the Executive and Judicial Branches lacked adequate power to counter legislative encroachments.

Federalist 48 acknowledges that legislative power is particularly difficult to check because, when compared to the executive and the judiciary, the limits on its scope are less certain. Courts are reactive rather than active; they can address only matters that are presented to them by litigants. The executive's ability to act is limited by the scope of existing law; that is, he can "execute" only within the legal regime established by the legislature. In contrast, absent express limitations on its authority, the Legislative Branch can extend its influence into whatever new areas of policy-making it wishes. Further, in a republic, where the citizens' participation in government is through a relatively small group of elected representatives, overreaching by the legislative body is not checked by its ponderous size, as would be the case in a pure democracy.

The conclusion of Federalist 48 is that "a mere demarcation on parchment of the constitutional limits of the several departments is not a sufficient guard against those encroachments which lead to a tyrannical concentration of all the powers of government in the same hands." In other words, it is not enough merely to *tell* any branch of government what its boundaries are; rather, meaningful limits are set by allocating real, countervailing power to the other branches

Federalist 51

The title of Federalist 51 states its thesis: "The Structure of the Government Must Furnish the Proper Checks and Balances Between the Different Departments." The essay explains that balance and stability must be maintained

> by so contriving the interior structure of the government as that its several constituent parts may, by their mutual relations, be the means of keeping each other in their proper places.
>
> * * *
>
> [T]he great security against a gradual concentration of the several powers in the same department, consists in giving to those who administer each department the necessary constitutional means and personal motives to resist encroachments of the others. The provision for defense must in this, as in all other cases, be made commensurate to the danger of attack. Ambition must be made to counteract ambition.

Nevertheless, despite the checks that are naturally provided by having an independent executive and judiciary, "in a republican government, the legislative authority necessarily predominates." Therefore, bicameralism and the possibility of executive veto act as further limits on legislative activity. Further, Federalist 51 reflects the Framers' expectation that the natural factionalism within a pluralistic society would act as an ever-present brake on the legislature going too far in any single direction:

> [S]o many separate descriptions of citizens . . . will render an unjust combination of a majority of the whole very improbable, if not impracticable . . . the society itself will be broken into so many parts, interests, and classes of citizens, that the rights of individuals, or of the minority, will be in little danger from interested combinations of the majority.

CHAPTER TWO:
INTRODUCTION TO CONSTITUTIONAL CHECKS AND BALANCES

THE PRINCIPAL CONSTITUTIONAL CHECKS ON THE THREE BRANCHES OF GOVERNMENT

The Constitution that was drafted at the Philadelphia Convention and advocated for in the Federalist Papers created a federal government with three co-equal branches: a bicameral legislature, an executive authority embodied in a single official elected separately from the legislature, and an independent judiciary designed to be largely insulated from politics. These branches, their powers, and the limitations upon them, are set forth in Articles I, II and III of the Constitution.

The Checks On The Legislative Branch

Bicameralism. A fundamental check on the activity of the legislature is that it is bicameral. An act of the legislature must be approved by each of two chambers, the members of which are elected at different times by different constituencies. (Indeed, for the first 125 years under the Constitution -- prior to the ratification of the Seventeenth Amendment -- senators were appointed by their state legislatures rather then elected by the citizens of their states.) The vast majority of legislative proposals offered during any Congress are not able to garner the support of both chambers.

Presentment and veto. Before an act becomes law, it must be presented to the executive -- the President, who may approve it or veto it. An act vetoed by the President may become law only if it is then passed by two-thirds super-majorities of both congressional chambers.

Judicial review. The Constitution provides what amounts to life tenure for federal judges once they are confirmed to the bench, and also provides that their compensation cannot be reduced. These provisions allow the judiciary to act independently of congressional or other political influence. And, as Chief Justice John Marshall explained in the landmark decision of *Marbury v. Madison*, 5 U.S. 137 (1803), "it is emphatically the province and duty of the judicial department to say what the law is." According to *Marbury* -- and according to custom and consensus over the course of more than two centuries since, if an act of Congress is inconsistent with the Constitution, the act fails. Although the Constitution does not expressly provide for this sort of judicial review -- and occasional invalidation -- of legislation, it was intended by the Framers. As Alexander Hamilton noted in Federalist 78:

> [T]he courts were designed to be an intermediate body between the people and the legislature, in order, among other things, to keep the latter within the limits assigned to their authority. A constitution is, in fact, and must be regarded by the judges, as a fundamental law. It therefore belongs to them to ascertain its meaning, as well as the meaning of any particular act proceeding from the legislative body. If there should happen to be an irreconcilable variance between the two, that which has the superior obligation and validity ought, of course, to be preferred; or, in other words, the Constitution ought to be preferred to the statute, the intention of the people to the intention of their agents.

Absence of executive power. The Legislative Branch lacks the means to enforce its own acts. Congress does not command the armed forces, does not direct law enforcement, and does not supervise the work of the President or other Executive Branch officials tasked with enforcing the laws that Congress enacts. Further, although, under Article II, Section 2, the Senate must approve (or may disapprove) the President's appointment of senior officials within the Executive Branch, it is not the appointing authority. By establishing separate and co-equal legislative and executive functions, the Framers divorced policy*making* (that is, legislating) from policy *enforcement*.

Enumerated powers. Although the scope of permissible congressional action has undoubtedly expanded far beyond what the Framers intended, largely through broad judicial interpretations of the Interstate Commerce Clause found in Article I, Section 8 ("the Congress shall have the power . . . to regulate commerce . . . among the several states"), the federal legislature is nevertheless a body with specific, enumerated powers rather than plenary power. The Framers intended that the legislature created by the Constitution would be able to engage in policymaking only in certain, carefully prescribed areas.

Prohibition on bills of attainder and ex post facto lawmaking. Section 9 of Article I contains specific prohibitions on the types of laws that Congress may pass. In particular, Congress is not permitted to punish persons legislatively who have not been found guilty of wrongdoing through the judicial process. Similarly, Congress is generally prohibited from passing legislation that retroactively criminalizes or otherwise punishes conduct that was not illegal when it occurred.

The Checks On The Executive Branch

Lacks power of the purse. Under Article II, Section 3, the President is obligated generally to "take care that the laws be faithfully executed"; however, he has available to do so only the resources that are given to him by the Legislative Branch. Similarly, while the President is commander in chief of the armed forces, the scale and the equipping of those armed forces is determined by the Legislative Branch. Aside from impeachment (see below), perhaps the greatest constitutional check on an overreaching executive is the ability of a determined Congress to constrain his actions by limiting his resources.

President does not declare war. Article I, Section 8 unequivocally grants to the people's representatives in Congress the power "to declare war." While many presidents have initiated military action without a formal declaration of war (see Chapter Nine), very large, long-term commitments of troops abroad still require congressional authorization. Thus, although the prosecution of armed conflict is left to the President as commander in chief, the fundamental decision whether to enter into such a conflict is allocated to the legislature.

Senate approval of treaties. The executive may enter into agreements with foreign powers, but such agreements only become binding treaties if they are ratified by a two-thirds majority in the Senate.

Senate approval of senior officials. The President selects the "officers of the United States" who will assist him with his executive responsibilities, and he also selects federal judges; however, such selectees may take office only upon confirmation by the Senate (except in the relatively infrequent instances where the President installs a selectee through a recess appointment).

Congressional override of veto. While the executive's veto is a check on the legislature, the legislature may override a veto if both chambers are able to muster a two-thirds super-majority. If there is sufficient will within the Legislative Branch, it can enact legislation that the President deems unwise; it may even direct the President to take action that he does not wish to take. Once a law is enacted -- even if it is over his veto, the President is obliged to "take care that [it is] faithfully executed."

Judicial review. Just as the Judicial Branch may review and pass judgment upon the work of the legislature, it may also review the action of the Executive Branch. One prominent historical example of such review is found in the *Youngstown* case discussed below, in which the Supreme Court invalidated President Truman's seizure of the nation's steel mills.

Impeachment. The ultimate check on the President (and other Executive Branch officials) is that he may face impeachment and removal from office at the hands of the legislature. As was demonstrated by the case of *Nixon v. United States* (see pages 227-31), there are very few -- and perhaps no -- legal standards or requirements for impeachment. It is a fundamentally political decision. As Gerald Ford remarked in reference his unsuccessful effort to impeach Justice William O. Douglas when Ford was the Republican Leader in the House of Representatives, "an impeachable offense is whatever a majority of the House of Representatives considers it to be at a given moment in history."

The Checks On The Judicial Branch

The judiciary is reactive only. The most profound limitation on the influence of the judiciary stems not so much from the tripartite structure of the government as from the essential role of the judiciary: It cannot initiate policy changes based on its own whim. Rather, it can act only if and when litigants present it with a dispute to be resolved, and then the nature and scope of the judiciary's response is bounded by the nature and scope of the dispute.

Executive and legislative involvement in judicial appointments. Once a federal judge takes the bench, he or she is not accountable to either of the political branches. This critical attribute of independence allows the Judicial Branch to act as an impartial check on the two other branches. However, one becomes a federal judge only if the President and the Senate first agree on the judge's suitability for the bench. The political branches do not oversee the work of judges, but they act as gatekeepers in determining who may become a judge.

Lacks power of the purse. That the Legislative Branch controls the purse strings is a check on the Judicial Branch just as it is a check on the Executive Branch. Although the compensation of judges "shall not be diminished during their continuance in office" (Article III, Section 1), the financial resources of the courts is something that is determined by Congress, not the courts themselves.

Impeachment. As is the case with members of the Executive Branch, members of the Judicial Branch may be removed from office if they fail to demonstrate "good behaviour" (Article III, Section 1).

No direct enforcement power. While the federal courts generally have broad authority to issue orders and direct remedies as necessary to resolve the matters before them, they lack the practical means to enforce their own rulings; they do not control armies or even police forces. Like the enforcement of legislative enactments, the enforcement of judicial rulings is left to another branch -- the executive. In theory, a President might simply refuse to enforce or abide by a ruling with which he strenuously disagrees, particularly a ruling on a matter of great national importance. In at least one historical circumstance, a President did just that. After suspending the writ of habeas corpus early in the Civil War, Lincoln ignored judicial rulings that denied him the right unilaterally to suspend habeas corpus – most notably, the ruling in *Ex parte Merryman*, 17. F. Cas. 144 (1861) by Chief Justice Roger Taney while riding circuit.

THE RELATIVE POWERS OF THE POLITICAL BRANCHES AND THE CLASSIC CASE: *YOUNGSTOWN*

History shows that the courts accord substantial deference to the exercise of Executive Branch power and only very infrequently invalidate executive action as illegal. Two rare instances in which the courts nullified executive orders are referenced below. In the second instance, discussed at pages 54-58, the D.C. Circuit determined that a Clinton Administration order relating to government contracting was inconsistent with American labor policy as reflected in the National Labor Relations Act. *Chamber of Commerce v. Reich*, 74 F.3d 1322 (D.C. Cir. 1996). The first instance is the Supreme Court's signal pronouncement on the separation of powers between the Executive and Legislative Branches of government. This is the decision in *Youngstown Sheet & Tube Co. v. Sawyer*, 343 U.S. 579 (1952). This case -- and particularly Justice Robert Jackson's concurring opinion -- has often been the lens through which subsequent separation of powers questions are analyzed. For example, Chief Justice John Roberts, during his September 2005 Senate confirmation hearings, explained that "the framework for analyzing [a conflict between the legislature and the executive over an exercise of executive power] is in the Youngstown Sheet and Tube case, the famous case coming out of President Truman's seizure of the steel mills . . . and the framework set forth in Justice Jackson's concurring opinion, which is the opinion that has sort of set the stage for subsequent cases . . ."

With the United States' involvement in the Korean War as the backdrop, the case arose from a dispute between steel manufacturers and the United Steelworkers of America, the union that represented employees of the major steel manufacturers. During collective bargaining, and even after attempted conciliation by the Federal Mediation and Conciliation Service and the Wage Stabilization Board, the companies and the union were unable to reach agreement on new terms and conditions of employment. On April 4, 1952, the union announced that a strike would begin on April 9. President Truman, believing that such a work stoppage in steel production would jeopardize national defense, invoked his inherent executive authority and authority as commander in chief, and ordered Secretary of Commerce Sawyer to seize and operate the steel mills. President Truman elected not to rely upon the "national emergency" provisions of the Taft-Hartley Act of 1947 because he had opposed and vetoed the legislation (which was then passed over his veto). The President notified Congress of his action, and Congress offered no legislative response.

The steel companies challenged the seizures in district court, asserting that there was no statutory or constitutional authority for the President to take such an extraordinary step. Notably, in the district court proceeding, Assistant Attorney General Holmes Baldridge argued that the President's executive authority is essentially unlimited:

> Judge Pine: Do you contend that the Executive has unlimited power in an emergency?
>
> Baldridge: If you carry it to its logical conclusion, that's what it is. But there are two limitations—one is the ballot box; the other is impeachment.
>
> Judge Pine: Is it your concept of Government . . . that the Constitution limits Congress, and it limits the Judiciary but does not limit the Executive?
>
> Baldridge: That's the way we read the Constitution.
>
> Judge Pine: Do you mean that if the President empowered [Secretary of Commerce] Sawyer to take you into custody and execute you, you'd have no power to enjoin him?
>
> Baldridge: I'll have to think that one over.

Baldridge's bold assertions about unlimited executive power played prominently in the appellate arguments of the steel companies. A six-justice majority of the Supreme Court rejected these assertions, and even the three dissenting justices who were willing to uphold the seizure of the mills were not willing to do so based on theories of unchecked -- and uncheckable -- executive power.

A half century later, another President was engaged in another armed conflict abroad, and his lawyers made similar claims of executive power so extensive that it trumped any legislative efforts to restrict the conduct of the executive.

In the aftermath of the devastating terrorist attacks of September 11, 2001, the Bush Administration commenced what it often referred to as the War on Terror. Many questions about the scope of executive power and its limits arose as a result of the War on Terror. Foremost among these was how detainees were to be treated, what laws applied to their treatment, and who had the authority to decide such matters. Early on, lawyers in the Department of Justice's Office of Legal Counsel were asked to advise the Administration on these questions, and some of that advice took the form of legal memoranda that were later severely criticized and eventually disavowed by the Administration. Distilled to their essence, the conclusion of these memos was that, when invoking his authority as commander in chief, the President's power is plenary and beyond any legal limitation that the Congress might seek to impose. Here is a representative excerpt:

Memorandum for William J. Haynes, II

General Counsel for the Department of Defense

March 14, 2003

[Authored by John C. Yoo, Deputy Assistant Attorney General]

> [The memo explains that it is intended to address "the legal standards governing military interrogations of unlawful alien combatants held outside the United States, and that it will examine applicable domestic and international law, including the U.S. criminal statute prohibiting torture abroad, 18 U.S.C. Sec. 2340A. In pertinent part, this statute makes it a criminal offense for any person "outside the United States [to] commit[] or attempt[] to commit torture." Torture is defined as an "act committed by a person acting under the color of law specifically intended to inflict severe physical or mental pain or suffering [] upon another person within his custody or physical control."]
>
> The September 11, 2001 terrorist attacks marked a state of international armed conflict between the United States and the al Qaeda terrorist organization. Pursuant to his Commander-in-Chief power, as supported by an act of Congress, the President has ordered the Armed Forces to carry out military operations against al Qaeda, which includes the power both to kill and to capture members of the enemy. Interrogation arises as a necessary and legitimate element of the detention of al Qaeda and Taliban members during an armed conflict.

* * *

The Framers understood the Commander-in-Chief Clause to grant the President the fullest range of power recognized at the time of the ratification as belonging to the military commander. In addition, the structure of the Constitution demonstrates that any power traditionally understood as pertaining to the executive -- which includes the conduct of warfare and the defense of the nation unless expressly assigned to Congress, is vested in the President. Article II, Section I makes this clear by stating that the "executive Power shall be vested in a President of the United States of America." That sweeping grant vests in the President the "executive power" and contrasts with the specific enumeration of the powers-those "herein"-granted to Congress in Article I . . . In wartime, it is for the President alone to decide what methods to use to best prevail against the enemy.

* * *

In order to respect the President's inherent constitutional authority to direct a military campaign against al Qaeda and its allies, general criminal laws must be construed as not applying to interrogations undertaken pursuant to his Commander-in-Chief authority. Congress cannot interfere with the President's exercise of his authority as Commander in Chief to control the conduct of operations during a war . . . As we have discussed above, the President's power to detain and interrogate enemy combatants arises out of his constitutional authority as Commander in Chief. Any construction of criminal laws that regulated the President's authority as Commander in Chief to determine the interrogation and treatment of enemy combatants would raise serious constitutional questions whether Congress had intruded on the President's constitutional authority. Moreover, we do not believe that Congress enacted general criminal provisions such as the prohibitions against assault, maiming, interstate stalking, and torture pursuant to any express authority that would allow it to infringe on the President's constitutional control over the operation of the Armed Forces in wartime. In our view, Congress may no more regulate the President's ability to detain and interrogate enemy combatants than it may regulate his ability to direct troop movements on the battlefield.

* * *

Any effort by Congress to regulate the interrogation of enemy combatants would violate the Constitution's sole vesting of the Commander-in-Chief authority in the President . . . Just as statutes that order the President to conduct warfare in a certain manner or for specific goals would be unconstitutional, so too are laws that would prevent the President from gaining the intelligence he believes necessary to prevent attacks upon the United States.

Other legal memoranda contained similar broad assertions of commander in chief authority that could not be subject to regulation or restriction by the Legislative Branch.

These memoranda were later repudiated by the Office of Legal Counsel, which stated that "these propositions are not consistent with the current views of OLC . . . the sweeping assertions in the opinions above that the President's Commander in Chief authority categorically precludes Congress from enacting any legislation concerning the detention, interrogation, prosecution, and transfer of enemy combatants are not sustainable." January 15, 2009 Memorandum for the Files Re: Status of Certain OLC Opinions Issued in the Aftermath of the Terrorist Attacks of September 11, 2001 (signed by Steven G. Bradbury, Principal Deputy Assistant Attorney General).

The *Youngstown* decision explains that, even though the President is the nation's chief executive, and even when the President is acting in his core capacity as commander in chief, his power is still subject to congressional oversight and limitation. Inexplicably, nowhere in Deputy Assistant Attorney General Yoo's 81-page, single-spaced legal memorandum excerpted above is the *Youngstown* decision mentioned. A review of that decision makes clear why the Office of Legal Counsel later declared that the conclusions of Yoo's memorandum "are not sustainable."

Youngstown Sheet & Tube Co. v. Sawyer

343 U.S. 579 (1952)[1]

MR. JUSTICE BLACK delivered the opinion of the Court.

We are asked to decide whether the President was acting within his constitutional power when he issued an order directing the Secretary of Commerce to take possession of and operate most of the Nation's steel mills. The mill owners argue that the President's order amounts

---

[1] Footnotes and some citations found in the original decision have been omitted from this excerpted version.

to lawmaking, a legislative function which the Constitution has expressly confided to the Congress, and not to the President. The Government's position is that the order was made on findings of the President that his action was necessary to avert a national catastrophe which would inevitably result from a stoppage of steel production, and that, in meeting this grave emergency, the President was acting within the aggregate of his constitutional powers as the Nation's Chief Executive and the Commander in Chief of the Armed Forces of the United States.

* * *

The President's power, if any, to issue the order must stem either from an act of Congress or from the Constitution itself. There is no statute that expressly authorizes the President to take possession of property as he did here. Nor is there any act of Congress to which our attention has been directed from which such a power can fairly be implied. Indeed, we do not understand the Government to rely on statutory authorization for this seizure. There are two statutes which do authorize the President to take both personal and real property under certain conditions. [The Selective Service Act of 1948 and the Defense Production Act of 1950.] The Government admits that these conditions were not met, and that the President's order was not rooted in either of the statutes. The Government refers to the seizure provisions of one of these statutes (§ 201(b) of the Defense Production Act) as "much too cumbersome, involved, and time-consuming for the crisis which was at hand." [Justice Black then notes that Congress refused to include a seizure provision in the Taft-Hartley Act of 1947.]

It is clear that, if the President had authority to issue the order he did, it must be found in some provision of the Constitution. And it is not claimed that express constitutional language grants this power to the President. The contention is that presidential power should be implied from the aggregate of his powers under the Constitution. Particular reliance is placed on provisions in Article II which say that "The executive Power shall be vested in a President . . ."; that "he shall take Care that the Laws be faithfully executed", and that he "shall be Commander in Chief of the Army and Navy of the United States."

The order cannot properly be sustained as an exercise of the President's military power as Commander in Chief of the Armed Forces. The Government attempts to do so by citing a number of cases upholding broad powers in military commanders engaged in day-to-day fighting in a theater of war. Such cases need not concern us here. Even though "theater of war" be an expanding concept, we cannot with faithfulness to our constitutional system hold that the Commander in Chief of the Armed Forces has the ultimate power as such to take possession of private property in order to keep labor disputes from stopping production. This is a job for the Nation's lawmakers, not for its military authorities.

Nor can the seizure order be sustained because of the several constitutional provisions that grant executive power to the President. In the framework of our Constitution, the President's power to see that the laws are faithfully executed refutes the idea that he is to be a lawmaker. The Constitution limits his functions in the lawmaking process to the recommending of laws he thinks wise and the vetoing of laws he thinks bad. And the Constitution is neither silent nor equivocal about who shall make laws which the President is to execute. The first section of the first article says that "All legislative Powers herein granted shall be vested in a Congress of the United States. . . ." After granting many powers to the Congress, Article I goes on to provide that Congress may "make all Laws which shall be necessary and proper for carrying into Execution the foregoing Powers, and all other Powers vested by this Constitution in the Government of the United States, or in any Department or Officer thereof."

The President's order does not direct that a congressional policy be executed in a manner prescribed by Congress -- it directs that a presidential policy be executed in a manner prescribed by the President. The preamble of the order itself, like that of many statutes, sets out reasons why the President believes certain policies should be adopted, proclaims these policies as rules of conduct to be followed, and again, like a statute, authorizes a government official to promulgate additional rules and regulations consistent with the policy proclaimed and needed to carry that policy into execution. The power of Congress to adopt such public policies as those proclaimed by the order is beyond question. It can authorize the taking of private property for public use. It can make laws regulating the relationships between employers and employees, prescribing rules designed to settle labor disputes, and fixing wages and working conditions in certain fields of our economy. The Constitution does not subject this lawmaking power of Congress to presidential or military supervision or control.

*   *   *

The Founders of this Nation entrusted the lawmaking power to the Congress alone in both good and bad times. It would do no good to recall the historical events, the fears of power, and the hopes for freedom that lay behind their choice. Such a review would but confirm our holding that this seizure order cannot stand.

The judgment of the District Court is

Affirmed.

MR. JUSTICE FRANKFURTER, concurring.

[Justice Frankfurter notes that he does not intend to define the entire scope of the President's power.]

The question before the Court comes in this setting. Congress has frequently -- at least 16 times since 1916 -- specifically provided for executive seizure of production, transportation, communications, or storage facilities. In every case, it has qualified this grant of power with limitations and safeguards. This body of enactments [summarized elsewhere in the opinion] demonstrates that Congress deemed seizure so drastic a power as to require that it be carefully circumscribed whenever the President was vested with this extraordinary authority. The power to seize has uniformly been given only for a limited period or for a defined emergency, or has been repealed after a short period. Its exercise has been restricted to particular circumstances such as "time of war or when war is imminent," the needs of "public safety" or of "national security or defense," or "urgent and impending need."

* * *

In adopting the provisions which it did, by the Labor Management Relations Act of 1947, for dealing with a "national emergency" arising out of a breakdown in peaceful industrial relations, Congress was very familiar with Governmental seizure as a protective measure. On a balance of considerations, Congress chose not to lodge this power in the President. It chose not to make available in advance a remedy to which both industry and labor were fiercely hostile . . . Congress could not more clearly and emphatically have withheld authority than it did in 1947.

* * *

By the Labor Management Relations Act of 1947, Congress said to the President, "You may not seize. Please report to us and ask for seizure power if you think it is needed in a specific situation." This, of course, calls for a report on the unsuccessful efforts to reach a voluntary settlement, as a basis for discharge by Congress of its responsibility -- which it has unequivocally reserved -- to fashion further remedies than it provided. But it is now claimed that the President has seizure power by virtue of the Defense Production Act of 1950 and its Amendments. And the claim is based on the occurrence of new events -- Korea and the need for stabilization, etc. -- although it was well known that seizure power was withheld by the Act of 1947, and although the President, whose specific requests for other authority were, in the main, granted by Congress, never suggested that, in view of the new events, he needed the power of seizure which Congress in its judgment had decided to withhold from him. The utmost that the Korean conflict may imply is that it may have been desirable to have given the President further authority, a freer hand in these matters. Absence of authority in the President to deal with a crisis does not imply want of power in the Government. Conversely, the fact that power exists in the Government does not vest it in the President. The need for new legislation does not enact it. Nor does it repeal or amend existing law.

No authority that has since been given to the President can, by any fair process of statutory construction, be deemed to withdraw the restriction or change the will of Congress as expressed by a body of enactments, culminating in the Labor Management Relations Act of 1947.

* * *

It is an inadmissibly narrow conception of American constitutional law to confine it to the words of the Constitution and to disregard the gloss which life has written upon them. In short, a systematic, unbroken, executive practice, long pursued to the knowledge of the Congress and never before questioned, engaged in by Presidents who have also sworn to uphold the Constitution, making as it were such exercise of power part of the structure of our government, may be treated as a gloss on "executive Power" vested in the President by § 1 of Art. II . . . [however], the record is barren of instances comparable to the one before us.

MR. JUSTICE JACKSON, concurring in the judgment and opinion of the Court.

[Justice Jackson noted the difficulty in, and the lack of clear legal precedent relevant to, deciding important cases about the scope of the federal government's authority and the power of the Executive within the tripartite federal government.]

The actual art of governing under our Constitution does not, and cannot, conform to judicial definitions of the power of any of its branches based on isolated clauses, or even single Articles torn from context. While the Constitution diffuses power the better to secure liberty, it also contemplates that practice will integrate the dispersed powers into a workable government. It enjoins upon its branches separateness but interdependence, autonomy but reciprocity. Presidential powers are not fixed but fluctuate depending upon their disjunction or conjunction with those of Congress. We may well begin by a somewhat over-simplified grouping of practical situations in which a President may doubt, or others may challenge, his powers, and by distinguishing roughly the legal consequences of this factor of relativity.

1. When the President acts pursuant to an express or implied authorization of Congress, his authority is at its maximum, for it includes all that he possesses in his own right plus all that Congress can delegate. In these circumstances, and in these only, may he be said (for what it may be worth) to personify the federal sovereignty. If his act is held unconstitutional under these circumstances, it usually means that the Federal Government, as an undivided whole, lacks power. A seizure executed by the President pursuant to an Act of Congress would be supported by the strongest of presumptions and the widest latitude of judicial interpretation, and the burden of persuasion would rest heavily upon any who might attack it.

2. When the President acts in absence of either a congressional grant or denial of authority, he can only rely upon his own independent powers, but there is a zone of twilight in which he and Congress may have concurrent authority, or in which its distribution is uncertain. Therefore, congressional inertia, indifference or quiescence may sometimes, at least, as a practical matter, enable, if not invite, measures on independent presidential responsibility. In this area, any actual test of power is likely to depend on the imperatives of events and contemporary imponderables, rather than on abstract theories of law.

3. When the President takes measures incompatible with the expressed or implied will of Congress, his power is at its lowest ebb, for then he can rely only upon his own constitutional powers minus

any constitutional powers of Congress over the matter. Courts can sustain exclusive presidential control in such a case only by disabling the Congress from acting upon the subject. Presidential claim to a power at once so conclusive and preclusive must be scrutinized with caution, for what is at stake is the equilibrium established by our constitutional system.

Into which of these classifications does this executive seizure of the steel industry fit? It is eliminated from the first by admission, for it is conceded that no congressional authorization exists for this seizure. That takes away also the support of the many precedents and declarations which were made in relation, and must be confined, to this category. Can it then be defended under flexible tests available to the second category? It seems clearly eliminated from that class, because Congress has not left seizure of private property an open field, but has covered it by three statutory policies inconsistent with this seizure. In cases where the purpose is to supply needs of the Government itself, two courses are provided: one, seizure of a plant which fails to comply with obligatory orders placed by the Government; another, condemnation of facilities, including temporary use under the power of eminent domain. The third is applicable where it is the general economy of the country that is to be protected, rather than exclusive governmental interests. None of these were invoked. In choosing a different and inconsistent way of his own, the President cannot claim that it is necessitated or invited by failure of Congress to legislate upon the occasions, grounds and methods for seizure of industrial properties.

This leaves the current seizure to be justified only by the severe tests under the third grouping, where it can be supported only by any remainder of executive power after subtraction of such powers as Congress may have over the subject. In short, we can sustain the President only by holding that seizure of such strike-bound industries is within his domain and beyond control by Congress. Thus, this Court's first review of such seizures occurs under circumstances which leave presidential power most vulnerable to attack and in the least favorable of possible constitutional postures.

* * *

The Solicitor General seeks the power of seizure in three clauses of the Executive Article, the first reading, "The executive Power shall be vested in a President of the United States of America." Lest I be thought to exaggerate, I quote the interpretation which his brief puts upon it: "In our view, this clause constitutes a grant of all the executive powers of which the Government is capable." If that be true, it is difficult to see why the forefathers bothered to add several specific items, including some trifling ones.

The example of such unlimited executive power that must have most impressed the forefathers was the prerogative exercised by George III, and the description of its evils in the Declaration of Independence leads me to doubt that they were creating their new Executive in his image. Continental European examples were no more appealing. And, if we seek instruction from our own times, we can match it only from the executive powers in those governments we disparagingly describe as totalitarian. I cannot accept the view that this clause is a grant in bulk of all conceivable executive power, but regard it as an allocation to the presidential office of the generic powers thereafter stated.

The clause on which the Government next relies is that "The President shall be Commander in Chief of the Army and Navy of the United States. . . ." These cryptic words have given rise to some of the most persistent controversies in our constitutional history. Of course, they imply something more than an empty title. But just what authority goes with the name has plagued presidential advisers who would not waive or narrow it by nonassertion, yet cannot say where it begins or ends. It undoubtedly puts the Nation's armed forces under presidential command. Hence, this loose appellation is sometimes advanced as support for any presidential action, internal or external, involving use of force, the idea being that it vests power to do anything, anywhere, that can be done with an army or navy.

That seems to be the logic of an argument tendered at our bar -- that the President having, on his own responsibility, sent American troops abroad derives from that act "affirmative power" to seize the means of producing a supply of steel for them. To quote,

"Perhaps the most forceful illustration of the scope of Presidential power in this connection is the fact that American troops in Korea, whose safety and effectiveness are so directly involved here, were sent to the field by an exercise of the President's constitutional powers."

Thus, it is said, he has invested himself with "war powers."

I cannot foresee all that it might entail if the Court should indorse this argument. Nothing in our Constitution is plainer than that declaration of a war is entrusted only to Congress. Of course, a state of war may, in fact, exist without a formal declaration. But no doctrine that the

Court could promulgate would seem to me more sinister and alarming than that a President whose conduct of foreign affairs is so largely uncontrolled, and often even is unknown, can vastly enlarge his mastery over the internal affairs of the country by his own commitment of the Nation's armed forces to some foreign venture. I do not, however, find it necessary or appropriate to consider the legal status of the Korean enterprise to discountenance argument based on it.

Assuming that we are in a war *de facto,* whether it is or is not a war *de jure,* does that empower the Commander in Chief to seize industries he thinks necessary to supply our army? The Constitution expressly places in Congress power "to raise and *support* Armies" and "to *provide* and *maintain* a Navy." (Emphasis supplied.) This certainly lays upon Congress primary responsibility for supplying the armed forces. Congress alone controls the raising of revenues and their appropriation, and may determine in what manner and by what means they shall be spent for military and naval procurement. I suppose no one would doubt that Congress can take over war supply as a Government enterprise. On the other hand, if Congress sees fit to rely on free private enterprise collectively bargaining with free labor for support and maintenance of our armed forces, can the Executive, because of lawful disagreements incidental to that process, seize the facility for operation upon Government-imposed terms?

There are indications that the Constitution did not contemplate that the title Commander in Chief *of the Army and Navy* will constitute him also Commander in Chief of the country, its industries and its inhabitants. He has no monopoly of "war powers," whatever they are. While Congress cannot deprive the President of the command of the army and navy, only Congress can provide him an army or navy to command. It is also empowered to make rules for the "Government and Regulation of land and naval Forces," by which it may, to some unknown extent, impinge upon even command functions.

* * *

We should not use this occasion to circumscribe, much less to contract, the lawful role of the President as Commander in Chief. I should indulge the widest latitude of interpretation to sustain his exclusive function to command the instruments of national force, at least when turned against the outside world for the security of our society. But, when it is turned inward not because of rebellion, but because of a lawful economic struggle between industry and labor, it should have no such indulgence. His command power is not such an absolute as might be implied from that office in a militaristic system, but is subject to limitations consistent with a constitutional Republic whose law and policymaking branch is a representative Congress. The purpose of lodging dual titles in one man was to insure that the civilian would control the military, not to enable the military to subordinate the presidential office. No penance would ever expiate the sin against free government of holding that a President can escape control of executive powers by law through assuming his military role. What the power of command may include I do not try to envision, but I think it is not a military prerogative, without support of law, to seize persons or property because they are important or even essential for the military and naval establishment.

The third clause in which the Solicitor General finds seizure powers is that "he shall take Care that the Laws be faithfully executed. . . . That authority must be matched against words of the Fifth Amendment that "No person shall be . . . deprived of life, liberty or property, without due process of law. . . ." One gives a governmental authority that reaches so far as there is law, the other gives a private right that authority shall go no farther. These signify about all there is of the principle that ours is a government of laws, not of men, and that we submit ourselves to rulers only if under rules.

The Solicitor General lastly grounds support of the seizure upon nebulous, inherent powers never expressly granted, but said to have accrued to the office from the customs and claims of preceding administrations. The plea is for a resulting power to deal with a crisis or an emergency according to the necessities of the case, the unarticulated assumption being that necessity knows no law.

Loose and irresponsible use of adjectives colors all nonlegal and much legal discussion of presidential powers. "Inherent" powers, "implied" powers, "incidental" powers, "plenary" powers, "war" powers and "emergency" powers are used, often interchangeably and without fixed or ascertainable meanings.

* * *

The appeal, however, that we declare the existence of inherent powers *ex necessitate* to meet an emergency asks us to do what many think would be wise, although it is something the forefathers omitted. They knew what emergencies were, knew the pressures they engender for authoritative action, knew, too, how they afford a ready pretext for usurpation. We may also suspect that they suspected that emergency powers would tend to kindle emergencies. Aside from suspension of the privilege of the writ of habeas corpus in time of rebellion or invasion, when the public safety may require it, they made no express provision for exercise of extraordinary authority because of a crisis. I do not think we rightfully may so amend their work, and, if we could, I am not convinced it would be wise to do so, although many modern nations have forthrightly recognized that war and economic crises may upset the normal balance between liberty and authority. Their experience with emergency powers may not be irrelevant to the argument here that we should say that the Executive, of his own volition, can invest himself with undefined emergency powers.

* * *

In the practical working of our Government, we already have evolved a technique within the framework of the Constitution by which normal executive powers may be considerably expanded to meet an emergency. Congress may and has granted extraordinary authorities which lie dormant in normal times but may be called into play by the Executive in war or upon proclamation of a national emergency. In 1939, upon congressional request, the Attorney General listed ninety-nine such separate statutory grants by Congress of emergency or wartime executive powers. They were invoked from time to time as need appeared. Under this procedure, we retain Government by law -- special, temporary law, perhaps, but law nonetheless. The public may know the extent and limitations of the powers that can be asserted, and persons affected may be informed from the statute of their rights and duties.

In view of the ease, expedition and safety with which Congress can grant and has granted large emergency powers, certainly ample to embrace this crisis, I am quite unimpressed with the argument that we should affirm possession of them without statute. Such power either has no beginning or it has no end. If it exists, it need submit to no legal restraint. I am not alarmed that it would plunge us straightway into dictatorship, but it is at least a step in that wrong direction.

MR. JUSTICE BURTON, concurring in both the opinion and judgment of the Court.

[Justice Burton noted that the Taft-Hartley Act offered a procedure for the President to utilize to avoid closure of the nation’s steel mills, but the President elected not to pursue that option.]

This brings us to a further crucial question. Does the President, in such a situation, have inherent constitutional power to seize private property which makes congressional action in relation thereto unnecessary? We find no such power available to him under the present circumstances. The present situation is not comparable to that of an imminent invasion or threatened attack. We do not face the issue of what might be the President's constitutional power to meet such catastrophic situations. Nor is it claimed that the current seizure is in the nature of a military command addressed by the President, as Commander-in-Chief, to a mobilized nation waging, or imminently threatened with, total war.

The controlling fact here is that Congress, within its constitutionally delegated power, has prescribed for the President specific procedures, exclusive of seizure, for his use in meeting the present type of emergency. Congress has reserved to itself the right to determine where and when to authorize the seizure of property in meeting such an emergency. Under these circumstances, the President's order of April 8 invaded the jurisdiction of Congress. It violated the essence of the principle of the separation of governmental powers. Accordingly, the injunction against its effectiveness should be sustained.

[JUSTICE CLARK concurred in the judgment, reasoning that the President probably has "inherent" or "implied" emergency powers under the Constitution; however, when Congress has passed legislation that directly addresses the situation, the President must abide by and work within that legislative framework. Here, either the Taft-Hartley Act or the Selective Service Act of 1948 might have permitted seizure of the steel mills, but President Truman chose not to invoke either of these, which left him without seizure authority.]

MR CHIEF JUSTICE VINSON, with whom MR. JUSTICE REED and MR. JUSTICE MINTON join, dissenting.

[Chief Justice Vinson noted that Congress had repeatedly appropriated funds for the Korean War; had enacted the Defense Production Act of 1950, which was aimed at strengthening the military; and had otherwise pursued a "legislative program" that the United States would undertake "to protect the free world from aggression." He also noted that President Truman had notified Congress of his intention to seize and operate the steel mills, and Congress had taken no action to disapprove. He then reviewed historical instances in which presidents had acted in significant ways without explicit statutory authorization -- for example, Jefferson's Louisiana Purchase, the announcement of the Monroe Doctrine, and Lincoln's blockade of Southern ports and issuance of the Emancipation Proclamation.]

Focusing now on the situation confronting the President on the night of April 8, 1952, we cannot but conclude that the President was performing his duty under the Constitution to "take Care that the Laws be faithfully executed" -- a duty described by President Benjamin Harrison as "the central idea of the office."

The President reported to Congress the morning after the seizure that he acted because a work stoppage in steel production would immediately imperil the safety of the Nation by preventing execution of the legislative programs for procurement of military equipment. And, while a shutdown could be averted by granting the price concessions requested by plaintiffs, granting such concessions would disrupt the price stabilization program also enacted by Congress. Rather than fail to execute either legislative program, the President acted to execute both.

Much of the argument in this case has been directed at straw men. We do not now have before us the case of a President acting solely on the basis of his own notions of the public welfare. Nor is there any question of unlimited executive power in this case. The President himself closed the door to any such claim when he sent his Message to Congress stating his purpose to abide by any action of Congress, whether approving or disapproving his seizure action. Here, the President immediately made sure that Congress was fully informed of the temporary action he had taken only to preserve the legislative programs from destruction until Congress could act.

* * *

There is no statute prohibiting seizure as a method of enforcing legislative programs. Congress has in no wise indicated that its legislation is not to be executed by the taking of private property (subject, of course, to the payment of just compensation) if its legislation cannot otherwise be executed. Indeed, the Universal Military Training and Service Act authorizes the seizure of any plant that fails to fill a Government contract or the properties of any steel producer that fails to allocate steel as directed for defense production. And the Defense Production Act authorizes the President to requisition equipment and condemn real property needed without delay in the defense effort. Where Congress authorizes seizure in instances not necessarily crucial to the defense program, it can hardly be said to have disclosed an intention to prohibit seizures where essential to the execution of that legislative program.

Whatever the extent of Presidential power on more tranquil occasions, and whatever the right of the President to execute legislative programs as he sees fit without reporting the mode of execution to Congress, the single Presidential purpose disclosed on this record is to faithfully execute the laws by acting in an emergency to maintain the *status quo,* thereby preventing collapse of the legislative programs until Congress could act. The President's action served the same purposes as a judicial stay entered to maintain the *status quo* in order to preserve the jurisdiction of a court. In his Message to Congress immediately following the seizure, the President explained the necessity of his action in executing the military procurement and anti-inflation legislative programs and expressed his desire to cooperate with any legislative proposals approving, regulating or rejecting the seizure of the steel mills. Consequently, there is no evidence whatever of any Presidential purpose to defy Congress or act in any way inconsistent with the legislative will.

In *United States v. Midwest Oil Co., supra,* this Court approved executive action where, as here, the President acted to preserve an important matter until Congress could act -- even though his action in that case was contrary to an express statute. In this case, there is no statute prohibiting the action taken by the President in a matter not merely important, but threatening the very safety of the Nation. Executive inaction in such a situation, courting national disaster, is foreign to the concept of energy and initiative in the Executive as created by the Founding Fathers. The Constitution was itself "adopted in a period of grave emergency. . . . While emergency does not create power, emergency may furnish the occasion for the exercise of power."

The Framers knew, as we should know in these times of peril, that there is real danger in Executive weakness. There is no cause to fear Executive tyranny so long as the laws of Congress are being faithfully executed. Certainly there is no basis for fear of dictatorship when the Executive acts, as he did in this case, only to save the situation until Congress could act.

DISCUSSION AND QUESTIONS

1. In writing for the majority, Justice Black refers to the "cases upholding broad powers in military commanders engaged in day-to-day fighting in a theater of war," and he characterizes the concept of "theater of war" as "an

expanding concept." Black seems to be suggesting that it makes a difference whether the President's actions are taking place within a theater of war -- if so, the scope of permissible commander in chief action is broadened -- but that steel mills in the United States are not within the theater of war, so the concept is inapplicable. In 1952, it was plain that the Korean War was not being fought in or near the territory of the United States. In contrast, the terrorist attacks of September 11, 2001 that led to the so-called "War on Terror" did occur within the borders of the United States and killed thousands of Americans. Undoubtedly, the international terrorists with whom the U.S. is "at war" would like to strike again within United States territory. Should the courts, therefore, view the United States as a "theater of war" in the War on Terror and permit the President to exercise more extensive commander in chief powers than the *Youngstown* court was willing to countenance? If the United States is arguably a "theater of war," does it matter -- and does it limit the President's scope of action -- that U.S. forces are not "engaged in day-to-day fighting" in that particular theater?

2. Justice Jackson's three-tier framework has become the best-known and most often-cited analytical tool for assessing challenged exercises of presidential authority. Justice Black also offers an excellent shorthand device for determining whether a president has overreached: "The President's order does not direct that a congressional policy be executed in a manner prescribed by Congress -- it directs that a presidential policy be executed in a manner prescribed by the President." Won't this formulation always serve us well -- if a President is executing his own policy rather than a congressional policy, the action is not legitimate? Are there situations where this analysis will not be applicable? Was it really applicable in the *Youngstown* case? After all, the Executive Branch was not even arguing that it was carrying out a congressional policy; it admitted that it was carrying out its own policy and was basing the authority to do so on the Constitution's grant of authority directly to the President.

3. Justice Jackson refers to Article II's Vesting Clause and says of it: "I cannot accept the view that this clause is a grant in bulk of all conceivable executive power, but regard it as an allocation to the presidential office of the generic powers thereafter stated." But doesn't the Vesting Clause quite plainly do precisely what Jackson rejects? Does it not vest in the President all of the executive power that is possessed by the federal government? If, as Jackson believes, the Vesting Clause vests the President with something less than "all conceivable executive power," then where does the executive power reside that is not vested in the President? In the Congress? In the courts? Elsewhere?

4. Note the rhetorical device that Chief Justice Vinson utilizes. He would uphold the seizure of the steel mills as a valid effort by the President to

execute not any particular law, but rather what Vinson describes as "legislative programs" relating to military procurement and national defense. That is, Vinson looked to various enactments and inferred from them a general congressional will favoring a vigorous national defense and the military procurement to support it. Once that generalized congressional will was identified (or contrived), Vinson concluded that it gave the president all the authorization he needed to seize the nation's privately-owned steel mills. Does the Constitution oblige the President to "take care that *legislative programs* be faithfully executed?" Does the Constitution authorize the President to review the body of existing statutory law, then divine some generalized "legislative program," and then take any unilateral action that the President deems appropriate to support that program, even if not specifically authorized by statute and, indeed, even if legislative history indicates that Congress specifically considered and rejected authorizing the President to take such action? Under Vinson's views of presidential authority, could a President look to statutes such as the Clean Air Act, Clean Water Act and Endangered Species Act, conclude that there is a "legislative program" to protect the environment, and then seize the property of any private entity that the President deems to be a polluter?

CHAPTER THREE: THE SCOPE OF EXECUTIVE POWER

Article II of the Constitution confers upon the President these affirmative grants of authority:

- "The executive power shall be vested in a President of the United States."
- "The President shall be Commander in Chief of the Army and Navy of the United States, and of the militia of the several states when called into the actual service of the United States."
- The President may grant reprieves and pardons.
- With the advice and consent of the Senate, the President may enter into treaties.
- The President may appoint ambassadors, judges, and other "officers of the United States." (Such appointments require Senate approval if they are not made during a recess of the Senate.)

The first bullet point above is a direct quote of the first sentence of Article II. This seemingly straightforward sentence has been the subject of much debate on the nature and scope of Presidential power. It indicates (1) that there is a specific, discernible executive power – *the* executive power – and (2) that this power resides, in its entirety, in the person of the President and nowhere else. It is difficult to interpret this simple declarative sentence in any other way. Nevertheless, neither Article II nor any other provision of the Constitution details precisely how far the "executive power" extends or where its limits can be found.

The Constitution's ambiguous reference to the power of the executive stands in stark contrast to the detailed explication of Legislative Branch powers that appears in Article I. The implications of this contrast are not clear. On the one hand, the Framers' relative precision in setting forth legislative powers may mean that they were more fearful of an overreaching legislature (as is suggested, for example, in Federalist 48) and believed that careful circumscription of such power was necessary. At the same time, they intended to give a more generalized, even plenary, power to the executive. This theory argues for an interpretation of Article II as a "sweeping grant" of executive power, as John Yoo argued in his memorandum of March 14, 2003 (see pages 15-17, above). On the other hand, the Framers may have believed that, by carefully enumerating the powers of the Legislative Branch, they were concomitantly limiting the power of the Executive Branch. According to this school of thought, except for the very few instances where the Constitution confers upon the executive an affirmative grant of authority such as the pardon power or the appointment power, the purpose of the Executive Branch is merely to *execute* on the policies enacted by the legislature. In other words, the proper function for "executive power" is to execute on the will of the people as expressed through their elected legislative representatives. If the legislature has chosen not to exercise its allotted authority in a particular area, there is no basis for the exercise of executive power in that area.

EXECUTIVE POWER IN FOREIGN AFFAIRS

As momentous and instructive as it is, the *Youngstown* decision excerpted and discussed in Chapter Two does not entirely resolve the debate about the scope of executive power. However, it strongly suggests that, in most circumstances, Executive Branch power does not extend far (if at all) beyond what has been legislatively authorized by Congress. And, even in emergencies, it very clearly is not unlimited, as Assistant Attorney General Baldridge argued in 1952 and Deputy Assistant Attorney General Yoo asserted 51 years later. Nevertheless, the courts have found certain powers and prerogatives to be inherent in the very nature of the executive. In particular -- and despite the absence of any express grant in the Constitution, the courts have concluded that the executive has particularly robust authority in the arena of foreign affairs. Indeed, in the following case, *United States v. Curtiss-Wright Export Corp.*, Justice George Sutherland refers to the "plenary and exclusive power of the President as the sole organ of the federal government in the field of international relations."

United States v. Curtiss-Wright Export Corp.

299 U.S. 304 (1936)[2]

MR. JUSTICE SUTHERLAND delivered the opinion of the Court.

[Justice Sutherland explains that this is a criminal case in which the defendants are charged with selling machine guns to Bolivia in violation of legislation that authorized the President to prohibit "the sale of arms and munitions of war in the United States to those countries now engaged in armed conflict in the Chaco [Boreal region of South America]." The legislation imposed criminal penalties for violations. Shortly after passage of this legislation, President Roosevelt issued a proclamation prohibiting the sale of arms to Bolivia and Paraguay and warning that violations of the prohibition would be prosecuted. The defendants were convicted of prohibited arms sales and now argue on appeal that the legislation under which they were convicted was an unconstitutional delegation of legislative authority to the President.]

* * *

[The defendants argue that] Congress abdicated its essential functions and delegated them to the Executive.

Whether, if the Joint Resolution had related solely to internal affairs, it would be open to the challenge that it constituted an unlawful delegation of legislative power to the Executive, we find it unnecessary to determine. The whole aim of the resolution is to affect a situation entirely external to the United States, and falling within the category of foreign affairs. The determination which we are called to make, therefore, is whether the Joint Resolution, as applied to that situation, is vulnerable to attack under the rule that forbids a delegation of the lawmaking power. In other words, assuming (but not deciding) that the challenged delegation, if it were confined to internal affairs, would be invalid, may it nevertheless be sustained on the ground that its exclusive aim is to afford a remedy for a hurtful condition within foreign territory?

It will contribute to the elucidation of the question if we first consider the differences between the powers of the federal government in respect of foreign or external affairs and those in respect of domestic

[2] Footnotes and some citations found in the original decision have been omitted from this excerpted version.

or internal affairs. That there are differences between them, and that these differences are fundamental, may not be doubted.

The two classes of powers are different, both in respect of their origin and their nature. The broad statement that the federal government can exercise no powers except those specifically enumerated in the Constitution, and such implied powers as are necessary and proper to carry into effect the enumerated powers, is categorically true only in respect of our internal affairs. In that field, the primary purpose of the Constitution was to carve from the general mass of legislative powers then possessed by the states such portions as it was thought desirable to vest in the federal government, leaving those not included in the enumeration still in the states. Carter v. Carter Coal Co., 298 U.S. 238, 294, 56 S.Ct. 855, 865. That this doctrine applies only to powers which the states had is self-evident. And since the states severally never possessed international powers, such powers could not have been carved from the mass of state powers but obviously were transmitted to the United States from some other source. During the Colonial period, those powers were possessed exclusively by and were entirely under the control of the Crown. By the Declaration of Independence, 'the Representatives of the United States of America' declared the United (not the several) Colonies to be free and independent states, and as such to have 'full Power to levy War, conclude Peace, contract Alliances, establish Commerce and to do all other Acts and Things which Independent States may of right do.'

As a result of the separation from Great Britain by the colonies, acting as a unit, the powers of external sovereignty passed from the Crown not to the colonies severally, but to the colonies in their collective and corporate capacity as the United States of America. Even before the Declaration, the colonies were a unit in foreign affairs, acting through a common agency-namely, the Continental Congress, composed of delegates from the thirteen colonies. That agency exercised the powers of war and peace, raised an army, created a navy, and finally adopted the Declaration of Independence. Rulers come and go; governments end and forms of government change; but sovereignty survives. A political society cannot endure without a supreme will somewhere. Sovereignty is never held in suspense. When, therefore, the external sovereignty of Great Britain in respect of the colonies ceased, it immediately passed to the Union. See Penhallow v. Doane, 3 Dall. 54, 80, 81, Fed.Cas. No. 10925. That fact was given practical application almost at once. The treaty of peace, made on September 3, 1783, was concluded between his Brittanic Majesty and the 'United States of America.' 8 Stat., European Treaties, 80.

The Union existed before the Constitution, which was ordained and established among other things to form 'a more perfect Union.' Prior to that event, it is clear that the Union, declared by the Articles of Confederation to be 'perpetual,' was the sole possessor of external sovereignty, and in the Union it remained without change save in so far as the Constitution in express terms qualified its exercise. The Framers' Convention was called and exerted its powers upon the irrefutable postulate that though the states were several their people in respect of foreign affairs were one.

* * *

It is important to bear in mind that we are here dealing not alone with an authority vested in the President by an exertion of legislative power, but with such an authority plus the very delicate, plenary and exclusive power of the President as the sole organ of the federal government in the field of international relations -- a power which does not require as a basis for its exercise an act of Congress, but which, of course, like every other governmental power, must be exercised in subordination to the applicable provisions of the Constitution. It is quite apparent that if, in the maintenance of our international relations, embarrassment -- perhaps serious embarrassment -- is to be avoided and success for our aims achieved, congressional legislation which is to be made effective through negotiation and inquiry within the international field must often accord to the President a degree of discretion and freedom from statutory restriction which would not be admissible were domestic affairs alone involved. Moreover, he, not Congress, has the better opportunity of knowing the conditions which prevail in foreign countries, and especially is this true in time of war. He has his confidential sources of information. He has his agents in the form of diplomatic, consular and other officials. Secrecy in respect of information gathered by them may be highly necessary, and the premature disclosure of it productive of harmful results.

* * *

[Many previous acts of Congress have delegated authority to the President in the realm of foreign affairs, such as the authority to institute and revoke embargoes, to permit and to prohibit the sale of arms, and to impose and repeal duties on imports.]

* * *

We deem it unnecessary to consider, seriatim, the several clauses which are said to evidence the unconstitutionality of the Joint

Resolution as involving an unlawful delegation of legislative power. It is enough to summarize by saying that, both upon principle and in accordance with precedent, we conclude there is sufficient warrant for the broad discretion vested in the President to determine whether the enforcement of the statute will have a beneficial effect upon the re-establishment of peace in the affected countries; whether he shall make proclamation to bring the resolution into operation; whether and when the resolution shall cease to operate and to make proclamation accordingly; and to prescribe limitations and exceptions to which the enforcement of the resolution shall be subject.

* * *

The judgment of the court below must be reversed and the cause remanded for further proceedings in accordance with the foregoing opinion.

It is so ordered.

DISCUSSION AND QUESTIONS

1. Prior to taking the bench, Justice Sutherland spent several years as a congressman and senator from the state of Utah. One might suspect that he would be particularly sensitive to the prerogatives of the Legislative Branch, yet he endorsed a sweeping view of executive authority in the arena of foreign affairs. To be sure, President Roosevelt had acted pursuant to a legislative grant of authority, but Justice Sutherland chose to go further than was strictly necessary to uphold the President's authority under the Joint Resolution. He states:

> We are here dealing not alone with an authority vested in the President by an exertion of legislative power, but with such an authority plus the very delicate, plenary and exclusive power of the President as the sole organ of the federal government in the field of international relations . . .

In Article I, Section 8, the Constitution expressly allocates to the Legislative Branch the power "to regulate commerce with foreign nations . . . to define and punish piracies and felonies committed on the high seas, and offenses against the law of nations; to declare war, grant letters of marque and reprisal, and make rules concerning captures on land and water." Further, at Article II, Section 2, the

Constitution provides that a treaty negotiated by the executive is valid only if "two thirds of the senators present concur." Is Justice Sutherland correct in characterizing the President as the "sole organ of the federal government" when it comes to foreign affairs, and in describing the President's power in this area as "plenary and exclusive"?

2. In reaching his conclusion about "plenary and exclusive" power for the executive in foreign affairs, Justice Sutherland reasons that the executive's authority in foreign affairs is derived differently than the legislature's authority to make domestic law. Although the enumerated and limited powers of the Congress in the domestic arena were delegated from the several sovereign states, "the states severally never possessed international powers." According to Justice Sutherland, the power over foreign affairs passed from the British Crown not to the states severally, but to the states acting collectively as the "Union." Therefore, "the investment of the federal government with powers of external sovereignty did not depend upon the affirmative grants of the Constitution." In other words, while the power of the federal government to act domestically is limited to whatever degree of power was delegated from the several states through the Constitution, the federal government's power in foreign affairs did not come via delegation from the states. If Justice Sutherland is correct about this, how then does he conclude that the government's authority in foreign affairs "like every other governmental power, must be exercised in subordination to the applicable provisions of the Constitution"? If the foreign affairs power pre-existed the Constitution, and if it was never possessed by the states, how then can it be limited by the Constitution, which is no more and no less than an agreement among the several states?

3. Is Justice Sutherland's essential premise -- that the individual states never possessed the power to act internationally -- correct? In The Declaration of Independence of 1776 the former British colonies announced to the world that:

> these United Colonies are . . . Free and Independent States; that they are Absolved from all Allegiance to the British Crown, and that all political connection between them and the State of Great Britain, is . . . totally dissolved; and that as Free and Independent States, they have full Power to levy War, conclude Peace, contract Alliances, establish Commerce, and to do all other Acts and Things which Independent States may of right do.

The former colonies refer to themselves as "united," but they also identify themselves as "independent states" (notably, not as one single independent state or nation) with full power to levy war, conclude peace, and contract alliances. This language suggests that, at the moment they severed ties with Great Britain, each of the several states viewed itself as an independent sovereign state possessing the full power of such a state to conduct international relations. That these several states were "united" in their existential struggle to reject British domination did not diminish such individual sovereignty.

Later, in the Articles of Confederation (ratified in 1781), the several states were careful to note that:

> Each state retains its sovereignty, freedom, and independence, and every power, jurisdiction, and right, which is not by this Confederation expressly delegated to the United States, in Congress assembled.

The states then proceeded in the document to delegate to the central government of the United States authority to conduct international affairs. For example, in Article IX, the several states delegated to the United States the authority to determine questions of peace and war, send and receive ambassadors, enter into treaties and alliances, and establish rules for captures. It is difficult to conclude that, prior to entering into the relationship embodied in the Articles, "the states severally never possessed international powers."

The formal pronouncements of the states at the moment of declaring independence and in the immediate aftermath indicate that each of the several states viewed itself as "independent," "sovereign," and possessing the full power of a sovereign state to conduct foreign relations.

4. If the President's power with regard to foreign affairs is truly "plenary and exclusive," must we conclude that there is nothing Congress can do to influence or limit the President's actions in this area? Suppose the President determined that it was in the long-term interests of the United States to enter into diplomatic relations with a particular nation, yet large majorities in the Congress felt to the contrary and passed legislation (overriding the President's veto with two-thirds majorities in each chamber) forbidding the President from doing so. Which branch's preference would control?

Forty-five years after its resounding endorsement of muscular executive power in *Curtiss-Wright*, the Supreme Court again had occasion to address the extent of Presidential prerogatives in foreign affairs in the case of *Dames & Moore v. Regan*. The *Dames & Moore* Court declined to indulge in absolutist language such as "plenary" and "exclusive" when describing the President's power to conduct foreign affairs; however, in a sense, the *Dames & Moore* decision goes further in its deference to executive power. In contrast to the circumstances presented in *Curtiss-Wright*, where President Roosevelt acted in direct conformity with a congressional enactment, the Court in *Dames & Moore* sustained executive action that was not expressly authorized by any statute.

After Iranian revolutionaries seized the U.S. embassy in Tehran in 1979, President Carter acted under the International Emergency Economic Powers Act (IEEPA) to freeze Iranian assets. He also granted a general "license" to permit judicial proceedings against Iranian assets. Later, however, he negotiated an agreement with Iran (the Algiers Accords of January 19, 1981) to send all claims to a special Claims Tribunal. As a result, President Carter "nullified" his previous license permitting claims to proceed in U.S. courts and ordered that all Iranian assets, by whomever held, be transferred to the U.S. Treasury. Shortly thereafter, President Reagan purported to "suspend" all claims pending against Iran in U.S. courts so they could be transferred to and resolved by the Claims Tribunal. Meanwhile, Dames & Moore had obtained a judgment against Iran, and here challenges the Presidents' "nullification" and "suspension" as unconstitutional.

Dames & Moore v. Regan

453 U.S. 654 (1981)[3]

JUSTICE REHNQUIST delivered the opinion of the Court.

The questions presented by this case touch fundamentally upon the manner in which our Republic is to be governed. Throughout the nearly two centuries of our Nation's existence under the Constitution, this subject has generated considerable debate. We have had the benefit of commentators such as John Jay, Alexander Hamilton, and James Madison writing in The Federalist Papers at the Nation's very inception, the benefit of astute foreign observers of our system such as Alexis de Tocqueville and James Bryce writing during the first century of the Nation's existence, and the benefit of many other treatises as well as more than 400 volumes of reports of decisions of this Court. As these writings reveal it is doubtless both futile and perhaps dangerous to find any epigrammatical explanation of how this country has been governed. Indeed, as Justice Jackson noted, "[a] judge . . . may be surprised at the poverty of really useful and

[3] Footnotes and some citations found in the original decision have been omitted from this excerpted version.

unambiguous authority applicable to concrete problems of executive power as they actually present themselves." Youngstown Sheet & Tube Co. v. Sawyer, 343 U.S. 579, 634 (1952) (concurring opinion).

Our decision today will not dramatically alter this situation, for the Framers "did not make the judiciary the overseer of our government." Id., at 594 (Frankfurter, J., concurring). We are confined to a resolution of the dispute presented to us. That dispute involves various Executive Orders and regulations by which the President nullified attachments and liens on Iranian assets in the United States, directed that these assets be transferred to Iran, and suspended claims against Iran that may be presented to an International Claims Tribunal. This action was taken in an effort to comply with an Executive Agreement between the United States and Iran.

* * *

The tensions present in any exercise of executive power under the tripartite system of Federal Government established by the Constitution have been reflected in opinions by Members of this Court more than once. The Court stated in United States v. Curtiss-Wright Export Corp., 299 U.S. 304, 319 -320 (1936):

> [W]e are here dealing not alone with an authority vested in the President by an exertion of legislative power, but with such an authority plus the very delicate, plenary and exclusive power of the President as the sole organ of the federal government in the field of international relations - a power which does not require as a basis for its exercise an act of Congress, but which, of course, like every other governmental power, must be exercised in subordination to the applicable provisions of the Constitution.

And yet 16 years later, Justice Jackson in his concurring opinion in Youngstown, supra, which both parties agree brings together as much combination of analysis and common sense as there is in this area, focused not on the "plenary and exclusive power of the President" but rather responded to a claim of virtually unlimited powers for the Executive by noting:

> The example of such unlimited executive power that must have most impressed the forefathers was the prerogative exercised by George III, and the description of its evils in the Declaration of

> Independence leads me to doubt that they were creating their new Executive in his image.

343 U.S., at 641.

As we now turn to the factual and legal issues in this case, we freely confess that we are obviously deciding only one more episode in the never-ending tension between the President exercising the executive authority in a world that presents each day some new challenge with which he must deal and the Constitution under which we all live and which no one disputes embodies some sort of system of checks and balances.

* * *

In nullifying post-November 14, 1979, attachments and directing those persons holding blocked Iranian funds and securities to transfer them to the Federal Reserve Bank of New York for ultimate transfer to Iran, President Carter cited five sources of express or inherent power. The Government, however, has principally relied on 203 of the IEEPA, 91 Stat. 1626, 50 U.S.C. 1702 (a) (1) (1976 ed., Supp. III), as authorization for these actions. Section 1702 (a) (1) provides in part:

> At the times and to the extent specified in section 1701 of this title, the President may, under such regulations as he may prescribe, by means of instructions, licenses, or otherwise -
>
> (A) investigate, regulate, or prohibit -
> (i) any transactions in foreign exchange,
> (ii) transfers of credit or payments between, by, through, or to any banking institution, to the extent that such transfers or payments involve any interest of any foreign country or a national thereof,
> (iii) the importing or exporting of currency or securities, and
>
> (B) investigate, regulate, direct and compel, nullify, void, prevent or prohibit, any acquisition, holding, withholding, use, transfer, withdrawal, transportation, importation or exportation of, or dealing in, or exercising any right, power, or privilege with respect to, or transactions involving, any property in which

> any foreign country or a national thereof has any interest;
>
> by any person, or with respect to any property, subject to the jurisdiction of the United States.

The Government contends that the acts of "nullifying" the attachments and ordering the "transfer" of the frozen assets are specifically authorized by the plain language of the above statute.

* * *

Because the President's action in nullifying the attachments and ordering the transfer of the assets was taken pursuant to specific congressional authorization, it is "supported by the strongest of presumptions and the widest latitude of judicial interpretation, and the burden of persuasion would rest heavily upon any who might attack it." Youngstown, 343 U.S., at 637 (Jackson, J., concurring). Under the circumstances of this case, we cannot say that petitioner has sustained that heavy burden. A contrary ruling would mean that the Federal Government as a whole lacked the power exercised by the President, see id., at 636-637, and that we are not prepared to say.

Although we have concluded that the IEEPA constitutes specific congressional authorization to the President to nullify the attachments and order the transfer of Iranian assets, there remains the question of the President's authority to suspend claims pending in American courts. Such claims have, of course, an existence apart from the attachments which accompanied them. In terminating these claims through Executive Order No. 12294, the President purported to act under authority of both the IEEPA and 22 U.S.C. 1732, the so-called "Hostage Act." 46 Fed. Reg. 14111 (1981).

[The Court concludes that neither the IEEPA nor the Hostage Act authorized the suspension of claims.]

Although we have declined to conclude that the IEEPA or the Hostage Act directly authorizes the President's suspension of claims for the reasons noted, we cannot ignore the general tenor of Congress' legislation in this area in trying to determine whether the President is acting alone or at least with the acceptance of Congress. As we have noted, Congress cannot anticipate and legislate with regard to every possible action the President may find it necessary to take or every possible situation in which he might act. Such failure of Congress specifically to delegate authority does not, "especially . . . in the areas of foreign policy and national security," imply "congressional disapproval" of action taken by the Executive. Haig v. Agee, ante, at 291. On the contrary, the enactment of legislation closely related to the question of the President's authority in a particular case which evinces legislative intent to accord the President broad discretion may be considered to "invite" "measures on independent presidential responsibility," Youngstown, 343 U.S., at 637 (Jackson, J., concurring). At least this is so where there is no contrary indication of legislative intent and when, as here, there is a history of congressional acquiescence in conduct of the sort engaged in by the President. It is to that history which we now turn.

Not infrequently in affairs between nations, outstanding claims by nationals of one country against the government of another country are "sources of friction" between the two sovereigns. United States v. Pink, 315 U.S. 203, 225 (1942). To resolve these difficulties, nations have often entered into agreements settling the claims of their respective nationals . . . Since 1952, the President has entered into at least 10 binding settlements with foreign nations, including an $80 million settlement with the People's Republic of China.

Crucial to our decision today is the conclusion that Congress has implicitly approved the practice of claim settlement by executive agreement. [The Court explains that Congress enacted, and has frequently amended, the International Claims Settlement Act of 1949, which facilitates the resolution of claims by U.S. nationals against foreign governments.]

* * *

Petitioner next asserts that Congress divested the President of the authority to settle claims when it enacted the Foreign Sovereign Immunities Act of 1976 (hereinafter FSIA). 28 U.S.C. 1330, 1602 et seq. The FSIA granted personal and subject-matter jurisdiction in the federal district courts over commercial suits brought by claimants against those foreign states which have waived immunity. 28 U.S.C. 1330. Prior to the enactment of the FSIA, a foreign government's immunity to suit was determined by the Executive Branch on a case-by-case basis. According to petitioner, the principal purpose of the FSIA was to depoliticize these commercial lawsuits by taking them out of the arena of foreign affairs - where the Executive Branch is subject to the pressures of foreign states seeking to avoid liability through a grant of immunity - and by placing them within the exclusive jurisdiction of the courts. Petitioner thus insists that the

President, by suspending its claims, has circumscribed the jurisdiction of the United States courts in violation of Art. III of the Constitution. We disagree. In the first place, we do not believe that the President has attempted to divest the federal courts of jurisdiction. Executive Order No. 12294 purports only to "suspend" the claims, not divest the federal court of "jurisdiction." As we read the Executive Order, those claims not within the jurisdiction of the Claims Tribunal will "revive" and become judicially enforceable in United States courts. This case, in short, illustrates the difference between modifying federal-court jurisdiction and directing the courts to apply a different rule of law. See United States v. Schooner Peggy, 1 Cranch 103 (1801). The President has exercised the power, acquiesced in by Congress, to settle claims and, as such, has simply effected a change in the substantive law governing the lawsuit. Indeed, the very example of sovereign immunity belies petitioner's argument. No one would suggest that a determination of sovereign immunity divests the federal courts of "jurisdiction." Yet, petitioner's argument, if accepted, would have required courts prior to the enactment of the FSIA to reject as an encroachment on their jurisdiction the President's determination of a foreign state's sovereign immunity.

* * *

It is telling that the Congress which enacted the FSIA considered but rejected several proposals designed to limit the power of the President to enter into executive agreements, including claims settlement agreements. It is quite unlikely that the same Congress that rejected proposals to limit the President's authority to conclude executive agreements sought to accomplish that very purpose sub silentio through the FSIA. And, as noted above, just one year after enacting the FSIA, Congress enacted the IEEPA, where the legislative history stressed that nothing in the IEEPA was to impede the settlement of claims of United States citizens. It would be surprising for Congress to express this support for settlement agreements had it intended the FSIA to eliminate the President's authority to make such agreements.

In light of all of the foregoing - the inferences to be drawn from the character of the legislation Congress has enacted in the area, such as the IEEPA and the Hostage Act, and from the history of acquiescence in executive claims settlement - we conclude that the President was authorized to suspend pending claims pursuant to Executive Order No. 12294. As Justice Frankfurter pointed out in Youngstown, 343 U.S., at 610 -611, "a systematic, unbroken, executive practice, long pursued to the knowledge of the Congress and never before questioned . . . may be treated as a gloss on `Executive Power' vested in the President by 1 of Art. II." Past practice does not, by itself, create power, but "long-continued practice, known to and acquiesced in by Congress, would raise a presumption that the [action] had been [taken] in pursuance of its consent . . . ." United States v. Midwest Oil Co., 236 U.S. 459, 474 (1915). See Haig v. Agee, ante, at 291-292. Such practice is present here and such a presumption is also appropriate. In light of the fact that Congress may be considered to have consented to the President's action in suspending claims, we cannot say that action exceeded the President's powers.

Our conclusion is buttressed by the fact that the means chosen by the President to settle the claims of American nationals provided an alternative forum, the Claims Tribunal, which is capable of providing meaningful relief.

* * *

Finally, we re-emphasize the narrowness of our decision. We do not decide that the President possesses plenary power to settle claims, even as against foreign governmental entities. As the Court of Appeals for the First Circuit stressed, "[t]he sheer magnitude of such a power, considered against the background of the diversity and complexity of modern international trade, cautions against any broader construction of authority than is necessary." Chas. T. Main Int'l, Inc. v. Khuzestan Water & Power Authority, 651 F.2d, at 814. But where, as here, the settlement of claims has been determined to be a necessary incident to the resolution of a major foreign policy dispute between our country and another, and where, as here, we can conclude that Congress acquiesced in the President's action, we are not prepared to say that the President lacks the power to settle such claims.

[The Court chooses not to address the merits of the petitioner's argument that the suspension of its claims against Iran is a taking that requires just compensation. That argument is not ripe.]

The judgment of the District Court is accordingly affirmed, and the mandate shall issue forthwith.

It is so ordered.

DISCUSSION AND QUESTIONS

1. The *Dames & Moore* decision can be seen as a predictable synthesis of the fundamental teachings of *Curtiss-Wright* and *Youngstown.* If *Curtiss-Wright* stands for the proposition that the President enjoys extraordinary freedom of action in the realm of foreign relations, and if *Youngstown* (particularly Justice Jackson's concurrence) instructs that presidential action enjoys great deference when it appears to be consistent with the will of the Congress, then the outcome in *Dames & Moore* is hardly surprising. When he "nullified" certain claims, the President was acting pursuant to express congressional authorization. When he "suspended" certain claims, the President was acting in a way that was consistent with apparent congressional policy, albeit policy that had not manifested itself in the form of an enacted statute.

2. The Constitution contemplates that presidents may enter into treaties (with Senate approval) and that such treaties "shall be the supreme law of the land" (along with the Constitution and federal statutes). Yet here, the international agreement under which Presidents Carter and Reagan were acting was an executive agreement between the United States and Iran, rather than a treaty approved by the Senate pursuant to Article II, Section 2. The Constitution gives no effect to such non-treaty international executive agreements; indeed, it does not mention them. Given that the Constitution specifies how a President may properly enter into an international agreement and give it binding force domestically, is the Court being unduly deferential to presidential power by facilitating domestic enforcement of an executive agreement that does not meet these constitutional specifications?

3. What if the President had gone a step further and, rather than transferring claims to an international settlement tribunal, had completely extinguished certain claims against Iran? In fact, that did happen, and the President's decision was upheld by the courts. As part of the agreement with Iran, any claims that the former hostages – held for 444 days against their will – might have asserted against Iran were extinguished. In effect, the President agreed on behalf of these hostages to waive any legal claims stemming from their captivity. The courts upheld this executive action under the reasoning of *Dames & Moore* and *Curtiss-Wright. See, e.g., Belk v. United States*, 858 F.2d 706 (Fed. Cir. 1988) (citing the same historical settlement authority relied on by the court in *Dames & Moore* and granting deference to "a policy decision made by the President during a time of crisis"). Extinguishing claims entirely is qualitatively different from settling claims. Is the outcome in *Belk* consistent with the statement in *Dames & Moore* that "crucial to our decision today is the conclusion that Congress has implicitly approved the practice of claim settlement by executive agreement"?

EXECUTIVE ACTION TAKEN VIA EXECUTIVE ORDER

When presidents take formal action of one kind or another, they often do so through executive orders. An executive order is sometimes characterized as a "proclamation" (often if it has only a ceremonial or commemorative purpose) and sometimes as a "directive" (for example, Presidents George H.W. Bush and Bill Clinton issued executive orders relating to national security matters as presidential "directives").

Most often, executive orders are instructions from the President to those who work for him in the Executive Branch. For instance, many presidents have issued directions to federal agencies as to criteria they must apply in awarding government contracts. Examples of two such executive orders appear in the *AFL-CIO v. Kahn* and *Chamber of Commerce v. Reich* cases discussed below. President Barack Obama continued this practice when, just days after taking office in January 2009, he issued several executive orders related to government contracting that many observers considered to reflect a pro-labor stance by the new Administration. These orders prohibited the government from reimbursing government contractors for costs associated with opposing union organizing efforts (Executive Order 13494) and required federal contractors to post in the workplace a notification of employees' organizational rights under the National Labor Relations Act (Executive Order 13496). A President might also issue an executive order that re-organizes an agency, that sets up a presidential commission to study and offer recommendations on a particular subject, that instructs the Executive Branch how it should respond to certain types of emergencies, or on myriad other matters relating to the policies and operations of the government.

Some executive orders, however, extend beyond the internal management of the government and have much wider-ranging effects. In some instances, a President may exercise important statutory authority through executive order, as Franklin Roosevelt did with his proclamation prohibiting the sale of arms to Bolivia and Paraguay in the *Curtiss-Wright* case. Some of the most consequential – and controversial – executive orders have involved a President's invocation of his commander in chief authority, such as Truman's order seizing privately-owned steel mills, which became the subject of the *Youngstown* decision, or Lincoln's unilateral suspension of the writ of habeas corpus during the Civil War (see pages 255-56).

Other notable executive orders include:

- In 1939, Franklin Roosevelt issued Executive Order 8248, which formally created and outlined the organization of the modern

Executive Office of the President. This executive order was issued pursuant to a specific legislative authorization contained in the Reorganization Act of 1939, which was intended to enable Roosevelt to remake and assert greater control over the Executive Branch. Among other things, this executive order expanded and formalized the status of the President's personal assistants in the "The White House Office" and created the Office of Management and Budget.

- In 1948, Harry Truman issued Executive Order 9981, which ended racial segregation in the Armed Forces of the United States. The operative language stated: "It is hereby declared to be the policy of the President that there shall be equality of treatment and opportunity for all persons in the armed services without regard to race, color, religion, or national origin." Although this was an unprecedented, controversial and huge step in terms of its societal impact, it was one that Truman could take unilaterally by invoking his authority as commander in chief.

- Perhaps the most well-known executive order in American history (although many are unaware that it was an executive order) is Abraham Lincoln's Emancipation Proclamation of 1863. Despite the widespread perception that Lincoln issued this executive order because he opposed slavery in principle and wanted to end it, the proclamation was explicitly based on Lincoln's authority as commander in chief and made clear that its legal justification was as a "war measure" implemented to help suppress the rebellion. The proclamation did not purport to free all slaves throughout the United States. It did not free slaves in border states that had not seceded, such as Kentucky, Maryland and Missouri; rather, it freed slaves only in states that were in open rebellion, and even then it exempted from its effects certain portions of Louisiana and Virginia that were under federal control, which were "left precisely as if this proclamation had not issued." The goal of the Emancipation Proclamation was not to end slavery altogether but, more specifically, to undermine the important social and economic institution of slavery in rebel states and thereby impede the war-fighting capacity of the Confederacy.

- In 1942, Franklin Roosevelt issued Executive Order 9066 -- one of the most notorious ever issued by any President. This executive order was premised on Roosevelt's power as commander in chief, and it authorized the military "to prescribe military areas . . . from which any or all persons may be excluded." The stated rationale for this step was "protection against espionage and against sabotage to national-defense material, national-defense premises, and national-defense utilities." Implementation of this executive order led to the exclusion of tens of thousands of American citizens of Japanese ancestry from their homes, mostly along the West Coast. To a much lesser degree, Americans of German and Italian ancestry were also affected. The vast majority of those who were excluded from military areas were transported to internment camps called "War Relocation Centers." Shortly after its issuance, Roosevelt's executive order was ratified by an act of Congress that imposed criminal penalties on those who violated military exclusion orders. Although this executive order effectively interned, against their will, tens of thousands of American citizens based on nothing more than their ancestry, it was upheld as a necessary war measure in the case of *Korematsu. v. United States*, 323 U.S. 214 (1944), discussed at pages 263-76.

AFL-CIO v. Kahn

618 F.2d 784 (D.C. Cir. 1979)[4]

J. SKELLY WRIGHT, Chief Judge:

This case presents the question whether Congress has authorized the President to deny Government contracts above $5 million to companies that fail or refuse to comply with the voluntary wage and price standards. We answer that question in the affirmative.

[In November of 1978, in an effort to combat conditions of extraordinarily high price inflation throughout the economy, President Carter issued Executive Order 12092, which established the Council on Wage and Price Stability. The Council established voluntary standards for wage and price increases to be considered non-inflationary. The order also directed that federal government contractors must comply with the Council's standards on wages and prices or face termination of existing contracts and debarment from competing for future federal contracts. Plaintiff labor unions complained that the order interfered with their right to collectively bargain for wages and challenged the President's authority to issue such an order.]

[4] Footnotes and some citations found in the original decision have been omitted from this excerpted version.

We note at the outset our disagreement with the contention that this case presents the same issue decided by the Supreme Court in Youngstown Sheet & Tube Co. v. Sawyer. In Youngstown President Truman argued that he could constitutionally seize and operate the steel mills, which had been closed by a labor dispute, under his "inherent powers" to deal with national emergencies and wartime situations. In arguing for the validity of Executive Order 12092, however, the Government relies entirely upon authority said to be delegated by statute, and makes no appeal to constitutional powers of the Executive that have not been confirmed by legislation. Thus, although both cases involve challenges to Executive actions, they raise sharply different legal questions. Although the separation of powers between Congress and the President was the dominant issue in Youngstown, here we primarily face a difficult problem of statutory interpretation. Appellees' challenge to the Executive Order is directed at the procurement aspect of the Order, not at the Council's authority under Council On Wage Price Stability Act [COWPSA] to promulgate voluntary standards. Thus the central issue in this case is whether the Federal Property and Administrative Services Act [FPASA] indeed grants to the President the powers he has asserted.

The FPASA was a response to the recommendation of the Hoover Commission in 1949 that the Government's method of doing business be streamlined and modernized. The statute was designed to centralize Government property management and to introduce into the public procurement process the same flexibility that characterizes such transactions in the private sector. These goals can be found in the terms "economy" and "efficiency" which appear in the statute and dominate the sparse record of the congressional deliberations.

The most important provision of the Act for this case, Section 205(a), provides that the President "may prescribe such policies and directives, not inconsistent with the provisions of this Act, as he shall deem necessary to effectuate the provisions of said Act."

* * *

"Economy" and "efficiency" are not narrow terms; they encompass those factors like price, quality, suitability, and availability of goods or services that are involved in all acquisition decisions . . . Section 205(a) grants the President particularly direct and broad-ranging authority over those larger administrative and management issues that involve the Government as a whole. And that direct presidential authority should be used in order to achieve a flexible management system capable of making sophisticated judgments in pursuit of economy and efficiency.

[The Court then surveyed other executive orders by which previous presidents had incorporated policy objectives into the federal procurement process.]

Any order based on Section 205(a) must accord with the values of "economy" and "efficiency." Because there is a sufficiently close nexus between those criteria and the procurement compliance program established by Executive Order 12092, we find that program to be authorized by the FPASA.

* * *

We do not deny that under Executive Order 12092 there may be occasional instances where a low bidder will not be awarded a contract. Nevertheless, we find no basis for rejecting the President's conclusion that any higher costs incurred in those transactions will be more than offset by the advantages gained in negotiated contracts and in those cases where the lowest bidder is in compliance with the voluntary standards and his bid is lower than it would have been in the absence of standards. Consequently, we conclude that Executive Order 12092 is in accord with the "economy and efficiency" touchstone of the FPASA. By acting to restrain procurement costs across the entire Government, the President was within his Section 205(a) powers.

[The Court then explained that President Carter's procurement program under Executive Order 12092 was not inconsistent with the Council on Wage and Price Stability Act. While that act made clear that it did not authorize the imposition of mandatory wage and price controls, this "is of no concern," because the Executive Order relies on the FPASA, not the COWPSA, for its authority. Further, when the government imposes conditions on government contractors, it is not coercively mandating that those conditions be met; enterprises that do not wish to meet the conditions may simply refrain from accepting government contracts.]

* * *

[Judge MACKINNON issued a lengthy dissent arguing that Executive Order 12092 went far beyond the limited authority delegated to the President by the FPASA. He also argued that history shows that Congress has zealously guarded its authority to set wage and price controls, and it never intended to delegate to the President any authority to impose mandatory wage and price controls on any company or industry, even those that do business with the government.]

Chamber of Commerce v. Reich

74 F.3d 1322 (D.C. Cir. 1996)[5]

SILBERMAN, Circuit Judge:

Appellants challenge President Clinton's Executive Order barring the federal government from contracting with employers who hire permanent replacements during a lawful strike. The district court determined that appellants' challenge is not judicially reviewable and, in any event, the Order is legal. We conclude that judicial review is available and that the Order conflicts with the National Labor Relations Act, and therefore we reverse.

President Clinton issued Executive Order No. 12,954, 60 Fed.Reg. 13,023 (1995), on March 8, 1995, pursuant to his authority under the Federal Property and Administrative Services Act, 40 U.S.C. § 471 *et seq.* (the Procurement Act), which declares:

> It is the policy of the executive branch in procuring goods and services that, to ensure the economical and efficient administration and completion of Federal Government contracts, contracting agencies shall not contract with employers that permanently replace lawfully striking employees.

Order at 13,023, § 1. The Order applies to all government contracts over $100,000. In 1994, federal procurement exceeded $400 billion and constituted approximately 6.5% of the gross domestic product. *See* STATISTICAL ABSTRACT OF THE UNITED STATES 451 (115th ed. 1995). As of 1993, approximately 26 million workers, 22% of the labor force, were employed by federal contractors and subcontractors. GENERAL ACCOUNTING OFFICE, REPORT TO SENATOR PAUL SIMON, WORKER PROTECTION: FEDERAL

[5] Footnotes and some citations found in the original decision have been omitted from this excerpted version.

CONTRACTORS AND VIOLATIONS OF LABOR LAW (Oct. 1995) (GAO REPORT).

The Order explains that the "balance" between allowing businesses to operate during a strike and preserving worker rights is disrupted when an employer hires permanent replacements during a strike. "It has been found" that the hiring of permanent replacements results in longer strikes, can change a "limited dispute into a broader, more contentious struggle," and results in the loss to the employer of the "accumulated knowledge, experience, skill, and expertise" of the striking workers. These consequences adversely affect federal contractors' ability to supply high quality and reliable goods and services.

The Secretary of Labor is charged with implementing and enforcing the Order. If the Secretary finds that a contractor has permanently replaced lawfully striking workers, the Secretary "may make a finding that it is appropriate to terminate the contract for convenience" unless the head of the contracting agency objects. The Secretary is also to debar contractors that have permanently replaced striking workers from future government contracts unless the "labor dispute precipitating the permanent replacement of lawfully striking workers has been resolved, as determined by the Secretary" or the head of the agency determines that there is a compelling reason to lift the debarment.

* * *

Appellants challenge the Executive Order on three separate grounds: that the Order transgresses an employer's statutory right (under the NLRA [National Labor Relations Act]) to hire permanent replacements to supplant "economic" strikers; that the Order also violates the very Procurement Act which it purports to implement because the President neglected to make findings tying the Order to savings in government procurement costs; and that this lack of presidential findings independently violates the Constitution since it would render the Procurement Act an unconstitutional delegation under *Panama Refining Co. v. Ryan,* 293 U.S. 388, 55 S.Ct. 241, 79 L.Ed. 446 (1935).

[The court addressed the government's procedural argument that the court lacked authority to review presidential action taken through executive order. Ample precedent, including but not limited to *Leedom v. Kyne,* 358 U.S. 184, 79 S.Ct. 180, 3 L.Ed.2d 210 (1958), instructs that there is a strong presumption in favor of judicial review of action taken by government officials that exceeds their legal authority.]

Appellants' most powerful argument on the merits, it strikes us, is their claim that the Executive Order is in conflict with the NLRA. If that is so, it is unnecessary to decide whether, in the absence of the NLRA, the President would be authorized (with or without appropriate findings) under the Procurement Act and the Constitution to issue the Executive Order. It is, in that regard, undisputed that the NLRA preserves to employers the right to permanently replace economic strikers as an offset to the employees' right to strike. Almost 60 years ago, the Supreme Court explained that an employer retained the right "to protect and continue his business by supplying places left vacant by strikers. And he is not bound to discharge those hired to fill the places of strikers, upon the election of the latter to resume their employment, in order to create places for them." *NLRB v. Mackay Radio & Tel. Co.,* 304 U.S. 333, 345-46, 58 S.Ct. 904, 910-11, 82 L.Ed. 1381 (1938). The Court has repeatedly approved and reaffirmed *Mackay Radio.*

* * *

The President's authority to pursue "efficient and economic" procurement, *see* 40 U.S.C. § 486(a), to be sure, has been interpreted to permit such broad ranging Executive Orders as 11,246 and 12,092, respectively guaranteeing equal employment opportunities, and restricting wage increases on the part of government contractors-measures which certainly reach beyond any narrow concept of efficiency and economy in procurement. But in those cases, the Third Circuit and this court did not perceive any conflict with another federal statute. Here, undeniably there is some tension between the President's Executive Order and the NLRA. To determine whether that tension constitutes unacceptable conflict we look to the extensive body of Supreme Court cases that mark out the boundaries of the field occupied by the NLRA. Since the progenitors of these cases originally arose in the context of state actions that were thought to interfere with the federal statute, they are referred to collectively as establishing the NLRA "pre-emption doctrine." The principles developed, however, have been applied equally to federal governmental behavior that is thought similarly to encroach into the NLRA's regulatory territory.

The Supreme Court has crafted two different types of NLRA pre-emption. *Metropolitan Life Ins. Co. v. Massachusetts,* 471 U.S. 724, 748, 105 S.Ct. 2380, 2393, 85 L.Ed.2d 728 (1985). *Garmon* pre-emption "forbids state and local regulation of activities that are 'protected by § 7 of the [NLRA], or constitute an unfair labor practice under § 8.' " [Citations omitted.] *Machinists* pre-emption, on the other hand, prohibits regulation of areas that Congress intended to be left "unregulated and to be controlled by the free play of economic forces." *Lodge 76, International Ass'n of Machinists & Aerospace Workers v. Wisconsin Employment Relations Comm'n,* 427 U.S. 132, 144, 96 S.Ct. 2548, 2555, 49 L.Ed.2d 396 (1976) (holding that a Wisconsin employment relations board could not find a refusal to work overtime, an action that did not violate the NLRA, an unfair labor practice). The underlying rationale is that union and management "proceed from contrary and to an extent antagonistic viewpoints and concepts of self-interest.... The presence of economic weapons in reserve, and their actual exercise on occasion by the parties, is part and parcel of the system that the Wagner and Taft-Hartley Acts have recognized." *NLRB v. Insurance Agents' Int'l Union,* 361 U.S. 477, 488-89, 80 S.Ct. 419, 426-27, 4 L.Ed.2d 454 (1960). In fact, *Machinists* itself refers to the "hiring of permanent replacements" as an economic weapon available to an employer. 427 U.S. at 153, 96 S.Ct. at 2559.

Nor, as we have noted, is there any doubt that *Machinists* "pre-emption" applies to federal as well as state action . . . The Court has described *Machinists* pre-emption as creating a "free zone from which all regulation, 'whether *federal* or State,' is excluded." *Golden State Transit Corp. v. Los Angeles,* 493 U.S. 103, 111, 110 S.Ct. 444, 451, 107 L.Ed.2d 420 (1989) (quoting *Machinists,* 427 U.S. at 153, 96 S.Ct. at 2559) (citation omitted); emphasis added); *see also Machinists,* 427 U.S. at 141, 96 S.Ct. at 2553 (explaining that *Machinists* pre-emption protects conduct that "Congress intended to be 'unrestricted by *any* governmental power to regulate' ") (quoting *Insurance Agents,* 361 U.S. at 488-89, 80 S.Ct. at 426-27) (emphasis added in *Machinists*).

* * *

It does not seem to us possible to deny that the President's Executive Order seeks to set a broad policy governing the behavior of thousands of American companies and affecting millions of American workers. The President has, of course, acted to set procurement policy rather than labor policy. But the former is quite explicitly based-and would have to be based-on his views of the latter. For the premise of the Executive Order is the proposition that the permanent replacement of strikers unduly prolongs and widens strikes and disrupts the proper "balance" between employers and employees. Whether that proposition is correct, or whether the prospect of permanent replacements deters strikes, and therefore an employer's right to permanently replace strikers is simply one element in the relative bargaining power of management and organized labor, is beside the point. Whatever one's views on the issue, it surely goes to the heart of United States labor relations policy.

* * *

In *Kahn,* we recognized that the imposition of wage and price controls as a condition of eligibility for government contractors could result in the government actually paying more for individual government contracts than might be so otherwise. 618 F.2d at 793. We thought, however, the President's judgment that the overall impact of those controls would reduce government procurement costs was entitled to deference . . . But labor relations policy is different because of the NLRA and its broad field of pre-emption. No state or federal official or government entity can alter the delicate balance of bargaining and economic power that the NLRA establishes, whatever his or its purpose may be.

* * *

We, therefore, conclude that the Executive Order is regulatory in nature and is pre-empted by the NLRA which guarantees the right to hire permanent replacements. The district court is hereby

Reversed.

DISCUSSION AND QUESTIONS

1. The D.C. Circuit's contrasting treatment of the executive orders in the *Kahn* and *Reich* cases pointedly illustrates the teaching of *Youngstown*. When the President acts pursuant to congressional authorization (as in *Kahn*), his action is very likely to be upheld. When the President acts in contravention of clear congressional intent (as in *Reich*), his power is, as Justice Jackson explained, "at its lowest ebb." As a practical matter, can there be any limits on what a President may do, so long as Congress agrees that he may do it? On the one hand, Franklin Roosevelt's forced relocation of tens of thousands of American citizens based on nothing but their Japanese ancestry -- which was ratified by Congress shortly after Roosevelt issued his order -- was upheld by the Supreme Court in the *Korematsu* case (see pages 264-74). On the other hand, with the enactment of the Line Item Veto Act in 1996, both

the Congress and President Clinton agreed that the President should be authorized to cancel from spending legislation specific items that he found objectionable; nevertheless, the Supreme Court invalidated such presidential action (and the Act) as unconstitutional in the case of *Clinton v. New York* (see pages 66-71).

2. Could the President, citing his belief that a terrorist attack against the heart of the federal government was imminent, issue an executive order sealing off the entire city of Washington, D.C. -- no one enters the city until further notice? Would such an order be legal if it were based only on the President's constitutional authority as commander in chief? Would such an order require congressional approval or ratification before it could be deemed a legal action by the executive? If such an order were to be issued (with or without congressional assent), how would it square with the citizen's "right to come to the seat of government" to assert claims, transact business or seek protection from the government? *Crandall v. Nevada*, 73 U.S. 35, 44 (1867); *see also*, *In re Slaughterhouse Cases*, 83 U.S. 36, 79 (1872) (citing *Crandall* and noting that the right of access to the seat of government is a privilege inherent in U.S. citizenship); U.S. Constitution, First Amendment (articulating the "right of the people . . . to petition the government for a redress of grievances").

3. Justice Jackson explained in *Youngstown* that "When the President acts pursuant to an express or implied authorization of Congress, his authority is at its maximum, for it includes all that he possesses in his own right plus all that Congress can delegate." In *Curtiss-Wright*, Congress had delegated to the President the discretion to criminalize (or not) certain conduct. In that case, the sale of arms to Bolivia or Paraguay was made a criminal offense because President Roosevelt issued a proclamation stating that it would be so. Given the strong presumption in favor of the legality of Executive Branch action when it is approved by Congress, are there any limits on what Congress may authorize the executive to do? What are the limits, and on what basis are they imposed? The simple answer is that Congress can legislatively authorize the President to exercise any or all power that is possessed by the federal government. As Justice Jackson phrased it in *Youngstown*, when the President acts with express congressional approval, he effectively "personif[ies] federal sovereignty." Therefore, the limitation on congressional delegation of authority to the Executive Branch is not *how much* authority can be delegated, but *how* the authority is delegated. In theory, when it delegates power to the Executive Branch, the Legislative Branch must set forth the restrictions on the scope of such authority and must provide guidance as to how such authority is to be used, in order to avoid an Executive Branch run amok. In practice, however, these limitations are

virtually meaningless. The Supreme Court has ruled that Congress may delegate its authority "under broad general directives" and need only provide the barest "intelligible principle" about how such authority is to be exercised. *Mistretta v. United States*, 488 U.S. 361, 372 (1989); *see also, Whitman v. American Trucking Associations, Inc.*, 531 U.S. 457, 472-75 (2001). The criteria for what constitutes a legally sufficient "intelligible principle" are so forgiving that even a concept as vague as "public interest" has been considered adequate statutory guidance. *National Broadcasting Company, Inc. v. United States*, 319 U.S. 190, 216, 224-25 (1943). In only two cases -- more than 75 years ago -- has the Supreme Court invalidated congressional delegations of power to the Executive Branch. *Panama Refining Co. v. Ryan*, 293 US 388 (1935); *Shechter Poultry Corp. v. United States*, 295 US 495 (1935). (For more on the delegation of power from the Legislative Branch to the Executive Branch, see Chapter Six, pages 177-94.)

PRESIDENTIAL SIGNING STATEMENTS

When signing a bill into law, a President will often issue a "signing statement," in which the President explains to the public and to his subordinates within the Executive Branch how he views the new law and, sometimes, how he intends to enforce it. The signing statement may also represent an effort to create legislative history to influence subsequent judicial interpretation of the statute. (Notably, in the 1980s, then-Attorney General Ed Meese convinced West Publishing to include presidential signing statements in its *United States Code Congressional and Administrative News* along with congressional records reflecting the legislative history of certain statutes.) A signing statement may be positive and laudatory toward the new enactment. For instance, on February 17, 2009, when President Barack Obama signed into law an economic stimulus package titled the American Recovery and Reinvestment Act of 2009, he issued a brief signing statement that unequivocally touted the expected benefits of the act. It said, in part:

> The Act provides a direct fiscal boost to help lift our Nation from the greatest economic crisis in our lifetimes and lay the foundation for further growth. This recovery plan will help to save or create as many as three to four million jobs by the end of 2010, the vast majority of them in the private sector. It will make the most significant investment in America's roads, bridges, mass transit, and other infrastructure since the construction of the interstate highway system. It will make investments to foster reform in education, double renewable energy while fostering efficiency in the use

of our energy, and improve quality while bringing down costs in healthcare. Middle-class families will get tax cuts and the most vulnerable will get the largest increase in assistance in decades.

On other occasions, however, presidents have used signing statements to criticize laws even as they are enacting them; to declare that a provision of a law is unconstitutional; or to offer a narrow interpretation of a law, along with a pronouncement that the President intends to enforce the law in some limited fashion. For example:

- In 1876, signing an appropriations bill, President Ulysses Grant stated that he would not spend money for local public works projects -- "under no circumstances will I allow expenditures upon works not clearly national."

- President Theodore Roosevelt signed a bill in 1909 that, among other things, purported to prevent him from obtaining advice from uncompensated presidential commissions. He explained that he would ignore this restriction: "Congress cannot prevent the president from seeking advice."

- In signing a merchant marine bill in 1920, President Woodrow Wilson announced that he would not enforce certain provisions that, in his opinion, would have violated various treaty obligations of the United States.

- In 1976, President Gerald Ford signed the Department of Defense Appropriation Act because it provided for necessary defense spending, but declared that he would treat "as a complete nullity" a provision that required approval from specific congressional committees before certain funds could be spent.

Despite the long history of presidents using signing statements to comment favorably or unfavorably on legislative enactments, the practice garnered unusual and vigorous criticism during the Administration of George W. Bush. President Bush sometimes inserted into signing statements the proviso that he would construe legislation "in a manner consistent with the constitutional authorities of the President to supervise the unitary executive branch." He also often invoked the "constitutional authority of the President to conduct the Nation's foreign relations" and his authority "as Commander in Chief of the Armed Forces." President Bush often announced, for example, that he would not be bound by legislative requirements that he report certain information to Congress within certain time frames; that he submit his policy decisions for review and approval by certain congressional committees; or that he accept congressional recommendations for certain presidential appointments. (See, e.g., March 6, 2006 Statement on Signing the USA PATRIOT Improvement and Reauthorization Act of 2005; December 20, 2006 Statement on Signing the Tax Relief and Health Care Act of 2006; September 30, 2003 Statement on Signing the Department of Defense Appropriations Act, 2004.) Perhaps because of his unabashed assertion of muscular executive powers in other areas (e.g., the detention and interrogation of enemy combatants, the use of warrantless wiretaps), President Bush's critics viewed his use of signing statements as an improper intrusion into the legislative realm. As Senator Patrick Leahy, Democratic Senator from Vermont and Ranking Member of the Senate Judiciary Committee, stated in June of 2006, "this Administration has taken what was otherwise a press release and transformed it into a proclamation stating which parts of the law the President will follow and which parts he will simply ignore." Senator Leahy characterized President Bush's "unprecedented" use of signing statements as "a grave threat to our constitutional system of checks and balances." Even the Republican Chairman of the Judiciary Committee, Senator Arlen Specter of Pennsylvania, described President Bush's signing statements as a "blatant encroachment" on Legislative Branch power.

As a result of such concerns about President Bush's signing statements, the American Bar Association generated a report on the subject, which concluded:

> If our constitutional system of separation of powers is to operate as the framers intended, the President must accept the limitations imposed on his office by the Constitution itself. The use of presidential signing statements to have the last word as to which laws will be enforced and which will not is inconsistent with those limitations and poses a serious threat to the rule of law.

Report of the ABA Task Force on Presidential Signing Statements and the Separation of Powers Doctrine, at 20 (August 2006). Based on its recommendations for reform with regard to presidential signing statements, the ABA Task Force was apparently concerned that presidents use signing statements essentially to rewrite legislation with which they have qualms, rather than veto it. According to the Task Force, when a President asserts that he will not enforce a certain legislative provision as drafted, he is "claim[ing] line-item veto authority that trespass[es] on the lawmaking powers of Congress." Id. at 25.

DISCUSSION AND QUESTIONS

1. Do presidential signing statements represent the "grave threat to our constitutional system of checks and balances" that Senator Leahy argued? To develop a meaningful answer to this question, one must consider what the actual effect is of a signing statement. Suppose a President signs into law the "X, Y and Z Act," and as he is doing so, announces that "I consider provision Z to be an unconstitutional infringement on the authority of the Executive Branch and will therefore treat this provision as a complete nullity." Suppose further that, contrary to his stated intention, the President then complies with provision Z – that is, he abides by the entire X, Y and Z Act as drafted. Has this President flouted the will of the Congress? Has he acted inconsistently with any law? Imagine other circumstances in which the President signs the X, Y and Z Act into law, issues no signing statement, and then refuses to comply with provision Z. In terms of evaluating whether the President is behaving in conformity with constitutional requirements, is it what the President *says* that matters, or is it what the President actually *does*?

2. The Constitution requires the President to "take care that the laws be faithfully executed." Article II, Section 3. Is the President obliged to enforce or abide by even those statutory provisions that he believes are unconstitutional for one reason or another? Or, does the President, as the embodiment of a separate and co-equal branch of the government, have an obligation to engage in – and act on – his own, independent assessment of a statute's constitutionality? In vetoing the re-chartering of the Second Bank of the United States on July 10, 1832, President Andrew Jackson contended:

> The Congress, the Executive, and the Court must each for itself be guided by its own opinion of the Constitution. Each public officer who takes an oath to support the Constitution swears that he will support it as he understands it, and not as it is understood by others. It is as much the duty of the House of Representatives, of the Senate, and of the President to decide upon the constitutionality of any bill or resolution which may be presented to them for passage or approval as it is of the supreme judges when it may be brought before them for judicial decision.

The ABA Task Force suggested that, by signaling his refusal to enforce what he believes to be an unconstitutional statutory provision, a President is seeking "to usurp judicial authority as the final arbiter of the constitutionality of congressional acts." ABA Task Force Report at 23. Is this really a concern? Even if a President follows through on his stated intention not to enforce a particular statutory provision, how is the disagreement between the Executive Branch and the Legislative Branch likely to be resolved? To put it in more concrete terms, suppose an appropriations bill directs the Executive Branch to spend certain funds on anti-terrorism measures in New York City, and the President, believing such a direction to be an unconstitutional infringement on his executive authority, refuses to expend those funds for that purpose. How is such a disagreement likely to be resolved? (Hint: Consider the line-item veto case, *Clinton v. New York*, discussed below at pages 66-74.)

3. Many critics of President Bush's extensive use of signing statements argued that, if the President disagrees with some aspect of a proposed law, he should use his constitutional veto power to reject the entire law rather than announce in a signing statement that he intends to interpret narrowly, or ignore entirely, selected portions. Indeed, this was one recommendation for reform that was urged by the ABA Task Force. Which is the better course? In the modern legislative process, some bills passed by Congress are literally thousands of pages long and contain hundreds of separate provisions – often relating to many different topics. If such a bill lands on the President's desk and he finds that just a handful of provisions are troubling, is it preferable that he veto the bill in its entirety, or that he sign the bill and make clear his intentions to interpret a few provisions in a fashion that makes them less objectionable? What are the likely short- and long-term consequences of each approach?

4. Is it appropriate for courts to look to presidential signing statements as an aid to interpreting statutes? On one hand, the President is not a legislator, does not participate (at least not directly) in the debates that occur in the House and Senate, and does not cast a vote for or against any piece of proposed legislation. On the other hand, except on the rare occasion of a veto override by two-thirds of each chamber, no legislation can become law without the President's approval, and only the President brings to the lawmaking process the perspective of a leader who was elected on a nationwide basis. Are the President's views on a particular statute more meaningful or less meaningful than a single congressman's views that might be reflected in a floor speech?

THE PRESIDENTIAL VETO

The word "veto" does not itself appear in the Constitution; however, this term – from the Latin meaning "I forbid" -- has long been the accepted description for circumstances in which one governmental official acts unilaterally to prevent action by others. This notion of individual veto power goes back at least to the Roman Republic, in which concurrence of both Consuls was necessary to take executive action; either could "veto" action desired by the other.

Article I, Section 7 of the Constitution provides that:

> Every bill which shall have passed the House of Representatives and the Senate, shall, before it becomes a law, be presented to the President of the United States; if he approve he shall sign it, but if not he shall return it with his objections to that house in which it shall have originated …

Section 7 goes on to explain that a law may be enacted over presidential objection with a two-thirds vote in each house. Further, if the President does not express his disapproval within ten days of being presented with a bill, the bill becomes law, "unless the Congress, by their adjournment prevent its return, in which case it shall not be a law." (When, under this last provision, the President holds a bill until Congress adjourns, it is said that he has exercised a "pocket veto.")

Most presidents exercise their veto power infrequently. For example, President George W. Bush was in office for more than five years before he first used his veto power (in July of 2006 on a bill promoting stem cell research). Over the course of two full terms, President Bill Clinton vetoed just 36 bills (plus the pocket veto of one other). During the 211-year period from 1789 through 2000, presidents used a total of 2550 regular and pocket vetoes, or an average of one per month (this average is skewed upward by a handful of presidents who exercised an extraordinary number of vetoes, such as Franklin Roosevelt and Harry Truman). See *Presidential Vetoes, 1789-2000*, Senate Publication 107-10 (Government Printing Office 2001). Nevertheless, the President's power to prevent congressional action by vetoing it is a critical element of the inter-branch checks and balances envisioned by the Framers. In Federalist No. 73, Alexander Hamilton explained the rationale for the presidential veto:

> Without [a veto], the [President] would be absolutely unable to defend himself against the depredations of the [Congress]. He might gradually be stripped of his authorities by successive resolutions, or annihilated by a single vote . . . But the power in question has a further use. It not only serves as a shield to the Executive, but it furnishes an additional security against the enaction of improper laws. It establishes a salutary check upon the legislative body, calculated to guard the community against the effects of faction, precipitancy, or of any impulse unfriendly to the public good, which may happen to influence a majority of that body.

According to the explanation offered by Hamilton, a President should feel free to veto not only legislation that he concludes is unconstitutional, but also legislation that is "unfriendly to the public good" -- that is, legislation that the President believes is simply *a bad idea.*

The presidential veto is a formidable tool, but it is a blunt instrument as well, because it is an all-or-nothing proposition. As the following case establishes, the President is not empowered to veto a particular portion or provision of legislation. When a bill is passed by both chambers and presented to the President, he has only the simple choice of approving the legislation in total or rejecting it in total. This all-or-nothing nature of the veto largely explains why vetoes are not used routinely by most presidents, and further explains the use of signing statements in an effort to limit or interpret narrowly certain statutory provisions that presidents find objectionable. If a President were to veto every piece of legislation that was not entirely to his liking, few bills would ever become law, including the appropriations bills that must be passed every year to fund the continuing operations of the government.

Clinton v. New York

524 U.S. 417 (1998)[6]

JUSTICE STEVENS delivered the opinion of the Court.

[The Line Item Veto Act was enacted in 1996. It authorized the President to sign new bills into law but then to "cancel in whole" individual spending items or tax benefits that he found objectionable. President Clinton used this cancellation power in 1997 to cancel payments to New York that were provided for by the Balanced Budget Act of 1997 and to cancel certain tax benefits for farmers' cooperatives under the Taxpayer Relief Act of 1997. He canceled these particular provisions after he signed each of the bills into law. The Line Item Veto Act required the President to transmit to Congress a special message notifying it of each cancellation.]

A cancellation takes effect upon receipt by Congress of the special message from the President. See §691b(a). If, however, a "disapproval bill" pertaining to a special message is enacted into law, the cancellations set forth in that message become "null and void." Ibid . The Act sets forth a detailed expedited procedure for the

[6] Footnotes and some citations found in the original decision have been omitted from this excerpted version.

consideration of a "disapproval bill," see §691d, but no such bill was passed for either of the cancellations involved in these cases.

A majority vote of both Houses is sufficient to enact a disapproval bill. The Act does not grant the President the authority to cancel a disapproval bill, see §691(c), but he does, of course, retain his constitutional authority to veto such a bill.

The effect of a cancellation is plainly stated in §691e, which defines the principal terms used in the Act. With respect to both an item of new direct spending and a limited tax benefit, the cancellation prevents the item "from having legal force or effect." 2 U. S. C. §§691e(4)(B)-(C) (1994 ed., Supp. II).

Thus, under the plain text of the statute, the two actions of the President that are challenged in these cases prevented one section of the Balanced Budget Act of 1997 and one section of the Taxpayer Relief Act of 1997 "from having legal force or effect." The remaining provisions of those statutes, with the exception of the second canceled item in the latter, continue to have the same force and effect as they had when signed into law.

In both legal and practical effect, the President has amended two Acts of Congress by repealing a portion of each. "[R]epeal of statutes, no less than enactment, must conform with Art. I." INS v. Chadha, 462 U.S. 919, 954 (1983). There is no provision in the Constitution that authorizes the President to enact, to amend, or to repeal statutes. Both Article I and Article II assign responsibilities to the President that directly relate to the lawmaking process, but neither addresses the issue presented by these cases. The President "shall from time to time give to the Congress Information on the State of the Union, and recommend to their Consideration such Measures as he shall judge necessary and expedient . . . ." Art. II, §3. Thus, he may initiate and influence legislative proposals. Moreover, after a bill has passed both Houses of Congress, but "before it become[s] a Law," it must be presented to the President. If he approves it, "he shall sign it, but if not he shall return it, with his Objections to that House in which it shall have originated, who shall enter the Objections at large on their Journal, and proceed to reconsider it." Art. I, §7, cl. 2.

His "return" of a bill, which is usually described as a "veto," is subject to being overridden by a two-thirds vote in each House.

There are important differences between the President's "return" of a bill pursuant to Article I, §7, and the exercise of the President's cancellation authority pursuant to the Line Item Veto Act. The constitutional return takes place before the bill becomes law; the statutory cancellation occurs after the bill becomes law. The constitutional return is of the entire bill; the statutory cancellation is of only a part. Although the Constitution expressly authorizes the President to play a role in the process of enacting statutes, it is silent on the subject of unilateral Presidential action that either repeals or amends parts of duly enacted statutes.

There are powerful reasons for construing constitutional silence on this profoundly important issue as equivalent to an express prohibition. The procedures governing the enactment of statutes set forth in the text of Article I were the product of the great debates and compromises that produced the Constitution itself. Familiar historical materials provide abundant support for the conclusion that the power to enact statutes may only "be exercised in accord with a single, finely wrought and exhaustively considered, procedure." Chadha, 462 U.S., at 951. Our first President understood the text of the Presentment Clause as requiring that he either "approve all the parts of a Bill, or reject it in toto."

What has emerged in these cases from the President's exercise of his statutory cancellation powers, however, are truncated versions of two bills that passed both Houses of Congress. They are not the product of the "finely wrought" procedure that the Framers designed.

[This case is distinguishable from *Field v. Clark*, 143 U.S. 649 (1892), in which a statute authorized the President to suspend or impose certain tariffs on foreign goods. In *Field v. Clark* and other cases in which the President exercises authority that is given to him *pursuant to* a statute, he is not re-writing or partially repealing the statute. In contrast, the line Item Veto Act purports to enable the President to modify statutes after they are passed by the Congress and signed by the President.]

Neither are we persuaded by the Government's contention that the President's authority to cancel new direct spending and tax benefit items is no greater than his traditional authority to decline to spend appropriated funds. The Government has reviewed in some detail the series of statutes in which Congress has given the Executive broad discretion over the expenditure of appropriated funds. For example, the First Congress appropriated "sum[s] not exceeding" specified amounts to be spent on various Government operations. See, e.g. , Act of Sept. 29, 1789, ch. 23, §1, 1 Stat. 95; Act of Mar. 26, 1790, ch. 4, §1, 1 Stat. 104; Act of Feb. 11, 1791, ch. 6, 1 Stat. 190. In those statutes, as in later years, the President was given wide discretion with respect to both the amounts to be spent and how the money would be allocated among different functions. It is argued that the Line Item Veto Act merely confers comparable discretionary authority over the expenditure of appropriated funds. The critical difference between this statute and all of its predecessors, however, is that unlike any of them, this Act gives the President the unilateral power to change the text of duly enacted statutes. None of the Act's predecessors could even arguably have been construed to authorize such a change.

*   *   *

If there is to be a new procedure in which the President will play a different role in determining the final text of what may "become a law," such change must come not by legislation but through the amendment procedures set forth in Article V of the Constitution. Cf. U. S. Term Limits, Inc. v. Thornton, 514 U.S. 779, 837 (1995).

The judgment of the District Court is affirmed.

It is so ordered.

[JUSTICE KENNEDY concurred, noting that the Framers allocated to the Legislative Branch and the Executive Branch their respective roles in enacting laws expressly to avoid the concentration of too much power in one branch. A violation of this fundamental separation of powers principle is not permissible just because "Congress surrendered its authority by its own hand" or because the violation results from the pursuit of desirable policy objectives.]

[JUSTICE BREYER , with whom JUSTICE O'CONNOR and JUSTICE SCALIA joined [in part], dissented. Justice Breyer first argued that, in the modern federal government, "a typical budget appropriations bill may have a dozen titles, hundreds of sections, and spread across more than 500 pages of the Statutes at Large . . . Congress cannot divide such a bill into thousands, or tens of thousands, of separate appropriations bills, each one of which the President would have to sign, or to veto, separately."

He then argued that "when the President 'canceled' the two appropriation measures now before us, he did not repeal any law nor did he amend any law. He simply followed the law, leaving the statutes, as they are literally written, intact." The President simply used authority granted to him by the Line Item Veto Act to prevent certain spending provisions and tax benefits from having legal force or effect. This is not a legislative function; rather, it is an appropriate executive function performed pursuant to a delegation of authority from Congress.]

JUSTICE SCALIA , with whom JUSTICE O'CONNOR joins, and with whom JUSTICE BREYER joins [in part], concurring in part and dissenting in part.

[Justice Scalia questions the standing of certain appellees, but agrees that the New York appellees do have standing to challenge the cancellation of payments to New York.]

The Presentment Clause requires, in relevant part, that "[e]very Bill which shall have passed the House of Representatives and the Senate, shall, before it becomes a Law, be presented to the President of the United States; If he approve he shall sign it, but if not he shall return it," U. S. Const., Art. I, §7, cl. 2. There is no question that enactment of the Balanced Budget Act complied with these requirements: the House and Senate passed the bill, and the President signed it into law. It was only after the requirements of the Presentment Clause had been satisfied that the President exercised his authority under the Line Item Veto Act to cancel the spending item. Thus, the Court's problem with the Act is not that it authorizes the President to veto parts of a bill and sign others into law, but rather that it authorizes him to "cancel" -- prevent from "having legal force or effect" -- certain parts of duly enacted statutes. [Thus, the real question presented by this case is not whether the Line Item Veto Act violates the Presentment Clause of Article I, Section 7; rather, it is whether the power given to the President by the Act constitutes an impermissible delegation of legislative authority to the executive.]

I turn, then, to the crux of the matter: whether Congress's authorizing the President to cancel an item of spending gives him a power that our history and traditions show must reside exclusively in the Legislative Branch.

* * *

Insofar as the degree of political, "law-making" power conferred upon the Executive is concerned, there is not a dime's worth of difference between Congress's authorizing the President to cancel a spending item, and Congress's authorizing money to be spent on a particular item at the President's discretion. And the latter has been done since the Founding of the Nation . . . Examples of appropriations committed to the discretion of the President abound in our history. During the Civil War, an Act appropriated over $76 million to be divided among various items "as the exigencies of the service may require," Act of Feb. 25, 1862, ch. 32, 12 Stat. 344-345. During the Great Depression, Congress appropriated $950 million "for such projects and/or purposes and under such rules and regulations as the President in his discretion may prescribe," Act of Feb. 15, 1934, ch. 13, 48 Stat. 351, and $4 billion for general classes of projects, the money to be spent "in the discretion and under the direction of the President," Emergency Relief Appropriation Act of 1935, 49 Stat. 115. The constitutionality of such appropriations has never seriously been questioned. Rather, "[t]hat Congress has wide discretion in the matter of prescribing details of expenditures for which it appropriates must, of course, be plain. Appropriations and other acts of Congress are replete with instances of general appropriations of large amounts, to be allotted and expended as directed by designated government agencies." Cincinnati Soap Co. v. United States, 301 U.S. 308, 321 - 322 (1937).

* * *

The short of the matter is this: Had the Line Item Veto Act authorized the President to "decline to spend" any item of spending contained in the Balanced Budget Act of 1997, there is not the slightest doubt that authorization would have been constitutional. What the Line Item Veto Act does instead-authorizing the President to "cancel" an item of spending -- is technically different. But the technical difference does not relate to the technicalities of the Presentment Clause, which have been fully complied with; and the doctrine of unconstitutional delegation, which is at issue here, is preeminently not a doctrine of technicalities. The title of the Line Item Veto Act, which was perhaps designed to simplify for public comprehension, or perhaps merely to comply with the terms of a campaign pledge, has succeeded in faking out the Supreme Court. The President's action it authorizes in fact is not a line-item veto and thus does not offend Art. I, §7; and insofar as the substance of that action is concerned, it is no different from what Congress has permitted the President to do since the formation of the Union.

DISCUSSION AND QUESTIONS

1. At first glance, *Clinton v. New York* appears to present a situation that falls within zone one of Justice Jackson's *Youngstown* framework: The President is exercising authority to cancel spending items pursuant to an express statutory

authorization from Congress. Justice Jackson stated that, in such circumstances, the President's "authority is at its maximum" and there is a strong presumption in favor of the validity of the action taken. Why, then, does the Supreme Court invalidate the line-item veto? As Justice Jackson explained in *Youngstown*, "if his act is held unconstitutional under these circumstances, it usually means that the Federal Government, as an undivided whole, lacks power." Justice Stevens' opinion in *Clinton v. New York* confirmed Justice Jackson's view in this regard. Justice Stevens found that "constitutional silence" on the question of the line-item veto is "equivalent to an express prohibition." Thus, even when the Executive Branch and the Legislative Branch are in complete agreement, they may not take action that is prohibited by the Constitution.

2. Congress sometimes chooses expressly to make legislation "severable," which permits the courts to invalidate an individual provision in the act without invalidating the entire act. For instance, the Federal Election Campaign Act (as amended) provides that:

> If any provision of this Act, or the application thereof to any person or circumstance, is held invalid, the validity of the remainder of the Act and the application of such provision to other persons and circumstances shall not be affected thereby.

2. U.S.C. §454. If Congress can authorize the Judicial Branch to "cancel" individual provisions within legislation, why is Congress prohibited from giving the same authority to the Executive Branch? If the courts find a particular provision of a statute to be unconstitutional but leave the remainder of the statute in force, hasn't the Judicial Branch repealed or amended a statute without conforming to the Presentment Clause in Article I, §7?

3. In *Clinton v. New York*, Congress enacted stand-alone legislation (the Line Item Veto Act) that purported to give the President authority to cancel spending items in subsequent, separate bills. Would it make a difference in the President's cancellation authority if it were granted in *each* spending bill rather than in a separate act. For example, imagine a spending bill that provided as follows:

> This spending bill contains a total of 200 spending provisions. At the time he signs this bill, the President may, at his sole discretion, strike whichever provisions he deems appropriate and leave the remaining provisions in full force and effect.

If the President signed the bill into law and then struck certain spending items, one could argue that he was not amending or repealing the bill; rather, he was acting in a way that was perfectly consistent with, and expressly authorized by, the very bill in question. Would this bill be closer to the way Justice Scalia characterized the effects of the Line Item Veto Act – the President is merely choosing not to spend certain funds pursuant to discretion given to him by the same bill that authorized the spending?

4. Is Justice Breyer correct that it is not feasible for Congress to pass smaller, more discrete spending bills that a President can veto or sign separately? What prevents Congress from doing just that? If Congress can pass an enormous appropriations bill containing thousands of spending items, why can it not pass each spending item as an individual bill? If Justice Breyer is correct in his conclusion that Congress is unable to legislate individual spending items separately, what makes him believe that the President is able to consider individual spending items separately for purposes of applying the line item veto?

What would be the effect of Justice Breyer's apparent willingness to let Congress fund anything and everything that it collectively wishes to fund, and then leave it to the President to set priorities and make the tough calls about spending through use of the line item veto? Would this be the appropriate allocation of responsibilities between these two branches of the government?

5. In a sense, the concept of the line item veto is similar to the concept of "impoundment." Impoundment is the authority that was historically asserted by presidents to refrain from spending certain appropriated funds. Many presidents, from Thomas Jefferson to Richard Nixon, contended that it was inherent in their executive authority that they could choose not to spend money that was given to the Executive Branch by Congress. Opponents of impoundment argued that, once Congress appropriates funds and directs that they be used in a certain fashion or for a particular purpose, the President's "take care" responsibility obliges him to spend the money as the law requires. *Train v. New York*, 420 U.S. 35 (1975) suggests that the opponents of impoundment have the stronger argument. In that case, President Nixon directed the Administrator of the Environmental Protection Agency to allot to certain states less money for controlling water pollution than was mandated by the Federal Water Pollution Control Act Amendments of 1972. The Supreme Court found that the allotment language of the statute was mandatory and rejected the Executive Branch's assertion of discretionary authority to withhold funding that was allocated by this mandatory language.

Under Title X of the Congressional Budget and Impoundment Control Act of 1974, Congress further restrained the President's theoretical impoundment authority. Pursuant to this act, unless he is statutorily given spending discretion with respect to certain funds, the President may not refuse to spend appropriated funds as directed. Rather, he may propose "rescissions" to Congress (which the Congress typically ignores).

Given the outcome in *Train* and the statutory restrictions that Congress has placed on impoundment, the President is probably required to spend funds that have been appropriated for a specific purpose. On the other hand, in actual practice, the Executive Branch is often given a fair degree of implicit (and sometimes explicit) discretion in precisely how funds are spent. When a lump sum is appropriated for the operations of an agency or to accomplish a given mission, the Executive Branch officials responsible for that agency or that mission enjoy discretion in how best to use the appropriated funds. *See, e.g., Lincoln v. Vigil*, 508 U.S. 182 (1993) (Indian Health Service within the Department of Health and Human Services enjoyed discretion to spend its lump sum appropriation as it deemed most effective to accomplish its statutory mission; it was not required to continue spending on direct clinical services for Indian children if not expressly directed to do so by Congress).

APPOINTMENT AND REMOVAL POWER

In classic separation of powers style, the Framers divided between the Executive Branch and the Legislative Branch the authority to appoint senior-most government officials. Article II, Section 2 of the Constitution provides that:

> [The President] shall nominate, and by and with the advice and consent of the Senate, shall appoint ambassadors, other public ministers and consuls, judges of the Supreme Court, and all other officers of the United States whose appointments are not herein otherwise provided for, and which shall be established by law. But the Congress may by law vest the appointment of such inferior officers as they think proper, in the President alone, in the courts of law, or in the heads of departments.

Thus, it is the President, in the first instance, who selects individuals for service at the highest levels of the federal government, and not only those who assist him in the Executive Branch, but also those who serve as judges in the Judicial Branch.

However, the President's selections become effective only if and when approval from the Legislative Branch comes in the form of "advice and consent" from the Senate.

An exception to the requirement for Senate confirmation occurs when the President makes a "recess appointment." In this regard, Article II, Section 2 states that "the President shall have power to fill up all vacancies that may happen during the recess of the Senate, by granting commissions which shall expire at the end of their next session."

What is clear from these provisions in Article II is that the Framers wanted both political branches to be involved in placing officials who were not elected but who would nevertheless exert heavy influence on the functioning of the government. It is also evident that the Framers did not want necessary appointments to be entirely stymied by an absent Senate. However, the language quoted above raises questions as to certain details. For example, if Senate approval is needed to place a particular official, is Senate approval also needed to remove that official? What is the distinction between an "officer" whose appointment requires Senate confirmation and an "inferior officer" who can be appointed without Senate confirmation? How long must the Senate be absent to constitute a "recess" of the Senate that permits the President to invoke his recess appointment power? The constitutional text supplied by the Framers did not expressly answer such important questions. Some gaps in the constitutional text have been filled in by the courts, while others have not.

The first question above was answered by the Supreme Court in the case of *United States v. Myers*, excerpted below As a matter of pure textual statutory interpretation, one might have concluded that impeachment was the exclusive method for removing an "officer" within the Executive Branch, just as it is the method for removing Article III judges. Article II explains (at Section 2) that Senate approval is required for the placement of an "officer," and then goes on (in Section 4) to state:

> The President, Vice President and all civil officers of the United States, shall be removed from office on impeachment for, and conviction of, treason, bribery, or other high crimes and misdemeanors.

Thus, the Constitution appears to set forth the method for appointing and the method for removing officers of the United States. No other removal method is identified. The basic canon of statutory interpretation, *expressio unius est exclusio alterius* (the expression of one excludes others), would seem to apply: because the Constitution expressly provides one and only one method for removing officials, that is the only method available. Nevertheless, a divided Supreme Court concluded in *Myers* that officers within the Executive Branch serve at the pleasure of the President and may be unilaterally removed by him.

Myers v. United States

272 U.S. 52 (1926)[7]

MR. CHIEF JUSTICE TAFT delivered the opinion of the Court.

This case presents the question whether under the Constitution the President has the exclusive power of removing executive officers of the United States whom he has appointed by and with the advice and consent of the Senate.

[Myers was a Postmaster in Portland, Oregon, who had been appointed by the President with advice and consent by the Senate. He was later terminated by the President with no involvement by the Senate. The administratrix of his estate now challenges that termination and seeks back pay. Myers' estate argues that Senate approval was necessary to appoint Myers, and Senate approval was also necessary to terminate him. The statute that enabled his appointment stated, in pertinent part: "Postmasters . . . shall be appointed and may be removed by the President by and with the advice and consent of the Senate."

Chief Justice Taft quotes Article II, Sections 1 through 4, and Article III, Section 1.]

The question where the power of removal of executive officers appointed by the President by and with the advice and consent of the Senate was vested, was presented early in the first session of the First Congress. There is no express provision respecting removals in the Constitution, except as section 4 of article 2, above quoted, provides for removal from office by impeachment.

[Chief Justice Taft engages in an extensive review of debates in the Constitutional Convention and in the first Congress under the Constitution on the subject of executive appointment and removal power.]

[7] Footnotes and some citations found in the original decision have been omitted from this excerpted version.

The vesting of the executive power in the President was essentially a grant of the power to execute the laws. But the President alone and unaided could not execute the laws. He must execute them by the assistance of subordinates. This view has since been repeatedly affirmed by this court. Wilcox v. Jackson, 13 Pet. 498, 513; United States v. Eliason, 16 Pet. 291, 302; Williams v. United States, 1 How. 290, 297; Cunningham v. Neagle, 135 U.S. 1, 63 , 10 S. Ct. 658; Russell Co. v. United States, 261 U.S. 514, 523 , 43 S. Ct. 428. As he is charged specifically to take care that they be faithfully executed, the reasonable implication, even in the absence of express words, was that as part of his executive power he should select those who were to act for him under his direction in the execution of the laws. The further implication must be, in the absence of any express limitation respecting removals, that as his selection of administrative officers is essential to the execution of the laws by him, so must be his power of removing those for whom he cannot continue to be responsible.

* * *

The requirement of the second section of article 2 that the Senate should advise and consent to the presidential appointments, was to be strictly construed. The words of section 2, following the general grant of executive power under section 1, were either an enumeration and emphasis of specific functions of the executive, not all inclusive, or were limitations upon the general grant of the executive power, and as such, being limitations, should not be enlarged beyond the words used. Madison, 1 Annals, 462, 463, 464. The executive power was given in general terms strengthened by specific terms where emphasis was regarded as appropriate, and was limited by direct expressions where limitation was needed, and the fact that no express limit was placed on the power of removal by the executive was convincing indication that none was intended. . . This principle as a rule of constitutional and statutory construction, then generally conceded, has been recognized ever since. Ex parte Hennen, 13 Pet. 230, 259; Reagan v. United States, 182 U.S. 419 , 21 S. Ct. 842; Shurtleff v. United States, 189 U.S. 311, 315 , 23 S. Ct. 535. The reason for the principle is that those in charge of and responsible for administering functions of government, who select their executive subordinates, need in meeting their responsibility to have the power to remove those whom they appoint.

* * *

The power to prevent the removal of an officer who has served under the President is different from the authority to consent to or reject his appointment. When a nomination is made, it may be presumed that the Senate is, or may become, as well advised as to the fitness of the nominee as the President, but in the nature of things the defects in ability or intelligence or loyalty in the administration of the laws of one who has served as an officer under the President are facts as to which the President, or his trusted subordinates, must be better informed than the Senate, and the power to remove him may therefore be regarded as confined for very sound and practical reasons, to the governmental authority which has administrative control. The power of removal is incident to the power of appointment, not to the power of advising and consenting to appointment, and when the grant of the executive power is enforced by the express mandate to take care that the laws be faithfully executed, it emphasizes the necessity for including within the executive power as conferred the exclusive power of removal.

[Chief Justice Taft explains that, when it creates Executive Branch offices through legislation, the Congress may define the powers and duration of such offices, and may even set forth the eligibility and qualifications for the officeholders; however, these Legislative Branch powers may not extend to the point of designating the person who may occupy the office. He continues to review the commentary of the Framers and of the members of the First Congress in support of the general proposition that the entire executive power is vested in the President, with the only qualifications being those that are expressly set forth in the Constitution, such as the requirement for Senate approval of treaties. He also reviews prior history and case law regarding appointment and removal of executive officers and Article III judges, including *Marbury v. Madison* and the Tenure of Office Act, which led to the impeachment of President Andrew Johnson. He concludes that legislative attempts to restrict the President's authority to remove senior Executive Branch officers is unconstitutional.]

The separate opinion of MR. JUSTICE McREYNOLDS.

*   *   *

The argument [of the Majority] runs thus: The Constitution gives the President all executive power of the national government, except as this is checked or controlled by some other definite provision; power to remove is executive and unconfined; accordingly, the President may remove at will. Further, the President is required to take care that the laws be faithfully executed; he cannot do this unless he may remove at will all officers whom he appoints; therefore he has such authority.

The argument assumes far too much. Generally, the actual ouster of an officer is executive action; but to prescribe the conditions under which this may be done is legislative. The act of hanging a criminal is executive; but to say when and where and how he shall be hanged is clearly legislative. Moreover, officers may be removed by direct legislation; the act of 1820 hereafter referred to did this. 'The essence of the legislative authority is to enact laws, or, in other words, to prescribe rules for the regulation of the society; while the execution of the laws, and the employment of the common strength, either for this purpose, or for the common defense, seem to comprise all the functions of the executive magistrate. The Federalist, No. LXXIV.

The Legislature may create post offices and prescribe qualifications, duties, compensation, and term. And it may protect the incumbent in the enjoyment of his term unless in some way restrained therefrom. The real question, therefore, comes to this: Does any constitutional provision definitely limit the otherwise plenary power of Congress over postmasters, when they are appointed by the President with the consent of the Senate? The question is not the much-mooted one whether the Senate is part of the appointing power under the Constitution and therefore must participate in removals.

Here the restriction is imposed by statute alone and thereby made a condition of the tenure.

* * *

Congress has long and vigorously asserted its right to restrict removals and there has been no common executive practice based upon a contrary view. The President has often removed, and it is admitted that he may remove, with either the express or implied assent of Congress; but the present theory is that he may override the declared will of that body. This goes far beyond any practice heretofore approved or followed; it conflicts with the history of the Constitution, with the ordinary rules of interpretation, and with the construction approved by Congress since the beginning and emphatically sanctioned by this court. To adopt it would be revolutionary.

* * *

If the framers of the Constitution had intended 'the executive power,' in article 2, 1, to include all power of an executive nature, they would not have added the carefully defined grants of section 2. They were scholarly men, and it exceeds belief 'that the known advocates in the convention for a jealous grant and cautious definition of federal powers should have silently permitted the introduction of words and phrases in a sense rendering fruitless the restrictions and definitions elaborated by them.' Why say, the President shall be commander-in-chief; may require opinions in writing of the principal officers in each of the executive departments; shall have power to grant reprieves and pardons; shall give information to Congress concerning the state of the union; shall receive ambassadors; shall take care that the laws be faithfully executed-if all of these things and more had already been vested in him by the general words? The Constitution is exact in statement. Holmes v. Jennison, 14 Pet. 540. That the general words of a grant are limited, when followed by those of special import, is an established canon; and an accurate writer would hardly think of emphasizing a general grant by adding special and narrower ones without explanation. 'An affirmative grant of special powers would be absured, as well as useless, if a general authority were intended.' Story on the Constitution, 448. 'The powers delegated by the proposed Constitution to the federal government are few and defined.' Federalist, No. XLIV. 'Affirmative words are often, in their operation, negative of other objects than those affirmed; and in this case a negative or exclusive sense must be given to them or they have no operation at all. It cannot be presumed that any clause in the Constitution is intended to be without effect, and therefore such a construction is inadmissible, unless the words require it.' Marbury v. Madison, at page 174.

In his address to the Senate (February 16 1835) on 'The Appointing an Removing Power,' Mr. Webster considered and demolished the theory that the first section of article 2 conferred all executive powers upon the President except as therein limited (Webster's Works (Little, B. & Co., 1866), vol. 4, pp. 179, 186; Debates of Congress), and showed that the right to remove must be regarded as an incident to that of appointment. He pointed out the evils of uncontrolled removals, and, I think, demonstrated that the claim of illimitable executive power here advanced has no substantial foundation. The argument is exhaustive and ought to be conclusive. A paragraph from it follows:

> It is true, that the Constitution declares that the executive power shall be vested in the President; but the first question which then arises is, What is executive power? What is the degree, and what are the limitations? Executive power is not a thing so well known, and so accurately defined, as that the written Constitution of a limited government can be supposed to have conferred it in the lump. What is executive power? What are its boundaries? What model or example had the framers of the Constitution in their

> minds, when they spoke of 'executive power'? Did they mean executive power as known in England, or as known in France, or as known in Russia? Did they take it as defined by Montesquieu, by Burlamaqui, or by De Lolme? All these differ from one another as to the extent of the executive power of government. What, then, was intended by 'the executive power'? Now, sir, I think it perfectly plain and manifest that, although the framers of the Constitution meant to confer executive power on the President, yet they meant to define and limit that power, and to confer no more than they did thus define and limit. When they say it shall be vested in a President, they mean that one magistrate, to be called a President, shall hold the executive authority; but they mean, further, that he shall hold this authority according to the grants and limitations of the Constitution itself.

MR. JUSTICE BRANDEIS, dissenting.

* * *

To imply a grant to the President of the uncontrollable power of removal from statutory inferior executive offices involves an unnecessary and indefensible limitation upon the constitutional power of Congress to fix the tenure of the inferior statutory offices.

* * *

The assertion that the mere grant by the Constitution of executive power confers upon the President as a prerogative the unrestricted power of appointment and of removal from executive offices, except so far as otherwise expressly provided by the Constitution, is clearly inconsistent also with those statutes which restrict the exercise by the President of the power of nomination. There is not a word in the Constitution which in terms authorizes Congress to limit the President's freedom of choice in making nominations for executive offices. It is to appointment as distinguished from nomination that the Constitution imposes in terms the requirement of Senatorial consent. But a multitude of laws have been enacted which limit the President's power to make nominations, and which through the restrictions imposed, may prevent the selection of the person deemed by him best fitted. Such restriction upon the power to nominate has been exercised by Congress continuously since the foundation of the government. Every President has approved one or more of such acts. Every President has consistently observed them. This is true of those offices

> to which he makes appointments without the advice and consent of the Senate as well as of those for which its consent is required.
>
> * * *
>
> The separation of the powers of government did not make each branch completely autonomous. It left each in some measure, dependent upon the others, as it left to each power to exercise, in some respects, functions in their nature executive, legislative and judicial. Obviously the President cannot secure full execution of the laws, if Congress denies to him adequate means of doing so. Full execution may be defeated because Congress declines to create offices indispensable for that purpose; or because Congress, having created the office, declines to make the indispensable appropriation; or because Congress, having both created the office and made the appropriation, prevents, by restrictions which it imposes, the appointment of officials who in quality and character are indispensable to the efficient execution of the law. If, in any such way, adequate means are denied to the President, the fault will lie with Congress. The President performs his full constitutional duty, if, with the means and instruments provided by Congress and within the limitations prescribed by it, he uses his best endeavors to secure the faithful execution of the laws enacted.

Notwithstanding the vigorous dissenting opinions in *Myers*, the essential holding of the Supreme Court seems straightforward: The Constitution empowers the President unilaterally to remove an executive officer, even if Senate approval was necessary for the appointment of such officer. However, just nine years later, another circumstance arose that revealed more nuance to, and more potential restrictions on, the President's removal power. While *Myers* answered the question of whether Senate approval was necessary for a removal, it left open the question of whether other restrictions could be placed on the removal of Senate-confirmed officials.

In *Humphrey's Executor v. United States*, the estate of Federal Trade Commissioner William Humphrey challenged President Roosevelt's putative removal of Humphrey from the FTC in 1933. After Humphrey rejected the President's requests that Humphrey resign, the President removed Humphrey from the FTC, not because of any misconduct or indolence, but because the President felt that Humphrey was not sufficiently devoted to the President's New Deal agenda. Humphrey died a short time later, and his estate argued that the President's removal of Humphrey was improper because the Federal Trade Commission Act, which created the FTC, provided that the President could remove a Commissioner only for "inefficiency, neglect of duty, or malfeasance in office."

Humphrey's Executor v. United States

295 U.S. 602 (1935)[8]

Mr. Justice SUTHERLAND delivered the opinion of the Court.

* * *

The question first to be considered is whether, by the provisions of section 1 of the Federal Trade Commission Act already quoted, the President's power is limited to removal for the specific causes enumerated therein.

* * *

The statute fixes a term of office, in accordance with many precedents. The first commissioners appointed are to continue in office for terms of three, four, five, six, and seven years, respectively; and their successors are to be appointed for terms of seven years-any commissioner being subject to removal by the President for inefficiency, neglect of duty, or malfeasance in office. The words of the act are definite and unambiguous.

The government says the phrase 'continue in office' is of no legal significance and, moreover, applies only to the first Commissioners. We think it has significance. It may be that, literally, its application is restricted as suggested; but it, nevertheless, lends support to a view contrary to that of the government as to the meaning of the entire requirement in respect of tenure; for it is not easy to suppose that Congress intended to secure the first commissioners against removal except for the causes specified and deny like security to their successors. Putting this phrase aside, however, the fixing of a definite term subject to removal for cause, unless there be some countervailing provision or circumstance indicating the contrary, which here we are unable to find, is enough to establish the legislative intent that the term is not to be curtailed in the absence of such cause. But if the intention of Congress that no removal should be made during the specified term except for one or more of the enumerated causes were not clear upon the face of the statute, as we think it is, it would be

[8] Footnotes and some citations found in the original decision have been omitted from this excerpted version.

made clear by a consideration of the character of the commission and the legislative history which accompanied and preceded the passage of the act.

The commission is to be nonpartisan; and it must, from the very nature of its duties, act with entire impartiality. It is charged with the enforcement of no policy except the policy of the law. Its duties are neither political nor executive, but predominantly quasi judicial and quasi legislative. Like the Interstate Commerce Commission, its members are called upon to exercise the trained judgment of a body of experts 'appointed by law and informed by experience.' Illinois Cent. &c. R.R. v. Inter. Com. Comm., 206 U.S. 441, 454 , 27 S.Ct. 700, 704; Standard Oil Co. v. United States, 283 U.S. 235, 238 , 239 S., 51 S.Ct. 429.

*   *   *

We conclude that the intent of the act is to limit the executive power of removal to the causes enumerated, the existence of none of which is claimed here; and we pass to the second question.

To support its contention that the removal provision of section 1, as we have just construed it, is an unconstitutional interference with the executive power of the President, the government's chief reliance is Myers v. United States, 272 U.S. 52, 47 S.Ct. 21. That case has been so recently decided, and the prevailing and dissenting opinions so fully review the general subject of the power of executive removal, that further discussion would add little of value to the wealth of material there collected. These opinions examine at length the historical, legislative, and judicial data bearing upon the question, beginning with what is called 'the decision of 1789' in the first Congress and coming down almost to the day when the opinions were delivered. They occupy 243 pages of the volume in which they are printed. Nevertheless, the narrow point actually decided was only that the President had power to remove a postmaster of the first class, without the advice and consent of the Senate as required by act of Congress. In the course of the opinion of the court, expressions occur which tend to sustain the government's contention, but these are beyond the point involved and, therefore, do not come within the rule of stare decisis. In so far as they are out of harmony with the views here set forth, these expressions are disapproved.

*   *   *

The office of a postmaster is so essentially unlike the office now involved that the decision in the Myers Case cannot be accepted as controlling our decision here. A postmaster is an executive officer restricted to the performance of executive functions. He is charged with no duty at all related to either the legislative or judicial power. The actual decision in the Myers Case finds support in the theory that such an officer is merely one of the units in the executive department and, hence, inherently subject to the exclusive and illimitable power of removal by the Chief Executive, whose subordinate and aid he is. Putting aside dicta, which may be followed if sufficiently persuasive but which are not controlling, the necessary reach of the decision goes far enough to include all purely executive officers. It goes no farther; much less does it include an officer who occupies no place in the executive department and who exercises no part of the executive power vested by the Constitution in the President.

The Federal Trade Commission is an administrative body created by Congress to carry into effect legislative policies embodied in the statute in accordance with the legislative standard therein prescribed, and to perform other specified duties as a legislative or as a judicial aid. Such a body cannot in any proper sense be characterized as an arm or an eye of the executive. Its duties are performed without executive leave and, in the contemplation of the statute, must be free from executive control. In administering the provisions of the statute in respect of 'unfair methods of competition,' that is to say, in filling in and administering the details embodied by that general standard, the commission acts in part quasi legislatively and in part quasi judicially.

* * *

The authority of Congress, in creating quasi legislative or quasi judicial agencies, to require them to act in discharge of their duties independently of executive control cannot well be doubted; and that authority includes, as an appropriate incident, power to fix the period during which they shall continue, and to forbid their removal except for cause in the meantime. For it is quite evident that one who holds his office only during the pleasure of another cannot be depended upon to maintain an attitude of independence against the latter's will.

* * *

The power of removal here claimed for the President falls within this principle, since its coercive influence threatens the independence of a commission, which is not only wholly disconnected from the executive department, but which, as already fully appears, was created by Congress as a means of carrying into operation legislative and judicial powers, and as an agency of the legislative and judicial departments.

* * *

The result of what we now have said is this: Whether the power of the President to remove an officer shall prevail over the authority of Congress to condition the power by fixing a definite term and precluding a removal except for cause will depend upon the character of the office; the Myers decision, affirming the power of the President alone to make the removal, is confined to purely executive officers; and as to officers of the kind here under consideration, we hold that no removal can be made during the prescribed term for which the officer is appointed, except for one or more of the causes named in the applicable statute.

To the extent that, between the decision in the Myers Case, which sustains the unrestrictable power of the President to remove purely executive officers, and our present decision that such power does not extend to an office such as that here involved, there shall remain a field of doubt, we leave such cases as may fall within it for future consideration and determination as they may arise.

The operative distinction between *Myers* and *Humphrey's Executor* is contained in Justice Sutherland's observation that "the Myers decision, affirming the power of the President alone to make the removal, is confined to purely executive officers." In contrast, Congress may restrict the President's ability to remove officials who perform quasi-judicial or quasi-legislative functions, because these officials must be free to "discharge [] their duties independently of executive control."

Notably, there was no dissent in *Humphrey's Executor*; apparently, the entire Supreme Court of 1935 agreed with the notion that there could be "quasi-judicial" and "quasi-legislative" officials within the federal government who do not reside squarely within the Executive Branch, the Legislative Branch or the Judicial Branch. Congress could, in effect, create hybrid institutions (such as, for example, the Federal Trade Commission, the National Labor Relations Board, and the Securities and Exchange Commission) that would be responsible for enforcing certain laws but would be independent of the Executive Branch and beyond direct control by the President. The unanimous Court in *Humphrey's Executor* neglects to reconcile this notion with the seemingly unequivocal mandate in Article II, Section 1 that "the executive power shall be vested in a President." To be sure, the Court concludes that an "independent" agency such as the FTC "cannot in any proper sense be characterized as an arm or an eye of the executive," yet it fails to explain how this can be so when the purpose of such an agency appears to be classically executive: "to carry into effect legislative policies embodied in the statute in accordance with the legislative standard therein prescribed." The Supreme Court of a half century later seemed to take a different view of what is and is not executive action when it explained: "Interpreting a law enacted by Congress to implement the legislative mandate is the very essence of 'execution' of the law." *Bowsher v. Synar*, 478 U.S. 714, 733 (1986).

Several decades after the decision in *Humphrey's Executor*, what appeared to be a bright line for appointment and removal purposes -- on the one hand, purely executive officers who are removable at the will of the President; on the other hand, officials performing quasi-legislative or quasi-judicial functions, whose removal can be conditional -- was blurred by the decision in *Morrison v. Olson.*

Morrison v. Olson was a challenge to the legitimacy of the Independent Counsel, which was created by the Ethics in Government Act of 1978. The Act was passed largely as a response to the Watergate scandal. In particular, the creation of the Independent Counsel was a direct response to a series of events during the Watergate investigation that became known as the Saturday Night Massacre.

In May of 1973, Attorney General Elliot Richardson appointed former Solicitor General Archibald Cox as Special Prosecutor to carry out an investigation related to the break-in at Democratic headquarters in the Watergate office complex. When the Senate committee investigating Watergate uncovered the existence of secret Oval Office audio tapes, Cox subpoenaed the tapes. President Richard Nixon initially refused to produce the tapes, and then offered a compromise by which Senator John Stennis (Democrat of Mississippi) would review the tapes and provide written summaries to Cox. When Cox rejected the Stennis Compromise and continued to pursue the tapes, Nixon ordered Attorney General Richardson to fire Cox. Richardson refused to do so and resigned. Nixon then ordered Deputy Attorney General William Ruckelshaus to fire Cox. Ruckelshaus refused to do so and resigned. Ultimately, Solicitor General Robert Bork complied with Nixon's direction and fired Cox. In response to his termination, Cox stated that "whether ours shall continue to be a government of laws and not of men is now for Congress and ultimately the American people." Although political pressure forced Nixon to appoint Special Prosecutor Leon Jaworski as Cox's successor, many in Congress and elsewhere concluded that a truly independent prosecutor was needed to address possible misconduct that might occur in the future at the highest levels of the Executive Branch.

Under the Ethics in Government Act, the Attorney General conducts a preliminary investigation into alleged misconduct by a senior Executive Branch official. If the Attorney General finds "reasonable grounds" warranting further investigation, he so informs a Special Division of the D.C. Circuit Court of Appeals, which then appoints an Independent Counsel. The Independent Counsel is imbued with the full investigative and prosecutorial powers of the Attorney General, and may be removed by the Attorney General only for "good cause."

In March of 1983, then-Assistant Attorney General Ted Olson testified before the House Judiciary Committee about the Justice Department's involvement the previous year in the Reagan Administration's handling of congressional subpoenas directed to the Environmental Protection Agency. In a 1985 report issued by the committee, it was suggested that Olson had given false and misleading testimony. As a result of the report, the Attorney General ordered a preliminary investigation, concluded that appointment of an Independent Counsel was appropriate, and sought and obtained such an appointment from the Special Division. Olson challenged the appointment of the Independent Counsel, Alexia Morrison, as unconstitutional. Olson argued that the Independent Counsel was carrying out classic executive functions -- investigation and prosecution of possible crimes -- but was neither appointed by the President with Senate confirmation nor removable by the President, which is impermissible under the Appointments Clause.

Morrison v. Olson

487 U.S. 654 (1988)[9]

CHIEF JUSTICE REHNQUIST delivered the opinion of the Court.

This case presents us with a challenge to the independent counsel provisions of the Ethics in Government Act of 1978, 28 U.S.C. 49, 591 et seq. (1982 ed., Supp. V). We hold today that these provisions of the Act do not violate the Appointments Clause of the Constitution, Art. II, 2, cl. 2, or the limitations of Article III, nor do they impermissibly interfere with the President's authority under Article II in violation of the constitutional principle of separation of powers.

---

[9] Footnotes and some citations found in the original decision have been omitted from this excerpted version.

* * *

The Appointments Clause of Article II reads as follows:

> [The President] shall nominate, and by and with the Advice and Consent of the Senate, shall appoint Ambassadors, other public Ministers and Consuls, Judges of the supreme Court, and all other Officers of the United States, whose Appointments are not herein otherwise provided for, and which shall be established by Law: but the Congress may by Law vest the Appointment of such inferior Officers, as they think proper, in the President alone, in the Courts of Law, or in the Heads of Departments.

U.S. Const., Art. II, 2, cl. 2.

The parties do not dispute that "[t]he Constitution for purposes of appointment . . . divides all its officers into two classes." United States v. Germaine, 99 U.S. 508, 509 (1879). As we stated in Buckley v. Valeo, 424 U.S. 1, 132 (1976): "Principal officers are selected by the President with the advice and consent of the Senate. Inferior officers Congress may allow to be appointed by the President alone, by the heads of departments, or by the Judiciary." The initial question is, accordingly, whether appellant [Independent Counsel Alexia Morrison] is an "inferior" or a "principal" officer. If she is the latter, as the Court of Appeals concluded, then the Act is in violation of the Appointments Clause.

The line between "inferior" and "principal" officers is one that is far from clear, and the Framers provided little guidance into where it should be drawn. See, e. g., 2 J. Story, Commentaries on the Constitution 1536, pp. 397-398 (3d ed. 1858) ("In the practical course of the government there does not seem to have been any exact line drawn, who are and who are not to be deemed inferior officers, in the sense of the constitution, whose appointment does not necessarily require the concurrence of the senate"). We need not attempt here to decide exactly where the line falls between the two types of officers, because in our view appellant clearly falls on the "inferior officer" side of that line. Several factors lead to this conclusion.

First, appellant is subject to removal by a higher Executive Branch official. Although appellant may not be "subordinate" to the Attorney General (and the President) insofar as she possesses a degree of independent discretion to exercise the powers delegated to her under the Act, the fact that she can be removed by the Attorney General indicates that she is to some degree "inferior" in rank and authority.

Second, appellant is empowered by the Act to perform only certain, limited duties. An independent counsel's role is restricted primarily to investigation and, if appropriate, prosecution for certain federal crimes. Admittedly, the Act delegates to appellant "full power and independent authority to exercise all investigative and prosecutorial functions and powers of the Department of Justice," 594(a), but this grant of authority does not include any authority to formulate policy for the Government or the Executive Branch, nor does it give appellant any administrative duties outside of those necessary to operate her office. The Act specifically provides that in policy matters appellant is to comply to the extent possible with the policies of the Department. 594(f).

Third, appellant's office is limited in jurisdiction. Not only is the Act itself restricted in applicability to certain federal officials suspected of certain serious federal crimes, but an independent counsel can only act within the scope of the jurisdiction that has been granted by the Special Division pursuant to a request by the Attorney General.

Finally, appellant's office is limited in tenure. There is concededly no time limit on the appointment of a particular counsel. Nonetheless, the office of independent counsel is "temporary" in the sense that an independent counsel is appointed essentially to accomplish a single task, and when that task is over the office is terminated, either by the counsel herself or by action of the Special Division. Unlike other prosecutors, appellant has no ongoing responsibilities that extend beyond the accomplishment of the mission that she was appointed for and authorized by the Special Division to undertake. In our view, these factors relating to the "ideas of tenure, duration . . . and duties" of the independent counsel, Germaine, supra, at 511, are sufficient to establish that appellant is an "inferior" officer in the constitutional sense.

* * *

This does not, however, end our inquiry under the Appointments Clause. Appellees argue that even if appellant is an "inferior" officer, the Clause does not empower Congress to place the power to appoint such an officer outside the Executive Branch. They contend that the Clause does not contemplate congressional authorization of "interbranch appointments," in which an officer of one branch is appointed by officers of another branch. The relevant language of the

Appointments Clause is worth repeating. It reads: ". . . but the Congress may by Law vest the Appointment of such inferior Officers, as they think proper, in the President alone, in the courts of Law, or in the Heads of Departments." On its face, the language of this "excepting clause" admits of no limitation on interbranch appointments. Indeed, the inclusion of "as they think proper" seems clearly to give Congress significant discretion to determine whether it is "proper" to vest the appointment of, for example, executive officials in the "courts of Law." We recognized as much in one of our few decisions in this area, Ex parte Siebold, supra, where we stated:

> It is no doubt usual and proper to vest the appointment of inferior officers in that department of the government, executive or judicial, or in that particular executive department to which the duties of such officers appertain. But there is no absolute requirement to this effect in the Constitution; and, if there were, it would be difficult in many cases to determine to which department an office properly belonged. . . .

* * *

We do not mean to say that Congress' power to provide for interbranch appointments of "inferior officers" is unlimited. In addition to separation-of-powers concerns, which would arise if such provisions for appointment had the potential to impair the constitutional functions assigned to one of the branches, Siebold itself suggested that Congress' decision to vest the appointment power in the courts would be improper if there was some "incongruity" between the functions normally performed by the courts and the performance of their duty to appoint . . . Congress, of course, was concerned when it created the office of independent counsel with the conflicts of interest that could arise in situations when the Executive Branch is called upon to investigate its own high-ranking officers. If it were to remove the appointing authority from the Executive Branch, the most logical place to put it was in the Judicial Branch. In the light of the Act's provision making the judges of the Special Division ineligible to participate in any matters relating to an independent counsel they have appointed, 28 U.S.C. 49(f) (1982 ed., Supp. V), we do not think that appointment of the independent counsel by the court runs afoul of the constitutional limitation on "incongruous" interbranch appointments.

* * *

We now turn to consider whether the Act is invalid under the constitutional principle of separation of powers. Two related issues must be addressed: The first is whether the provision of the Act restricting the Attorney General's power to remove the independent counsel to only those instances in which he can show "good cause," taken by itself, impermissibly interferes with the President's exercise of his constitutionally appointed functions. The second is whether, taken as a whole, the Act violates the separation of powers by reducing the President's ability to control the prosecutorial powers wielded by the independent counsel.

Two Terms ago we had occasion to consider whether it was consistent with the separation of powers for Congress to pass a statute that authorized a Government official who is removable only by Congress to participate in what we found to be "executive powers." Bowsher v. Synar, 478 U.S. 714, 730 (1986). We held in Bowsher that "Congress cannot reserve for itself the power of removal of an officer charged with the execution of the laws except by impeachment." Id., at 726. A primary antecedent for this ruling was our 1926 decision in Myers v. United States, 272 U.S. 52 . Myers had considered the propriety of a federal statute by which certain postmasters of the United States could be removed by the President only "by and with the advice and consent of the Senate." There too, Congress' attempt to involve itself in the removal of an executive official was found to be sufficient grounds to render the statute invalid. As we observed in Bowsher, the essence of the decision in Myers was the judgment that the Constitution prevents Congress from "draw[ing] to itself . . . the power to remove or the right to participate in the exercise of that power. To do this would be to go beyond the words and implications of the [Appointments Clause] and to infringe the constitutional principle of the separation of governmental powers." Myers, supra, at 161.

Unlike both Bowsher and Myers, this case does not involve an attempt by Congress itself to gain a role in the removal of executive officials other than its established powers of impeachment and conviction. The Act instead puts the removal power squarely in the hands of the Executive Branch; an independent counsel may be removed from office, "only by the personal action of the Attorney General, and only for good cause." 596(a)(1). There is no requirement of congressional approval of the Attorney General's removal decision, though the decision is subject to judicial review.

[Chief Justice Rehnquist goes on to review and distinguish between *Myers* and *Humphrey's Executor*. The principle that explains the different outcomes in these cases was that, in *Myers*, the official in question performed purely executive functions, while in *Humphrey's Executor*, the official performed quasi-legislative and quasi-judicial functions. However, the question is not quite as simple as whether the official in question performs purely executive functions; rather, "the real question is whether the removal restrictions are of such a nature that they impede the President's ability to perform his constitutional duty, and the functions of the officials in question must be analyzed in that light." Here, the power to remove has been somewhat limited by the "good cause" requirement for removal; however, this is not a situation where the President has been completely denied the power to remove. The limitation here does not impermissibly burden the President in his ability "to control or supervise the independent counsel." Further: "Although the counsel exercises no small amount of discretion and judgment in deciding how to carry out his or her duties under the Act, we simply do not see how the President's need to control the exercise of that discretion is so central to the functioning of the Executive Branch as to require as a matter of constitutional law that the counsel be terminable at will by the President."]

Notwithstanding the fact that the counsel is to some degree "independent" and free from executive supervision to a greater extent than other federal prosecutors, in our view these features of the Act give the Executive Branch sufficient control over the independent counsel to ensure that the President is able to perform his constitutionally assigned duties.

JUSTICE SCALIA, dissenting.

[Justice Scalia reviews the factual circumstances leading to the appointment of the Independent Counsel. The situation began as an acrimonious dispute between the Legislative Branch and the Executive Branch about information that Congress sought from the EPA. This led some in Congress, still resentful about how the Executive Branch handled the underlying dispute, to urge the Attorney General to seek appointment of an Independent Counsel.]

As a general matter, the Act before us here requires the Attorney General to apply for the appointment of an independent counsel within 90 days after receiving a request to do so, unless he determines within that period that "there are no reasonable grounds to believe that further investigation or prosecution is warranted." 28 U.S.C. 592(b)(1). As a practical matter, it would be surprising if the Attorney General had any choice (assuming this statute is constitutional) but to seek appointment of an independent counsel to pursue the charges against the principal object of the congressional request, Mr. Olson. Merely the political consequences (to him and the President) of seeming to break the law by refusing to do so would have been substantial.

* * *

Congress has effectively compelled a criminal investigation of a high-level appointee of the President in connection with his actions arising out of a bitter power dispute between the President and the Legislative Branch . . . The decisions regarding the scope of that further investigation, its duration, and, finally, whether or not prosecution should ensue, are likewise beyond the control of the President and his subordinates.

* * *

To repeat, Article II, 1, cl. 1, of the Constitution provides: "The executive Power shall be vested in a President of the United States."

[T]his does not mean some of the executive power, but all of the executive power. It seems to me, therefore, that the decision of the Court of Appeals invalidating the present statute must be upheld on fundamental separation-of-powers principles if the following two questions are answered affirmatively: (1) Is the conduct of a criminal prosecution (and of an investigation to decide whether to prosecute) the exercise of purely executive power? (2) Does the statute deprive the President of the United States of exclusive control over the exercise of that power? Surprising to say, the Court appears to concede an affirmative answer to both questions, but seeks to avoid the inevitable conclusion that since the statute vests some purely executive power in a person who is not the President of the United States it is void.

* * *

It effects a revolution in our constitutional jurisprudence for the Court . . . to sit in judgment of whether "the President's need to control the exercise of [the independent counsel's] discretion is so central to the functioning of the Executive Branch" as to require complete control . . . It is not for us to determine, and we have never presumed to determine, how much of the purely executive powers of government must be within the full control of the President. The Constitution prescribes that they all are.

*   *   *

> Besides weakening the Presidency by reducing the zeal of his staff, it must also be obvious that the institution of the independent counsel enfeebles him more directly in his constant confrontations with Congress, by eroding his public support. Nothing is so politically effective as the ability to charge that one's opponent and his associates are not merely wrongheaded, naive, ineffective, but, in all probability, "crooks." And nothing so effectively gives an appearance of validity to such charges as a Justice Department investigation and, even better, prosecution. The present statute provides ample means for that sort of attack, assuring that massive and lengthy investigations will occur, not merely when the Justice Department in the application of its usual standards believes they are called for, but whenever it cannot be said that there are "no reasonable grounds to believe" they are called for. The statute's highly visible procedures assure, moreover, that unlike most investigations these will be widely known and prominently displayed.

*   *   *

> In sum, this statute does deprive the President of substantial control over the prosecutory functions performed by the independent counsel, and it does substantially affect the balance of powers.

> [Justice Scalia goes on to question the characterization of the Independent Counsel as an "inferior officer" and to criticize the blurring of what had appeared to be a clear Constitutional line of demarcation between officials whose duties are purely executive under *Myers* and, in contrast, those whose duties are quasi-legislative or quasi-judicial under *Humphrey's Executor*. He concludes by expressing concern that the Independent Counsel is not directly controlled by the President and, therefore, not subject to the normal political and institutional checks on abuses of prosecutorial discretion.]

Although the outcome of the Supreme Court litigation was not in former Assistant Attorney General Olson's favor, the ultimate result of the Independent Counsel's investigation was. After interviewing Olson, Independent Counsel Morrison announced that she would not seek an indictment and, in December 1988, issued a report exonerating him. Olson sought from the Special Division reimbursement of the almost $1.3 million in attorneys' fees that he had incurred as a result of the investigation, and the court awarded close to $900,000. *In re Theodore B. Olson*, 884 F.2d 1415 (D.C. Cir. 1989). Ted Olson went on to become one of the most influential lawyers in the United States, arguing dozens of cases in the Supreme Court and acting as Solicitor General during the first term of President George W. Bush.

DISCUSSION AND QUESTIONS

1. In remarks to the Federalist Society shortly after the decision in *Morrison v. Olson*, Samuel Alito (later to become a Justice of the United States Supreme Court) stated that the decision "hit the doctrine of separation of powers about as hard as heavyweight champ Mike Tyson usually hits his opponents," and opined that the ruling had "restricted the executive's constitutionally guaranteed appointment power." Introduction by Samuel Alito, "Debate: After the Independent Counsel Decision: Is Separation of Powers Dead," 26 *Am. Crim. L. Rev.* 1667 (1989). Are Justice Scalia and Samuel Alito correct? Given that the Constitution vests "*the* executive power" (emphasis added) in the President, can a federal official exercise purely executive functions such as investigating and prosecuting crimes without being selected by and directly answerable to the President? Even Chief Justice Rehnquist, writing for the eight-member majority, concedes that the Independent Counsel is "to some degree 'independent' and free from executive supervision." Yet, Justice Rehnquist concludes that the President nonetheless fundamentally retains the ability to supervise and control the Independent Counsel. If the Constitution, without limitation, places "the" executive power in the President, and imposes upon the President the unlimited responsibility to "take care that the laws be faithfully executed," can it be constitutionally appropriate to limit the President's oversight of the officials who assist him with his core executive responsibilities?

2. Justice Scalia expresses concern that the Independent Counsel's investigation of Ted Olson is merely a political exercise set in motion at the behest of Congress. He argues that no Attorney General will refuse to seek appointment of an independent counsel if Congress insists that he do so in any highly publicized matter. Is Justice Scalia correct? When the independent counsel law was in effect, most attorneys general did seek appointment of an independent counsel when asked to do so. However, in 1997, Attorney General Janet Reno declined to request appointment of an independent counsel in response to Republican allegations of improper fundraising by President Clinton and Vice President Gore during their 1996 re-election campaign. In any event, if Justice Scalia's concern is about investigations that occur because of political pressure, is that a problem that is limited to the independent counsel statute? Special prosecutors were appointed prior to the

enactment of, and have been appointed since the expiration of, the independent counsel law. Indeed, as a result of the Watergate scandal, several officials in the Nixon Administration were investigated and successfully prosecuted by a special prosecutor whose appointment was the direct result of congressional pressure placed on the Attorney General. When a politically motivated Congress pushes for an investigation of the Executive Branch, does it signify a threat to the proper separation of powers? Or, to the contrary, is it consistent with the Framers' anticipated functioning of separation of powers?

3. Chief Justice Rehnquist uses "central to the functioning of the executive branch" as the test for determining which officials must be terminable at the will of the President. In the federal government today, there are hundreds of cabinet and sub-cabinet positions that require presidential appointment after Senate confirmation. These include, for example:

- The Assistant Secretary for Policy Development and Research within the Department of Housing and Urban Development;
- The Assistant Secretary for Legislation and Congressional Affairs within the Department of Education;
- The Assistant Secretary for Planning and Evaluation within the Department of Health and Human Services; and
- The Assistant Secretary for Disability Employment Policy within the Department of Labor.

Such officials would seem to be "officers of the United States" within the meaning of Article II, Section 2 (the President, "with the advice and consent of the Senate, shall appoint . . . officers of the United States"). Yet, are such officials truly "central to the functioning of the executive branch"? Would the President be substantially impaired in carrying out his executive responsibilities under the Constitution if he were unable to remove at will the Assistant Secretary for Planning and Evaluation at HHS, or the Assistant Secretary for Disability Employment Policy at DOL? If the answer to this question is "no," then could not Congress, when it creates such positions, impose a "good cause" or similar restriction on the President's removal power? For that matter, could not Congress retroactively impose such restrictions on positions that already exist? Indeed, could not Congress restrict the President's power to remove a great many -- or even most -- officials within the Executive Branch? Among the hundreds of cabinet and sub-cabinet positions currently in existence, how many would the majority in *Morrison v. Olson* consider to be "central to the functioning of the executive branch"?

4. The progression from *Myers* to *Humphrey's Executor* to *Morrison* suggests a trend by which the Judicial Branch acquiesced to ever-increasing restrictions on the President's power to remove federal officials. However, in 2010, in the case of *Free Enterprise Fund v. Public Company Accounting Oversight Board*, 561 U.S. _____, 130 S. Ct. 3138 (2010), the Supreme Court rejected multilayered restrictions on the President's authority to remove an officer who "determines the policy and enforces the laws of the United States."

As a result of corporate accounting scandals around the turn of the twenty-first century, Congress passed the Sarbanes-Oxley Act of 2002, which, among other things, created the five-member Public Company Accounting Oversight Board (PCAOB) to oversee the activities of firms that provide auditing services for publicly-traded companies. Pursuant to the enabling legislation, the members of the PCAOB are appointed by the members of the Securities and Exchange Commission and can be removed only by the SEC and only for good cause. The SEC itself is an independent agency whose presidentially-appointed members are removable only for cause. Consequently, members of the PCAOB are free from direct presidential oversight and are insulated from presidential removal by two layers of "good cause" limitation. The Supreme Court invalidated this double-layered disconnection from presidential supervision and held that the members of the PCAOB must be deemed removable at will by the SEC. Writing for the Majority, Chief Justice John Roberts, explained the ruling:

> We hold that such multilevel protection from removal is contrary to Article II's vesting of the executive power in the President. The President cannot "take Care that the Laws be faithfully executed" if he cannot oversee the faithfulness of the officers who execute them. Here the President cannot remove an officer who enjoys more than one level of good-cause protection, even if the President determines that the officer is neglecting his duties or discharging them improperly. That judgment is instead committed to another officer, who may or may not agree with the President's determination, and whom the President cannot remove simply because that officer disagrees with him. This contravenes the President's constitutional obligation to ensure the faithful execution of the laws.
>
> * * *
>
> The Act before us . . . not only protects Board members from removal except for good cause, but

> withdraws from the President any decision on whether that good cause exists. That decision is vested instead in other tenured officers -- the Commissioners -- none of whom is subject to the President's direct control. The result is a Board that is not accountable to the President, and a President who is not responsible for the Board.

RECESS APPOINTMENTS

A glaring deficiency in the national government under the Articles of Confederation was that governmental authority effectively lapsed when the legislature was not in session (see Chapter One, page 4). Consequently, a crucial reason for creating a perpetual executive separate and apart from the legislature was to ensure that the business of governing did not cease just because Congress was in recess. Consistent with this rationale, the Framers anticipated that, on occasion, the President would need to fill important vacancies in his Administration (or in the courts) even when the Senate was not available to advise and consent on the President's appointments. As Alexander Hamilton explained in Federalist No. 67, "it would have been improper to oblige [the Senate] to be continually in session for the appointment of officers . . . vacancies might happen in their recess, which it might be necessary for the public service to fill without delay." As a result, the Framers provided, at Article II, Section 2:

> The President shall have power to fill up all vacancies that may happen during the recess of the Senate, by granting commissions which shall expire at the end of their next session.

Thus, the President is empowered to forgo Senate confirmation for officials whom he wishes to appoint when the Senate is in recess.

The plain meaning of the Recess Appointments Clause would seem to require that the vacancy at issue must arise literally "during" the Senate's recess rather than before the recess (and therefore while the Senate is in session). However, in practice, both the Executive Branch and the courts have interpreted the clause more broadly to include not only vacancies that first arise during a recess, but also vacancies that occur prior to, and continue to exist during, a recess. *See, e.g.*, *Evans v. Stephens*, 387 F.3d 1220, 1226-27 (11th Cir. 2004) (*en banc* court concluded that President could use recess appointment to fill a judicial vacancy that occurred prior to, but existed during, a Senate recess because the purpose of the Recess Appointments Clause is "to keep important offices filled and the government functioning"); *United States v. Woodley*, 751 F.2d 1008, 1012 (9th Cir. 1985) (it would be an "absurd result" to require that all offices vacant at the time the Senate recesses must remain vacant until the Senate reconvenes); *United States v. Allocco*, 305 F.2d 704, 712 (2d. Cir. 1962) (limiting the applicability of the clause only to vacancies that arise during a recess "would create executive paralysis and do violence to the orderly functioning of our complex government").

Thus, according to custom and decisional precedent, a vacancy "happens" during a Senate recess if it *exists* during a Senate recess, regardless of when the vacancy was initially created.

Another term used in the Recess Appointments Clause has been the subject of more debate: The word "recess" appears only twice in the Constitution and is not defined. Consequently, there has historically been a question about how long a Senate absence must last to constitute a "recess" within the meaning of Article II, Section 2 and thereby permit the President to invoke his recess appointment power. The prevailing view for more than a century after the Constitution's ratification was that the President could make recess appointments only during the *inter*session recess of the Senate; that is, during the *sine die* adjournment between sessions of Congress that generally occurs once each year. It was not believed that the clause applied to *intra*session recesses -- shorter breaks that occur during a session -- such as the traditional week-long Independence Day and Memorial Day recesses. This view was reflected in 1901 in a formal opinion by Attorney General Philander C. Knox. Knox relied heavily on Article II, Section 2's use of the definite article "the" when referring to "*the* recess of the Senate." He concluded that there could be only one recess contemplated by the clause, and it must be the recess that occurs most predictably and tends to be the longest. 23 Op. A.G. 599 (1901).

Twenty years later, however, Knox's conclusion was rejected in an opinion by Attorney General Harry Daugherty. Daugherty concluded that a recess appointment made during a 29-day intrasession recess was valid. His conclusion was largely pragmatic: If there were a prohibition on appointments during lengthy recesses, whether they occur during a session or between sessions, "the painful and inevitable result will be measurably to prevent the exercise of government functions." 33 Op. A.G. 20, 23 (1921). However, Daugherty was able to support his conclusion not only by reference to practicality but also by reference to the Senate's own views about the recess appointment power. In 1905, the Senate Judiciary Committee took up the question of what constitutes a "recess" within the meaning of Article II, Section 2. The committee issued a report finding that a recess for this purpose is:

> when the Senate is not sitting in regular or extraordinary session as a branch of the Congress or in extraordinary session for the discharge of executive functions; when its members owe no duty of attendance; when its chamber is empty; when, because of its absence, it can not receive communications from the President or participate as a body in making appointments

S. Rept. No. 4389, 58th Cong., 3d Sess. 2 (1905); 39 Cong. Rec. 3823-24 (1905). The Judiciary Committee report could be interpreted to mean that recess appointments may be made at any moment that the Senate is not actually meeting and doing business. However, Attorney General Daugherty believed that brief intrasession recesses, such as those lasting only five or ten days, would not support exercise of the President's recess appointment power.

More recently, the views of the Department of Justice under different administrations have coalesced around the conclusion that a recess of more than three days is needed before a recess appointment can properly be made. *See, e.g., New Process Steel v. National Labor Relations Board*, No. 08-1457, Transcript of Oral Argument, at 50 (U.S. 2010) (Deputy Solicitor General Neal Katyal explaining to Chief Justice Roberts "our office has opined the recess has to be longer than three days" before a recess appointment can occur); *Evans v. Stephens*, No. 04-828, Brief for the United States in Opposition to Petition for a Writ of Certiorari, at 11 (U.S. 2005).

Consistent with the modern view of the Department of Justice, in late 2007 and through most of 2008, Democratic Senate Majority Leader Harry Reid held "pro forma" sessions of the Senate to prevent Republican President George W. Bush from making recess appointments. Under this regime, even when the Senate was, for all practical purposes, in recess for a week or more-- no business was scheduled or done, most senators were out of town -- a lone Democratic senator would enter an otherwise empty Senate chamber, take to the Senate President's dais, bang the gavel, and pretend that the Senate was "in session" for just a few seconds. This exercise occurred at least every fourth day, on the theory that it technically prevented the Senate from being in recess for more than three days and thereby prevented President Bush from exercising his recess appointment power.

Notwithstanding the opinions of the Department of Justice and Senator Reid, the best reading of the Constitution as a whole indicates that a "recess" for purposes of presidential appointments occurs on any day that the Senate fails to meet with a quorum to do business. Aside from Article II, Section 2, the Constitution's only other use of the term "recess" occurs in Article I, Section 3. This section contains a provision that has been superseded by the Seventeenth Amendment; however, this provision, nonetheless, reveals what the Framers meant when they referred to a legislative "recess." Prior to 1913, pursuant to Article I, Section 3, senators were chosen by the legislatures of their respective states. Article I, Section 3 provided that, if Senate vacancies occurred "during the *recess* of the legislature of any state," the governor could fill them through temporary appointments that would last "until the next *meeting* of the legislature, which shall then fill such vacancies" (emphasis added). Thus, a legislative body is in recess whenever it is not meeting. A valid "meeting" requires the assembly of a quorum that is capable of conducting business. The Constitution mandates, at Amendment XX, Section 2, that Congress must assemble at least once per year on a specified date (prior to enactment of the Twentieth Amendment, this mandate appeared at Article I, Section 4). It would be absurd -- and therefore not a permissible interpretation -- for the Constitution to require that Congress assemble at least once annually for a meeting, yet permit a meeting of fewer members than are necessary to accomplish anything. Further, Article I, Section 3 anticipated that a "meeting" of the state legislature would result in the selection of a new senator; this could occur only if the legislative body enjoyed a quorum capable of conducting business.

Given how the terms "recess" and "meeting" are used in Article I, Section 3, it is clear that a legislative body is in recess whenever it is not meeting with a quorum able to do business. There is no reason to believe that the Framers meant anything different when they discussed recess appointments in Article II, Section 2. Consequently, the President may exercise his power to make recess appointments on any day that the Senate is not meeting with a quorum capable of conducting business.

In any event, no court has ever invalidated a recess appointment made pursuant to Article II, Section 2 because the Senate recess in question was too brief to justify a recess appointment. Indeed, in what is perhaps the boldest presidential use of recess appointments ever, Theodore Roosevelt appointed more than 160 individuals during what he asserted was a "constructive recess" of the Senate that lasted only seconds. On December 7, 1903, the Senate of the 58th Congress closed its first session and opened its second session, and did so in only the time required to bang the gavel to mark the end of the first session and then bang it again to mark the beginning of the second session. Although senators were present and Senate business continued unabated, Roosevelt deemed the moment between the first session and the second session to be an intersession recess during which appointments could be made without Senate confirmation. Although Roosevelt was criticized for the maneuver, none of his appointments was successfully challenged.

CHAPTER FOUR: EXECUTIVE PRIVILEGES AND IMMUNITIES

EXECUTIVE PRIVILEGE

The Watergate scandal of the 1970s not only tested separation of powers theories; it also illuminated certain aspects of the powers distributed among the branches. One area in which new light was shed became known as "executive privilege." Simply put, executive privilege is the power of the Executive Branch to withhold certain information from disclosure to the other branches. Although the privilege is not expressly set forth in the Constitution, its existence as an inherent power of the executive was confirmed by the Supreme Court in the case of *United States v. Nixon*.

After the apprehension of the burglars at the Watergate complex in June of 1972, the Senate convened a Select Committee, chaired by Senator Sam Ervin, to investigate possible links between the burglary and President's Nixon's re-election campaign. Under questioning by Minority Counsel Fred Thompson (later a successful actor and senator from Tennessee), former White House aide Alexander Butterfield revealed the existence of an audio taping system in the Oval Office. As a result of this disclosure, Special Prosecutor Leon Jaworski subpoenaed presidential audio tapes that he believed might contain evidence of wrongdoing. (Jaworski succeeded Archibald Cox as Special Prosecutor. See Chapter Three, page 87, for more on Archibald Cox and the Saturday Night Massacre.) President Nixon moved to quash the subpoenas, and the dispute quickly made its way to the Supreme Court. Chief Justice Burger wrote the decision for a unanimous court, finding that there is an executive privilege based in the Constitution, but that, in the case at hand, the privilege must give way to the prosecutor's need for the evidence.

United States v. Nixon

418 U.S. 683 (1974)[10]

MR. CHIEF JUSTICE BURGER delivered the opinion of the Court.

[In the District Court proceedings, the Special Prosecutor subpoenaed from the President various materials needed for the prosecution of several Watergate conspirators, including White House audio tapes. The President claimed executive privilege and moved to quash. The

[10] Footnotes and some citations found in the original decision have been omitted from this excerpted version.

President also argued that the matter was non-justiciable because it was an "intra-executive" dispute.]

In the District Court, the President's counsel argued that the court lacked jurisdiction to issue the subpoena because the matter was an intra-branch dispute between a subordinate and superior officer of the Executive Branch and hence not subject to judicial resolution. That argument has been renewed in this Court with emphasis on the contention that the dispute does not present a "case" or "controversy" which can be adjudicated in the federal courts. The President's counsel argues that the federal courts should not intrude into areas committed to the other branches of Government. He views the present dispute as essentially a "jurisdictional" dispute within the Executive Branch which he analogizes to a dispute between two congressional committees. Since the Executive Branch has exclusive authority and absolute discretion to decide whether to prosecute a case, Confiscation Cases, 7 Wall. 454 (1869); United States v. Cox, 342 F.2d 167, 171 (CA5), cert. denied sub nom. Cox v. Hauberg, 381 U.S. 935 (1965), it is contended that a President's decision is final in determining what evidence is to be used in a given criminal case.

* * *

Our starting point is the nature of the proceeding for which the evidence is sought - here a pending criminal prosecution. It is a judicial proceeding in a federal court alleging violation of federal laws and is brought in the name of the United States as sovereign. Berger v. United States, 295 U.S. 78, 88 (1935). Under the authority of Art. II, 2, Congress has vested in the Attorney General the power to conduct the criminal litigation of the United States Government. 28 U.S.C. 516. It has also vested in him the power to appoint subordinate officers to assist him in the discharge of his duties. 28 U.S.C. 509, 510, 515, 533. Acting pursuant to those statutes, the Attorney General has delegated the authority to represent the United States in these particular matters to a Special Prosecutor with unique authority and tenure. The regulation gives the Special Prosecutor explicit power to contest the invocation of executive privilege in the process of seeking evidence deemed relevant to the performance of these specially delegated duties. 38 Fed. Reg. 30739, as amended by 38 Fed. Reg. 32805.

So long as this regulation is extant it has the force of law . . . it is theoretically possible for the Attorney General to amend or revoke the regulation defining the Special Prosecutor's authority. But he has not done so. So long as this regulation remains in force the Executive

Branch is bound by it, and indeed the United States as the sovereign composed of the three branches is bound to respect and to enforce it.

* * *

The demands of and the resistance to the subpoena present an obvious controversy in the ordinary sense, but that alone is not sufficient to meet constitutional standards. In the constitutional sense, controversy means more than disagreement and conflict; rather it means the kind of controversy courts traditionally resolve. Here at issue is the production or nonproduction of specified evidence deemed by the Special Prosecutor to be relevant and admissible in a pending criminal case. It is sought by one official of the Executive Branch within the scope of his express authority; it is resisted by the Chief Executive on the ground of his duty to preserve the confidentiality of the communications of the President. Whatever the correct answer on the merits, these issues are "of a type which are traditionally justiciable." United States v. ICC, 337 U.S., at 430.

* * *

[Now] we turn to the claim that the subpoena should be quashed because it demands "confidential conversations between a President and his close advisors that it would be inconsistent with the public interest to produce." App. 48a. The first contention is a broad claim that the separation of powers doctrine precludes judicial review of a President's claim of privilege. The second contention is that if he does not prevail on the claim of absolute privilege, the court should hold as a matter of constitutional law that the privilege prevails over the subpoena duces tecum.

* * *

In support of his claim of absolute privilege, the President's counsel urges two grounds, one of which is common to all governments and one of which is peculiar to our system of separation of powers. The first ground is the valid need for protection of communications between high Government officials and those who advise and assist them in the performance of their manifold duties; the importance of this confidentiality is too plain to require further discussion. Human experience teaches that those who expect public dissemination of their remarks may well temper candor with a concern for appearances and for their own interests to the detriment of the decisionmaking process. Whatever the nature of the privilege of confidentiality of Presidential communications in the exercise of Art. II powers, the privilege can be said to derive from the supremacy of each branch within its own assigned area of constitutional duties. Certain powers and privileges flow from the nature of enumerated powers; the protection of the confidentiality of Presidential communications has similar constitutional underpinnings.

The second ground asserted by the President's counsel in support of the claim of absolute privilege rests on the doctrine of separation of powers. Here it is argued that the independence of the Executive Branch within its own sphere, Humphrey's Executor v. United States, 295 U.S. 602, 629 -630 (1935); Kilbourn v. Thompson, 103 U.S. 168, 190 -191 (1881), insulates a President from a judicial subpoena in an ongoing criminal prosecution, and thereby protects confidential Presidential communications.

However, neither the doctrine of separation of powers, nor the need for confidentiality of high-level communications, without more, can sustain an absolute, unqualified Presidential privilege of immunity from judicial process under all circumstances. The President's need for complete candor and objectivity from advisers calls for great deference from the courts. However, when the privilege depends solely on the broad, undifferentiated claim of public interest in the confidentiality of such conversations, a confrontation with other values arises. Absent a claim of need to protect military, diplomatic, or sensitive national security secrets, we find it difficult to accept the argument that even the very important interest in confidentiality of Presidential communications is significantly diminished by production of such material for in camera inspection with all the protection that a district court will be obliged to provide.

The impediment that an absolute, unqualified privilege would place in the way of the primary constitutional duty of the Judicial Branch to do justice in criminal prosecutions would plainly conflict with the function of the courts under Art. III. In designing the structure of our Government and dividing and allocating the sovereign power among three co-equal branches, the Framers of the Constitution sought to provide a comprehensive system, but the separate powers were not intended to operate with absolute independence.

* * *

Since we conclude that the legitimate needs of the judicial process may outweigh Presidential privilege, it is necessary to resolve those competing interests in a manner that preserves the essential functions of each branch. The right and indeed the duty to resolve that question does not free the Judiciary from according high respect to the representations made on behalf of the President. United States v. Burr, 25 F. Cas. 187, 190, 191-192 (No. 14,694) (CC Va. 1807).

The expectation of a President to the confidentiality of his conversations and correspondence, like the claim of confidentiality of judicial deliberations, for example, has all the values to which we accord deference for the privacy of all citizens and, added to those values, is the necessity for protection of the public interest in candid, objective, and even blunt or harsh opinions in Presidential decision-making. A President and those who assist him must be free to explore alternatives in the process of shaping policies and making decisions and to do so in a way many would be unwilling to express except privately. These are the considerations justifying a presumptive privilege for Presidential communications. The privilege is fundamental to the operation of Government and inextricably rooted in the separation of powers under the Constitution. In Nixon v. Sirica, 159 U.S. App. D.C. 58, 487 F.2d 700 (1973), the Court of Appeals held that such Presidential communications are "presumptively privileged," id., at 75, 487 F.2d, at 717, and this position is accepted by both parties in the present litigation. We agree with Mr. Chief Justice Marshall's observation, therefore, that "[i]n no case of this kind would a court be required to proceed against the president as against an ordinary individual." United States v. Burr, 25 F. Cas., at 192.

But this presumptive privilege must be considered in light of our historic commitment to the rule of law. This is nowhere more profoundly manifest than in our view that "the twofold aim [of criminal justice] is that guilt shall not escape or innocence suffer." Berger v. United States, 295 U.S., at 88 . We have elected to employ an adversary system of criminal justice in which the parties contest all issues before a court of law. The need to develop all relevant facts in the adversary system is both fundamental and comprehensive. The ends of criminal justice would be defeated if judgments were to be founded on a partial or speculative presentation of the facts. The very integrity of the judicial system and public confidence in the system depend on full disclosure of all the facts, within the framework of the rules of evidence. To ensure that justice is done, it is imperative to the function of courts that compulsory process be available for the production of evidence needed either by the prosecution or by the defense.

*   *   *

In this case the President challenges a subpoena served on him as a third party requiring the production of materials for use in a criminal prosecution; he does so on the claim that he has a privilege against disclosure of confidential communications. He does not place his claim of privilege on the ground they are military or diplomatic secrets. As to these areas of Art. II duties the courts have traditionally shown the utmost deference to Presidential responsibilities. In C. & S. Air Lines v. Waterman S. S. Corp., 333 U.S. 103, 111 (1948), dealing with Presidential authority involving foreign policy considerations, the Court said:

> The President, both as Commander-in-Chief and as the Nation's organ for foreign affairs, has available intelligence services whose reports are not and ought not to be published to the world. It would be intolerable that courts, without the relevant information, should review and perhaps nullify actions of the Executive taken on information properly held secret.

*　　*　　*

No case of the Court, however, has extended this high degree of deference to a President's generalized interest in confidentiality. Nowhere in the Constitution, as we have noted earlier, is there any explicit reference to a privilege of confidentiality, yet to the extent this interest relates to the effective discharge of a President's powers, it is constitutionally based.

The right to the production of all evidence at a criminal trial similarly has constitutional dimensions. The Sixth Amendment explicitly confers upon every defendant in a criminal trial the right "to be confronted with the witnesses against him" and "to have compulsory process for obtaining witnesses in his favor." Moreover, the Fifth Amendment also guarantees that no person shall be deprived of liberty without due process of law. It is the manifest duty of the courts to vindicate those guarantees, and to accomplish that it is essential that all relevant and admissible evidence be produced.

In this case we must weigh the importance of the general privilege of confidentiality of Presidential communications in performance of the President's responsibilities against the inroads of such a privilege on the fair administration of criminal justice. The interest in preserving confidentiality is weighty indeed and entitled to great respect. However, we cannot conclude that advisers will be moved to temper the candor of their remarks by the infrequent occasions of disclosure

> because of the possibility that such conversations will be called for in the context of a criminal prosecution.
>
> On the other hand, the allowance of the privilege to withhold evidence that is demonstrably relevant in a criminal trial would cut deeply into the guarantee of due process of law and gravely impair the basic function of the courts. A President's acknowledged need for confidentiality in the communications of his office is general in nature, whereas the constitutional need for production of relevant evidence in a criminal proceeding is specific and central to the fair adjudication of a particular criminal case in the administration of justice. Without access to specific facts a criminal prosecution may be totally frustrated. The President's broad interest in confidentiality of communications will not be vitiated by disclosure of a limited number of conversations preliminarily shown to have some bearing on the pending criminal cases.
>
> We conclude that when the ground for asserting privilege as to subpoenaed materials sought for use in a criminal trial is based only on the generalized interest in confidentiality, it cannot prevail over the fundamental demands of due process of law in the fair administration of criminal justice. The generalized assertion of privilege must yield to the demonstrated, specific need for evidence in a pending criminal trial.

DISCUSSION AND QUESTIONS

1. *United States v. Nixon* preceded *Morrison v. Olson* by 14 years. Did the unanimous decision in *Nixon* presage the seven-justice majority opinion in *Morrison*? (Hint: In retrospect, could the justiciability determination in *Nixon* be seen as a preview of how the *Morrison* court would treat the fundamental separation of powers issue that it was asked to address?)

2. In *Nixon*, eight justices (Justice Rehnquist took no part in the decision) believed there could be a dispute between the President and a federal prosecutor that required resolution by the Judicial Branch. How does this conclusion square with the Constitution's unqualified grant of "the executive power" to the President? If only one institution can possess the executive power, how can it come to pass that judicial intervention is needed when there is a disagreement between officials carrying out purely executive functions?

3. The Court finds that executive privilege is a constitutional privilege based on the inherent nature and function of the Executive Branch. Yet, "the legitimate needs of the judicial process may outweigh Presidential privilege." The conclusion that executive privilege is subject to a balancing test and will sometimes be trumped by the needs of the Judicial Branch begs the question: Why is this constitutional privilege so readily limited when another constitutional privilege, the Fifth Amendment protection against self-incrimination, is virtually absolute? Are the privileges treated differently only because one is implicit and the other is explicit? Further, why should a privilege based in the Constitution give way in judicial proceedings -- even criminal proceedings -- when other, non-constitutional privileges, such as the attorney-client privilege and the spousal privilege, do not?

4. In outlining the contours of the privilege that it is recognizing, the *Nixon* court refers to "the President's need for complete candor and objectivity from advisers" and "the expectation of a President to the confidentiality of his conversations and correspondence." This phrasing suggests that the President must be personally and directly involved in the communications at issue for the privilege to attach. Should executive privilege protect only those communications to which the President is a party, or should it be more broadly construed to encompass communications among his advisors in which he is not a direct participant. Given the rationale for the privilege, is there any less need for its protection when presidential advisors are conferring among themselves about how they will advise the President than when they are actually giving advice to the President?

Later decisions arising from the Administration of Bill Clinton filled in some of the gaps left by *Nixon* in terms of understanding the scope and nature of executive privilege.

In 1994, an Independent Counsel was appointed to investigate alleged acceptance of gifts by then-Secretary of Agriculture (and former congressman) Mike Espy. During grand jury proceedings, the Independent Counsel sought the production of documents developed or relied upon by the White House Counsel during an internal investigation of Espy, which had been conducted at the direction of President Clinton. In response to a grand jury subpoena, President Clinton withheld several dozen documents based on executive privilege and "deliberative process" privilege. In resolving the resulting dispute about whether the documents should be produced, the D.C. Circuit confirmed that there are (at least) two specific categories of privilege enjoyed by the Executive Branch. The first is a privilege relating to presidential communications. This is the implied constitutional privilege that was announced by the Supreme Court in *Nixon*. The second is (consistent with the assertions of President Clinton) a common law privilege that protects internal deliberations among officials within the Executive Branch as they evaluate and make decisions about matters within their scope of responsibility. According to the D.C. Circuit, the privilege for presidential communications can attach to communications that do not directly involve the President; however, application of the privilege is limited to the White House staff in "operational proximity" to presidential decision-making and does not extend beyond the White House into other departments of agencies. Further, the privilege applies only to communications related to decision-making on official government matters. *See In re Sealed Case*, 121 F.3d 729 (1997). (Ultimately, Espy was indicted, tried and acquitted on all charges. After the verdict, several jurors expressed dismay and disdain for the Independent Counsel's case.)

Ten years later, the teaching of the Espy case was largely reaffirmed in *Judicial Watch, Inc. v. Department of Justice*, 365 F.3d 1108 (2004). Judicial Watch was a government watchdog organization looking into the propriety of pardons given by President Clinton. Through the Freedom of Information Act, they sought from the Department of Justice thousands of documents generated and relied on within the Office of the Pardon Attorney and others in the Department of Justice. The D.C. Circuit rejected the government's effort to apply the presidential communications privilege to information that had only been used within the Department of Justice and had not been solicited or received by the President or his closest advisors within the White House staff. If such information is to be protected at all, explained the court, it must be by the deliberative process privilege rather than the presidential communications privilege.

EXECUTIVE IMMUNITY

Events of the Nixon presidency led to the Supreme Court's acknowledgment of an implied constitutional privilege for presidential communications. A few years later, litigation involving President Nixon also gave the Court the opportunity to find that the chief executive enjoys an implied absolute immunity from liability for his official acts.

Nixon v. Fitzgerald

457 U.S. 731 (1982)[11]

JUSTICE POWELL delivered the opinion of the Court.

[11] Footnotes and some citations found in the original decision have been omitted from this excerpted version.

The plaintiff in this lawsuit seeks relief in civil damages from a former President of the United States. The claim rests on actions allegedly taken in the former President's official capacity during his tenure in office. The issue before us is the scope of the immunity possessed by the President of the United States.

[In 1970, Plaintiff Fitzgerald was removed from his position as an analyst with the Air Force, supposedly due to a reorganization and reduction in force that eliminated his position. He claims that he was terminated in retaliation for testimony that he had given in Congressional hearings slightly more than one year earlier, where he revealed large cost overruns and technical defects in the performance of the C5-A transport airplane. There was some evidence that President Nixon had knowledge of, or was involved in, the decision to terminate Fitzgerald's federal employment, and the Civil Service Commission concluded that Fitzgerald had been terminated for impermissible reasons (although not necessarily in direct retaliation for his congressional whistle-blowing). Fitzgerald sued President Nixon and others in his Administration for damages stemming from his termination.

Historically, governmental officials have enjoyed a qualified -- not absolute -- immunity from civil liability for their official acts. This qualified immunity evolved in the law because it is in the public interest that governmental officials be able to carry out their official responsibilities independently and without constant fear of potential liability for actions taken in good faith.]

This case now presents the claim that the President of the United States is shielded by absolute immunity from civil damages liability. In the case of the President the inquiries into history and policy, though mandated independently by our cases, tend to converge. Because the Presidency did not exist through most of the development of common law, any historical analysis must draw its evidence primarily from our constitutional heritage and structure. Historical inquiry thus merges almost at its inception with the kind of "public policy" analysis appropriately undertaken by a federal court. This inquiry involves policies and principles that may be considered implicit in the nature of the President's office in a system structured to achieve effective government under a constitutionally mandated separation of powers.

Here a former President asserts his immunity from civil damages claims of two kinds. He stands named as a defendant in a direct action under the Constitution and in two statutory actions under federal laws of general applicability. In neither case has Congress taken express legislative action to subject the President to civil liability for his official acts.

Applying the principles of our cases to claims of this kind, we hold that petitioner, as a former President of the United States, is entitled to absolute immunity from damages liability predicated on his official acts. We consider this immunity a functionally mandated incident of the President's unique office, rooted in the constitutional tradition of the separation of powers and supported by our history. Justice Story's analysis remains persuasive:

> There are . . . incidental powers, belonging to the executive department, which are necessarily implied from the nature of the functions, which are confided to it. Among these, must necessarily be included the power to perform them . . . . The president cannot, therefore, be liable to arrest, imprisonment, or detention, while he is in the discharge of the duties of his office; and for this purpose his person must be deemed, in civil cases at least, to possess an official inviolability.

3 J. Story, Commentaries on the Constitution of the United States 1563, pp. 418-419 (1st ed. 1833).

The President occupies a unique position in the constitutional scheme. Article II, 1, of the Constitution provides that "[t]he executive Power shall be vested in a President of the United States . . . ." This grant of authority establishes the President as the chief constitutional officer of the Executive Branch, entrusted with supervisory and policy responsibilities of utmost discretion and sensitivity. These include the enforcement of federal law - it is the President who is charged constitutionally to "take Care that the Laws be faithfully executed"; the conduct of foreign affairs - a realm in which the Court has recognized that "[i]t would be intolerable that courts, without the relevant information, should review and perhaps nullify actions of the Executive taken on information properly held secret"; and management of the Executive Branch - a task for which "imperative reasons requir[e] an unrestricted power [in the President] to remove the most important of his subordinates in their most important duties."

In arguing that the President is entitled only to qualified immunity, the respondent relies on cases in which we have recognized immunity of this scope for governors and cabinet officers. E. g., Butz v. Economou, 438 U.S. 478 (1978); Scheuer v. Rhodes, 416 U.S. 232 (1974). We find these cases to be inapposite. The President's unique status under the Constitution distinguishes him from other executive officials.

Because of the singular importance of the President's duties, diversion of his energies by concern with private lawsuits would raise unique risks to the effective functioning of government. As is the case with prosecutors and judges - for whom absolute immunity now is established - a President must concern himself with matters likely to "arouse the most intense feelings." Pierson v. Ray, 386 U.S., at 554 . Yet, as our decisions have recognized, it is in precisely such cases that there exists the greatest public interest in providing an official "the maximum ability to deal fearlessly and impartially with" the duties of his office. Ferri v. Ackerman, 444 U.S. 193, 203 (1979). This concern is compelling where the officeholder must make the most sensitive and far-reaching decisions entrusted to any official under our constitutional system. Nor can the sheer prominence of the President's office be ignored. In view of the visibility of his office and the effect of his actions on countless people, the President would be an easily identifiable target for suits for civil damages. Cognizance of this personal vulnerability frequently could distract a President from his public duties, to the detriment of not only the President and his office but also the Nation that the Presidency was designed to serve.

* * *

In defining the scope of an official's absolute privilege, this Court has recognized that the sphere of protected action must be related closely to the immunity's justifying purposes. Frequently our decisions have held that an official's absolute immunity should extend only to acts in performance of particular functions of his office . . . In view of the special nature of the President's constitutional office and functions, we think it appropriate to recognize absolute Presidential immunity from damages liability for acts within the "outer perimeter" of his official responsibility.

Under the Constitution and laws of the United States the President has discretionary responsibilities in a broad variety of areas, many of them highly sensitive. In many cases it would be difficult to determine which of the President's innumerable "functions" encompassed a particular action.

* * *

Here respondent argues that petitioner Nixon would have acted outside the outer perimeter of his duties by ordering the discharge of an employee who was lawfully entitled to retain his job in the absence of "`such cause as will promote the efficiency of the service.'" Brief for Respondent 39, citing 5 U.S.C. 7512(a). Because Congress has granted this legislative protection, respondent argues, no federal official could, within the outer perimeter of his duties of office, cause Fitzgerald to be dismissed without satisfying this standard in prescribed statutory proceedings.

This construction would subject the President to trial on virtually every allegation that an action was unlawful, or was taken for a forbidden purpose. Adoption of this construction thus would deprive absolute immunity of its intended effect. It clearly is within the President's constitutional and statutory authority to prescribe the manner in which the Secretary will conduct the business of the Air Force. See 10 U.S.C. 8012(b). Because this mandate of office must include the authority to prescribe reorganizations and reductions in force, we conclude that petitioner's alleged wrongful acts lay well within the outer perimeter of his authority.

A rule of absolute immunity for the President will not leave the Nation without sufficient protection against misconduct on the part of the Chief Executive. There remains the constitutional remedy of impeachment. In addition, there are formal and informal checks on Presidential action that do not apply with equal force to other executive officials. The President is subjected to constant scrutiny by the press. Vigilant oversight by Congress also may serve to deter Presidential abuses of office, as well as to make credible the threat of impeachment. Other incentives to avoid misconduct may include a desire to earn reelection, the need to maintain prestige as an element of Presidential influence, and a President's traditional concern for his historical stature.

The existence of alternative remedies and deterrents establishes that absolute immunity will not place the President "above the law." For the President, as for judges and prosecutors, absolute immunity merely precludes a particular private remedy for alleged misconduct in order to advance compelling public ends.

* * *

JUSTICE WHITE, with whom JUSTICE BRENNAN, JUSTICE MARSHALL, and JUSTICE BLACKMUN join, dissenting.

The four dissenting Members of the Court in Butz v. Economou, 438 U.S. 478 (1978), argued that all federal officials are entitled to absolute immunity from suit for any action they take in connection with their official duties. That immunity would extend even to actions taken with express knowledge that the conduct was clearly contrary to the controlling statute or clearly violative of the Constitution. Fortunately, the majority of the Court rejected that approach: We held that although public officials perform certain functions that entitle them to absolute immunity, the immunity attaches to particular functions - not to particular offices. Officials performing functions for which immunity is not absolute enjoy qualified immunity; they are liable in damages only if their conduct violated well-established law and if they should have realized that their conduct was illegal.

The Court now applies the dissenting view in Butz to the Office of the President: A President, acting within the outer boundaries of what Presidents normally do, may, without liability, deliberately cause serious injury to any number of citizens even though he knows his conduct violates a statute or tramples on the constitutional rights of those who are injured. Even if the President in this case ordered Fitzgerald fired by means of a trumped-up reduction in force, knowing that such a discharge was contrary to the civil service laws, he would be absolutely immune from suit. By the same token, if a President, without following the statutory procedures which he knows apply to himself as well as to other federal officials, orders his subordinates to wiretap or break into a home for the purpose of installing a listening device, and the officers comply with his request, the President would be absolutely immune from suit. He would be immune regardless of the damage he inflicts, regardless of how violative of the statute and of the Constitution he knew his conduct to be, and regardless of his purpose.

The Court intimates that its decision is grounded in the Constitution. If that is the case, Congress cannot provide a remedy against Presidential misconduct and the criminal laws of the United States are wholly inapplicable to the President. I find this approach completely unacceptable. I do not agree that if the Office of President is to operate effectively, the holder of that Office must be permitted, without fear of liability and regardless of the function he is performing, deliberately to inflict injury on others by conduct that he knows violates the law.

* * *

Taken at face value, the Court's position that as a matter of constitutional law the President is absolutely immune should mean that he is immune not only from damages actions but also from suits for injunctive relief, criminal prosecutions and, indeed, from any kind of judicial process. But there is no contention that the President is immune from criminal prosecution in the courts under the criminal laws enacted by Congress or by the States for that matter. Nor would such a claim be credible. The Constitution itself provides that impeachment shall not bar "Indictment, Trial, Judgment and Punishment, according to Law." Art. I, 3, cl. 7. Similarly, our cases indicate that immunity from damages actions carries no protection from criminal prosecution. Supra, at 765-766.

Neither can there be a serious claim that the separation-of-powers doctrine insulates Presidential action from judicial review or insulates the President from judicial process. No argument is made here that the President, whatever his liability for money damages, is not subject to the courts' injunctive powers. See, e. g., Youngstown Sheet & Tube Co., supra; Korematsu v. United States, 323 U.S. 214 (1944); Panama Refining Co. v. Ryan, 293 U.S. 388 (1935). Petitioner's attempt to draw an analogy to the Speech or Debate Clause, Brief for Petitioner 45, one purpose of which is "to prevent . . . accountability before a possibly hostile judiciary," Gravel v. United States, 408 U.S., at 617 , breaks down at just this point. While the Speech or Debate Clause guarantees that "for any Speech or Debate" Congressmen "shall not be questioned in any other Place," and, thus, assures that Congressmen, in their official capacity, shall not be the subject of the courts' injunctive powers, no such protection is afforded the Executive. Indeed, as the cases cited above indicate, it is the rule, not the exception, that executive actions - including those taken at the immediate direction of the President - are subject to judicial review. Regardless of the possibility of money damages against the President, then, the constitutionality of the President's actions or their legality under the applicable statutes can and will be subject to review. Indeed, in this very case, respondent Fitzgerald's dismissal was set aside by the Civil Service Commission as contrary to the applicable regulations issued pursuant to authority granted by Congress.

* * *

The functional approach to the separation-of-powers doctrine and the Court's more recent immunity decisions converge on the following principle: The scope of immunity is determined by function, not office. The wholesale claim that the President is entitled to absolute immunity in all of his actions stands on no firmer ground than did the claim that all Presidential communications are entitled to an absolute privilege, which was rejected in favor of a functional analysis, by a unanimous Court in United States v. Nixon, 418 U.S. 683 (1974). Therefore, whatever may be true of the necessity of such a broad immunity in certain areas of executive responsibility, the only question that must be answered here is whether the dismissal of employees falls within a constitutionally assigned executive function, the performance of which would be substantially impaired by the possibility of a private action for damages. I believe it does not.

* * *

Because of the importance of this case, it is appropriate to examine the reasoning of the majority opinion.

* * *

First, the majority informs us that the President occupies a "unique position in the constitutional scheme," including responsibilities for the administration of justice, foreign affairs, and management of the Executive Branch. True as this may be, it says nothing about why a "unique" rule of immunity should apply to the President. The President's unique role may indeed encompass functions for which he is entitled to a claim of absolute immunity. It does not follow from that, however, that he is entitled to absolute immunity either in general or in this case in particular.

For some reason, the majority believes that this uniqueness of the President shifts the burden to respondent to prove that a rule of absolute immunity does not apply. The respondent has failed in this effort, the Court suggests, because the President's uniqueness makes "inapposite" any analogy to our cases dealing with other executive officers. Even if this were true, it would not follow that the President is entitled to absolute immunity; it would only mean that a particular argument is out of place. But the fact is that it is not true. There is nothing in the President's unique role that makes the arguments used in those other cases inappropriate.

Second, the majority contends that because the President's "visibility" makes him particularly vulnerable to suits for civil damages, a rule of absolute immunity is required. The force of this argument is surely undercut by the majority's admission that "there is no historical record of numerous suits against the President." Even granting that a Bivens cause of action did not become available until 1971, in the 11 years since then there have been only a handful of suits. Many of these are

> frivolous and dealt with in a routine manner by the courts and the Justice Department. There is no reason to think that, in the future, the protection afforded by summary judgment procedures would not be adequate to protect the President, as they currently protect other executive officers from unfounded litigation . . .
>
> Finally, the Court suggests that potential liability "frequently could distract a President from his public duties." Unless one assumes that the President himself makes the countless high-level executive decisions required in the administration of government, this rule will not do much to insulate such decisions from the threat of liability. The logic of the proposition cannot be limited to the President; its extension, however, has been uniformly rejected by this Court. See Butz v. Economou, 438 U.S. 478 (1978); Harlow v. Fitzgerald, post, p. 800. Furthermore, in no instance have we previously held legal accountability in itself to be an unjustifiable cost. The availability of the courts to vindicate constitutional and statutory wrongs has been perceived and protected as one of the virtues of our system of delegated and limited powers. As I argued in Part I, our concern in fashioning absolute immunity rules has been that liability may pervert the decisionmaking process in a particular function by undercutting the values we expect to guide those decisions. Except for the empty generality that the President should have "`the maximum ability to deal fearlessly and impartially with' the duties of his office," ante, at 752, the majority nowhere suggests a particular, disadvantageous effect on a specific Presidential function. The caution that comes from requiring reasonable choices in areas that may intrude on individuals' legally protected rights has never before been counted as a cost.

DISCUSSION AND QUESTIONS

1. Under the majority's view, are there any circumstances in which the President would not enjoy absolute immunity from civil liability? What if a President were to order the interrogation of a suspected terrorist by methods that were later held to constitute torture? Torture is a criminal violation of U.S. (and international) law. Can a President be operating "within the 'outer perimeter' of his official responsibility" if he orders his subordinates to engage in criminal conduct? Justice White, in dissent, seems to think that, under the majority's view, the answer to this question is "yes." Is he correct -- is this the necessary consequence of the rule set forth by the majority?

2. During the second term of Republican President George W. Bush, certain White House aides and senior officials in the Department of Justice faced allegations that they had fired several United States Attorneys for improper political reasons, including their perception that certain U.S. Attorneys were too timid in prosecuting public corruption among Democrats. Under 18 U.S.C. Section 1503, it is obstruction of justice to "corruptly ... endeavor to influence ... or impede any ... officer ... of any court of the United States ... in the discharge of his duty ... or corruptly ... influence ... or impede ... the due administration of justice ..." Suppose a President fired an official within the Department of Justice in an effort to impede that official's investigation of one of the President's political allies and, in response, the official asserted civil claims against the President. Would the President enjoy absolute immunity on the theory that hiring and firing Executive Branch officials falls within his official duties? Or would the President lose his immunity because obstruction of justice cannot be considered to be within even the "outer perimeter" of presidential responsibilities?

3. Justice White notes that, through the Speech and Debate Clause, the Constitution expressly grants to members of Congress immunity for their official conduct, while it offers no such express protection to the President. The Framers knew how to provide immunity when they wished to do so; should we infer from the absence of express immunity for the President that the Framers intended for the President to face civil liability for his official acts? Is it likely that the Framers even considered that the nations' chief executive might be sued for civil damages?

4. Justice Powell looks to the "unique" and "singular" nature of the presidency in concluding that absolute immunity is appropriate. Given the reasoning of *Fitzgerald*, should there be any degree of immunity accorded to the *Vice President* for his conduct in office? In the minutes immediately following the terrorist attacks of September 11, 2001, Vice President Dick Cheney was involved in coordinating response efforts from a White House bunker while President George W. Bush was traveling outside of Washington. According to the official findings of the National Commission on Terrorist Attacks Upon the United States (popularly known as the "9/11 Commission"), Vice President Cheney authorized military fighter jets over Washington, D.C. to shoot down unauthorized aircraft that approached the city. *The 9/11 Commission Report* (Authorized Edition, 2004) at 41-42. The Constitution gives no role to the Vice President in matters of national security or military affairs. (Further, the Vice President has no place in the statutory chain of command. Under the Goldwater-Nichols Department of Defense Reorganization Act of 1986, the chain of command runs from the President to the Secretary of Defense to combatant commanders. 10 U.S.C. §162(b).) Under the reasoning of *Fitzgerald*, if the Vice President were to order governmental action that resulted in personal injuries or

property damage, would he enjoy absolute immunity from civil liability? Proponents of vice presidential immunity might argue that, when the Vice President exercises executive authority in the same fashion that the President normally would, he should benefit from immunity similar to the President's immunity. Opponents of vice presidential immunity might argue that the Constitution gives to the Vice President no executive authority whatsoever; consequently, any executive action by the Vice President would, by definition, exceed the "outer perimeter" of his responsibilities.

Clinton v. Jones

520 U.S. 681 (1997)[12]

JUSTICE STEVENS delivered the opinion of the Court.

This case raises a constitutional and a prudential question concerning the Office of the President of the United States. Respondent, a private citizen, seeks to recover damages from the current occupant of that office based on actions allegedly taken before his term began. The President submits that in all but the most exceptional cases the Constitution requires federal courts to defer such litigation until his term ends and that, in any event, respect for the office warrants such a stay. Despite the force of the arguments supporting the President's submissions, we conclude that they must be rejected.

* * *

[Bill Clinton is the sitting President of the United States. This case involves claims for civil damages arising from alleged sexual harassment that Clinton directed at the plaintiff, Paula Jones, in 1991 when Clinton was Governor of Arkansas. The President, asserting presidential immunity, moved "to dismiss . . . without prejudice and to toll any statutes of limitation [that may be applicable] until he is no longer President, at which time the plaintiff may refile the instant suit."]

Petitioner's principal submission -- that "in all but the most exceptional cases," the Constitution affords the President temporary immunity from civil damages litigation arising out of events that occurred before he took office -- cannot be sustained on the basis of precedent.

---

[12] Footnotes and some citations found in the original decision have been omitted from this excerpted version.

Only three sitting Presidents have been defendants in civil litigation involving their actions prior to taking office. Complaints against Theodore Roosevelt and Harry Truman had been dismissed before they took office; the dismissals were affirmed after their respective inaugurations. Two companion cases arising out of an automobile accident were filed against John F. Kennedy in 1960 during the Presidential campaign. After taking office, he unsuccessfully argued that his status as Commander in Chief gave him a right to a stay under the Soldiers' and Sailors' Civil Relief Act of 1940. The motion for a stay was denied by the District Court, and the matter was settled out of court. Thus, none of those cases sheds any light on the constitutional issue before us.

The principal rationale for affording certain public servants immunity from suits for money damages arising out of their official acts is inapplicable to unofficial conduct. In cases involving prosecutors, legislators, and judges we have repeatedly explained that the immunity serves the public interest in enabling such officials to perform their designated functions effectively without fear that a particular decision may give rise to personal liability. We explained in Ferri v. Ackerman, 444 U.S. 193 (1979):

> As public servants, the prosecutor and the judge represent the interest of society as a whole. The conduct of their official duties may adversely affect a wide variety of different individuals, each of whom may be a potential source of future controversy. The societal interest in providing such public officials with the maximum ability to deal fearlessly and impartially with the public at large has long been recognized as an acceptable justification for official immunity. The point of immunity for such officials is to forestall an atmosphere of intimidation that would conflict with their resolve to perform their designated functions in a principled fashion.

Id., at 202-204.

That rationale provided the principal basis for our holding that a former President of the United States was "entitled to absolute immunity from damages liability predicated on his official acts," Fitzgerald, 457 U.S., at 749 . See id., at 752 (citing Ferri v. Ackerman). Our central concern was to avoid rendering the President "unduly cautious in the discharge of his official duties." 457 U.S., at 752, n. 32.

This reasoning provides no support for an immunity for unofficial conduct. As we explained in Fitzgerald, "the sphere of protected action must be related closely to the immunity's justifying purposes." Id., at 755. Because of the President's broad responsibilities, we recognized in that case an immunity from damages claims arising out of official acts extending to the "outer perimeter of his authority." Id., at 757. But we have never suggested that the President, or any other official, has an immunity that extends beyond the scope of any action taken in an official capacity. See id., at 759 (Burger, C. J., concurring) (noting that "a President, like Members of Congress, judges, prosecutors, or congressional aides -- all having absolute immunity -- are not immune for acts outside official duties"); see also id., at 761, n. 4.

Moreover, when defining the scope of an immunity for acts clearly taken within an official capacity, we have applied a functional approach. "Frequently our decisions have held that an official's absolute immunity should extend only to acts in performance of particular functions of his office." Id., at 755. Hence, for example, a judge's absolute immunity does not extend to actions performed in a purely administrative capacity. See Forrester v. White, 484 U.S. 219, 229 -230 (1988). As our opinions have made clear, immunities are grounded in "the nature of the function performed, not the identity of the actor who performed it." Id., at 229.
Petitioner's effort to construct an immunity from suit for unofficial acts grounded purely in the identity of his office is unsupported by precedent.

* * *

Petitioner's strongest argument supporting his immunity claim is based on the text and structure of the Constitution. He does not contend that the occupant of the Office of the President is "above the law," in the sense that his conduct is entirely immune from judicial scrutiny. The President argues merely for a postponement of the judicial proceedings that will determine whether he violated any law. His argument is grounded in the character of the office that was created by Article II of the Constitution, and relies on separation of powers principles that have structured our constitutional arrangement since the founding.

As a starting premise, petitioner contends that he occupies a unique office with powers and responsibilities so vast and important that the public interest demands that he devote his undivided time and attention to his public duties. He submits that -- given the nature of the office -- the doctrine of separation of powers places limits on the authority of the Federal Judiciary to interfere with the Executive Branch that would be transgressed by allowing this action to proceed.

* * *

Rather than arguing that the decision of the case will produce either an aggrandizement of judicial power or a narrowing of executive power, petitioner contends that -- as a byproduct of an otherwise traditional exercise of judicial power -- burdens will be placed on the President that will hamper the performance of his official duties . . . As a factual matter, petitioner contends that this particular case -- as well as the potential additional litigation that an affirmance of the Court of Appeals judgment might spawn -- may impose an unacceptable burden on the President's time and energy, and thereby impair the effective performance of his office.

Petitioner's predictive judgment finds little support in either history or the relatively narrow compass of the issues raised in this particular case. As we have already noted, in the more than 200 year history of the Republic, only three sitting Presidents have been subjected to suits for their private actions. If the past is any indicator, it seems unlikely that a deluge of such litigation will ever engulf the Presidency. As for the case at hand, if properly managed by the District Court, it appears to us highly unlikely to occupy any substantial amount of petitioner's time.

Of greater significance, petitioner errs by presuming that interactions between the Judicial Branch and the Executive, even quite burdensome interactions, necessarily rise to the level of constitutionally forbidden impairment of the Executive's ability to perform its constitutionally mandated functions.

* * *

First, we have long held that when the President takes official action, the Court has the authority to determine whether he has acted within the law. Perhaps the most dramatic example of such a case is our holding that President Truman exceeded his constitutional authority when he issued an order directing the Secretary of Commerce to take possession of and operate most of the Nation's steel mills in order to avert a national catastrophe. Youngstown Sheet & Tube Co. v. Sawyer, 343 U.S. 579 (1952). Despite the serious impact of that decision on the ability of the Executive Branch to accomplish its assigned mission, and the substantial time that the President must

> necessarily have devoted to the matter as a result of judicial involvement, we exercised our Article III jurisdiction to decide whether his official conduct conformed to the law. Our holding was an application of the principle established in Marbury v. Madison, 1 Cranch 137 (1803), that "[i]t is emphatically the province and duty of the judicial department to say what the law is." Id., at 177.
>
> Second, it is also settled that the President is subject to judicial process in appropriate circumstances. Although Thomas Jefferson apparently thought otherwise, Chief Justice Marshall, when presiding in the treason trial of Aaron Burr, ruled that a subpoena duces tecum could be directed to the President. United States v. Burr, 25 F. Cas. 30 (No. 14, 692d) (CC Va. 1807). We unequivocally and emphatically endorsed Marshall's position when we held that President Nixon was obligated to comply with a subpoena commanding him to produce certain tape recordings of his conversations with his aides. United States v. Nixon, 418 U.S. 683 (1974). As we explained, "neither the doctrine of separation of powers, nor the need for confidentiality of high level communications, without more, can sustain an absolute, unqualified Presidential privilege of immunity from judicial process under all circumstances." Id., at 706.
>
> * * *
>
> [W]e are persuaded that it was an abuse of discretion for the District Court to defer the trial until after the President leaves office. Such a lengthy and categorical stay takes no account whatever of the respondent's interest in bringing the case to trial. The complaint was filed within the statutory limitations period -- albeit near the end of that period -- and delaying trial would increase the danger of prejudice resulting from the loss of evidence, including the inability of witnesses to recall specific facts, or the possible death of a party.
>
> [JUSTICE BREYER filed a concurring opinion.]

<u>DISCUSSION AND QUESTIONS</u>

1. Six months after the *Jones* decision was issued, President Clinton was sitting for a deposition and was being questioned by a lawyer for Paula Jones. Among other things, the President was asked about alleged sexual contacts with, or advances toward, other women, including former White House intern Monica

Lewinsky. The President testified that "I have never had sexual relations with Monica Lewinsky. I've never had an affair with her." Transcript of January 17, 1998 Deposition of President William J. Clinton at 78. A short time later, his deposition testimony became the subject of an investigation by Independent Counsel Kenneth Starr. Eleven months after his deposition, President Clinton was impeached by the House of Representatives for perjury and obstruction of justice. Was the unanimous *Jones* court correct in predicting that "it seems unlikely that a deluge of such litigation will ever engulf the Presidency. As for the case at hand, if properly managed by the District Court, it appears to us highly unlikely to occupy any substantial amount of petitioner's time"? Or, did the *Jones* court unwisely abandon Justice Powell's reasoning 15 years earlier in *Fitzgerald* that, "because of the singular importance of the President's duties, diversion of his energies by concern with private lawsuits would raise unique risks to the effective functioning of government"? Former University of Texas football coach Darrell Royal famously preferred the running game to the passing game. His view of the forward pass was "three things can happen, and two of them are bad." Would a more prescient Supreme Court have taken a similar approach to subjecting a sitting President to civil litigation for his personal conduct: Several things can happen, and most of them are bad?

2. In the *Jones* case, President Clinton was denied any form of immunity -- even a stay of litigation -- for conduct that occurred *before* he took office as President. Would the same result obtain if a plaintiff were to sue the sitting President for conduct that occurs while the President is in office? In February 2006, Vice President Dick Cheney accidentally shot one of his companions during a quail hunt in Texas. If a President were involved in a similar mishap while in office, would his injured hunting companion be permitted to pursue civil claims, just as Paula Jones did against President Clinton?

3. Both the *Fitzgerald* and *Jones* cases address civil claims. The Supreme Court has not had occasion to determine whether a sitting President can be criminally prosecuted while in office. Justice White dissents in *Fitzgerald* and observes that the natural consequence of the majority's reasoning there is that "Congress cannot provide a remedy against Presidential misconduct and the criminal laws of the United States are wholly inapplicable to the President." He also notes, however, that such a result would be untenable because the Constitution itself appears to contemplate that the President remains subject to criminal prosecution. To be sure, the Constitution provides, in Article I, Section 3, that a party "convicted" after impeachment shall be "subject to indictment, trial, judgment and punishment, according to law." This suggests that a President who is removed from office through the impeachment process remains liable for criminal conduct in which he

may have engaged. But the Constitution does not directly answer the question whether a President can be subject to criminal prosecution while still in office. In the presidential hunting accident hypothesized above, imagine that the local prosecutor believed the President had been criminally negligent and sought to prosecute the President. Do separation of power principles permit the judiciary to subject the sitting President of the United States to a criminal trial and potential criminal liability, possibly to include incarceration? Does it matter whether the criminal trial is to occur in state court or federal court? Is it likely that the Framers intended for the commander in chief and repository of "the executive power" to be subject to criminal prosecution and confinement?

CHAPTER FIVE: LEGISLATIVE BRANCH INVESTIGATION AND OVERSIGHT

CONGRESS' POWER OF INQUIRY

Most important historical and social developments in recent American history have been punctuated with congressional investigations. Examples abound. In the twentieth century, some of the best known were the Army-McCarthy hearings and investigations by the House Un-American Activities Committee of the late 1940s and early 1950s, which probed alleged Communist sympathizers in the United States and Communist infiltration into the government; the Church Committee of the 1970s, which investigated alleged abuses of and by the intelligence services; the Iran-Contra hearings of the 1980s, which investigated alleged illegal weapons sales and hostage negotiations by the Reagan Administration; and, of course, the Watergate hearings, which investigated all manner of alleged improprieties by President Richard M. Nixon and his Administration and eventually led to his resignation.

Such congressional investigation -- including active oversight of the Executive Branch -- goes back to the early days of the republic. Congress' "power of inquiry" has been accepted as an appropriate and necessary corollary of its legislative function. If it is to legislate effectively, the Legislative Branch must have the power to inform itself fully about the matters under consideration. And the legislature can act as an effective check on the executive only if the legislature is able to apprise itself of how well or poorly the executive is fulfilling its responsibilities. Moreover, its power of inquiry would be of little use if it were unable to require witnesses to testify or if it were forced to rely on the goodwill of the other branches to enforce its investigative requests. Consequently, Congress' power of inquiry includes its "inherent contempt" power -- that is, the authority to compel witnesses to provide information through arrest and contempt proceedings if necessary.

One of the earliest cases to address Congress' inherent contempt power sprang from an alleged bribe. After John Anderson was accused of attempting to bribe a Congressman, the House of Representatives called him to appear for a hearing at which he was represented by counsel and permitted to call witnesses. Anderson was found to have offered the bribe and therefore to be in contempt of Congress, and was given into the custody of Thomas Dunn, the House's Sergeant-At-Arms, for confinement and punishment. Anderson sued Dunn for battery and false imprisonment, arguing that the House had no authority to hold and punish an individual for contempt.

Anderson v. Dunn

19 U.S. 204 (1821)[13]

MR. JUSTICE JOHNSON delivered the opinion of the Court.

It is certainly true, that there is no power given by the constitution to either House to punish for contempts, except when committed by their own members. Nor does the judicial or criminal power given to the United States, in any part, expressly extend to the infliction of punishment for contempt of either House, or any one coordinate branch of the government. Shall we, therefore, decide, that no such power exists?

It is true, that such a power, if it exists, must be derived from implication, and the genius and spirit of our institutions are hostile to the exercise of implied powers. Had the faculties of man been competent to the framing of a system of government which would have left nothing to implication, it cannot be doubted, that the effort would have been made by the framers of the Constitution. But what is the fact? There is not in the whole of that admirable instrument a grant of powers which does not draw after it others, not expressed, but vital to their exercise; not substantive and independent, indeed, but auxiliary and subordinate.

* * *

[I]f there is one maxim which necessarily rides over all others in the practical application of government, it is that the public functionaries must be left at liberty to exercise the powers which the people have entrusted to them. The interests and dignity of those who created them, require the exertion of the powers indispensable to the attainment of the ends of their creation.

* * *

On this principle it is that courts of justice are universally acknowledged to be vested, by their very creation, with power to impose silence, respect, and decorum in their presence, and submission to their lawful mandates, and, as a corollary to this proposition, to preserve themselves and their officers from the approach and insults of pollution.

[13] Footnotes and some citations found in the original decision have been omitted from this excerpted version.

*   *   *

But it is contended that, if this power in the House of Representatives is to be asserted on the plea of necessity, the ground is too broad, and the result too indefinite; that the executive, and every coordinate, and even subordinate, branch of the Government may resort to the same justification, and the whole assume to themselves, in the exercise of this power, the most tyrannical licentiousness.

This is unquestionably an evil to be guarded against, and if the doctrine may be pushed to that extent, it must be a bad doctrine, and is justly denounced.

But what is the alternative? The argument obviously leads to the total annihilation of the power of the House of Representatives to guard itself from contempts, and leaves it exposed to every indignity and interruption that rudeness, caprice, or even conspiracy, may meditate against it. This result is fraught with too much absurdity not to bring into doubt the soundness of any argument from which it is derived. That a deliberate assembly, clothed with the majesty of the people and charged with the care of all that is dear to them; composed of the most distinguished citizens, selected and drawn together from every quarter of a great nation; whose deliberations are required by public opinion to be conducted under the eye of the public, and whose decisions must be clothed with all that sanctity which unlimited confidence in their wisdom and purity can inspire; that such an assembly should not possess the power to suppress rudeness, or repel insult is a supposition too wild to be suggested. And, accordingly, to avoid the pressure of these considerations, it has been argued that the right of the respective Houses to exclude from their presence, and their absolute control within their own walls, carry with them the right to punish contempts committed in their presence; while the absolute legislative power given to Congress within this District enables them to provide by law against all other insults against which there is any necessity for providing.

*   *   *

But although the offence be held undefinable, it is justly contended that the punishment need not be indefinite. Nor is it so.

We are not now considering the extent to which the punishing power of Congress, by a legislative act, may be carried. On that subject, the bounds of their power are to be found in the provisions of the Constitution.

The present question is what is the extent of the punishing power which the deliberative assemblies of the Union may assume and exercise on the principle of self-preservation?

Analogy, and the nature of the case, furnish the answer -- "the least possible power adequate to the end proposed;" which is the power of imprisonment. It may, at first view, and from the history of the practice of our legislative bodies, be thought to extend to other inflictions. But every other will be found to be mere commutation for confinement; since commitment alone is the alternative where the individual proves contumacious. And even to the duration of imprisonment a period is imposed by the nature of things, since the existence of the power that imprisons is indispensable to its continuance, and although the legislative power continues perpetual, the legislative body ceases to exist on the moment of its adjournment or periodical dissolution. It follows that imprisonment must terminate with that adjournment.

* * *

But it is argued, that the inference, if any, arising under the Constitution is against the exercise of the powers here asserted by the House of Representatives; that the express grant of power to punish their members respectively, and to expel them, by the application of a familiar maxim, raises an implication against the power to punish any other than their own members.

This argument proves too much, for its direct application would lead to the annihilation of almost every power of Congress. To enforce its laws upon any subject without the sanction of punishment is obviously impossible. Yet there is an express grant of power to punish in one class of cases and one only, and all the punishing power exercised by Congress in any cases, except those which relate to piracy and offences against the laws of nations, is derived from implication. Nor did the idea ever occur to anyone that the express grant in one class of cases repelled the assumption of the punishing power in any other.

* * *

Judgment affirmed.

DISCUSSION AND QUESTIONS

1. The Court implies an inherent contempt power in the Legislative Branch that is necessary for its "self-preservation." Regardless of whether it's sensible for Congress to make and enforce contempt findings, isn't this something that could be handled legislatively rather than through judicial creation of power that looks very much like the sort of power that is ordinarily shared between the Executive and Judicial Branches – jailing individuals for their misconduct? If Congress felt that it needed some sort of contempt power, could it not have enacted a statute defining and setting forth appropriate punishments for contempt of Congress?

2. The Court in *Anderson* implies a constitutional entitlement in a branch of government based on that branch's role and responsibilities, just as there is an implied executive privilege and an implied power in the courts to issue and enforce ancillary orders in support of their proper functioning. If there is an inherent contempt power in the Legislative Branch, why should there not be an inherent contempt power also for the Executive Branch? If, in *Anderson*, the House of Representatives could unilaterally try and jail a citizen for attempting to bribe one of its members, why couldn't the President unilaterally try and jail a citizen suspected of attempting to bribe a cabinet official? Surely the integrity and proper functioning of the Executive Branch is just as threatened by bribery as is the integrity and functioning of the Legislative Branch. But there is no inherent contempt power in the Executive; why not? What is the distinction?

3. The Court in *Anderson* validates action by the Legislative Branch – trying and jailing an individual – that is normally viewed as a shared responsibility of the Executive and Judicial Branches, and which is normally attended by other constitutional safeguards of individual rights, such as the Fifth Amendment right to avoid self-incrimination, the Sixth Amendment right to counsel, and the Eighth Amendment prohibition against cruel and unusual punishment. The *Anderson* decision is unclear as to whether such safeguards must be part of congressional inherent contempt proceedings. Does the Court's decision allude to any checks on potential abuses of the inherent contempt power? First, the Court explains that any inherent contempt detention may last only until the chamber adjourns. Second, the Court notes that the members of the legislative body imposing the penalty are "the most distinguished citizens, selected and drawn together from every quarter of a great nation, whose deliberations are required by public opinion to be conducted under the eye of the public." The Court may view the electoral process itself as the ultimate check; legislators who support the overzealous exercise of the inherent contempt power must do so publicly and will presumably be called to account by voters.

4. Could the Congress use its inherent contempt power to enforce its legislative enactments? For example, if Congress passed a law against counterfeiting, could it then unilaterally punish an alleged counterfeiter because he demonstrated "contempt" of a congressional act? No. Article II of the Constitution expressly allocates to the President the responsibility for enforcing the laws. The inherent contempt power is not about enforcing the laws enacted by Congress; rather, it is about preserving the effectiveness of the legislative process.

A little more than half a century after *Anderson* was decided, in the case of *Kilbourn v. Thompson*, 103 U.S. 168 (1880), the Supreme Court placed some limits on the seemingly expansive inherent contempt power described in *Anderson*. In *Kilbourn*, the contemnor was found in contempt of Congress and taken into custody by the Sergeant-At-Arms for refusing to answer questions and produce documents before a special House committee that was investigating the failure of a real estate pool. He sued the Sergeant-At-Arms and various House members for false arrest.

Kilbourn v. Thompson

103 U.S. 168 (1880)[14]

MR. JUSTICE MILLER, after stating the case, delivered the opinion of the court.

The argument before us has assumed a very wide range, and includes the discussion of almost every suggestion that can well be conceived on the subject. The two extremes of the controversy are the proposition on the part of the plaintiff that the House of Representatives has no power whatever to punish for a contempt of its authority, and, on the part of defendants, that such power undoubtedly exists, and when that body has formally exercised it, it must be presumed that it was right fully exercised.

This latter proposition assumes the form of expression sometimes used with reference to courts of justice of general jurisdiction that, having the power to punish for contempts, the judgment of the House that a person is guilty of such contempt is conclusive everywhere.

---

[14] Footnotes and some citations found in the original decision have been omitted from this excerpted version.

Conceding for the sake of the argument that there are cases in which one of the two bodies that constitute the Congress of the United States may punish for contempt of its authority or disregard of its orders, it will scarcely be contended by the most ardent advocate of their power in that respect that it is unlimited.

The powers of Congress itself, when acting through the concurrence of both branches, are dependent solely on the Constitution. Such as are not conferred by that instrument, either expressly or by fair implication from what is granted, are "reserved to the States respectively, or to the people." Of course, neither branch of Congress, when acting separately, can lawfully exercise more power than is conferred by the Constitution on the whole body, except in the few instances where authority is conferred on either House separately, as in the case of impeachments. No general power of inflicting punishment by the Congress of the United States is found in that instrument. It contains in the provision that no "person all be deprived of life, liberty, or property, without due process of law" the strongest implication against punishment by order of the legislative body. It has been repeatedly decided by this court, and by others of the highest authority, that this means a trial in which the rights of the party shall be decided by a tribunal appointed by law, which tribunal is to be governed by rules of law previously established. An act of Congress which proposed to adjudge a man guilty of a crime and inflict the punishment would be conceded by all thinking men to be unauthorized by anything in the Constitution. That instrument, however, is not wholly silent as to the authority of the separate branches of Congress to inflict punishment. It authorizes each House to punish its own members. By the second clause of the fifth section of the first article,

"Each House may determine the rules of its proceedings, punish its members for disorderly behavior, and, with the concurrence of two-thirds, expel a member,"

and, by the clause immediately preceding, it "may be authorized to compel the attendance of absent members in such manner and under such penalties as each House may provide."

These provisions are equally instructive in what they authorize and in what they do not authorize. There is no express power in that instrument conferred on either House of Congress to punish for contempts.

The advocates of this power have, therefore, resorted to an implication of its existence founded on two principal arguments. These are, 1, its exercise by the House of Commons of England, from which country we, it is said, have derived our system of parliamentary law; and 2d, the necessity of such a power to enable the two Houses of Congress to perform the duties and exercise the power which the Constitution has conferred on them.

[The court then reviewed extensively the English precedents relating to a supposed inherent contempt power enjoyed by the English Parliament.]

We are of opinion that the right of the House of Representatives to punish the citizen for a contempt of its authority or a breach of its privileges can derive no support from the precedents and practices of the two Houses of the English Parliament, nor from the adjudged cases in which the English courts have upheld these practices. Nor, taking what has fallen from the English judges, and especially the later cases on which we have just commented, is much aid given to the doctrine that this power exists as one necessary to enable either House of Congress to exercise successfully their function of legislation.

This latter proposition is one which we do not propose to decide in the present case, because we are able to decide it without passing upon the existence or nonexistence of such power in aid of the legislative function.

As we have already said, the Constitution expressly empowers each House to punish its own members for disorderly behavior. We see no reason to doubt that this punishment may, in a proper case, be imprisonment, and that it may be for refusal to obey some rule on that subject made by the House for the preservation of order.

So also, the penalty which each House is authorized to inflict in order to compel the attendance of absent members may be imprisonment, and this may be for a violation of some order or standing rule on that subject.

Each House is, by the Constitution, made the judge of the election and qualification of its members. In deciding on these, it has an undoubted right to examine witnesses and inspect papers, subject to the usual rights of witnesses in such cases, and it may be that a witness would be subject to like punishment at the hands of the body engaged in trying a contested election, for refusing to testify, that he would if the case were pending before a court of judicature.

The House of Representatives has the sole right to impeach officers of the government, and the Senate to try them. Where the question of such impeachment is before either body acting in its appropriate sphere on that subject, we see no reason to doubt the right to compel the attendance of witnesses, and their answer to proper questions, in the same manner and by the use of the same means that courts of justice can in like cases.

Whether the power of punishment in either House by fine or imprisonment goes beyond this or not, we are sure that no person can be punished for contumacy as a witness before either House unless his testimony is required in a matter into which that House has jurisdiction to inquire, and we feel equally sure that neither of these bodies possesses the general power of making inquiry into the private affairs of the citizen.

*   *   *

In looking to the preamble and resolution under which the committee acted, before which Kilbourn refused to testify, we are of opinion that the House of Representatives not only exceeded the limit of its own authority, but assumed a power which could only be properly exercised by another branch of the government, because it was, in its nature, clearly judicial.

*   *   *

We are of opinion, for these reasons, that the resolution of the House of Representatives authorizing the investigation was in excess of the power conferred on that body by the Constitution; that the committee, therefore, had no lawful authority to require Kilbourn to testify a a witness beyond what he voluntarily chose to tell; that the orders and resolutions of the House, and the warrant of the speaker, under which Kilbourn was imprisoned are, in like manner, void for want of jurisdiction in that body, and that his imprisonment was without any lawful authority.

At this point of the inquiry we are met by Anderson v. Dunn, 6 Wheat. 204, which in many respects is analogous to the case now under consideration.

*   *   *

> [T]hough the grounds of the decision are not very clearly stated, we take them to be that there is in some cases a power in each House of Congress to punish for contempt; that this power is analogous to that exercised by courts of justice, and that it being the well established doctrine that, when it appears that a prisoner is held under the order of a court of general jurisdiction for a contempt of its authority, no other court will discharge the prisoner or make further inquiry into the cause of his commitment. That this is the general rule, though somewhat modified since that case was decided, as regards the relations of one court to another, must be conceded.
>
> But we do not concede that the Houses of Congress possess this general power of punishing for contempt. The cases in which they can do this are very limited, as we have already attempted to show. If they are proceeding in a matter beyond their legitimate cognizance, we are of opinion that this can be shown, and we cannot give our assent to the principle that, by the mere act of asserting a person to be guilty of a contempt, they thereby establish their right to fine and imprison him, beyond the power of any court or any other tribunal whatever to inquire into the grounds on which the order was made.
>
> *   *   *
>
> We must, therefore, hold, notwithstanding what is said in the case of *Anderson v. Dunn,* that the resolution of the House of Representatives finding Kilbourn guilty of contempt, and the warrant of its speaker for his commitment to prison, are not conclusive in this case, and, in fact, are no justification, because, as the whole plea shows, the House was without authority in the matter.
>
> *   *   *
>
> *So ordered.*

DISCUSSION AND QUESTIONS

1. The *Kilbourn* Court is far more skeptical about the inherent contempt power than the *Anderson* Court several decades earlier, but the *Kilbourn* decision does not reject the power entirely. How does the *Kilbourn* Court limit the inherent contempt power of Congress? If a congressional chamber were to invoke its inherent contempt power today, how (if at all) would the *Kilbourn* ruling limit the exercise of that power? Are the recognized limits on the scope of congressional inquiry broader or narrower than when *Kilbourn* was decided? Would it still be fair to say that

"neither [chamber] possesses the general power of making inquiry into the private affairs of the citizen"?

2. The Court notes that the Constitution forbids a deprivation of liberty without due process, which "means a trial in which the rights of the party shall be decided by a tribunal appointed by law, which tribunal is to be governed by rules of law previously established." Is the Court instructing that, even in the narrow circumstances where the Legislative Branch may invoke its inherent contempt power, it must afford to the alleged contemnor all the traditional attributes of constitutional due process? If an otherwise valid inherent contempt proceeding in the Senate failed to permit access to counsel for the accused, or required the accused to testify against himself, would the courts entertain a challenge to the proceedings on those grounds? Would the Court's extremely deferential approach reflected in *Nixon v. United States* (see Chapter Eight, pages 227-31) apply to such proceedings as it applied to impeachment proceedings?

Between 1795 and 1857, there were 14 inherent contempt proceedings in the House and Senate. Although some were successful in the sense that they resulted in either the punishment of the contemnor or the contemnor producing requested information, such proceedings were similar to adversarial trials and therefore required time and legislative resources. Further, the punishment that could be imposed was viewed by some as inadequate because confinement of a contemnor could not extend beyond the pertinent chamber's adjournment. As a result, in 1857 Congress created a statutory alternative to its inherent contempt power, which is codified at 2 U.S.C. Sections 192 and 194. In pertinent part, these provisions state:

> Every person who having been summoned as a witness by the authority of either House of Congress [or any committee] to give testimony or to produce papers upon any matter under inquiry . . . willfully makes default, or who, having appeared, refuses to answer any question pertinent to the question under inquiry, shall be deemed guilty of a misdemeanor, punishable by a fine of not more than $1,000 nor less than $100 and imprisonment in a common jail for not less than one month nor more than twelve months.
>
> Whenever a witness summoned as mentioned in section 192 of this title fails to appear to testify or fails to produce any books, papers, records, or documents, as required, or whenever any witness so summoned refuses to answer any question pertinent to the subject under inquiry . . . it shall be the duty of the said President of the Senate or Speaker of the House, as the case may be, to certify, and he shall so certify [the matter] to the appropriate United States attorney,

> whose duty it shall be to bring the matter before the grand jury for its action.

With the availability of statutory relief for contempt of Congress, use of the inherent contempt power became less frequent. It was last used in 1934, when William MacCracken was arrested and imprisoned by the Senate Sergeant-At-Arms for permitting the destruction of documents that had been subpoenaed by a Senate committee investigating how the Postmaster General awarded contracts for the carriage of mail. In his petition for habeas corpus relief, MacCracken did not dispute the validity of the congressional subpoena and did not deny the allegation that he had permitted the destruction of documents; rather, he asserted that Congress' inherent contempt power could only be used to coerce compliance, not to punish past behavior.

Jurney v. MacCracken

294 U.S. 125 (1935)[15]

MR. JUSTICE BRANDEIS delivered the opinion of the Court.

* * *

First. The main contention of MacCracken is that the so-called power to punish for contempt may never be exerted, in the case of a private citizen, solely *qua* punishment. The argument is that the power may be used by the legislative body merely as a means of removing an existing obstruction to the performance of its duties; that the power to punish ceases as soon as the obstruction has been removed or its removal has become impossible, and hence that there is no power to punish a witness who, having been requested to produce papers, destroys them after service of the subpoena. The contention rests upon a misconception of the limitations upon the power of the Houses of Congress to punish for contempt. It is true that the scope of the power is narrow . . . But, where the offending act was of a nature to obstruct the legislative process, the fact that the obstruction has since been removed, or that its removal has become impossible, is without legal significance.

* * *

[15] Footnotes and some citations found in the original decision have been omitted from this excerpted version.

Here, we are concerned not with an extension of congressional privilege, but with vindication of the established and essential privilege of requiring the production of evidence. For this purpose, the power to punish for a past contempt is an appropriate means. *Compare Ex parte Nugent,* Fed.Cas. No. 10,375; *Stewart v. Blaine,* 1 MacArthur 453. The apprehensions expressed from time to time in congressional debates, in opposition to particular exercises of the contempt power, concerned not the power to punish, as such, but the broad, undefined privileges which it was believed might find sanction in that power. The ground for such fears has since been effectively removed by the decisions of this Court which hold that assertions of congressional privilege are subject to judicial review, *Kilbourn v. Thompson, supra,* and that the power to punish for contempt may not be extended to slanderous attacks which present no immediate obstruction to legislative processes, *Marshall v. Gordon, supra.*

Second. The power of either House of Congress to punish for contempt was not impaired by the enactment in 1857 of the statute, R.S. § 102, making refusal to answer or to produce papers before either House or one of its committees a misdemeanor. *Compare Sinclair v. United States,* 279 U. S. 263. The statute was enacted not because the power of the Houses to punish for a past contempt was doubted, but because imprisonment limited to the duration of the session was not considered sufficiently drastic a punishment for contumacious witnesses. That the purpose of the statute was merely to supplement the power of contempt by providing for additional punishment was recognized in *In re Chapman,* 166 U. S. 661, 166 U. S. 671-672:

> We grant that Congress could not divest itself, or either of its houses, of the essential and inherent power to punish for contempt in cases to which the power of either house properly extended; but, because Congress, by the Act of 1857, sought to aid each of the houses in the discharge of its constitutional functions, it does not follow that any delegation of the power in each to punish for contempt was involved, and the statute is not open to objection on that account.

Punishment, purely as such, through contempt proceedings, legislative or judicial, is not precluded because punishment may also be inflicted for the same act as a statutory offense.

*   *   *

The judgment of the Court of Appeals [ordering the petitioner's release] should be reversed, and that of the Supreme Court of the District [dismissing the habeas petition] should be affirmed.

Reversed.

DISCUSSION AND QUESTIONS

1. *Jurney* makes clear that Congress' inherent contempt power is not limited to a civil contempt-type coercive detention where the contemnor "holds the keys to his jail cell" and may purge himself of contempt by choosing to comply with the wishes of the body that he has offended. Rather, the inherent contempt power includes the ability to punish simply for the sake of punishing. Why then may the term of confinement extend only to the end of the legislative session? If a witness called before a Senate committee just two weeks before the adjournment of the Senate willfully destroyed documents properly requested by the committee, would just a few days of confinement seem an appropriate penalty? Could a witness be subject to punishment *after* Congress reconvenes if it is then discovered that the witness had improperly withheld information *before* Congress adjourned?

2. Under *Jurney*, a congressional chamber may punish for the sake of punishing; however, *Jurney* does not change the pronouncement in *Anderson* more than a century earlier that physical confinement is the only form of punishment that is available. Courts can impose financial penalties on contemnors; by what rationale is the Legislative Branch prohibited from doing so? The *Anderson* Court seems to think the limitation is obvious and doesn't explain the source of the limitation ("commitment alone is the alternative where the individual proves contumacious"). If the rationale underlying the inherent contempt power is that the Congress must be able to deter conduct that interferes with its legislative functioning, which is so critical to our constitutional form of government, would it not be useful to permit other punishment options? Imagine a situation in which a Senate committee is conducting a high-profile investigation into possible public corruption, and is doing so in the last month of the current Congress. Would an obstreperous witness be more likely to acquiesce to the committee's demands for his testimony if he faced confinement until the end of the Congress, or if he faced a potential fine of, say, $250,000?

3. The contempt statute set forth above makes contempt of Congress a misdemeanor and imposes a penalty of confinement for up to twelve months (in

addition to a comparatively minor financial penalty). By its terms, this statutory provision works in a strictly punitive fashion; it does not contemplate that a convicted contemnor may purge himself of contempt and thereby reduce his time of confinement. Is this statutory alternative more or less likely to lead to witness compliance than Congress' inherent contempt power, under which a chamber may confine a contemnor in an effort to induce his compliance with its demands for information?

4. The contempt statute set forth above purports to impose a "duty" on the U.S. Attorney to prosecute congressional contemnors. Is this likely to be an effective device against a witness from the Executive Branch who refuses to provide requested testimony by invoking executive privilege? In early 2008, the House of Representatives referred to the Department of Justice for prosecution two alleged contemnors -- White House Chief of Staff Josh Bolten and former White House Counsel Harriet Miers -- who had cited executive privilege in refusing to respond to congressional subpoenas. Then-Attorney General Michael Mukasey promptly informed House Speaker Nancy Pelosi that "the department will not bring the congressional contempt citations before a grand jury or take any other action to prosecute Mr. Bolten or Ms. Miers." The House then instituted civil litigation in federal court to enforce its subpoenas against Bolten and Miers, which resulted in the *Committee on the Judiciary, U.S. House of Representatives v. Miers* decision, excerpted below at pages 150-54. Attorney General Mukasey's response was consistent with existing Department of Justice opinions concluding that the Executive Branch will not prosecute its own personnel who are simply following the directions of the President.

Although the inherent contempt power has not been used in more than seven decades, Congress' "power of inquiry" is alive and well and in constant use. It has been recognized since the earliest days of the republic and was resoundingly reaffirmed by the Supreme Court as a result of the Teapot Dome scandal of the 1920s. President Harding's Interior Secretary (and former Senator from New Mexico), Albert Fall, gave no-bid, sweetheart leases on oil-rich federal lands in Wyoming and California to oil magnates Harry Sinclair and Edward Doheny in exchange for bribes (Fall was convicted of bribery but Sinclair and Doheny were acquitted). After newspapers broke the story about the shady dealings related to the oil leases, the Senate Committee on Public Lands commenced an investigation led by Senator Thomas Walsh. That investigation led to two Supreme Court cases affirming the right of the Congress to compel witnesses to appear and testify. In the first case, *McGrain v. Daugherty*, Congress utilized its inherent power to enforce compliance with a subpoena. In the second case, *Sinclair v. United States*, the uncooperative witness was charged and convicted under the contempt statute.

McGrain v. Daugherty

273 U.S. 135 (1927)[16]

MR. JUSTICE VAN DEVANTER delivered the opinion of the Court.

This is an appeal from the final order in a proceeding in habeas corpus discharging a recusant witness held in custody under process of attachment issued from the United States Senate in the course of an investigation which it was making of the administration of the Department of Justice.

[The opinion explains that the Senate passed a resolution authorizing the investigation of former Attorney General Harry Daugherty for his failure to investigate and prosecute the conspirators involved in the Teapot Dome Scandal, as well as other alleged mis- and nonfeasance in his leadership of the Department of Justice.]

The resolution also authorized the committee to send for books and papers, to subpoena witnesses, to administer oaths, and to sit at such times and places as it might deem advisable.

In the course of the investigation, the committee issued and caused to be duly served on Mally S. Daugherty -- who was a brother of Harry M. Daugherty and president of the Midland National Bank of Washington Court House, Ohio -- a subpoena commanding him to appear before the committee for the purpose of giving testimony bearing on the subject under investigation, and to bring with him the

"deposit ledgers of the Midland National Bank since November 1, 1920; also note files and transcript of owners of every safety vault; also records of income drafts; also records of any individual account or accounts showing withdrawals of amounts of $25,000 or over during above period."

The witness failed to appear.

A little later in the course of the investigation, the committee issued and caused to be duly served on the same witness another subpoena, commanding him to appear before it for the purpose of giving testimony relating to the subject under consideration, nothing being said in this subpoena about bringing records, books, or papers. The

[16] Footnotes and some citations found in the original decision have been omitted from this excerpted version.

witness again failed to appear, and no excuse was offered by him for either failure.

[As a result of Daugherty's failure to appear, the Senate passed a resolution directing the sergeant-at-arms to find Daugherty, take him into custody, and "bring the said M.S. Daugherty before the bar of the Senate, then and there to answer such questions pertinent to the matter under inquiry." The sergeant-at-arms assigned this responsibility to his deputy, John McGrain, who found Daugherty in Cincinnati and took him into custody. Daugherty filed a habeas corpus petition in federal district court, and the petition was granted. This appeal followed.]

We have given the case earnest and prolonged consideration because the principal questions involved are of unusual importance and delicacy. They are (a) whether the Senate, or the House of Representatives, both being on the same plane in this regard, has power, through its own process, to compel a private individual to appear before it or one of its committees and give testimony needed to enable it efficiently to exercise a legislative function belonging to it under the Constitution, and (b) whether it sufficiently appears that the process was being employed in this instance to obtain testimony for that purpose.

* * *

The first of the principal questions, the one which the witness particularly presses on our attention, is, as before shown, whether the Senate -- or the House of Representatives, both being on the same plane in this regard -- has power, through its own process, to compel a private individual to appear before it or one of its committees and give testimony needed to enable it efficiently to exercise a legislative function belonging to it under the Constitution.

The Constitution provides for a Congress, consisting of a Senate and House of Representatives, and invests it with "all legislative powers" granted to the United States, and with power "to make all laws which shall be necessary and proper" for carrying into execution these powers and "all other powers" vested by the Constitution in the United States or in any department or officer thereof. Art. I, Secs. 1, 8. Other provisions show that, while bills can become laws only after being considered and passed by both houses of Congress, each house is to be distinct from the other, to have its own officers and rules, and to exercise its legislative function independently. Art. I, §§ 2, 3, 5, 7. But there is no provision expressly investing either house with power to make investigations and exact testimony to the end that it may exercise its legislative function advisedly and effectively. So the question arises whether this power is so far incidental to the legislative function as to be implied.

In actual legislative practice, power to secure needed information by such means has long been treated as an attribute of the power to legislate. It was so regarded in the British Parliament and in the colonial legislatures before the American Revolution, and a like view has prevailed and been carried into effect in both houses of Congress and in most of the state legislatures.

[The Court then reviewed historical exercises of investigative authority by the House and Senate, and also by state legislatures, and noted past judicial rulings that upheld both the investigative authority and the contempt power of the Legislative Branch.]

With this review of the legislative practice, congressional enactments, and court decisions, we proceed to a statement of our conclusions on the question.

We are of opinion that the power of inquiry -- with process to enforce it -- is an essential and appropriate auxiliary to the legislative function. It was so regarded and employed in American legislatures before the Constitution was framed and ratified. Both houses of Congress took this view of it early in their history -- the House of Representatives with the approving votes of Mr. Madison and other members whose service in the convention which framed the Constitution gives special significance to their action -- and both houses have employed the power accordingly up to the present time.

* * *

A legislative body cannot legislate wisely or effectively in the absence of information respecting the conditions which the legislation is intended to affect or change, and where the legislative body does not itself possess the requisite information -- which not infrequently is true -- recourse must be had to others who do possess it. Experience has taught that mere requests for such information often are unavailing, and also that information which is volunteered is not always accurate or complete, so some means of compulsion are essential to obtain what is needed. All this was true before and when the Constitution was framed and adopted. In that period, the power of inquiry, with enforcing process, was regarded and employed as a necessary and appropriate attribute of the power to legislate -- indeed, was treated as inhering in it. Thus, there is ample warrant for thinking, as we do, that the constitutional provisions which commit the legislative function to the two houses are intended to include this attribute to the end that the function may be effectively exercised.

The contention is earnestly made on behalf of the witness that this power of inquiry, if sustained, may be abusively and oppressively exerted. If this be so, it affords no ground for denying the power. The same contention might be directed against the power to legislate, and, of course, would be unavailing. We must assume for present purposes that neither houses will be disposed to exert the power beyond its proper bounds, or without due regard to the rights of witnesses. But if, contrary to this assumption, controlling limitations or restrictions are disregarded, the decisions in *Kilbourn v. Thompson* and *Marshall v. Gordon* point to admissible measures of relief. And it is a necessary deduction from the decisions in *Kilbourn v. Thompson* and *In re Chapman* that a witness rightfully may refuse to answer where the bounds of the power are exceeded or the questions are not pertinent to the matter under inquiry.

[The Court then concluded that the investigation of former Attorney General Daugherty's conduct in office was not effectively a criminal proceeding against him personally, but was a legitimate effort at legislative oversight of an executive agency.]

We conclude that the investigation was ordered for a legitimate object; that the witness wrongfully refused to appear and testify before the committee and was lawfully attached; that the Senate is entitled to have him give testimony pertinent to the inquiry, either at its bar or before the committee, and that the district court erred in discharging him from custody under the attachment.

* * *

What has been said requires that the final order in the district court discharging the witness from custody be reversed.

Final order reversed.

DISCUSSION AND QUESTIONS

1. The *Daugherty* Court suggests that a chamber of Congress is no more likely to abuse its investigative power than its power to legislate. Are the two really comparable? A chamber's power to legislate is subject to structural constitutional checks, including bicameralism and presentment to the President. Neither of these checks applies when a chamber exercises its investigative (and contempt) authority.

2. Two years later, in the case of *Sinclair v. United States*, 279 U.S. 263 (1929), the Court reaffirmed the legislature's power of inquiry when it upheld oilman Harry Sinclair's conviction under the 1857 contempt of Congress statute for refusing to answer questions related to the Teapot Dome Scandal. Sinclair probably could have avoided prosecution if he had invoked his Fifth Amendment privilege not to incriminate himself, which is a constitutional privilege that cannot be trumped by Congress' power of inquiry. However, Sinclair instead based his refusal to answer on the notion that the matter under investigation had become a subject of judicial inquiry in the form of civil litigation and criminal investigations, which effectively divested Congress of the power to inquire further on the matter. Would it make sense for the courts to impose a prudential limitation on Congress' power of inquiry when a congressional investigation might interfere with ongoing judicial proceedings? Is there a separation of powers basis for such a limitation (that is, the Judiciary Branch protects the integrity of its role against legislative encroachment), or do separation of powers considerations militate in the other direction (that is, the unelected Judiciary Branch should refrain from second-guessing what are and are not suitable matters for investigation by the elected representatives of the people)?

CONGRESS' POWER OF INQUIRY VERSUS EXECUTIVE PRIVILEGE

As the Supreme Court determined in *United States v. Nixon* (see Chapter Four, pages 103-09), the Executive Branch enjoys an inherent privilege to avoid the disclosure of certain confidential communications deemed necessary to the President's proper fulfillment of his executive responsibilities. What happens when the executive's asserted need for confidentiality runs into the legislature's asserted need for information that is in the possession of Executive Branch officials?

A classic example of such a dispute arose in the early 1980s, when the House Committee on Energy and Commerce was investigating the Environmental Protection Agency's (EPA) enforcement of the Superfund hazardous waste cleanup law. The Committee submitted multiple requests for documents, and the EPA -- pursuant to instructions from the Department of Justice -- responded by producing some documents but withholding others based on asserted executive privilege for "enforcement sensitive" materials. Frustrated with what he perceived to be a pattern of non-responsiveness, Committee Chairman John Dingell issued to EPA Administrator Anne Gorsuch a subpoena that required her to appear and bring certain documents that had been withheld. Shortly thereafter, Administrator Gorsuch was also subpoenaed by another subcommittee engaged in a related investigation. Attorney General William French Smith sent a letter to the committee chairmen explaining that the requested information would be withheld based on executive privilege for matters of internal Executive Branch deliberations and law enforcement strategy. House Counsel Stan Brand responded by arguing that Congress is entitled to engage in vigorous oversight of the Executive Branch and that disclosure to Congress is different from public disclosure. The Department of Justice maintained that it could not rely on congressional assurances that confidentiality would be preserved and also cited concerns about potential congressional interference in ongoing Executive Branch enforcement actions.

In response to Executive Branch defiance, the House voted to hold Administrator Gorsuch in contempt of Congress. The U.S. Attorney refused to prosecute Gorsuch under the contempt of Congress statute and the Justice Department immediately initiated litigation against the House seeking to prevent enforcement of the subpoenas and the contempt finding. The U.S. District Court dismissed the case, explaining that, in a dispute of this nature between co-equal branches, "judicial intervention should be delayed until all possibilities for settlement have been exhausted." *United States v. House of Representatives*, 556 F. Supp. 150, 152 (D.D.C. 1983). The court reasoned that judicial intervention might become necessary should Administrator Gorsuch become a defendant in a criminal proceeding, but the dispute had not yet reached that point. The court urged the parties that "compromise and cooperation, rather than confrontation, should be the[ir] aim." Id. at 153.

Ultimately, the district judge was correct. A settlement was reached that permitted the investigating committees to review the requested documents in closed session, but not to retain possession of the documents. Such disputes involving Congress' power of inquiry versus claims of executive privilege are typically resolved in this fashion and are almost never decided by the courts. A way is found to provide the essential information Congress needs while taking steps to minimize the risk that sensitive information will be leaked. For example, a similar compromise was reached in another showdown in the early 1980s when the Congress demanded from the Department of the Interior certain documents that the Attorney General characterized as "quintessentially deliberative, pre-decisional materials" not subject to disclosure. Ultimately, a compromise permitted committee members to review, but not copy, the requested materials.

In 2008, one such inter-branch dispute did play out in federal court and resulted in a rare decision on the merits. The House Judiciary Committee was investigating the highly controversial firings of nine U.S. Attorneys by President George W. Bush, which many alleged had been politically motivated and some characterized as potentially constituting criminal obstruction of justice. The committee sought information about the firings from former White House Counsel Harriet Miers and White House Chief of Staff Josh Bolten. The committee issued subpoenas for these individuals to testify and produce relevant documents. The Administration offered to make the witnesses available for unsworn and unrecorded interviews, which could not cover the witnesses' communications with the President or others on the White House staff. No compromise was reached and, pursuant to a claim of executive privilege asserted by President Bush, Miers and Bolten both refused to appear before the committee. The House determined that Miers and Bolten were in contempt of the House, and Speaker Nancy Pelosi referred the matter to the U.S. Attorney to pursue a criminal contempt action. Attorney General Michael Mukasey responded by saying that the Department of Justice would not pursue criminal action against Executive Branch officials who were simply following the President's orders. With the Executive Branch unwilling to proceed against its own members, the committee initiated a civil action on its own behalf seeking enforcement of the subpoenas. Miers and Bolten asserted that the committee lacked standing to pursue a civil action against them, and that, in any event, as two of the President's closest advisors, they should have absolute immunity from compelled testimony before the legislature.

Committee on the Judiciary, U.S. House of Representatives v. Harriet Miers, et al.

558 F. Supp. 2d 53 (D.D.C. 2008) [17]

MEMORANDUM OPINION BY U.S. DISTRICT JUDGE JOHN D. BATES

[The Court reviewed the procedural background of the case, including the committee's investigation, the witnesses' refusal to comply with subpoenas, and subsequent unsuccessful efforts to reach a compromise.]

The undisputed factual record . . . establishes the following. Notwithstanding a prolonged period of negotiation, the parties reached a self-declared impasse with respect to the document production and testimony at issue here. Faced with that reality, the

[17] Footnotes and citations to the record found in the original decision have been omitted from this excerpted version.

full House of Representatives voted to hold Ms. Miers and Mr. Bolten in contempt of Congress and certified the Contempt Report to the U.S. Attorney for the District of Columbia to pursue criminal enforcement of the contempt citations. The Attorney General then directed the U.S. Attorney not to proceed against Ms. Miers and Mr. Bolten. The Committee, then, filed this suit seeking civil enforcement of its subpoena authority by way of declaratory and injunctive relief.

[The Court considered and rejected the Executive Branch's assertion that the House committee lacked standing. The Court reasoned that the House has standing as an institution to enforce subpoenas necessary to carry out its oversight functions, and the committee was expressly authorized by a House resolution to represent the institution. The Court distinguished this situation from previous cases in which individual plaintiffs lacked standing because they did not represent the interests of the institution or because the alleged injury to the institution was not sufficiently particularized.]

[T]he Committee has issued subpoenas to two high-ranking executive branch officials who have refused to comply, citing executive privilege. The Committee's attempt to pursue criminal prosecution of its contempt of Congress citation was thwarted by the Executive. Exercise of Congress's inherent contempt power through arrest and confinement of a senior executive official would provoke an unseemly constitutional confrontation that should be avoided. Cf. United States v. Nixon, 418 U.S. at 691-92 (concluding that forcing the President to disobey a court order to obtain appellate review would create an unseemly, unnecessary constitutional confrontation between the branches). Thus, the Committee filed this suit to vindicate both its right to the information that is the subject of the subpoena and its institutional prerogative to compel compliance with its subpoenas. A harm to either interest satisfies the injury-in-fact standing requirement. Clear judicial precedent, along with persuasive reasoning in [Department of Justice Office of Legal Counsel ("OLC")] opinions, establishes that the Committee has standing to pursue this action and, moreover, that this type of dispute is justiciable in federal court. Consequently, the Executive's motion to dismiss for lack of standing will be denied.

* * *

[T]here can be no question that Congress has a right -- derived from its Article I legislative function -- to issue and enforce subpoenas, and a corresponding right to the information that is the subject of such subpoenas. Several Supreme Court decisions have confirmed that fact. See, e.g., Eastland, 421 U.S. at 504-05 ("The power to investigate and to do so through compulsory process plainly falls within [the] definition [of Congress's legislative function]."); Barenblatt, 360 U.S. at 111 ("The scope of the power of inquiry, in short, is as penetrating and far-reaching as the potential power to enact and appropriate under the Constitution."); Watkins v. United States, 354 U.S. 178, 187-88 (1957) ("It is unquestionably the duty of all citizens to cooperate with the Congress in its efforts to obtain the facts needed for intelligent legislative action. It is their unremitting obligation to respond to subpoenas, to respect the dignity of the Congress and its committees, and to testify fully with respect to matters within the province of proper investigations."); McGrain, 273 U.S. at 175 ("[T]he constitutional provisions which commit the legislative function to the two houses are intended to include this attribute to the end that the function may be effectively exercised."). The Court can identify no reason why that right cannot be vindicated by recourse to the federal courts through the [Declaratory Judgment Act].

* * *

[T]he Executive takes the Committee to task for failing to utilize its inherent contempt authority. But there are serious problems presented by the prospect of inherent contempt, not the least of which is that the Executive is attempting to have it both ways on this point. To begin with, prosecution pursuant to inherent contempt is a method of "inflicting punishment on an individual who failed" to comply with a subpoena. See Olson OLC Opinion at 137. As OLC has recognized, a civil action, by contrast, is directed towards "obtaining any unprivileged documents necessary to assist [Congress's] lawmaking function." Id. Put another way, the two remedies serve different purposes, although it is true that threatening prosecution under inherent contempt may lead to the production of documents. But unlike a civil action for subpoena enforcement, that is not the primary goal of inherent contempt. Second, imprisoning current (and even former) senior presidential advisors and prosecuting them before the House would only exacerbate the acrimony between the two branches and would present a grave risk of precipitating a constitutional crisis. Indeed, one can easily imagine a stand-off between the Sergeant-at-Arms and executive branch law enforcement officials concerning taking Mr. Bolten into custody and detaining him. See Cooper OLC Opinion at 86 ("[I]t seems most unlikely that Congress could dispatch the Sergeant at-Arms to arrest and imprison an Executive Branch official who claimed executive privilege."). Such unseemly, provocative clashes should be avoided, and there is no need to run the risk of such mischief when a civil action can resolve the same issues in an orderly fashion. Third, even if the Committee did exercise inherent contempt, the disputed issue would in all likelihood end up before this Court, just by a different vehicle -- a writ of habeas corpus brought by Ms. Miers and Mr. Bolten. In either event there would be judicial resolution of the underlying issue.

* * *

The Executive maintains that absolute immunity shields Ms. Miers from compelled testimony before Congress. Although the exact reach of this proposed doctrine is not clear, the Executive insists that it applies only to "a very small cadre of senior advisors." The argument starts with the assertion that the President himself is absolutely immune from compelled congressional testimony. There is no case that stands for that exact proposition, but the Executive maintains that the conclusion flows logically from Nixon v. Fitzgerald, 457 U.S. 731 (1982), where the Supreme Court held that the President "is entitled to absolute immunity from damages liability predicated on his official acts." Id. at 749. "Any such [congressional] power of compulsion over the President," the Executive asserts, "would obviously threaten his independence and autonomy from Congress in violation of separation of powers principles." The Executive then contends that "[those] same principles apply just as clearly to the President's closest advisers." Because senior White House advisers "have no operational authority over government agencies . . . [t]heir sole function is to advise and assist the President in the exercise of his duties." Therefore, they must be regarded as the President's "alter ego." In a similar context, the Supreme Court has extended Speech or Debate Clause immunity to legislative aides who work closely with Members of Congress. See Gravel v. United States, 408 U.S. 606, 616-17 (1972). Accordingly, forcing close presidential advisors to testify before Congress would be tantamount to compelling the President himself to do so, a plainly untenable result in the Executive's view. Indeed, as the Executive would have it, "[w]ere the President's closest advisers subject to compelled testimony there would be no end to the demands that effectively could be placed upon the President himself." Unfortunately for the Executive, this line of argument has been virtually foreclosed by the Supreme Court. In Harlow v. Fitzgerald, 457 U.S. 800 (1982), the plaintiff sued "senior White House aides" for civil damages arising out of the defendants' official actions. Id. at 802. The defendants argued that they were "entitled to a blanket protection of absolute immunity as an incident of their offices as Presidential aides." Id. at 808. The Supreme Court rejected that position. Notwithstanding the absolute immunity extended to legislators, judges, prosecutors, and the President himself, the Court emphasized that "[f]or executive officials in general, however, our cases make plain that qualified immunity represents the norm." Id. at 807. Although there can be no doubt regarding "the importance to the President of loyal and efficient subordinates in executing his duties of office, . . . these factors, alone, [are] insufficient to justify absolute immunity." Id. at 808-09 (discussing Butz v. Economou, 438 U.S. 478 (1978)).

* * *

There are powerful reasons supporting the rejection of absolute immunity as asserted by the Executive here. If the Court held otherwise, the presumptive presidential privilege could be transformed into an absolute privilege and Congress's legitimate interest in inquiry could be easily thwarted. Indeed, even in the Speech or Debate context -- which has an explicit textual basis and confers absolute immunity -- Members of Congress must still establish that their actions were legislative in nature before invoking the protection of the Clause. See, e.g., Rayburn, 497 F.3d at 660; Jewish War Veterans of the U.S. of Am. v. Gates, 506 F. Supp. 2d 30, 54 (D.D.C. 2007). Members cannot simply assert, without more, that the Speech or Debate Clause shields their activities and thereby preclude all further inquiry. Yet that is precisely the treatment that the Executive requests here. Similarly, if the Executive's absolute immunity argument were to prevail, Congress could be left with no recourse to obtain information that is plainly not subject to any colorable claim of executive privilege. For instance, surely at least some of the questions that the Committee intends to ask Ms. Miers would not elicit a response subject to an assertion of privilege; so, too, for responsive documents, many of which may even have been produced already. The Executive's proposed absolute immunity would thus deprive Congress of even non-privileged information. That is an unacceptable result.

DISCUSSION AND QUESTIONS

1. In situations like those relating to the Gorsuch subpoenas of the early 1980s and the investigation into the U.S. Attorney firings more than 20 years later, the concerns raised by the Executive Branch typically fall into three categories: (1) leaks of sensitive information; (2) chilling candid deliberations and advice within the Executive Branch; and (3) congressional interference into Executive Branch activity.

Most often, a way is found for congressional investigators to obtain the substantive information they want without retaining a permanent record in their possession. For example, they are permitted to interview witnesses but not to take sworn testimony on the record, or they are permitted to review but not copy documents. Given these sorts of compromises, it seems that the most compelling concern is that of leaks. The compromises reached are focused on avoiding leaks to the public of sensitive information, because Congress is not given possession of the sources of the information.

2. Given that the overriding concern of the executive is the avoidance of leaks, could a settlement with congressional investigators take the form of a legally enforceable contract pursuant to which Congress is subject to injunctive relief or some sort of penalty if it leaks information provided by the Executive Branch that it has promised to keep confidential?

3. If there had been no compromise after Judge Bates rendered his decision in *Miers*, the former White House Counsel would have been obliged to appear before the Judiciary Committee and respond to its questions. She then could have asserted executive privilege on a question-by-question basis. At that point, what would be the task for a reviewing court: would it merely need to determine whether the question seeks privileged information because, if so, the question need not be answered? Or, would the analysis require the additional step of weighing the protection of the privilege against the Congress' need for the information? Would the court engage in an analysis like that in *United States v. Nixon* (see Chapter Four, pages 103-09)? Should a different analysis take place when privileged information is sought for a congressional inquiry as compared to a criminal proceeding?

CHAPTER SIX: CONSTRAINTS ON LEGISLATIVE ACTION

BICAMERALISM AND PRESENTMENT

As was noted in Chapter Two, a fundamental check on legislative action is found in the bicameralism and presentment requirements of Article I, Section 7. Before proposed legislation can become enforceable law, it must pass both the House of Representatives and the Senate, and must be presented to the President for his approval. (In infrequent cases, the President's disapproval -- his veto -- can be overcome by two-thirds majorities in each chamber.) All affirmative exertions of Legislative Branch power -- that is, anything that looks remotely like lawmaking -- must undergo this process of bicameralism and presentment. This basic principle was affirmed in the case of *Immigration and Naturalization Service v. Chadha.*

Immigration and Naturalization Service v. Chadha

462 U.S. 919 (1983)[18]

CHIEF JUSTICE BURGER delivered the opinion of the Court.

We granted certiorari in Nos. 80-2170 and 80-2171, and postponed consideration of the question of jurisdiction in No. 80-1832. Each presents a challenge to the constitutionality of the provision in 244(c)(2) of the Immigration and Nationality Act, 66 Stat. 216, as amended, 8 U.S.C. 1254(c) (2), authorizing one House of Congress, by resolution, to invalidate the decision of the Executive Branch, pursuant to authority delegated by Congress to the Attorney General of the United States, to allow a particular deportable alien to remain in the United States.

[Chadha is a British citizen born in Kenya who overstayed his visa in the United States and faced deportation. Pursuant to his statutory authority, the Attorney General suspended the deportation proceedings and, as required by the Immigration and Nationality Act (the "Act"), reported his decision to Congress. The Act authorized either chamber to override such a decision by the Attorney General if "either the Senate or the House of Representatives passes a resolution stating in substance that it does not favor the suspension of such deportation." On the recommendation of a single sub-committee

[18] Footnotes and some citations found in the original decision have been omitted from this excerpted version.

chairman and with virtually no debate, the House passed a resolution reversing the decision of the Attorney General. The House's resolution was not treated as a legislative act and, thus, was not submitted to either the Senate or the President for further consideration. The resolution had the effect of exposing Chadha once again to deportation. He challenged the Act's one-house veto provision as unconstitutional.]

[The court next addressed various challenges to its jurisdiction, such as arguments that the case presented no real case or controversy and that it presented a non-justiciable political question, and determined that it did have jurisdiction to resolve the case on the merits.]

We turn now to the question whether action of one House of Congress under 244(c)(2) violates strictures of the Constitution. We begin, of course, with the presumption that the challenged statute is valid. Its wisdom is not the concern of the courts; if a challenged action does not violate the Constitution, it must be sustained:

"Once the meaning of an enactment is discerned and its constitutionality determined, the judicial process comes to an end. We do not sit as a committee of review, nor are we vested with the power of veto." TVA v. Hill, 437 U.S. 153, 194 -195 (1978).

By the same token, the fact that a given law or procedure is efficient, convenient, and useful in facilitating functions of government, standing alone, will not save it if it is contrary to the Constitution. Convenience and efficiency are not the primary objectives - or the hallmarks - of democratic government and our inquiry is sharpened rather than blunted by the fact that congressional veto provisions are appearing with increasing frequency in statutes which delegate authority to executive and independent agencies:

> Since 1932, when the first veto provision was enacted into law, 295 congressional veto-type procedures have been inserted in 196 different statutes as follows: from 1932 to 1939, five statutes were affected; from 1940-49, nineteen statutes; between 1950-59, thirty-four statutes; and from 1960-69, forty-nine. From the year 1970 through 1975, at least one hundred sixty-three such provisions were included in eighty-nine laws.

Abourezk, The Congressional Veto: A Contemporary Response to Executive Encroachment on Legislative Prerogatives, 52 Ind. L. Rev. 323, 324 (1977).

*   *   *

Explicit and unambiguous provisions of the Constitution prescribe and define the respective functions of the Congress and of the Executive in the legislative process. Since the precise terms of those familiar provisions are critical to the resolution of these cases, we set them out verbatim. Article I provides:

> All legislative Powers herein granted shall be vested in a Congress of the United States, which shall consist of a Senate and House of Representatives.

Art. I, 1.

> Every Bill which shall have passed the House of Representatives and the Senate, shall, before it becomes a law, be presented to the President of the United States . . . .

Art. I, 7, cl. 2.

> Every Order, Resolution, or Vote to which the Concurrence of the Senate and House of Representatives may be necessary (except on a question of Adjournment) shall be presented to the President of the United States; and before the Same shall take Effect, shall be approved by him, or being disapproved by him, shall be repassed by two thirds of the Senate and House of Representatives, according to the Rules and Limitations prescribed in the Case of a Bill.

Art. I, 7, cl. 3.

These provisions of Art. I are integral parts of the constitutional design for the separation of powers. We have recently noted that "[t]he principle of separation of powers was not simply an abstract generalization in the minds of the Framers: it was woven into the document that they drafted in Philadelphia in the summer of 1787." Buckley v. Valeo, 424 U.S., at 124. Just as we relied on the textual provision of Art. II, 2, cl. 2, to vindicate the principle of separation of powers in Buckley, we see that the purposes underlying the Presentment Clauses, Art. I, 7, cls. 2, 3, and the bicameral requirement of Art. I, 1, and 7, cl. 2, guide our resolution of the important question presented in these cases. The very structure of the Articles delegating and separating powers under Arts. I, II, and III exemplifies the concept of separation of powers, and we now turn to Art. I.

[The court then reviewed the legislative history and judicial precedent emphasizing the importance role played by bicameralism and presentment in constitutional separation of powers.]

We see therefore that the Framers were acutely conscious that the bicameral requirement and the Presentment Clauses would serve essential constitutional functions. The President's participation in the legislative process was to protect the Executive Branch from Congress and to protect the whole people from improvident laws. The division of the Congress into two distinctive bodies assures that the legislative power would be exercised only after opportunity for full study and debate in separate settings. The President's unilateral veto power, in turn, was limited by the power of two-thirds of both Houses of Congress to overrule a veto thereby precluding final arbitrary action of one person . . . It emerges clearly that the prescription for legislative action in Art. I, 1, 7, represents the Framers' decision that the legislative power of the Federal Government be exercised in accord with a single, finely wrought and exhaustively considered, procedure.

* * *

Examination of the action taken here by one House pursuant to 244(c)(2) reveals that it was essentially legislative in purpose and effect. In purporting to exercise power defined in Art. I, 8, cl. 4, to "establish an uniform Rule of Naturalization," the House took action that had the purpose and effect of altering the legal rights, duties, and relations of persons, including the Attorney General, Executive Branch officials and Chadha, all outside the Legislative Branch. Section 244(c)(2) purports to authorize one House of Congress to require the Attorney General to deport an individual alien whose deportation otherwise would be canceled under 244. The one-House veto operated in these cases to overrule the Attorney General and mandate Chadha's deportation; absent the House action, Chadha would remain in the United States. Congress has acted and its action has altered Chadha's status.

* * *

[W]e see that when the Framers intended to authorize either House of Congress to act alone and outside of its prescribed bicameral legislative role, they narrowly and precisely defined the procedure for such action. There are four provisions in the Constitution, explicit and unambiguous, by which one House may act alone with the unreviewable force of law, not subject to the President's veto:

(a) The House of Representatives alone was given the power to initiate impeachments. Art. I, 2, cl. 5;

(b) The Senate alone was given the power to conduct trials following impeachment on charges initiated by the House and to convict following trial. Art. I, 3, cl. 6;

(c) The Senate alone was given final unreviewable power to approve or to disapprove Presidential appointments. Art. II, 2, cl. 2;

(d) The Senate alone was given unreviewable power to ratify treaties negotiated by the President. Art. II, 2, cl. 2.

Clearly, when the Draftsmen sought to confer special powers on one House, independent of the other House, or of the President, they did so in explicit, unambiguous terms. These carefully defined exceptions from presentment and bicameralism underscore the difference between the legislative functions of Congress and other unilateral but important and binding one-House acts provided for in the Constitution. These exceptions are narrow, explicit, and separately justified; none of them authorize the action challenged here. On the contrary, they provide further support for the conclusion that congressional authority is not to be implied and for the conclusion that the veto provided for in 244(c)(2) is not authorized by the constitutional design of the powers of the Legislative Branch.

Since it is clear that the action by the House under 244(c)(2) was not within any of the express constitutional exceptions authorizing one House to act alone, and equally clear that it was an exercise of legislative power, that action was subject to the standards prescribed in Art. I. The bicameral requirement, the Presentment Clauses, the President's veto, and Congress' power to override a veto were intended to erect enduring checks on each Branch and to protect the people from the improvident exercise of power by mandating certain prescribed steps. To preserve those checks, and maintain the separation of powers, the carefully defined limits on the power of each Branch must not be eroded. To accomplish what has been attempted by one House of Congress in this case requires action in conformity with the express procedures of the Constitution's prescription for legislative action: passage by a majority of both Houses and presentment to the President.

* * *

The choices we discern as having been made in the Constitutional Convention impose burdens on governmental processes that often seem clumsy, inefficient, even unworkable, but those hard choices were consciously made by men who had lived under a form of government that permitted arbitrary governmental acts to go unchecked. There is no support in the Constitution or decisions of this Court for the proposition that the cumbersomeness and delays often encountered in complying with explicit constitutional standards may be avoided, either by the Congress or by the President. See Youngstown Sheet & Tube Co. v. Sawyer, 343 U.S. 579 (1952). With all the obvious flaws of delay, untidiness, and potential for abuse, we have not yet found a better way to preserve freedom than by making the exercise of power subject to the carefully crafted restraints spelled out in the Constitution.

* * *

JUSTICE POWELL, concurring in the judgment.

The Court's decision, based on the Presentment Clauses, Art. I, 7, cls. 2 and 3, apparently will invalidate every use of the legislative veto. The breadth of this holding gives one pause. Congress has included the veto in literally hundreds of statutes, dating back to the 1930's. Congress clearly views this procedure as essential to controlling the delegation of power to administrative agencies. One reasonably may disagree with Congress' assessment of the veto's utility, but the respect due its judgment as a coordinate branch of Government cautions that our holding should be no more extensive than necessary to decide these cases. In my view, the cases may be decided on a narrower ground. When Congress finds that a particular person does not satisfy the statutory criteria for permanent residence in this country it has assumed a judicial function in violation of the principle of separation of powers. Accordingly, I concur only in the judgment.

* * *

On its face, the House's action appears clearly adjudicatory. The House did not enact a general rule; rather it made its own determination that six specific persons did not comply with certain statutory criteria. It thus undertook the type of decision that traditionally has been left to other branches. Even if the House did not make a de novo determination, but simply reviewed the Immigration and Naturalization Service's findings, it still assumed a function ordinarily entrusted to the federal courts.

* * *

The impropriety of the House's assumption of this function is confirmed by the fact that its action raises the very danger the Framers sought to avoid - the exercise of unchecked power. In deciding whether Chadha deserves to be deported, Congress is not subject to any internal constraints that prevent it from arbitrarily depriving him of the right to remain in this country. Unlike the judiciary or an administrative agency, Congress is not bound by established substantive rules. Nor is it subject to the procedural safeguards, such as the right to counsel and a hearing before an impartial tribunal, that are present when a court or an agency adjudicates individual rights. The only effective constraint on Congress' power is political, but Congress is most accountable politically when it prescribes rules of general applicability. When it decides rights of specific persons, those rights are subject to "the tyranny of a shifting majority."

* * *

JUSTICE WHITE, dissenting.

Today the Court not only invalidates 244(c)(2) of the Immigration and Nationality Act, but also sounds the death knell for nearly 200 other statutory provisions in which Congress has reserved a "legislative veto." For this reason, the Court's decision is of surpassing importance. And it is for this reason that the Court would have been well advised to decide the cases, if possible, on the narrower grounds of separation of powers, leaving for full consideration the constitutionality of other congressional review statutes operating on such varied matters as war powers and agency rulemaking, some of which concern the independent regulatory agencies.

The prominence of the legislative veto mechanism in our contemporary political system and its importance to Congress can hardly be overstated. It has become a central means by which Congress secures the accountability of executive and independent agencies. Without the legislative veto, Congress is faced with a

Hobson's choice: either to refrain from delegating the necessary authority, leaving itself with a hopeless task of writing laws with the requisite specificity to cover endless special circumstances across the entire policy landscape, or in the alternative, to abdicate its law-making function to the Executive Branch and independent agencies. To choose the former leaves major national problems unresolved; to opt for the latter risks unaccountable policymaking by those not elected to fill that role.

* * *

[Justice White reviews the enormous expansion of government since the Depression and the use of the legislative veto as a congressional check on the sprawling bureaucracy.]

If the legislative veto were as plainly unconstitutional as the Court strives to suggest, its broad ruling today would be more comprehensible. But, the constitutionality of the legislative veto is anything but clear-cut. The issue divides scholars, courts, Attorneys General, and the two other branches of the National Government. If the veto devices so flagrantly disregarded the requirements of Art. I as the Court today suggests, I find it incomprehensible that Congress, whose Members are bound by oath to uphold the Constitution, would have placed these mechanisms in nearly 200 separate laws over a period of 50 years.

The reality of the situation is that the constitutional question posed today is one of immense difficulty over which the Executive and Legislative Branches - as well as scholars and judges - have understandably disagreed. That disagreement stems from the silence of the Constitution on the precise question: The Constitution does not directly authorize or prohibit the legislative veto. Thus, our task should be to determine whether the legislative veto is consistent with the purposes of Art. I and the principles of separation of powers which are reflected in that Article and throughout the Constitution. We should not find the lack of a specific constitutional authorization for the legislative veto surprising, and I would not infer disapproval of the mechanism from its absence.

From the summer of 1787 to the present the Government of the United States has become an endeavor far beyond the contemplation of the Framers. Only within the last half century has the complexity and size of the Federal Government's responsibilities grown so greatly that the Congress must rely on the legislative veto as the most effective if not the only means to insure its role as the Nation's lawmaker. But the wisdom of the Framers was to anticipate that the Nation would grow and new problems of governance would require different solutions. Accordingly, our Federal Government was intentionally chartered with the flexibility to respond to contemporary needs without losing sight of fundamental democratic principles.

* * *

The Court's holding today that all legislative-type action must be enacted through the lawmaking process ignores that legislative authority is routinely delegated to the Executive Branch, to the independent regulatory agencies, and to private individuals and groups.

* * *

[B]y virtue of congressional delegation, legislative power can be exercised by independent agencies and Executive departments without the passage of new legislation. For some time, the sheer amount of law - the substantive rules that regulate private conduct and direct the operation of government - made by the agencies has far outnumbered the lawmaking engaged in by Congress through the traditional process. There is no question but that agency rulemaking is lawmaking in any functional or realistic sense of the term.

* * *

If Congress may delegate lawmaking power to independent and Executive agencies, it is most difficult to understand Art. I as prohibiting Congress from also reserving a check on legislative power for itself. Absent the veto, the agencies receiving delegations of legislative or quasi-legislative power may issue regulations having the force of law without bicameral approval and without the President's signature. It is thus not apparent why the reservation of a veto over the exercise of that legislative power must be subject to a more exacting test. In both cases, it is enough that the initial statutory authorizations comply with the Art. I requirements.

DISCUSSION AND QUESTIONS

1. Chief Justice Burger and Justice Powell agree that the one-house legislative veto is unconstitutional, but for different reasons. Burger views the

House's action against Chadha as "essentially legislative in purpose and effect." Powell characterizes the House's action as "clearly adjudicatory" -- the House "assumed a function ordinarily entrusted to the federal courts." Which is the better view? If a governmental body is determining the status or rights of a specific person in specific circumstances, does it look more like a legislative or an adjudicative undertaking?

2. Doesn't Justice White make a valid point when he notes that a great deal of lawmaking takes place in the modern United States without bicameralism and presentment? How can Chief Justice Burger's reasoning -- that every exercise of legislative power must include bicameralism and presentment -- be squared with the enormous amount of lawmaking that occurs every year across the alphabet-soup of federal regulatory agencies such as the FTC, SEC, EEOC, FDA, EPA, OSHA and many others? (Hint: See the *Mistretta* and *American Trucking Association* cases discussed in Chapter Six.) Congress can authorize independent and Executive Branch agencies essentially to make law by issuing regulations that do not require bicameralism and presentment; why, then, cannot Congress authorize one of its own chambers also to make law without bicameralism and presentment? Put another way, if, as *Chadha* teaches, the latter proposition is prohibited by the Constitution, what is it in the Constitution that permits the former proposition?

3. Chief Justice Burger and Justice White both note that the legislative veto has been used in hundreds of statutes over the course of several decades prior to the *Chadha* decision, with little to no challenge from the Executive Branch or other institutions. Nonetheless, the court is willing to invalidate this relatively well-accepted tool of legislative oversight. In *Youngstown*, Justice Frankfurter expressed in his concurring opinion the view that "a systematic, unbroken, executive practice, long pursued to the knowledge of the Congress and never before questioned" can create a "gloss" on executive power. 343 U.S. at 610-11. In *Dames & Moore*, Justice Rehnquist relied on the same notion in finding that the President was authorized to suspend claims against a foreign nation even though such executive action was not expressly authorized by the Constitution or any statute. If a long-accepted practice can create a "gloss" on executive power and a presumption of validity for executive action, should not the same presumption apply to legislative action? Is there more reason to look to custom and practice when evaluating the limits of executive power than when evaluating the limits on legislative power?

4. Justice White wants to retain the legislative veto at least as much for practical reasons as for legal reasons. He believes it is a necessary tool of legislative oversight: "It has become a central means by which Congress secures the accountability of executive and independent agencies . . . the complexity and size of

the Federal Government's responsibilities [has] grown so greatly that the Congress must rely on the legislative veto as the most effective if not the only means to insure its role as the Nation's lawmaker." Is Justice White correct? Aren't there other effective tools available to a Congress that wishes to assert itself? Are any of the following viable alternatives to the total loss of congressional control that Justice White seems to fear will be the result of taking away the legislative veto?

- Executive Branch agencies, independent agencies, and the "complexity and size of the federal government" are all creatures of the Legislative Branch's creation. If the scope of government and size of the bureaucracy have grown too large for Congress to handle, could not Congress take action to reduce them?

- If Congress wishes to secure the accountability of executive and independent agencies, can it not pass more specific laws describing precisely what such agencies may and may not do, and thereby circumscribe their discretion?

- Congressional action trumps agency action. If an agency were to issue a regulation or make a decision that offends Congress, could not Congress overturn that agency action through a legislative enactment?

- Congress has the power of the purse; agencies have only the resources that Congress appropriates for them. If an agency were to take action with which Congress disagrees, could not Congress respond by reducing the agency's funding? And don't agencies know this?

- Most agency heads and many other senior officials are subject to Senate confirmation. Can the Senate use its important role in the appointment process to guard against the appointment of officials who are likely to defy the will of Congress?

CONGRESS LACKS EXECUTIVE POWER

As noted in Chapter Two, one of the most basic checks on the Legislative Branch is that it may not itself exercise executive authority. For example, the Legislative Branch may not appoint "officers of the United States" under Article II,

Section 2, because that power is reserved for the President. *Buckley v. Valeo*, 424 U.S. 1 (1973). Further, cases like *Humphrey's Executor* and *Morrison v. Olson* (see Chapter Three) reveal that Congress may place certain restrictions on the President's power to remove the appointed officials who assist him; however, as the next case illustrates, Congress may not retain for itself the power to remove officials who perform executive functions (except through impeachment, as is expressly set forth in the Constitution). To do so would intrude impermissibly into the supervision of executive actors and, therefore, executive action.

Widespread concern over federal budget deficits in the 1980s led to passage of the Gramm-Rudman-Hollings Balanced Budget and Emergency Deficit Control Act of 1985. Among other things, the Act provided for automatic spending reductions if certain budget-cutting targets were not met. The mechanism for implementing these reductions involved the Comptroller General, who was also the head of the General Accounting Office, directing the President to "sequester" (that is, to refrain from spending) certain appropriated funds. As head of the General Accounting Office, the Comptroller General is appointed by the President with the advice and consent of the Senate, but he is removable only by a joint resolution of Congress (or impeachment).

Bowsher v. Synar

478 U.S. 714 (1986)[19]

CHIEF JUSTICE BURGER delivered the opinion of the Court.

The question presented by these appeals is whether the assignment by Congress to the Comptroller General of the United States of certain functions under the Balanced Budget and Emergency Deficit Control Act of 1985 violates the doctrine of separation of powers.

[Under the Act, the Comptroller General receives independent reports from the Office of Management and Budget and Congressional Budget Office estimating the size of the budget deficit for the coming year. the Comptroller General then reports to the President his own conclusions about the size of the deficit, and also specifies spending reductions that are necessary to meet budget targets. The President must then issue a "sequestration" order that implements the specified reductions. There is a "fallback" provision that bypasses the

[19] Footnotes and some citations found in the original decision have been omitted from this excerpted version.

Comptroller General and provides for legislative enactment of spending cuts on an expedited basis.

The Act is now challenged by several members of Congress and the National Treasury Employees Union, which represents federal employees affected by spending cuts.]

We noted recently that "[t]he Constitution sought to divide the delegated powers of the new Federal Government into three defined categories, Legislative, Executive, and Judicial." INS v. Chadha, 462 U.S. 919, 951 (1983). The declared purpose of separating and dividing the powers of government, of course, was to "diffus[e] power the better to secure liberty." Youngstown Sheet & Tube Co. v. Sawyer, 343 U.S. 579, 635 (1952) (Jackson, J., concurring). Justice Jackson's words echo the famous warning of Montesquieu, quoted by James Madison in The Federalist No. 47, that "`there can be no liberty where the legislative and executive powers are united in the same person, or body of magistrates' . . . ." The Federalist No. 47, p. 325 (J. Cooke ed. 1961).

Even a cursory examination of the Constitution reveals the influence of Montesquieu's thesis that checks and balances were the foundation of a structure of government that would protect liberty. The Framers provided a vigorous Legislative Branch and a separate and wholly independent Executive Branch, with each branch responsible ultimately to the people. The Framers also provided for a Judicial Branch equally independent with "[t]he judicial Power . . . extend[ing] to all Cases, in Law and Equity, arising under this Constitution, and the Laws of the United States." Art. III, 2.

Other, more subtle, examples of separated powers are evident as well. Unlike parliamentary systems such as that of Great Britain, no person who is an officer of the United States may serve as a Member of the Congress. Art. I, 6. Moreover, unlike parliamentary systems, the President, under Article II, is responsible not to the Congress but to the people, subject only to impeachment proceedings which are exercised by the two Houses as representatives of the people. Art. II, 4. And even in the impeachment of a President the presiding officer of the ultimate tribunal is not a member of the Legislative Branch, but the Chief Justice of the United States. Art. I, 3.

That this system of division and separation of powers produces conflicts, confusion, and discordance at times is inherent, but it was deliberately so structured to assure full, vigorous, and open debate on the great issues affecting the people and to provide avenues for the operation of checks on the exercise of governmental power.

The Constitution does not contemplate an active role for Congress in the supervision of officers charged with the execution of the laws it enacts. The President appoints "Officers of the United States" with the "Advice and Consent of the Senate . . . ." Art. II. 2. Once the appointment has been made and confirmed, however, the Constitution explicitly provides for removal of Officers of the United States by Congress only upon impeachment by the House of Representatives and conviction by the Senate. An impeachment by the House and trial by the Senate can rest only on "Treason, Bribery or other high Crimes and Misdemeanors." Art. II, 4. A direct congressional role in the removal of officers charged with the execution of the laws beyond this limited one is inconsistent with separation of powers.

* * *

To permit an officer controlled by Congress to execute the laws would be, in essence, to permit a congressional veto. Congress could simply remove, or threaten to remove, an officer for executing the laws in any fashion found to be unsatisfactory to Congress. This kind of congressional control over the execution of the laws, Chadha makes clear, is constitutionally impermissible.

* * *

Appellants urge that the Comptroller General performs his duties independently and is not subservient to Congress. We agree with the District Court that this contention does not bear close scrutiny.
The critical factor lies in the provisions of the statute defining the Comptroller General's office relating to removability. Although the Comptroller General is nominated by the President from a list of three individuals recommended by the Speaker of the House of Representatives and the President pro tempore of the Senate, see 31 U.S.C. 703(a)(2), and confirmed by the Senate, he is removable only at the initiative of Congress. He may be removed not only by impeachment but also by joint resolution of Congress "at any time" resting on any one of the following bases:

> (i) permanent disability;
> (ii) inefficiency;
> (iii) neglect of duty;
> (iv) malfeasance; or
> (v) a felony or conduct involving moral turpitude.

31 U.S.C. 703(e)(1)B.

This provision was included, as one Congressman explained in urging passage of the Act, because Congress "felt that [the Comptroller General] should be brought under the sole control of Congress, so that Congress at any moment when it found he was inefficient and was not carrying on the duties of his office as he should and as the Congress expected, could remove him without the long, tedious process of a trial by impeachment." 61 Cong. Rec. 1081 (1921).

* * *

[T]he dissent is simply in error to suggest that the political realities reveal that the Comptroller General is free from influence by Congress. The Comptroller General heads the General Accounting Office (GAO), "an instrumentality of the United States Government independent of the executive departments," 31 U.S.C. 702(a), which was created by Congress in 1921 as part of the Budget and Accounting Act of 1921, 42 Stat. 23. Congress created the office because it believed that it "needed an officer, responsible to it alone, to check upon the application of public funds in accordance with appropriations." H. Mansfield, The Comptroller General: A Study in the Law and Practice of Financial Administration 65 (1939).

It is clear that Congress has consistently viewed the Comptroller General as an officer of the Legislative Branch. The Reorganization Acts of 1945 and 1949, for example, both stated that the Comptroller General and the GAO are "a part of the legislative branch of the Government." 59 Stat. 616; 63 Stat. 205. Similarly, in the Accounting and Auditing Act of 1950, Congress required the Comptroller General to conduct audits "as an agent of the Congress." 64 Stat. 835.

Over the years, the Comptrollers General have also viewed themselves as part of the Legislative Branch. In one of the early Annual Reports of Comptroller General, the official seal of his office was described as reflecting

> the independence of judgment to be exercised by the General Accounting Office, subject to the control of the legislative branch. . . . The combination represents an agency of the Congress independent of other authority auditing and checking the expenditures of the Government as required by law and subjecting any questions arising in that connection to quasi-judicial determination.

GAO Ann. Rep. 5-6 (1924).

Later, Comptroller General Warren, who had been a Member of Congress for 15 years before being appointed Comptroller General, testified: "During most of my public life, . . . I have been a member of the legislative branch. Even now, although heading a great agency, it is an agency of the Congress, and I am an agent of the Congress." To Provide for Reorganizing of Agencies of the Government: Hearings on H. R. 3325 before the House Committee on Expenditures, 79th Cong., 1st Sess., 69 (1945) (emphasis added). And, in one conflict during Comptroller General McCarl's tenure, he asserted his independence of the Executive Branch, stating: "Congress . . . is . . . the only authority to which there lies an appeal from the decision of this office. . . . I may not accept the opinion of any official, inclusive of the Attorney General, as controlling my duty under the law." 2 Comp. Gen. 784, 786-787 (1923) (disregarding conclusion of the Attorney General, 33 Op. Atty. Gen. 476 (1923), with respect to interpretation of compensation statute).

Against this background, we see no escape from the conclusion that, because Congress has retained removal authority over the Comptroller General, he may not be entrusted with executive powers. The remaining question is whether the Comptroller General has been assigned such powers in the Balanced Budget and Emergency Deficit Control Act of 1985.

The primary responsibility of the Comptroller General under the instant Act is the preparation of a "report." This report must contain detailed estimates of projected federal revenues and expenditures. The report must also specify the reductions, if any, necessary to reduce the deficit to the target for the appropriate fiscal year. The reductions must be set forth on a program-by-program basis.

* * *

Appellants suggest that the duties assigned to the Comptroller General in the Act are essentially ministerial and mechanical so that their performance does not constitute "execution of the law" in a meaningful sense. On the contrary, we view these functions as plainly entailing execution of the law in constitutional terms. Interpreting a law enacted by Congress to implement the legislative mandate is the very essence of "execution" of the law. Under 251, the Comptroller General must exercise judgment concerning facts that affect the application of the Act. He must also interpret the provisions of the Act to determine precisely what budgetary calculations are required. Decisions of that kind are typically made by officers charged with executing a statute.

The executive nature of the Comptroller General's functions under the Act is revealed in 252(a)(3) which gives the Comptroller General the ultimate authority to determine the budget cuts to be made. Indeed, the Comptroller General commands the President himself to carry out, without the slightest variation (with exceptions not relevant to the constitutional issues presented), the directive of the Comptroller General as to the budget reductions:

> The [presidential] order must provide for reductions in the manner specified in section 251(a)(3), must incorporate the provisions of the [Comptroller General's] report submitted under section 251(b), and must be consistent with such report in all respects. The President may not modify or recalculate any of the estimates, determinations, specifications, bases, amounts, or percentages set forth in the report submitted under section 251(b) in determining the reductions to be specified in the order with respect to programs, projects, and activities, or with respect to budget activities, within an account . . . .

[Section] 252(a)(3) (emphasis added).

By placing the responsibility for execution of the Balanced Budget and Emergency Deficit Control Act in the hands of an officer who is subject to removal only by itself, Congress in effect has retained control over the execution of the Act and has intruded into the executive function. The Constitution does not permit such intrusion.

JUSTICE STEVENS, with whom JUSTICE MARSHALL joins, concurring in the judgment.

When this Court is asked to invalidate a statutory provision that has been approved by both Houses of the Congress and signed by the President, particularly an Act of Congress that confronts a deeply vexing national problem, it should only do so for the most compelling constitutional reasons. I agree with the Court that the "Gramm-Rudman-Hollings" Act contains a constitutional infirmity so severe that the flawed provision may not stand. I disagree with the Court, however, on the reasons why the Constitution prohibits the Comptroller General from exercising the powers assigned to him by

251(b) and 251(c)(2) of the Act. It is not the dormant, carefully circumscribed congressional removal power that represents the primary constitutional evil. Nor do I agree with the conclusion of both the majority and the dissent that the analysis depends on a labeling of the functions assigned to the Comptroller General as "executive powers." Rather, I am convinced that the Comptroller General must be characterized as an agent of Congress because of his longstanding statutory responsibilities; that the powers assigned to him under the Gramm-Rudman-Hollings Act require him to make policy that will bind the Nation; and that, when Congress, or a component or an agent of Congress, seeks to make policy that will bind the Nation, it must follow the procedures mandated by Article I of the Constitution - through passage by both Houses and presentment to the President. In short, Congress may not exercise its fundamental power to formulate national policy by delegating that power to one of its two Houses, to a legislative committee, or to an individual agent of the Congress such as the Speaker of the House of Representatives, the Sergeant at Arms of the Senate, or the Director of the Congressional Budget Office. INS v. Chadha, (1983). That principle, I believe, is applicable to the Comptroller General.

In assessing the role of the Comptroller General, it is appropriate to consider his already existing statutory responsibilities. Those responsibilities leave little doubt that one of the identifying characteristics of the Comptroller General is his statutorily required relationship to the Legislative Branch.

[A review of the Comptroller General's various statutory roles and responsibilities over several decades establishes that the office exists to serve, is accountable to, and is part of, the Legislative Branch.]

The Court concludes that the Gramm-Rudman-Hollings Act impermissibly assigns the Comptroller General "executive powers." Justice White's dissent agrees that "the powers exercised by the Comptroller under the Act may be characterized as `executive' in that they involve the interpretation and carrying out of the Act's mandate." This conclusion is not only far from obvious but also rests on the unstated and unsound premise that there is a definite line that distinguishes executive power from legislative power.

* * *

One reason that the exercise of legislative, executive, and judicial powers cannot be categorically distributed among three mutually exclusive branches of Government is that governmental power cannot always be readily characterized with only one of those three labels. On the contrary, as our cases demonstrate, a particular function, like a chameleon, will often take on the aspect of the office to which it is assigned.

*   *   *

The Gramm-Rudman-Hollings Act assigns to the Comptroller General the duty to make policy decisions that have the force of law. The Comptroller General's report is, in the current statute, the engine that gives life to the ambitious budget reduction process. It is the Comptroller General's report that "provide[s] for the determination of reductions" and that "contain[s] estimates, determinations, and specifications for all of the items contained in the report" submitted by the Office of Management and Budget and the Congressional Budget Office. 251(b). It is the Comptroller General's report that the President must follow and that will have conclusive effect. 252. It is, in short, the Comptroller General's report that will have a profound, dramatic, and immediate impact on the Government and on the Nation at large.

Article I of the Constitution specifies the procedures that Congress must follow when it makes policy that binds the Nation: its legislation must be approved by both of its Houses and presented to the President.

*   *   *

[T]o decide this case there is no need to consider the Decision of 1789, the President's removal power, or the abstract nature of "executive powers." Once it is clear that the Comptroller General, whose statutory duties define him as an agent of Congress, has been assigned the task of making policy determinations that will bind the Nation, the question is simply one of congressional process. There can be no doubt that the Comptroller General's statutory duties under Gramm-Rudman-Hollings do not follow the constitutionally prescribed procedures for congressional lawmaking.

In short, even though it is well settled that Congress may delegate legislative power to independent agencies or to the Executive, and thereby divest itself of a portion of its lawmaking power, when it elects to exercise such power itself, it may not authorize a lesser representative of the Legislative Branch to act on its behalf. It is for this reason that I believe 251(b) and 251(c)(2) of the Act are unconstitutional.

[JUSTICE WHITE dissents. He agrees that the Comptroller General is assigned executive duties under the Act, but he disagrees that the statutory removal process makes the Comptroller General subservient to Congress. Because removal requires a joint resolution of Congress and agreement by the President, the Comptroller General "is one of the most independent officers in the entire federal establishment. Those who have studied the office agree that the procedural and substantive limits on the power of Congress and the President to remove the Comptroller make dislodging him against his will practically impossible."]

DISCUSSION AND QUESTIONS

1. Chief Justice Burger believes that, in ordering particular spending cuts, the Comptroller is exercising executive power. Justice Stevens seems to believe that the same behavior represents an exercise of legislative power. Whose is the better view? Is it not a classic function of the Legislative Branch to make policy determinations about how many dollars the government should spend and how those dollars should be spent? On the other hand, for much of the nation's history, presidents believed that they possessed the authority to "impound" -- that is, to refrain from spending -- appropriated funds. (For a brief explanation of impoundment, see Chapter Three, pages 73-74.) Interestingly, just three years earlier, in the Chadha case, there was a similar disagreement about the proper characterization of governmental power. There, Chief Justice Burger concluded that the one-house legislative veto determining an individual's immigration status was legislative in nature, while Justice Powell believed that it was adjudicative. Is it possible correctly to categorize any given governmental action as clearly "executive," "legislative," or "adjudicative"? If not, how can the courts (or anyone) be confident in a determination that a particular action by a particular branch is or is not properly within that branch's permissible scope of authority?

2. As Chief Justice Burger explains, the Gramm-Rudman-Hollings Act "gives the Comptroller General the ultimate authority to determine the budget cuts to be made . . . the Comptroller General commands the President himself to carry out . . . the directive of the Comptroller General as to the budget reductions." Put aside for the moment the debate about whether the Comptroller is part of the Legislative Branch. Regardless of the branch in which the position resides, may Congress give *anyone* the authority to tell the President how to carry out his executive duties? Imagine that, instead of placing authority in the Comptroller General, the Gramm-

Rudman-Hollings Act created a new position titled the "Budget Chief," administratively placed the position within the Executive Office of the President, made the official removable by the President for "good cause," and empowered the Budget Chief to "command the President to make budget reductions determined by the Budget Chief, which may not be disregarded or modified in any way by the President." Would such an allocation of authority pass constitutional muster? Would it be consistent with the unequivocal mandate in Article II, Section 1 that "the executive power shall be vested in a President of the United States"?

NON-DELEGATION

In theory, if perhaps not in current practice, there are limits on the extent to which the Legislative Branch can delegate its authority to other governmental actors. The Constitution states, at Article I, Section 1, that "All legislative powers herein granted shall be vested in a Congress of the United States." The plain meaning of this declaration would seem to be that any and all law-making at the federal level must be by Congress; there is no "legislative power" that resides in any other governmental body or actor. Yet, as the dissenting Byron White correctly noted in *Chadha*, most lawmaking occurs not in Congress, but within the countless independent and Executive Branch agencies to which Congress has given various specialized portfolios of responsibility:

> For some time, the sheer amount of law - the substantive rules that regulate private conduct and direct the operation of government - made by the agencies has far outnumbered the lawmaking engaged in by Congress through the traditional process. There is no question but that agency rulemaking is lawmaking in any functional or realistic sense of the term.

Chadha, 426 U.S. at 985-86.

Examples of delegated law-making abound. For instance, rather than regulate in detail the public securities markets, Congress created the Securities and Exchange Commission and authorized the SEC to promulgate the detailed rules that govern these markets. Rather than specify precisely how the American workplace in all its incarnations shall be made safe, Congress created the Occupational Safety and Health Administration and directed it to develop regulations addressing the multitude of health and safety concerns across all workplaces. Rather than explain in minute detail how employers can avoid running afoul of various laws prohibiting discrimination in employment, Congress created the Equal Employment Opportunity Commission, which issues regulations delineating permissible and impermissible employer conduct. Rather than instruct national banks about the legal nuances of their responsibilities toward depositors, sound banking procedures, and accounting practices, Congress directed the Comptroller of the Currency to develop these instructions, in the form of extensive regulations that appear in Title 12 of the Code of Federal Regulations.

The principal criticism of such delegation (aside from the truism that it is not contemplated by the plain text of the Constitution) is that it enables the people's elected legislators to avoid accountability. With the ability to delegate law-making authority, legislators in Congress can pass a law in a particular area of public concern and assert that they have "taken action" on the matter. But then it falls to unelected (and effectively anonymous) bureaucrats to work out the detailed burdens and responsibilities that are likely to alienate those who are affected by the resulting regulations. In other words, through delegation, Congress enjoys the twin benefits of (1) leaving the toughest decisions to others and (2) distancing itself from the consequences of those decisions. The severest critics of delegation characterize it as an abdication of legislative responsibility.

In the United States of the twenty-first century, the notion that there might be limits on how far Congress can go in authorizing other governmental actors to make policy seems almost quaint. As of this writing (late 2010), the last time the Supreme Court declared as invalid any congressional delegation of authority was 75 years ago. Two cases in 1935 represent the zenith of the non-delegation doctrine: *Panama Refining Co. v. Ryan*, 293 U.S. 388 (1935) and *Schechter Poultry Corp. v. United States*, 295 U.S. 495 (1935).

In the mid-1930s, the Administration of President Franklin Delano Roosevelt was engaged in its New Deal battle against the Great Depression. The centerpiece of early New Deal efforts was the National Industrial Recovery Act (NIRA), which President Roosevelt signed in 1933, and which empowered the government to engage in widespread regulation of industry and the marketplace. Among the many actions taken by the President pursuant to NIRA was the issuance of a Code of Fair Competition for the Petroleum Industry, which set production limits for petroleum products and allocated the amounts produced on a state-by-state basis. Transportation of so-called "hot oil" -- that which exceeded regulated limits -- was criminalized. The Supreme Court observed that NIRA "gives to the President an unlimited authority to determine the policy and to lay down the prohibition, or not to lay it down, as he may see fit." *Panama Refining*, 293 U.S. at 415. The Court further explained that the Constitution allows Congress

> the necessary resources of flexibility and practicality, which will enable it to perform its function in laying down policies and

> establishing standards, while leaving to selected instrumentalities the making of subordinate rules within prescribed limits and the determination of facts to which the policy as declared by the Legislature is to apply.

Id. at 421. Nevertheless,

> there are limits of delegation which there is no constitutional authority to transcend. We think that section 9(c) [of NIRA] goes beyond those limits. As to the transportation of oil production in excess of state permission, the Congress has declared no policy, has established no standard, has laid down no rule. There is no requirement, no definition of circumstances and conditions in which the transportation is to be allowed or prohibited.

Id. at 430. Because Congress had offered in NIRA no standard, no policy, no guidance that would cabin the exercise of executive authority, it had effectively left it entirely to the President to determine the policy and set the legal limits for the production of oil. Chief Justice Hughes, writing for an eight-justice majority, held this to be an unconstitutional delegation of legislative power.

Schechter Poultry represented another challenge to regulations issued under NIRA, in this case the "Live Poultry Code," which was approved by the President in 1934 and purported to promote competition in the live poultry industry in and around New York City through the regulation of wages, working hours, and various trade practices. The Code was issued pursuant to Section 3 of NIRA, which was a generalized authorization for the President to promulgate "codes of fair competition" for any trades or industries in which there was a perceived need. Among other things, the Schechter brothers were accused of violating minimum wage and maximum hours provisions of the Code and for selling chickens that were not properly inspected. In assessing whether Section 3 of NIRA was an unconstitutional delegation of law-making authority, the Court stated that, as a general proposition, "Congress cannot delegate legislative power to the President to exercise an unfettered discretion to make whatever laws he thinks may be needed or advisable for the rehabilitation and expansion of trade or industry." 295 U.S. at 537-38. It then went on to invalidate the unqualified discretion given to the President:

> Section 3 of the Recovery Act is without precedent. It supplies no standards for any trade, industry, or activity. It does not undertake to prescribe rules of conduct to be applied to particular states of fact determined by appropriate administrative procedure. Instead of prescribing rules of conduct, it authorizes the making of codes to prescribe them. For that legislative undertaking, Section 3 sets up no

> standards, aside from the statement of the general aims of rehabilitation, correction, and expansion described in Section 1. In view of the scope of that broad declaration and of the nature of the few restrictions that are imposed, the discretion of the President in approving or prescribing codes, and thus enacting laws for the government of trade and industry throughout the country, is virtually unfettered. We think that the code-making authority thus conferred is an unconstitutional delegation of legislative power.

Id. at 541-42.

(The *Schechter Poultry* Court not only invalidated Section 3 of NIRA as an improper delegation of legislative power; it went further and effectively declared the entire act unconstitutional because it exceeded Congress' power to regulate interstate commerce. NIRA was an effort by the federal government to regulate not only true interstate commerce, but also intrastate commerce -- such as the buying and selling of poultry within New York State. The Court narrowly interpreted Congress' interstate commerce power by distinguishing between activities that *directly* affect interstate commerce and those that only *indirectly* affect interstate commerce. The Court concluded that Congress may not engage in "regulation of intrastate transactions which affect interstate commerce only indirectly." Id. at 551. This restrictive reading of Congress' interstate commerce power was soon reversed. In *National Labor Relations Board v. Jones & Laughlin Steel Corp.*, 301 U.S. 1 (1937), the Supreme Court rejected a challenge to another major New Deal enactment, the National Labor Relations Act (also known as the Wagner Act, after its chief legislative proponent, Senator Robert Wagner of New York). There, Chief Justice Hughes, writing for divided court, said:

> Although activities may be intrastate in character when separately considered, if they have such a close and substantial relation to interstate commerce that their control is essential or appropriate to protect that commerce from burdens and obstructions, Congress cannot be denied the power to exercise that control.

Id. at 37. Even broader interpretation of the interstate commerce power came in subsequent cases, such as *Wickard v. Filburn*, 317 U.S. 111 (1942), in which the Court concluded that Congress' power to regulate wheat production extended even to wheat grown by a single farmer for his personal use. The immense judicial expansion of congressional power under the Interstate Commerce Clause since the mid-1930s has facilitated federal government growth and widespread regulation of American life that the Framers could not have imagined.)

Panama Refining and *Schechter Poultry* represent an anomalous moment in the jurisprudence of non-delegation. No subsequent Supreme Court decision has invalidated any act of Congress as an impermissible delegation of legislative authority. Indeed, the teaching of more recent decisions -- illustrated by the *Mistretta* and *Whitman* decisions excerpted below -- is that Congress need only supply some "intelligible principle," broadly defined, to support a delegation of law-making authority to another governmental actor.

Mistretta v. United States

488 U.S. 361 (1989)[20]

JUSTICE BLACKMUN delivered the opinion of the Court.

[We consider here the constitutionality of federal Sentencing Guidelines developed by the United States Sentencing Commission, a body that was created by the Sentencing Reform Act of 1984. In an effort to address perceived arbitrariness, inconsistency and unfairness in federal criminal sentencing, Congress created the seven-member Sentencing Commission as "an independent commission in the judicial branch of the United States." The Commission's role is to set specific, consistent and determinate sentences for the wide variety of federal crimes, which would be binding on the courts. Petitioner Mistretta was sentenced under the Guidelines for cocaine possession and now argues that the Guidelines are unconstitutional as an excessive delegation of congressional law-making authority.]

Petitioner argues that in delegating the power to promulgate sentencing guidelines for every federal criminal offense to an independent Sentencing Commission, Congress has granted the Commission excessive legislative discretion in violation of the constitutionally based nondelegation doctrine. We do not agree.

The nondelegation doctrine is rooted in the principle of separation of powers that underlies our tripartite system of Government. The Constitution provides that "[a]ll legislative Powers herein granted shall be vested in a Congress of the United States," U.S. Const., Art. I, 1, and we long have insisted that "the integrity and maintenance of the system of government ordained by the Constitution" mandate that Congress generally cannot delegate its legislative power to another Branch. Field v. Clark, 143 U.S. 649, 692 (1892). We also have

[20] Footnotes and some citations found in the original decision have been omitted from this excerpted version.

recognized, however, that the separation-of-powers principle, and the nondelegation doctrine in particular, do not prevent Congress from obtaining the assistance of its coordinate Branches. In a passage now enshrined in our jurisprudence, Chief Justice Taft, writing for the Court, explained our approach to such cooperative ventures: "In determining what [Congress] may do in seeking assistance from another branch, the extent and character of that assistance must be fixed according to common sense and the inherent necessities of the government co-ordination." J. W. Hampton, Jr., & Co. v. United States, 276 U.S. 394, 406 (1928). So long as Congress "shall lay down by legislative act an intelligible principle to which the person or body authorized to [exercise the delegated authority] is directed to conform, such legislative action is not a forbidden delegation of legislative power." Id., at 409.

Applying this "intelligible principle" test to congressional delegations, our jurisprudence has been driven by a practical understanding that in our increasingly complex society, replete with ever changing and more technical problems, Congress simply cannot do its job absent an ability to delegate power under broad general directives . . . "The Constitution has never been regarded as denying to the Congress the necessary resources of flexibility and practicality, which will enable it to perform its function." Panama Refining Co. v. Ryan, 293 U.S. 388, 421 (1935). Accordingly, this Court has deemed it "constitutionally sufficient if Congress clearly delineates the general policy, the public agency which is to apply it, and the boundaries of this delegated authority." American Power & Light Co. v. SEC, 329 U.S. 90, 105 (1946).

Until 1935, this Court never struck down a challenged statute on delegation grounds . . . After invalidating in 1935 two statutes as excessive delegations, see A. L. A. Schechter Poultry Corp. v. United States, 295 U.S. 495 , and Panama Refining Co. v. Ryan, supra, we have upheld, again without deviation, Congress' ability to delegate power under broad standards. See, e. g., Lichter v. United States, 334 U.S. 742, 785 -786 (1948) (upholding delegation of authority to determine excessive profits); American Power & Light Co. v. SEC, 329 U.S., at 105 (upholding delegation of authority to Securities and Exchange Commission to prevent unfair or inequitable distribution of voting power among security holders); Yakus v. United States, 321 U.S. 414, 426 (1944) (upholding delegation to Price Administrator to fix commodity prices that would be fair and equitable, and would effectuate purposes of Emergency Price Control Act of 1942); FPC v. Hope Natural Gas Co., 320 U.S. 591, 600 (1944) (upholding delegation to Federal Power Commission to determine just and reasonable rates); National Broadcasting Co. v. United States, 319 U.S. 190, 225 -226 (1943) (upholding delegation to Federal Communications Commission to regulate broadcast licensing "as public interest, convenience, or necessity" require).

In light of our approval of these broad delegations, we harbor no doubt that Congress' delegation of authority to the Sentencing Commission is sufficiently specific and detailed to meet constitutional requirements.

Congress charged the Commission with three goals: to "assure the meeting of the purposes of sentencing as set forth" in the Act; to "provide certainty and fairness in meeting the purposes of sentencing, avoiding unwarranted sentencing disparities among defendants with similar records . . . while maintaining sufficient flexibility to permit individualized sentences," where appropriate; and to "reflect, to the extent practicable, advancement in knowledge of human behavior as it relates to the criminal justice process." 28 U.S.C. 991(b)(1). Congress further specified four "purposes" of sentencing that the Commission must pursue in carrying out its mandate: "to reflect the seriousness of the offense, to promote respect for the law, and to provide just punishment for the offense"; "to afford adequate deterrence to criminal conduct"; "to protect the public from further crimes of the defendant"; and "to provide the defendant with needed . . . correctional treatment." 18 U.S.C. 3553(a)(2).

In addition, Congress prescribed the specific tool - the guidelines system - for the Commission to use in regulating sentencing. More particularly, Congress directed the Commission to develop a system of "sentencing ranges" applicable "for each category of offense involving each category of defendant." 28 U.S.C. 994(b). Congress instructed the Commission that these sentencing ranges must be consistent with pertinent provisions of Title 18 of the United States Code and could not include sentences in excess of the statutory maxima. Congress also required that for sentences of imprisonment, "the maximum of the range established for such a term shall not exceed the minimum of that range by more than the greater of 25 percent or 6 months, except that, if the minimum term of the range is 30 years or more, the maximum may be life imprisonment." 994(b)(2). Moreover, Congress directed the Commission to use current average sentences "as a starting point" for its structuring of the sentencing ranges. 994(m).

[Congress also outlined various factors in categorizing crimes and defendants, and offered other guidance for the Commission in developing appropriate sentences such as taking into account whether the offense was violent, whether it resulted in injury, and other aggravating and mitigating factors.]

We cannot dispute petitioner's contention that the Commission enjoys significant discretion in formulating guidelines. The Commission does have discretionary authority to determine the relative severity of federal crimes and to assess the relative weight of the offender characteristics that Congress listed for the Commission to consider. See 994(c) and (d) (Commission instructed to consider enumerated factors as it deems them to be relevant). The Commission also has significant discretion to determine which crimes have been punished too leniently, and which too severely. 994(m). Congress has called upon the Commission to exercise its judgment about which types of crimes and which types of criminals are to be considered similar for the purposes of sentencing.

But our cases do not at all suggest that delegations of this type may not carry with them the need to exercise judgment on matters of policy. In Yakus v. United States, 321 U.S. 414 (1944), the Court upheld a delegation to the Price Administrator to fix commodity prices that "in his judgment will be generally fair and equitable and will effectuate the purposes of this Act" to stabilize prices and avert speculation. See id., at 420. In National Broadcasting Co. v. United States, 319 U.S. 190 (1943), we upheld a delegation to the Federal Communications Commission granting it the authority to promulgate regulations in accordance with its view of the "public interest."

* * *

Developing proportionate penalties for hundreds of different crimes by a virtually limitless array of offenders is precisely the sort of intricate, labor-intensive task for which delegation to an expert body is especially appropriate. Although Congress has delegated significant discretion to the Commission to draw judgments from its analysis of existing sentencing practice and alternative sentencing models, "Congress is not confined to that method of executing its policy which involves the least possible delegation of discretion to administrative officers." Yakus v. United States, 321 U.S., at 425 - 426. We have no doubt that in the hands of the Commission "the criteria which Congress has supplied are wholly adequate for carrying out the general policy and purpose" of the Act. Sunshine Coal Co. v. Adkins, 310 U.S. 381, 398 (1940).

[The Court then rejected Mistretta's argument that placing the Sentencing Commission within the Judicial Branch violated separation of powers principles. The sentencing of crimes has always been a function shared among the branches, and judges have traditionally played a critical role in sentencing. It is not an improper intrusion into the role of the judiciary to place the Sentencing Commission within the Judicial Branch and to require that some members of the Commission be judges.]

JUSTICE SCALIA, dissenting.

While the products of the Sentencing Commission's labors have been given the modest name "Guidelines," see 28 U.S.C. 994(a)(1); United States Sentencing Commission Guidelines Manual (June 15, 1988), they have the force and effect of laws, prescribing the sentences criminal defendants are to receive. A judge who disregards them will be reversed, 18 U.S.C. 3742. I dissent from today's decision because I can find no place within our constitutional system for an agency created by Congress to exercise no governmental power other than the making of laws.

* * *

Precisely because the scope of delegation is largely uncontrollable by the courts, we must be particularly rigorous in preserving the Constitution's structural restrictions that deter excessive delegation. The major one, it seems to me, is that the power to make law cannot be exercised by anyone other than Congress, except in conjunction with the lawful exercise of executive or judicial power.

The whole theory of lawful congressional "delegation" is not that Congress is sometimes too busy or too divided and can therefore assign its responsibility of making law to someone else; but rather that a certain degree of discretion, and thus of lawmaking, inheres in most executive or judicial action, and it is up to Congress, by the relative specificity or generality of its statutory commands, to determine - up to a point - how small or how large that degree shall be. Thus, the courts could be given the power to say precisely what constitutes a "restraint of trade," see Standard Oil Co. of New Jersey v. United States, 221 U.S. 1 (1911), or to adopt rules of procedure, see Sibbach v. Wilson & Co., 312 U.S. 1, 22 (1941), or to prescribe by rule the manner in which their officers shall execute their judgments, Wayman v. Southard, 10 Wheat. 1, 45 (1825), because that "lawmaking" was ancillary to their exercise of judicial powers. And the Executive could be given the power to adopt policies and rules specifying in detail what radio and television licenses will be in the "public interest, convenience or necessity," because that was ancillary to the exercise of its executive powers in granting and policing licenses and making a "fair and equitable allocation" of the electromagnetic spectrum. See Federal Radio Comm'n v. Nelson Brothers Bond & Mortgage Co., 289 U.S. 266, 285 (1933). Or to take examples closer to the case before us: Trial judges could be given the power to determine what factors justify a greater or lesser sentence within the statutorily prescribed limits because that was ancillary to their exercise of the judicial power of pronouncing sentence upon individual defendants. And the President, through the Parole Commission subject to his appointment and removal, could be given the power to issue Guidelines specifying when parole would be available, because that was ancillary to the President's exercise of the executive power to hold and release federal prisoners. See 18 U.S.C. 4203(a)(1) and (b); 28 CFR 2.20 (1988).

* * *

The focus of controversy, in the long line of our so-called excessive delegation cases, has been whether the degree of generality contained in the authorization for exercise of executive or judicial powers in a particular field is so unacceptably high as to amount to a delegation of legislative powers. I say "so-called excessive delegation" because although that convenient terminology is often used, what is really at issue is whether there has been any delegation of legislative power, which occurs (rarely) when Congress authorizes the exercise of executive or judicial power without adequate standards. Strictly speaking, there is no acceptable delegation of legislative power . . . In the present case, however, a pure delegation of legislative power is precisely what we have before us. It is irrelevant whether the standards are adequate, because they are not standards related to the exercise of executive or judicial powers; they are, plainly and simply, standards for further legislation.

The lawmaking function of the Sentencing Commission is completely divorced from any responsibility for execution of the law or adjudication of private rights under the law. It is divorced from responsibility for execution of the law not only because the Commission is not said to be "located in the Executive Branch" (as I shall discuss presently, I doubt whether Congress can "locate" an entity within one Branch or another for constitutional purposes by merely saying so); but, more importantly, because the Commission neither exercises any executive power on its own, nor is subject to the control of the President who does . . . And the Commission's lawmaking is completely divorced from the exercise of judicial powers since, not being a court, it has no judicial powers itself, nor is it subject to the control of any other body with judicial powers. The power to make law at issue here, in other words, is not ancillary but quite naked. The situation is no different in principle from what would exist if Congress gave the same power of writing sentencing laws to a congressional agency such as the General Accounting Office, or to members of its staff.

* * *

By reason of today's decision, I anticipate that Congress will find delegation of its lawmaking powers much more attractive in the future. If rulemaking can be entirely unrelated to the exercise of judicial or executive powers, I foresee all manner of "expert" bodies, insulated from the political process, to which Congress will delegate various portions of its lawmaking responsibility. How tempting to create an expert Medical Commission (mostly M.D.'s, with perhaps a few Ph.D.'s in moral philosophy) to dispose of such thorny, "no-win" political issues as the withholding of life-support systems in federally funded hospitals, or the use of fetal tissue for research. This is an undemocratic precedent that we set - not because of the scope of the delegated power, but because its recipient is not one of the three Branches of Government. The only governmental power the Commission possesses is the power to make law; and it is not the Congress.

Whitman v. American Trucking Associations, Inc.

531 U.S. 457 (2001)[21]

JUSTICE SCALIA delivered the opinion of the Court.

[This is a challenge to the Environmental Protection Agency's interpretation of a section of the Clean Air Act that instructs the EPA to set standards for ambient air quality that "are requisite to protect the public health" with "an adequate margin of safety." The Court of Appeals found EPA's interpretation of the pertinent statutory language to constitute an unconstitutional delegation of legislative power because EPA "lack[ed] any determinate criteria for drawing lines. It has failed to state intelligibly how much is too much."]

[21] Footnotes and some citations found in the original decision have been omitted from this excerpted version.

In a delegation challenge, the constitutional question is whether the statute has delegated legislative power to the agency. Article I, §1, of the Constitution vests "[a]ll legislative Powers herein granted ... in a Congress of the United States." This text permits no delegation of those powers, *Loving* v. *United States,* 517 U. S. 748, 771 (1996); see *id.,* at 776-777 (*Scalia, J.*, concurring in part and concurring in judgment), and so we repeatedly have said that when Congress confers decisionmaking authority upon agencies *Congress* must "lay down by legislative act an intelligible principle to which the person or body authorized to [act] is directed to conform." *J. W. Hampton, Jr., & Co.* v. *United States,* 276 U. S. 394, 409 (1928). We have never suggested that an agency can cure an unlawful delegation of legislative power by adopting in its discretion a limiting construction of the statute . . . The idea that an agency can cure an unconstitutionally standardless delegation of power by declining to exercise some of that power seems to us internally contradictory. The very choice of which portion of the power to exercise -- that is to say, the prescription of the standard that Congress had omitted -- would *itself* be an exercise of the forbidden legislative authority. Whether the statute delegates legislative power is a question for the courts, and an agency's voluntary self-denial has no bearing upon the answer.
We agree with the Solicitor General that the text of §109(b)(1) of the CAA at a minimum requires that "[f]or a discrete set of pollutants and based on published air quality criteria that reflect the latest scientific knowledge, [the] EPA must establish uniform national standards at a level that is requisite to protect public health from the adverse effects of the pollutant in the ambient air." Tr. of Oral Arg. in No. 99-1257, p. 5. Requisite, in turn, "mean[s] sufficient, but not more than necessary." *Id.,* at 7. These limits on the EPA's discretion are strikingly similar to the ones we approved in *Touby* v. *United States,* 500 U. S. 160 (1991), which permitted the Attorney General to designate a drug as a controlled substance for purposes of criminal drug enforcement if doing so was " `necessary to avoid an imminent hazard to the public safety.' " *Id.,* at 163. They also resemble the Occupational Safety and Health Act provision requiring the agency to "`set the standard which most adequately assures, to the extent feasible, on the basis of the best available evidence, that no employee will suffer any impairment of health'" -- which the Court upheld in *Industrial Union Dept., AFL-CIO* v. *American Petroleum Institute,* 448 U. S. 607, 646 (1980), and which even then-Justice Rehnquist, who alone in that case thought the statute violated the nondelegation doctrine, see *id.,* at 671 (opinion concurring in judgment), would have upheld if, like the statute here, it did not permit economic costs to be considered. See *American Textile Mfrs. Institute, Inc.* v. *Donovan,* 452 U. S. 490, 545 (1981) (*Rehnquist, J.,* dissenting).

The scope of discretion §109(b)(1) allows is in fact well within the outer limits of our nondelegation precedents. In the history of the Court we have found the requisite "intelligible principle" lacking in only two statutes, one of which provided literally no guidance for the exercise of discretion, and the other of which conferred authority to regulate the entire economy on the basis of no more precise a standard than stimulating the economy by assuring "fair competition." See *Panama Refining Co.* v. *Ryan,* 293 U. S. 388 (1935); *A. L. A. Schechter Poultry Corp.* v. *United States,* 295 U. S. 495 (1935). We have, on the other hand, upheld the validity of §11(b)(2) of the Public Utility Holding Company Act of 1935, 49 Stat. 821, which gave the Securities and Exchange Commission authority to modify the structure of holding company systems so as to ensure that they are not "unduly or unnecessarily complicate[d]" and do not "unfairly or inequitably distribute voting power among security holders." *American Power & Light Co.* v. *SEC,* 329 U. S. 90, 104 (1946). We have approved the wartime conferral of agency power to fix the prices of commodities at a level that "`will be generally fair and equitable and will effectuate the [in some respects conflicting] purposes of th[e] Act.'" *Yakus* v. *United States,* 321 U. S. 414, 420, 423-426 (1944). And we have found an "intelligible principle" in various statutes authorizing regulation in the "public interest." See, *e.g., National Broadcasting Co.* v. *United States,* 319 U. S. 190, 225-226 (1943) (FCC's power to regulate airwaves); *New York Central Securities Corp.* v. *United States,* 287 U. S. 12, 24-25 (1932) (ICC's power to approve railroad consolidations). In short, we have "almost never felt qualified to second-guess Congress regarding the permissible degree of policy judgment that can be left to those executing or applying the law." *Mistretta* v. *United States,* 488 U. S. 361, 416 (1989) (*Scalia, J.,* dissenting); see *id.,* at 373 (majority opinion).

It is true enough that the degree of agency discretion that is acceptable varies according to the scope of the power congressionally conferred. See *Loving* v. *United States, supra,* at 772-773; *United States* v. *Mazurie,* 419 U. S. 544, 556-557 (1975). While Congress need not provide any direction to the EPA regarding the manner in which it is to define "country elevators," which are to be exempt from new-stationary-source regulations governing grain elevators, see §7411(i), it must provide substantial guidance on setting air standards that affect the entire national economy. But even in sweeping regulatory schemes we have never demanded, as the Court of Appeals did here, that statutes provide a "determinate criterion" for saying "how much [of the regulated harm] is too much." 175 F. 3d, at 1034. In *Touby*, for example, we did not require the statute to decree how "imminent" was too imminent, or how "necessary" was necessary enough, or even -- most relevant here -- how "hazardous" was too hazardous. 500 U. S., at 165-167. Similarly, the statute at issue in *Lichter* authorized agencies to recoup "excess profits" paid under wartime Government contracts, yet we did not insist that Congress specify how much profit was too much. 334 U. S., at 783-786. It is therefore not conclusive for delegation purposes that, as respondents argue, ozone and particulate matter are "nonthreshold" pollutants that inflict a continuum of adverse health effects at any airborne concentration greater than zero, and hence require the EPA to make judgments of degree. "[A] certain degree of discretion, and thus of lawmaking, inheres in most executive or judicial action." *Mistretta* v. *United States, supra,* at 417 (*Scalia, J.,* dissenting) (emphasis deleted); see 488 U. S., at 378-379 (majority opinion). Section 109(b)(1) of the CAA, which to repeat we interpret as requiring the EPA to set air quality standards at the level that is "requisite" -- that is, not lower or higher than is necessary -- to protect the public health with an adequate margin of safety, fits comfortably within the scope of discretion permitted by our precedent.

We therefore reverse the judgment of the Court of Appeals remanding for reinterpretation that would avoid a supposed delegation of legislative power.

JUSTICE THOMAS, concurring.

I agree with the majority that §109's directive to the agency is no less an "intelligible principle" than a host of other directives that we have approved. *Ante*, at 13-15. I also agree that the Court of Appeals' remand to the agency to make its own corrective interpretation does not accord with our understanding of the delegation issue. *Ante*, at 12. I write separately, however, to express my concern that there may nevertheless be a genuine constitutional problem with §109, a problem which the parties did not address.

The parties to this case who briefed the constitutional issue wrangled over constitutional doctrine with barely a nod to the text of the Constitution. Although this Court since 1928 has treated the "intelligible principle" requirement as the only constitutional limit on congressional grants of power to administrative agencies, see *J. W. Hampton, Jr., & Co.* v. *United States*, 276 U. S. 394, 409 (1928), the Constitution does not speak of "intelligible principles." Rather, it speaks in much simpler terms: "*All* legislative Powers herein granted shall be vested in a Congress." U. S. Const., Art. 1, §1 (emphasis added). I am not convinced that the intelligible principle doctrine serves to prevent all cessions of legislative power. I believe that there are cases in which the principle is intelligible and yet the significance of the delegated decision is simply too great for the decision to be called anything other than "legislative."

As it is, none of the parties to this case has examined the text of the Constitution or asked us to reconsider our precedents on cessions of legislative power. On a future day, however, I would be willing to address the question whether our delegation jurisprudence has strayed too far from our Founders' understanding of separation of powers.

JUSTICE STEVENS, with whom JUSTICE SOUTER joins, concurring in part and concurring in the judgment.

* * *

The Court has two choices. We could choose to articulate our ultimate disposition of this issue by frankly acknowledging that the power delegated to the EPA is "legislative" but nevertheless conclude that the delegation is constitutional because adequately limited by the terms of the authorizing statute. Alternatively, we could pretend, as the Court does, that the authority delegated to the EPA is somehow not "legislative power." Despite the fact that there is language in our opinions that supports the Court's articulation of our holding, I am persuaded that it would be both wiser and more faithful to what we have actually done in delegation cases to admit that agency rulemaking authority is "legislative power."

The proper characterization of governmental power should generally depend on the nature of the power, not on the identity of the person exercising it. See Black's Law Dictionary 899 (6th ed. 1990) (defining "legislation" as, *inter alia*, "[f]ormulation of rule[s] for the future"); 1 K. Davis & R. Pierce, Administrative Law Treatise §2.3, p. 37 (3d ed. 1994) ("If legislative power means the power to make rules of conduct that bind everyone based on resolution of major policy issues, scores of agencies exercise legislative power routinely by promulgating what are candidly called `legislative rules' "). If the [air quality standards] that the EPA promulgated had been prescribed by Congress, everyone would agree that those rules would be the product of an exercise of "legislative power." The same characterization is appropriate when an agency exercises rulemaking authority pursuant to a permissible delegation from Congress.

My view is not only more faithful to normal English usage, but is also fully consistent with the text of the Constitution. In Article I, the

> Framers vested "All legislative Powers" in the Congress, Art. I., §1, just as in Article II they vested the "executive Power" in the President, Art. II, §1. Those provisions do not purport to limit the authority of either recipient of power to delegate authority to others. See *Bowsher* v. *Synar,* 478 U. S. 714, 752 (1986) (*Stevens, J.,* concurring in judgment) ("Despite the statement in Article I of the Constitution that `All legislative powers herein granted shall be vested in a Congress of the United States,' it is far from novel to acknowledge that independent agencies do indeed exercise legislative powers"); *INS* v. *Chadha,* 462 U. S. 919, 985-986 (1983) (White, J., dissenting) ("[L]egislative power can be exercised by independent agencies and Executive departments ..."); 1 Davis §2.6, p. 66 ("The Court was probably mistaken from the outset in interpreting Article I's grant of power to Congress as an implicit limit on Congress' authority to delegate legislative power"). Surely the authority granted to members of the Cabinet and federal law enforcement agents is properly characterized as "Executive" even though not exercised by the President. Cf. *Morrison* v. *Olson,* 487 U. S. 654, 705-706 (1988) (*Scalia, J.,* dissenting) (arguing that the independent counsel exercised "executive power" unconstrained by the President).
>
> It seems clear that an executive agency's exercise of rulemaking authority pursuant to a valid delegation from Congress is "legislative." As long as the delegation provides a sufficiently intelligible principle, there is nothing inherently unconstitutional about it. Accordingly . . . I would hold that when Congress enacted §109, it effected a constitutional delegation of legislative power to the EPA.

DISCUSSION AND QUESTIONS

1. What would the Framers say about Congress delegating substantive lawmaking authority to unelected officials? Does it seem likely that, when the Framers vested "all legislative powers" in the Congress, they anticipated that rules for the equities markets would be set by a Securities and Exchange Commission, that rules regarding safety in the workplace would be crafted by an Occupational Safety and Health Commission, and that rules governing banking would be determined by a Comptroller of the Currency?

2. In *Mistretta*, Justice Blackmun justifies the work of the Sentencing Commission largely based on what he deems to be the practical demands of modern American society: "our jurisprudence [on delegation] has been driven by a practical

understanding that in our increasingly complex society, replete with ever changing and more technical problems, Congress simply cannot do its job absent an ability to delegate power under broad general directives." Is Blackmun's premise correct? Is it true that Congress cannot fulfill its constitutional responsibilities without delegating lawmaking authority to dozens of regulatory agencies? Article I, Section 8 enumerates Congress' authority to legislate in approximately 20 (depending somewhat on how one counts) substantive areas. The 111th Congress (2009-10) included 22 committees in the House, 21 committees in the Senate, at least two joint House-Senate committees, several thousands of staffers (some staffers work for individual members and some staffers serve committees), and a budget of close to $5 billion. Is it too much to expect that thirty-plus committees and thousands of paid staffers with financial resources in the multiple billions of dollars should be capable of developing comprehensive legislation within Congress' 20 assigned areas of responsibility?

Is there another way to interpret the asserted necessity for delegation? If Congress is attempting to regulate American society to such a degree that it is incapable of doing the job on its own -- even with thousands of staffers and billions of dollars, might this be an indication that Congress is simply going too far, that it is exceeding the proper limits of its responsibilities? With respect to criminal sentencing in particular, Justice Blackmun reasons that "[d]eveloping proportionate penalties for hundreds of different crimes by a virtually limitless array of offenders is precisely the sort of intricate, labor-intensive task for which delegation to an expert body is especially appropriate." Alternatively, might it also be reasonable to conclude that, if Congress is unable to determine the proper penalties for the many crimes it has defined, perhaps it has criminalized too much behavior? Given the scope of Congress' constitutionally enumerated powers, is there justification for "hundreds" of federal crimes to be set forth in the U.S. Code?

3. Interestingly, Justice Scalia wrote the majority opinion in *Whitman* but was the lone dissenter in *Mistretta*. In simple terms, he seems to think that it is permissible for Congress to delegate a significant amount of discretion to other governmental actors who are enforcing the law (as in *Whitman*), but it is impermissible for Congress to delegate to other governmental actors true lawmaking power (as in *Mistretta*). The majority of the Court, however, appears to subscribe to the notion that Congress may delegate actual lawmaking power, so long as it provides an "intelligible principle" that will guide and limit the application of that delegated lawmaking power. In *Mistretta*, isn't Justice Scalia correct in asserting that Congress has delegated to the Sentencing Commission a core legislative function? Historically, has it not been the province of the legislature to set the penalties for crimes -- not just at the federal level, but throughout the states, and indeed, in other

nations that are governed as representative democracies? If Congress may delegate to another governmental institution the responsibility for determining criminal penalties, is there any legislative function that Congress is not permitted to delegate? Could Congress establish an independent commission to determine not just criminal penalties, but substantive crimes -- that is, a commission would decide what sort of behavior is to be considered criminal? Could Congress set up a "Budget Board" that would take over the difficult responsibility for deciding how Americans should be taxed and how tax revenues should be spent? If not, why not, given the reasoning of an eight-justice majority in *Mistretta*?

4. In what might be the most extraordinary example of "delegation" in United States history, Congress created a commission to choose the President. The Twelfth Amendment assigns to the Congress, jointly assembled, the task of counting Electoral College votes for President, and to the House of Representatives the responsibility for choosing the President if no candidate earns a clear majority among the Electoral College. In the vigorously disputed election of 1876, Democrat Samuel Tilden won a majority of the popular vote and enjoyed a lead over Republican Rutherford B. Hayes among the Electoral College; however, disputes about how to award the electoral votes from several states prevented Tilden from claiming a clear Electoral College majority. Congress created a 15-member Electoral Commission to determine how to award the disputed Electoral College votes. The Commission consisted of five members of the House of Representatives, five senators, and five Supreme Court justices. Four of the justices were named in the act that created the Commission, and these four were to choose the fifth justice, who would also be the fifteenth member of the Electoral Commission. The first 14 members of the Commission were equally divided between Republicans and Democrats. It was anticipated that the fifteenth member would be Justice David Davis, who was viewed as a political independent (even though he had been appointed to the bench by Republican President Abraham Lincoln and had been Lincoln's campaign manager at the 1860 Republican convention). However, shortly before the Commission was to begin its work, the Illinois legislature appointed Davis to the Senate. As a result, the seat that had been intended for Davis went to Justice Joseph P. Bradley, a Republican, and the final composition of the Electoral Commission was seven Democrats and eight Republicans. Ultimately, on party-line votes, the Commission awarded all disputed electoral votes to Hayes, the Republican, who thereby gained a one-vote majority in the Electoral College and became the nineteenth President of the United States.

CHAPTER SEVEN: CONGRESSIONAL PRIVILEGE

As explained above in Chapter Four, the courts have found *implied* privileges and immunities for the chief executive based on the nature of the office and its responsibilities. In contrast, the Framers chose to place in the Constitution *express* privileges for members of the Legislative Branch. These are set forth at Article I, Section 6:

> The senators and representatives . . . shall in all cases, except treason, felony and breach of the peace, be privileged from arrest during their attendance at the session of their respective houses, and in going to and returning from the same; and for any speech or debate in either house, they shall not be questioned in any other place.

This provision sets forth two privileges. The first is a privilege from "arrest," which was enjoyed by British members of Parliament prior to the American Revolution and appeared in the Articles of Confederation. The Framers included it in the Constitution because, in the late eighteenth century, arrest in civil matters was not uncommon (see *Long v. Ansell*, 293 U.S. 76 (1934)), and had occasionally been used by British monarchs to intimidate and interfere with the work of Parliament. The Framers wished for the people's elected representatives to be able to go about their legislative business without fear of arrest for civil matters. The privilege excludes from its coverage "treason, felony and breach of the peace," which has been interpreted broadly to include any criminal matter. As a result, the constitutional privilege from arrest offers to legislators no immunity of any sort in any criminal matter. This principle is best illustrated by the case of *Williamson v. United States*, 207 U.S. 425 (1908). Williamson was a sitting congressman who was convicted of suborning perjury. He argued that the privilege from arrest prevented any court from imposing a sentence of imprisonment during his congressional term. The Supreme Court disagreed, concluding that the privilege from arrest applies only in civil matters and provides no protection in criminal matters.

The second privilege found in Article I, Section 6 is the privilege from being "questioned" for "any speech or debate." This legislative privilege was recognized at least as early as 1689 when it was included in the English Bill of Rights, which stated that "the freedom of speech and debates or proceedings in parliament ought not to be impeached or questioned in any court or place out of parliament." As Justice Harlan explained in *United States v. Johnson*, 383 U.S. 169, 178 (1966), the privilege

> was the culmination of a long struggle for parliamentary supremacy. Behind these simple phrases lies a history of conflict between the Commons and the Tudor and Stuart monarchs during which successive monarchs utilized the criminal and civil law to suppress and intimidate critical legislators. Since the Glorious Revolution in Britain, and throughout United States history, the privilege has been recognized as an important protection of the independence and integrity of the legislature.

The principal question raised in applying this privilege is, what conduct is encompassed within the concept of "speech or debate"? In the first case in which the Supreme Court applied the privilege, *Kilbourn v. Thompson*, 103 U.S. 168 (1881), the Court offered what appears to be a broad definition of "speech or debate": "things generally done in a session of the House by one of its members in relation to the business before it." *Id.* at 204. In more recent decades, however, the Court has set some outside parameters on the privilege. In *United States v. Brewster*, 408 U.S. 501 (1972), the Court explained that taking a bribe does not fall within the official duties of a member of Congress, so the Speech or Debate Clause does not preclude prosecution for bribery. The same year, in *Gravel v. United States*, and then again seven years later, in *Hutchinson v. Proxmire*, the Court further elucidated the nuances of the privilege.

Gravel v. United States

408 U.S. 606 (1972)[22]

Opinion of the Court by MR. JUSTICE WHITE, announced by MR. JUSTICE BLACKMUN.

These cases arise out of the investigation by a federal grand jury into possible criminal conduct with respect to the release and publication of a classified Defense Department study entitled History of the United States Decision-Making Process on Viet Nam Policy. This document, popularly known as the Pentagon Papers, bore a Defense security classification of Top Secret-Sensitive. The crimes being investigated included the retention of public property or records with intent to convert (18 U.S.C. 641), the gathering and transmitting of

[22] Footnotes and some citations found in the original decision have been omitted from this excerpted version.

national defense information (18 U.S.C. 793), the concealment or removal of public records or documents (18 U.S.C. 2071), and conspiracy to commit such offenses and to defraud the United States (18 U.S.C. 371).

Among the witnesses subpoenaed were Leonard S. Rodberg, an assistant to Senator Mike Gravel of Alaska and a resident fellow at the Institute of Policy Studies, and Howard Webber, Director of M. I. T. Press. Senator Gravel, as intervenor, filed motions to quash the subpoenas and to require the Government to specify the particular questions to be addressed to Rodberg. He asserted that requiring these witnesses to appear and testify would violate his privilege under the Speech or Debate Clause of the United States Constitution, Art. I, 6, cl. 1.

It appeared that on the night of June 29, 1971, Senator Gravel, as Chairman of the Subcommittee on Buildings and Grounds of the Senate Public Works Committee, convened a meeting of the subcommittee and there read extensively from a copy of the Pentagon Papers. He then placed the entire 47 volumes of the study in the public record. Rodberg had been added to the Senator's staff earlier in the day and assisted Gravel in preparing for and conducting the hearing. Some weeks later there were press reports that Gravel had arranged for the papers to be published by Beacon Press and that members of Gravel's staff had talked with Webber as editor of M. I. T. Press.

The District Court overruled the motions to quash and to specify questions but entered an order proscribing certain categories of questions. United States v. Doe, 332 F. Supp. 930 (Mass. 1971). The Government's contention that for purposes of applying the Speech or Debate Clause the courts were free to inquire into the regularity of the subcommittee meeting was rejected. Because the Clause protected all legislative acts, it was held to shield from inquiry anything the Senator did at the subcommittee meeting and "certain acts done in preparation therefore." Id., at 935. The Senator's privilege also prohibited "inquiry into things done by Dr. Rodberg as the Senator's agent or assistant which would have been legislative acts, and therefore privileged, if performed by the Senator personally." Id., at 937-938. The trial court, however, held the private publication of the documents was not privileged by the Speech or Debate Clause. Id., at 936.

[The Court of Appeals largely agreed with the District Court, but extended the privilege somewhat by concluding that neither the senator nor his aides could be questioned about plans for the private publication of the Pentagon Papers. The United States appealed the ruling that the Speech or Debate Privilege could be applied to the acts of legislative aides, and Senator Gravel appealed the ruling that private publication was not protected by the privilege.]

* * *

[T]he United States strongly urges that because the Speech or Debate Clause confers a privilege only upon "Senators and Representatives," Rodberg himself has no valid claim to constitutional immunity from grand jury inquiry. In our view, both courts below correctly rejected this position. We agree with the Court of Appeals that for the purpose of construing the privilege a Member and his aide are to be "treated as one," United States v. Doe, 455 F.2d, at 761; or, as the District Court put it: the "Speech or Debate Clause prohibits inquiry into things done by Dr. Rodberg as the Senator's agent or assistant which would have been legislative acts, and therefore privileged, if performed by the Senator personally." United States v. Doe, 332 F. Supp., at 937-938. Both courts recognized what the Senate of the United States urgently presses here: that it is literally impossible, in view of the complexities of the modern legislative process, with Congress almost constantly in session and matters of legislative concern constantly proliferating, for Members of Congress to perform their legislative tasks without the help of aides and assistants; that the day-to-day work of such aides is so critical to the Members' performance that they must be treated as the latter's alter egos; and that if they are not so recognized, the central role of the Speech or Debate Clause -- to prevent intimidation of legislators by the Executive and accountability before a possibly hostile judiciary, United States v. Johnson, 383 U.S. 169, 181 (1966) -- will inevitably be diminished and frustrated.

* * *

The United States fears the abuses that history reveals have occurred when legislators are invested with the power to relieve others from the operation of otherwise valid civil and criminal laws. But these abuses, it seems to us, are for the most part obviated if the privilege applicable to the aide is viewed, as it must be, as the privilege of the Senator, and invocable only by the Senator or by the aide on the Senator's behalf, and if in all events the privilege available to the aide is confined to those services that would be immune legislative conduct if performed by the Senator himself. This view places beyond the Speech or Debate Clause a variety of services characteristically performed by aides for Members of Congress, even though within the scope of their employment. It likewise provides no protection for criminal conduct threatening the security of the person or property of others, whether performed at the direction of the Senator in preparation for or in execution of a legislative act or done without his knowledge or direction. Neither does it immunize Senator or aide from testifying at trials or grand jury proceedings involving third-party crimes where the questions do not require testimony about or impugn a legislative act. Thus our refusal to distinguish between Senator and aide in applying the Speech or Debate Clause does not mean that Rodberg is for all purposes exempt from grand jury questioning.

We are convinced also that the Court of Appeals correctly determined that Senator Gravel's alleged arrangement with Beacon Press to publish the Pentagon Papers was not protected speech or debate within the meaning of Art. I, 6, cl. 1, of the Constitution.

Prior cases have read the Speech or Debate Clause "broadly to effectuate its purposes," United States v. Johnson, 383 U.S., at 180, and have included within its reach anything "generally done in a session of the House by one of its members in relation to the business before it." Kilbourn v. Thompson, 103 U.S., at 204; United States v. Johnson, 383 U.S., at 179. Thus, voting by Members and committee reports are protected; and we recognize today -- as the Court has recognized before, Kilbourn v. Thompson, 103 U.S., at 204; Tenney v. Brandhove, 341 U.S., 367, 377-378 (1951) -- that a Member's conduct at legislative committee hearings, although subject to judicial review in various circumstances, as is legislation itself, may not be made the basis for a civil or criminal judgment against a Member because that conduct is within the "sphere of legitimate legislative activity." Id., at 376.

But the Clause has not been extended beyond the legislative sphere. That Senators generally perform certain acts in their official capacity as Senators does not necessarily make all such acts legislative in nature. Members of Congress are constantly in touch with the Executive Branch of the Government and with administrative agencies -- they may cajole, and exhort with respect to the administration of a federal statute -- but such conduct, though generally done, is not protected legislative activity. United States v. Johnson decided at least this much. "No argument is made, nor do we think that it could be successfully contended, that the Speech or Debate Clause reaches conduct, such as was involved in the attempt to influence the Department of Justice, that is in no wise related to the due functioning of the legislative process." 383 U.S., at 172. Cf. Burton v. United States, 202 U.S., at 367-368.

* * *

Here, private publication by Senator Gravel through the cooperation of Beacon Press was in no way essential to the deliberations of the Senate; nor does questioning as to private publication threaten the integrity or independence of the Senate by impermissibly exposing its deliberations to executive influence. The Senator had conducted his hearings; the record and any report that was forthcoming were available both to his committee and the Senate. Insofar as we are advised, neither Congress nor the full committee ordered or authorized the publication. We cannot but conclude that the Senator's arrangements with Beacon Press were not part and parcel of the legislative process.

There are additional considerations. Article I, 6, cl. 1, as we have emphasized, does not purport to confer a general exemption upon Members of Congress from liability or process in criminal cases. Quite the contrary is true. While the Speech or Debate Clause recognized speech, voting, and other legislative acts as exempt from liability that might otherwise attach, it does not privilege either Senator or aide to violate an otherwise valid criminal law in preparing for or implementing legislative acts. If republication of these classified papers would be a crime under an Act of Congress, it would not be entitled to immunity under the Speech or Debate Clause. It also appears that the grand jury was pursuing this very subject in the normal course of a valid investigation. The Speech or Debate Clause does not in our view extend immunity to Rodberg, as a Senator's aide, from testifying before the grand jury about the arrangement between Senator Gravel and Beacon Press or about his own participation, if any, in the alleged transaction, so long as legislative acts of the Senator are not impugned.

[JUSTICE STEWART dissented in part.]

MR. JUSTICE DOUGLAS, dissenting.

I would construe the Speech or Debate Clause [1] to insulate Senator Gravel and his aides from inquiry concerning the Pentagon Papers, and Beacon Press from inquiry concerning publication of them, for that publication was but another way of informing the public as to what had gone on in the privacy of the Executive Branch concerning the conception and pursuit of the so-called "war" in Vietnam.

* * *

As to Senator Gravel's efforts to publish the Subcommittee record's contents, wide dissemination of this material as an educational service is as much a part of the Speech or Debate Clause philosophy as mailing under a frank a Senator's or a Congressman's speech across the Nation. As mentioned earlier, "[i]t is the proper duty of a representative body to look diligently into every affair of government and to talk much about what it sees. . . . The informing function of Congress should be preferred even to its legislative function." W. Wilson, Congressional Government 303 (1885), quoted with approval in Tenney v. Brandhove, supra, at 377 n. 6. "From the earliest times in its history, the Congress has assiduously performed an 'informing function,'" Watkins v. United States, 354 U.S. 178, 200 n. 33. "Legislators have an obligation to take positions on controversial political questions so that their constituents can be fully informed by them." Bond v. Floyd, 385 U.S. 116, 136.

We said in United States v. Johnson, 383 U.S. 169, 179, that the Speech or Debate Clause established a "legislative privilege" that protected a member of Congress against prosecution "by an unfriendly executive and conviction by a hostile judiciary" in order, as Mr. Justice Harlan put it, to ensure "the independence of the legislature." That hostility emanates from every stage of the present proceedings. It emphasizes the need to construe the Speech or Debate Clause generously, not niggardly. If republication of a Senator's speech in a newspaper carries the privilege, as it doubtless does, then republication of the exhibits introduced at a hearing before Congress must also do so. That means that republication by Beacon Press is within the ambit of the Speech or Debate Clause and that the confidences of the Senator in arranging it are not subject to inquiry "in any other Place" than the Congress.

* * *

MR. JUSTICE BRENNAN, with whom MR. JUSTICE DOUGLAS, and MR. JUSTICE MARSHALL, join, dissenting.

* * *

In holding that Senator Gravel's alleged arrangement with Beacon Press to publish the Pentagon Papers is not shielded from extra-senatorial inquiry by the Speech or Debate Clause, the Court adopts what for me is a far too narrow view of the legislative function. The Court seems to assume that words spoken in debate or written in congressional reports are protected by the Clause, so that if Senator Gravel had recited part of the Pentagon Papers on the Senate floor or copied them into a Senate report, those acts could not be questioned "in any other Place." Yet because he sought a wider audience, to publicize information deemed relevant to matters pending before his own committee, the Senator suddenly loses his immunity and is exposed to grand jury investigation and possible prosecution for the republication. The explanation for this anomalous result is the Court's belief that "Speech or Debate" encompasses only acts necessary to the internal deliberations of Congress concerning proposed legislation. "Here," according to the Court, "private publication by Senator Gravel through the cooperation of Beacon Press was in no way essential to the deliberations of the Senate." Therefore, "the Senator's arrangements with Beacon Press were not part and parcel of the legislative process."

Thus, the Court excludes from the sphere of protected legislative activity a function that I had supposed lay at the heart of our democratic system. I speak, of course, of the legislator's duty to inform the public about matters affecting the administration of government. That this "informing function" falls into the class of things "generally done in a session of the House by one of its members in relation to the business before it," Kilbourn v. Thompson, 103 U.S. 168, 204 (1881), was explicitly acknowledged by the Court in Watkins v. United States, 354 U.S. 178 (1957). In speaking of the "power of the Congress to inquire into and publicize corruption, maladministration or inefficiency in agencies of the Government," the Court noted that "[f]rom the earliest times in its history, the Congress has assiduously performed an `informing function' of this nature." Id., at 200 n. 33.

* * *

Unlike the Court, therefore, I think that the activities of Congressmen in communicating with the public are legislative acts protected by the Speech or Debate Clause. I agree with the Court that not every task performed by a legislator is privileged; intervention before Executive departments is one that is not. But the informing function carries a far more persuasive claim to the protections of the Clause. It has been recognized by this Court as something "generally done" by Congressmen, the Congress itself has established special concessions designed to lower the cost of such communication, and, most important, the function furthers several well-recognized goals of representative government. To say in the face of these facts that the informing function is not privileged merely because it is not necessary to the internal deliberations of Congress is to give the Speech or Debate Clause an artificial and narrow reading unsupported by reason.

Hutchinson v. Proxmire

443 U.S. 111 (1979)[23]

MR. CHIEF JUSTICE BURGER delivered the opinion of the Court.

[Senator William Proxmire, Democratic senator from Wisconsin, became well-known for awarding a "Golden Fleece Award of the Month" to government programs that he believed were wasting taxpayer dollars. In April 1975, he gave the award to several federal agencies that had funded Plaintiff Hutchinson's research into aggression, which included the use of monkeys as test subjects. Proxmire first announced the award in a speech on the floor of the Senate, which included remarks like this:

> The funding of this nonsense makes me almost angry enough to scream and kick or even clench my jaw. It seems to me it is outrageous. Dr. Hutchinson's studies should make the taxpayers as well as his monkeys grind their teeth. In fact, the good doctor has made a fortune from his monkeys and in the process made a monkey out of the American taxpayer. It is time for the Federal Government to get out of this "monkey business." In view of the transparent worthlessness of Hutchinson's study of jaw-grinding and biting by angry or hard-drinking monkeys, it is time we put a stop to the bite Hutchinson and the bureaucrats who fund him have been taking of the taxpayer.

Proxmire then issued a press release excerpting the speech, later sent a newsletter describing the award to roughly 100,000 recipients, and appeared on television to discuss the award. Plaintiff Hutchinson claims that Proxmire and the legislative assistant who helped publicize the award defamed him and injured him in his career. Proxmire and his legislative assistant argue that the claims are precluded by the Speech or Debate Clause.]

---

[23] Footnotes and some citations found in the original decision have been omitted from this excerpted version.

In support of the Court of Appeals holding that newsletters and press releases are protected by the Speech or Debate Clause, respondents rely upon both historical precedent and present-day congressional practices. They contend that impetus for the Speech or Debate Clause privilege in our Constitution came from the history of parliamentary efforts to protect the right of members to criticize the spending of the Crown and from the prosecution of a Speaker of the House of Commons for publication of a report outside of Parliament. Respondents also contend that in the modern day very little speech or debate occurs on the floor of either House; from this they argue that press releases and newsletters are necessary for Members of Congress to communicate with other Members. For example, in his deposition Proxmire testified:

> I have found in 19 years in the Senate that very often a statement on the floor of the Senate or something that appears in the Congressional Record misses the attention of most members of the Senate, and virtually all members of the House, because they don't read the Congressional Record. If they are handed a news release, or something, that is going to call it to their attention . . . .

Respondents also argue that an essential part of the duties of a Member of Congress is to inform constituents, as well as other Members, of the issues being considered.

* * *

[I]t is clear that nothing in history or in the explicit language of the Clause suggests any intention to create an absolute privilege from liability or suit for defamatory statements made outside the Chamber. In Brewster, [408 U.S.] at 507, we observed:

> The immunities of the Speech or Debate Clause were not written into the Constitution simply for the personal or private benefit of Members of Congress, but to protect the integrity of the legislative process by insuring the independence of individual legislators.

* * *

Claims under the Clause going beyond what is needed to protect legislative independence are to be closely scrutinized. In Brewster we took note of this:

> The authors of our Constitution were well aware of the history of both the need for the privilege and the abuses that could flow from too sweeping safeguards. In order to preserve other values, they wrote the privilege so that it tolerates and protects behavior on the part of Members not tolerated and protected when done by other citizens, but the shield does not extend beyond what is necessary to preserve the integrity of the legislative process.

408 U.S., at 517 (emphasis added).

Indeed, the precedents abundantly support the conclusion that a Member may be held liable for republishing defamatory statements originally made in either House. We perceive no basis for departing from that long-established rule.

Mr. Justice Story in his Commentaries, for example, explained that there was no immunity for republication of a speech first delivered in Congress:

> Therefore, although a speech delivered in the house of commons is privileged, and the member cannot be questioned respecting it elsewhere; yet, if he publishes his speech, and it contains libellous matter, he is liable to an action and prosecution therefor, as in common cases of libel. And the same principles seem applicable to the privilege of debate and speech in congress. No man ought to have a right to defame others under colour of a performance of the duties of his office. And if he does so in the actual discharge of his duties in congress, that furnishes no reason, why he should be enabled through the medium of the press to destroy the reputation, and invade the repose of other citizens. It is neither within the scope of his duty, nor in furtherance of public rights, or public policy. Every citizen has as good a right to be protected by the laws from malignant scandal, and false charges, and defamatory imputations, as a member of congress has to utter them in his seat.

2 J. Story, Commentaries on the Constitution 863, p. 329 (1833).

* * *

In Gravel v. United States, 408 U.S., at 622 -626, we recognized that the doctrine denying immunity for republication had been accepted in the United States:

> [P]rivate publication by Senator Gravel . . . was in no way essential to the deliberations of the Senate; nor does questioning as to private publication threaten the integrity or independence of the Senate by impermissibly exposing its deliberations to executive influence.

Id., at 625.

* * *

We reach a similar conclusion here. A speech by Proxmire in the Senate would be wholly immune and would be available to other Members of Congress and the public in the Congressional Record. But neither the newsletters nor the press release was "essential to the deliberations of the Senate" and neither was part of the deliberative process.

* * *

Respondents also argue that newsletters and press releases are privileged as part of the "informing function" of Congress. Advocates of a broad reading of the "informing function" sometimes tend to confuse two uses of the term "informing." In one sense, Congress informs itself collectively by way of hearings of its committees. It was in that sense that Woodrow Wilson used "informing" in a statement quoted by respondents. In reality, Wilson's statement related to congressional efforts to learn of the activities of the Executive Branch and administrative agencies; he did not include wideranging inquiries by individual Members on subjects of their choice. Moreover, Wilson's statement itself clearly implies a distinction between the informing function and the legislative function:

> Unless Congress have and use every means of acquainting itself with the acts and the disposition of the administrative agents of the government, the country must be helpless to learn how it is being served; and unless Congress both scrutinize these things and sift them by every form of discussion, the

> country must remain in embarrassing, crippling ignorance of the very affairs which it is most important that it should understand and direct. The informing function of Congress should be preferred even to its legislative function. . . . [T]he only really self-governing people is that people which discusses and interrogates its administration.

W. Wilson, Congressional Government 303 (1885).

It is in this narrower Wilsonian sense that this Court has employed "informing" in previous cases holding that congressional efforts to inform itself through committee hearings are part of the legislative function.
The other sense of the term, and the one relied upon by respondents, perceives it to be the duty of Members to tell the public about their activities. Valuable and desirable as it may be in broad terms, the transmittal of such information by individual Members in order to inform the public and other Members is not a part of the legislative function or the deliberations that make up the legislative process. As a result, transmittal of such information by press releases and newsletters is not protected by the Speech or Debate Clause.

* * *

MR. JUSTICE BRENNAN, dissenting.

I disagree with the Court's conclusion that Senator Proxmire's newsletters and press releases fall outside the protection of the speech-or-debate immunity. In my view, public criticism by legislators of unnecessary governmental expenditures, whatever its form, is a legislative act shielded by the Speech or Debate Clause.

<u>DISCUSSION AND QUESTIONS</u>

1. The majorities in both *Gravel* and *Proxmire* conclude that any publication or distribution of information beyond the halls of Congress is not protected by the Speech or Debate Clause. In contrast, Justice Brennan asserts in both cases that communicating with the public is a classic function of elected legislators that should be protected. Who has the better view of the legislator's role? Is it not integral to the proper functioning of a representative democracy that the people and their representatives be able to engage in free and open communications?

If an elected legislator can fairly be viewed as an agent of his constituents, mustn't he be permitted to communicate with them accurately and comprehensively about his activities on their behalf? Does it serve the goals of representative democracy to give a legislator unlimited freedom of speech within the legislative chamber, but then prohibit him from relating to his constituents how he expressed himself?

2. The *Gravel* and *Proxmire* cases preceded (slightly) the regular television coverage of the Senate and House by C-SPAN. If Senator Proxmire had criticized Hutchinson's research on the floor of the Senate in the 1990s, his speech might have been transmitted to viewers of C-SPAN across the United States. If so, would the transmitted remarks be protected by the Speech or Debate Clause (because the remarks were made within the Senate chamber) or would they be unprotected (because they were communicated outside the Senate chamber)?

3. Imagine that Senator A delivers a speech on the floor of the Senate in which he makes defamatory remarks about someone, and then Senator B reproduces those remarks (fully attributed to Senator A's floor speech) in a newsletter to constituents -- can either senator be held liable for the defamatory remarks? The defamation law of many states includes a "fair report" privilege that shields accurate reports of legislative and other governmental proceedings. See, e,g., Georgia Code Annotated §51-5-7(5); Louisiana Revised Statutes Annotated §14:49; Michigan Comp. Laws §600.2911(3); 12 Oklahoma Stat. Ann. §1443.1; *see also* Restatement of Torts (Second) §611 (fair report privilege applies to "[t]he publication of defamatory matter concerning another in a report of an official action or proceeding or of a meeting open to the public that deals with a matter of public concern . . . if the report is accurate and complete or a fair abridgement of the occurrence reported."). Should Senator B be held liable for merely reporting accurately privileged statements that were made by another? If the answer is "no," then would it make sense to hold Senator A liable for reporting in a newsletter what he himself said in a privileged floor speech (as Senator Proxmire did)?

4. In *Gravel,* the Court extended the protection of the speech or debate privilege to congressional aides when they are acting as the "alter ego" of their respective member, but application of the privilege is confined to circumstances in which an aide is performing "those services that would be immune legislative conduct if performed by the Senator himself." To some degree then, there is a privilege that insulates the *conduct* of congressional aides against liability and even against scrutiny by the other branches. What is left unclear by *Gravel* (and other decisions discussing the privilege) is whether there is a privilege for *communications* between a member and his aides, as there is for communications between the President and his closest aides. In *United States v. Nixon* (see Chapter Four, pages

103-09), the Supreme Court discovered a privilege for communications between the President and his aides based on

> the public interest in candid, objective, and even blunt or harsh opinions in Presidential decision-making. A President and those who assist him must be free to explore alternatives in the process of shaping policies and making decisions and to do so in a way many would be unwilling to express except privately.

Does a similar "public interest" militate in favor or preserving the confidentiality of communications between legislators and their aides? Should a member of Congress and those who assist him be free to explore alternatives in shaping legislative policies and making legislative decisions without concern that their communications will be publicly disclosed?

In 2006, an unprecedented test of the Speech or Debate Clause occurred when the FBI, in the course of a criminal investigation, served a search warrant on the office of a sitting congressman. The resulting decision by the D.C. Circuit (appeal from which was not accepted by the Supreme Court) offered new insights into the scope of the clause.

United States v. Rayburn House Office Building, Room 2113

497 F.3d 654 (D.C. Cir. 2007)[24]

> Before: GINSBURG, Chief Judge, and HENDERSON and ROGERS, Circuit Judges.
>
> Opinion for the Court filed by Circuit Judge ROGERS.
>
> This is an appeal from the denial of a motion, filed pursuant to Rule 41(g) of the Federal Rules of Criminal Procedure, seeking the return of all materials seized by the Executive upon executing a search warrant for non-legislative materials in the congressional office of a sitting Member of Congress. The question on appeal is whether the procedures under which the search was conducted were sufficiently protective of the legislative privilege created by the Speech or Debate Clause, Article I, Section 6, Clause 1 of the United States Constitution. Our precedent establishes that the testimonial privilege

[24] Footnotes and some citations found in the original decision have been omitted from this excerpted version.

under the Clause extends to non-disclosure of written legislative materials. See Brown & Williamson Tobacco Corp. v. Williams, 62 F.3d 408, 420 (D.C.Cir.1995). Given the Department of Justice's voluntary freeze of its review of the seized materials and the procedures mandated on remand by this court in granting the Congressman's motion for emergency relief pending appeal, the imaging and keyword search of the Congressman's computer hard drives and electronic media exposed no legislative material to the Executive, and therefore did not violate the Speech or Debate Clause, but the review of the Congressman's paper files when the search was executed exposed legislative material to the Executive and accordingly violated the Clause. Whether the violation requires, as the Congressman suggests, the return of all seized items, privileged as well as non-privileged, depends upon a determination of which documents are privileged and then, as to the non-privileged documents, a balancing of the separation of powers underlying the Speech or Debate Clause and the Executive's Article II, Section 3 law enforcement interest in the seized materials.

[In the course of investigating Congressman William Jefferson (Democrat from Louisiana) for bribery and wire fraud, the Department of Justice obtained a warrant authorizing the search of his congressional office. Special procedures were used in an effort to avoid improper seizure and retention of legislative materials protected by the Speech or Debate Privilege. The agents who searched the office and seized papers and copied electronic files responsive to the warrant turned these materials over to a "filter team," which then reviewed the seized materials to determine whether any were not responsive to the warrant or subject to speech or debate protection. Non-responsive or privileged materials were to be returned to Congressman Jefferson and not made available to the prosecution team. Congressman Jefferson asserts that the search of his office and the seizure of materials violated the Speech or Debate Clause, and demands the return of all materials taken.]

The Speech or Debate Clause provides that “for any Speech or Debate in either House, [members of Congress] shall not be questioned in any other Place.” U.S. Const. art. I, § 6, cl. 1. The version of the Clause adopted by the Founders closely resembles the language adopted in the English Bill of Rights of 1689, which came out of the long struggle for governmental supremacy between the English monarchs and the Parliament, during which the criminal and civil law were used to intimidate legislators. By the time of the Constitutional Convention, the privilege embodied in the Speech or Debate Clause was “recognized as an important protection of the independence and integrity of the legislature," United States v. Johnson, 383 U.S. 169 (1966), and was to serve as a protection against possible "prosecution by an unfriendly executive and conviction by a hostile judiciary," id. at 179.

In defining the protections afforded by the Clause, the Supreme Court has limited the scope to conduct that is an integral part of "the due functioning of the legislative process." United States v. Brewster, 408 U.S. 501, 513, 92 S.Ct. 2531, 33 L.Ed.2d 507 (1972). The Congressman does not dispute that congressional offices are subject to the operation of the Fourth Amendment and thus subject to a search pursuant to a search warrant issued by the federal district court. The Executive acknowledges, in connection with the execution of a search warrant, that there is a role for a Member of Congress to play in exercising the Member's rights under the Speech or Debate Clause. The parties disagree on precisely when that should occur and what effect any violation of the Member's Speech or Debate rights should have. The Congressman contends that the exercise of his privilege under the Clause must precede the disclosure of the contents of his congressional office to agents of the Executive and that any violation of the privilege requires return of all of the seized materials. The Executive offers that the special procedures described in the warrant affidavit "are more than sufficient to protect Rep[resentative] Jefferson's rights under the Clause," and that any violation of the privilege does not deprive the Executive of the right to retain all non-privileged materials within the scope of the search warrant.

The Supreme Court has not spoken to the precise issue at hand. May 20-21, 2006 was the first time a sitting Member's congressional office has been searched by the Executive. The Court has made clear, however, in the context of a grand jury investigation, that "[t]he Speech or Debate Clause was designed to assure a co-equal branch of the government wide freedom of speech, debate, and deliberation without intimidation or threats from the Executive Branch." Gravel v. United States, 408 U.S. 606, 616, 92 S.Ct. 2614, 33 L.Ed.2d 583 (1972). Although in Gravel the Court held that the Clause embraces a testimonial privilege, id. at 616, to date the Court has not spoken on whether the privilege conferred by the Clause includes a non-disclosure privilege. However, this court has.

Beginning with the observation that the prohibition in the Speech or Debate Clause is "deceptively simple," this court held in Brown & Williamson, 62 F.3d at 415, that the Clause includes a non-disclosure privilege, id. at 420. Noting that the purpose of the Speech or Debate Clause is "'to insure that the legislative function the Constitution allocates to Congress may be performed independently,' without regard to the distractions of private civil litigation or the periods of criminal prosecution," id. at 415 (quoting Eastland v. U.S. Servicemen's Fund, 421 U.S. 491, 502, 95 S.Ct. 1813, 44 L.Ed.2d 324 (1975)), the court rejected the view that the testimonial immunity of the Speech or Debate Clause applies only when Members or their aides are personally questioned.

Documentary evidence can certainly be as revealing as oral communications -- even if only indirectly when, as here, the documents in question do not detail specific congressional actions. But indications as to what Congress is looking at provide clues as to what Congress is doing, or might be about to do-and this is true whether or not the documents are sought for the purpose of inquiring into (or frustrating) legislative conduct or to advance some other goals.

* * *

Thus, our opinion in Brown & Williamson makes clear that a key purpose of the privilege is to prevent intrusions in the legislative process and that the legislative process is disrupted by the disclosure of legislative material, regardless of the use to which the disclosed materials are put. See 62 F.3d at 419. The bar on compelled disclosure is absolute, see Eastland, 421 U.S. at 503, and there is no reason to believe that the bar does not apply in the criminal as well as the civil context.

* * *

The search of Congressman Jefferson's office must have resulted in the disclosure of legislative materials to agents of the Executive. Indeed, the application accompanying the warrant contemplated it. In order to determine whether the documents were responsive to the search warrant, FBI agents had to review all of the papers in the Congressman's office, of which some surely related to legislative acts. This compelled disclosure clearly tends to disrupt the legislative process: exchanges between a Member of Congress and the Member's staff or among Members of Congress on legislative matters may legitimately involve frank or embarrassing statements; the possibility of compelled disclosure may therefore chill the exchange of views with respect to legislative activity. This chill runs counter to the Clause's purpose of protecting against disruption of the legislative process.

*　*　*

The special procedures outlined in the warrant affidavit would not have avoided the violation of the Speech or Debate Clause because they denied the Congressman any opportunity to identify and assert the privilege with respect to legislative materials before their compelled disclosure to Executive agents. Indeed, the Congressman, his attorney, and counsel for the House of Representatives were denied entry into Room 2113 once the FBI arrived. The special procedures described in the warrant affidavit called for review by FBI agents and the several members of the Justice Department filter team before the Congressman would be afforded an opportunity to identify potentially privileged materials.

*　*　*

Accordingly, we hold that a search that allows agents of the Executive to review privileged materials without the Member's consent violates the Clause.

*　*　*

Accordingly, we hold that the Congressman is entitled to the return of all legislative materials (originals and copies) that are protected by the Speech or Debate Clause seized from Rayburn House Office Building Room 2113 on May 20-21, 2006.

[Circuit Judge HENDERSON filed a separate opinion in which she reasoned that a search of a congressional office during the course of a criminal investigation is not the sort of "questioning" that is prohibited by the Speech or Debate Clause. The precedent makes clear that members of Congress are not immune to criminal prosecution. Searching the existing records of a member is not the same as requiring the member to produce the records himself or requiring him to submit to questions. Execution of a warrant requires no affirmative action by the member, so it should not be considered an impermissible Executive Branch intrusion into the legislative process.]

DISCUSSION AND QUESTIONS

1. The D.C. Circuit finds that the speech or debate privilege includes an entitlement for legislators to avoid disclosure of "legislative materials" so as "to prevent intrusions in the legislative process." The rationale seems to be that the Executive Branch is not entitled to examine the plans or activities of the Legislative Branch, because such monitoring might lead to active interference with the work of the legislature. Congress possesses the "power of inquiry" to investigate matters in which it is interested, and this includes the power to engage in oversight of the Executive Branch (subject to the fairly narrow limitations of executive privilege). (See Chapter Five.) Does the constitutional separation of powers envisioned by the Framers contemplate that the Legislative Branch may engage in investigation and oversight of the Executive Branch, while the Executive Branch is prohibited from inquiring into the work of the Legislative Branch? If so, on what basis?

2. Should the non-disclosure element of the speech or debate privilege described by Judge Rogers also protect confidential communications between members and their staffs? If a purpose of the privilege is to maintain the confidentiality of the legislative process, then should not the communications between members and their aides about the business of the legislature also be privileged?

3. Part of the Republican House members' "Contract with America" in the 1994 elections was the Congressional Accountability Act ("CAA"), which was enacted by the 104th Congress in 1995. The Act required members (and others within the Legislative Branch) to abide by various workplace laws that already applied to the private sector and, in many cases, to the Executive Branch, such as Title VII of the Civil Rights Act, the Fair Labor Standards Act and the Americans with Disabilities Act. In theory, the CAA makes members of Congress liable for violations of workplace protections embodied in these other statutes. When plaintiffs initiated litigation under the CAA, some members defended themselves by claiming that the Speech or Debate Clause prevents them from being held accountable for personnel decisions. The D.C. Circuit ruled in *Fields v. Office of Eddie Bernice Johnson*, 459 F.3d 1 (2006) that the clause does not automatically bar all claims under the CAA because personnel decisions are not legislative acts. That is, hiring, firing, and other personnel decisions relating to members' aides are not within the core legislative activities of Congress and, therefore, are not themselves covered by the privilege. However, the privilege may, nonetheless, be applicable -- and may effectively bar a plaintiff's claims -- if proving or defending against the claims would involve inquiry into legislative acts or the motivation for legislative acts.

CHAPTER EIGHT:
THE JUDICIAL BRANCH AS UMPIRE
AND THE POLITICAL QUESTION DOCTRINE

Alexander Hamilton explained in Federalist 78 that "the interpretation of the laws is the proper and peculiar province of the courts." Chief Justice John Marshall confirmed in *Marbury v. Madison* that "it is emphatically the province and duty of the judicial department to say what the law is." The courts, therefore, are predictably where questions about the scope or allocation of governmental power are answered. In particular, as the non-political (or perhaps, the least overtly political) branch, the judiciary is best suited to resolve dispassionately disputes between the two political branches about their respective roles and responsibilities under the Constitution. Nonetheless, there are occasionally circumstances in which the courts will decline to involve themselves in such disputes, based on what has become known as the "political question doctrine."

Although it is not set forth in the Constitution, the political question doctrine has become a recurring and important theme in separation of powers jurisprudence. It is a judicially created doctrine that, in practical terms, permits the courts to abstain from ruling on certain disputes because they are more political in nature than legal. These are disputes that, although sometimes immensely important, are not readily susceptible of judicial resolution because the question presented is so clearly committed to another branch, or because the question is one that courts simply are not well suited to answer.

The doctrine was first enunciated by the Supreme Court in *Luther v. Borden*, 48 U.S. 1 (1849). Martin Luther was a participant in the Dorr Rebellion in Rhode Island in 1841 and 1842. The rebel "Dorrites," led by Thomas Dorr, protested against the archaic Rhode Island government that was still based on the original Rhode Island charter of 1663, and which granted suffrage only to landowners. Among other things, the rebels sought suffrage for all free white males, and they held their own convention to draft a new state constitution to that effect. Luther was arrested by state authorities and his home was searched. In response, he initiated a lawsuit for trespass and asserted that the authorities who had acted against him were illegitimate because the charter government was not the "republican form of government" mandated by the Guarantee Clause in Article IV, Section 4 of the Constitution. The Supreme Court held that the judiciary was not the proper branch to determine what is or is not a proper Article IV republican form of government. The Court concluded that this was a quintessentially political question; it is entirely for Congress to decide what government is the established one in a state, as well as its "republican character." Id. at 42.

The *Luther* holding was reiterated 63 years later in *Pacific States Telephone v. Oregon*, 223 U.S. 118 (1912). This was a challenge to Oregon's initiative system on the grounds that direct democracy -- the enactment of legislation by the citizenry rather than the elected legislature -- was antithetical to the notion of republican government. The Court again held that this was the sort of question best answered by Congress and not the courts, and was therefore a non-justiciable political question.

Given the origins of the political question doctrine in disputes about voting rights, it is fitting that the best-known and most often cited explication of the doctrine came in another case about voting rights. It may be ironic, though, that the Court in this case chose not to apply the doctrine and determined that the case should be decided on the merits.

Baker v. Carr was a challenge to Tennessee's voting districts under the Equal Protection Clause of the Fourteenth Amendment. Despite the requirement of the state's constitution to reapportion state voting districts every 10 years, Tennessee had not reapportioned in 60 years. Over this period, the population in certain rural districts had substantially decreased and the population in certain suburban and urban districts had substantially increased, which meant that each rural voter's vote effectively carried more weight in electing state legislators. Some Tennessee voters sued, claiming that the failure to reapportion and the resulting misallocation of representation in the state legislature violated the Equal Protection Clause of the Fourteenth Amendment. In response, state officials sought to characterize this as a classically political question, likening this dispute to a question whether Tennessee was providing a republican form of government. The Supreme Court disagreed, but in doing so, said much about the political question doctrine and its application.

Baker v. Carr

369 U.S. 186 (1962)[25]

MR. JUSTICE BRENNAN delivered the opinion of the Court.

[The Court reviewed the decision below and addressed questions of jurisdiction and standing. The court below had found the matter to be non-justiciable because the precedent indicated that federal courts will not intervene to order reapportionment. Justice Brennan explains that this dispute does not arise under the Guarantee Clause (which was

[25] Footnotes and some citations found in the original decision have been omitted from this excerpted version.

held non-justiciable in prior cases such as *Luther* and *Pacific StatesTelephone*) but under the Equal Protection Clause.]

[In explaining why this case does not present a non-justiciable political question,] we deem it necessary first to consider the contours of the "political question" doctrine.

Our discussion, even at the price of extending this opinion, requires review of a number of political question cases, in order to expose the attributes of the doctrine - attributes which, in various settings, diverge, combine, appear, and disappear in seeming disorderliness. Since that review is undertaken solely to demonstrate that neither singly nor collectively do these cases support a conclusion that this apportionment case is nonjusticiable, we of course do not explore their implications in other contexts . . . The nonjusticiability of a political question is primarily a function of the separation of powers. Much confusion results from the capacity of the "political question" label to obscure the need for case-by-case inquiry. Deciding whether a matter has in any measure been committed by the Constitution to another branch of government, or whether the action of that branch exceeds whatever authority has been committed, is itself a delicate exercise in constitutional interpretation, and is a responsibility of this Court as ultimate interpreter of the Constitution. To demonstrate this requires no less than to analyze representative cases and to infer from them the analytical threads that make up the political question doctrine.

* * *

Foreign relations: There are sweeping statements to the effect that all questions touching foreign relations are political questions. Not only does resolution of such issues frequently turn on standards that defy judicial application, or involve the exercise of a discretion demonstrably committed to the executive or legislature; but many such questions uniquely demand single-voiced statement of the Government's views. Yet it is error to suppose that every case or controversy which touches foreign relations lies beyond judicial cognizance. Our cases in this field seem invariably to show a discriminating analysis of the particular question posed, in terms of the history of its management by the political branches, of its susceptibility to judicial handling in the light of its nature and posture in the specific case, and of the possible consequences of judicial action. For example, though a court will not ordinarily inquire whether a treaty has been terminated, since on that question "governmental action . . . must be regarded as of controlling importance," if there has been no conclusive "governmental action" then a court can construe a treaty and may find it provides the answer. Compare Terlinden v. Ames, 184 U.S. 270, 285, with Society for the Propagation of the Gospel in Foreign Parts v. New Haven, 8 Wheat. 464, 492-495.

[As a general proposition, the political question will prevent a court from deciding when hostilities have ceased in an armed conflict.]

Validity of enactments: In Coleman v. Miller, this Court held that the questions of how long a proposed amendment to the Federal Constitution remained open to ratification, and what effect a prior rejection had on a subsequent ratification, were committed to congressional resolution and involved criteria of decision that necessarily escaped the judicial grasp. Similar considerations apply to the enacting process: "The respect due to coequal and independent departments," and the need for finality and certainty about the status of a statute contribute to judicial reluctance to inquire whether, as passed, it complied with all requisite formalities. Field v. Clark, 143 U.S. 649, 672, 676-677; see Leser v. Garnett, 258 U.S. 130, 137. But it is not true that courts will never delve into a legislature's records upon such a quest: If the enrolled statute lacks an effective date, a court will not hesitate to seek it in the legislative journals in order to preserve the enactment. Gardner v. The Collector, 6 Wall. 499. The political question doctrine, a tool for maintenance of governmental order, will not be so applied as to promote only disorder.

*   *   *

It is apparent that several formulations which vary slightly according to the settings in which the questions arise may describe a political question, although each has one or more elements which identify it as essentially a function of the separation of powers. Prominent on the surface of any case held to involve a political question is found a textually demonstrable constitutional commitment of the issue to a coordinate political department; or a lack of judicially discoverable and manageable standards for resolving it; or the impossibility of deciding without an initial policy determination of a kind clearly for nonjudicial discretion; or the impossibility of a court's undertaking independent resolution without expressing lack of the respect due coordinate branches of government; or an unusual need for unquestioning adherence to a political decision already made; or the potentiality of embarrassment from multifarious pronouncements by various departments on one question.

[The Court then reviewed the decision in *Luther v. Borden* and other cases involving the Guarantee Clause and noted that such cases presented non-justiciable political questions because the clause "is not a repository of judicially manageable standards which a court could utilize independently in order to identify a State's lawful government."]

We come, finally, to the ultimate inquiry whether our precedents as to what constitutes a nonjusticiable "political question" bring the case before us under the umbrella of that doctrine. A natural beginning is to note whether any of the common characteristics which we have been able to identify and label descriptively are present. We find none: The question here is the consistency of state action with the Federal Constitution. We have no question decided, or to be decided, by a political branch of government coequal with this Court. Nor do we risk embarrassment of our government abroad, or grave disturbance at home if we take issue with Tennessee as to the constitutionality of her action here challenged. Nor need the appellants, in order to succeed in this action, ask the Court to enter upon policy determinations for which judicially manageable standards are lacking. Judicial standards under the Equal Protection Clause are well developed and familiar, and it has been open to courts since the enactment of the Fourteenth Amendment to determine, if on the particular facts they must, that a discrimination reflects no policy, but simply arbitrary and capricious action.

* * *

We conclude that the complaint's allegations of a denial of equal protection present a justiciable constitutional cause of action upon which appellants are entitled to a trial and a decision. The right asserted is within the reach of judicial protection under the Fourteenth Amendment.

The judgment of the District Court is reversed and the cause is remanded for further proceedings consistent with this opinion.

Reversed and remanded.

[JUSTICE DOUGLAS and JUSTICE CLARK filed concurring opinions in which they agreed that the alleged mis-apportionment in Tennessee should be subject to a remedy under the Equal Protection Clause.

JUSTICE FRANKFURTER and JUSTICE HARLAN each separately dissented, arguing essentially that extensive precedent counsels against the judiciary involving itself in what is quintessentially a political question -- the structure of government and the apportioning of representation within a state by that state's legislature.]

DISCUSSION AND QUESTIONS

1. In a passage that has often been cited (in whole or in part) in subsequent decisions involving asserted political questions, Justice Brennan described the circumstances in which such non-justiciable questions arise:

> Prominent on the surface of any case held to involve a political question is found [1] a textually demonstrable constitutional commitment of the issue to a coordinate political department; or [2] a lack of judicially discoverable and manageable standards for resolving it; or [3] the impossibility of deciding without an initial policy determination of a kind clearly for nonjudicial discretion; or [4] the impossibility of a court's undertaking independent resolution without expressing lack of the respect due coordinate branches of government; or [5] an unusual need for unquestioning adherence to a political decision already made; or [6] the potentiality of embarrassment from multifarious pronouncements by various departments on one question.

How useful is this explanation to future governmental decision-makers or to future litigants? It is hardly unheard of for the courts to reverse actions taken by the two political branches; this occurs every time a federal statute is invalidated and every time a regulation, ruling or decision by an executive agency is successfully challenged in the courts. Do not all such rulings, to some degree, reflect a "lack of [] respect due coordinate branches of government" or create "the potentiality of embarrassment from multifarious pronouncements by various departments on one question"? The very role of the Judicial Branch in government under the Constitution requires that sometimes it must disagree with the other branches on important questions. In *Chadha*, the Judicial Branch disagreed with the Legislative Branch about the legislative veto (see Chapter Six, pages 157-65). In *Bowsher v. Synar*, the Judicial Branch disagreed with the Legislative Branch about the proper role of the Comptroller General (see Chapter Six, pages 168-76). In *Clinton v. New York*, the Judicial Branch disagreed with both of the other branches about the line item veto (see Chapter Three, pages 66-71). In *Youngstown*, the Judicial Branch disagreed with the Executive Branch about the scope of executive authority (see Chapter Two, pages 17-30). In the *Hamdan* and *Boumediene* cases, the Judicial Branch disagreed with the Executive Branch about the treatment of combatants detained during armed conflict (see Chapter Ten, pages 328-39, 342-55). In all of these cases, the Judicial Branch determined it was appropriate to resolve the matter on the merits, even though such resolution involved "multifarious pronouncements by various departments" and arguably a "lack of [] respect" for other branches.

The slipperiness used in explaining the doctrine and the inconsistency of its application over time have caused some commentators to express skepticism about the legitimacy of the doctrine. See, e.g., Jared S. Pettinato, *Executing the Political Question Doctrine*, 33 N. Ky. L. Rev. 61, 63 (2006) (opining that, since Brennan laid out the six prongs of the doctrine, "the Supreme Court has eroded each prong until they have become trivial affectations upon a nebulous standard . . . [s]imply put, the *Baker* factors have no cohesive guiding principle"); Michael Lewis Seidman, *The Secret Life of the Political Question Doctrine*, 37 J. Marshall L. Rev. 441, 442-43 (2004) ("the effort to make the political question problem into a 'doctrine' -- to bound it by a rule of law -- is a fool's errand"; "the court has never -- and never can -- develop constitutional rules that control the political judgments . . . that it regularly makes"; "the political question doctrine is the most dangerous concept in all of constitutional law").

2. The Supreme Court has said that the six characteristics of political question cases that are outlined by Justice Brennan in *Baker* are "probably listed in descending order of both importance and clarity." *Vieth v. Jubelirer*, 541 U.S. 267, 277-78 (2004). In practice, the first two characteristics are the ones that tell the tale. Political question cases are characterized by the presence of either -- and often the presence of both -- a clear constitutional commitment of the issue to another branch or the absence of judicially manageable standards.

THE UNCERTAINTY INHERENT IN THE DOCTRINE

In some cases, the application of the political question doctrine would seem to be straightforward and, indeed, even obvious. One such case arose from the Kent State shootings in May of 1970. In that tragedy, Ohio National Guardsmen were engaged in crowd control efforts in response to anti-war protests by students of Kent State University. For reasons that are still debated, and after tear gas and other methods were used in attempts to disperse the protesters, members of the Guard fired on students, killing four and wounding several others. Several investigations followed, as well as litigation that included the case of *Gilligan v. Morgan*, 413 U.S. 1 (1973), which was ultimately resolved by the Supreme Court on political question grounds. Students sued the Governor of Ohio claiming that the Ohio National Guard had violated their civil rights in various ways. They sought injunctive relief in the form of restraints on when and how the Guard could be deployed in the future. As Chief Justice Burger, writing for a five-justice majority, noted, "this is not a case in which damages are sought . . . Nor is it an action seeking a restraining order against some specified and imminently threatened unlawful action. Rather, it is a broad call on judicial power to assume continuing regulatory jurisdiction over the activities of the Ohio National Guard." Chief Justice Burger went on to explain why the dispute was not susceptible of judicial resolution:

> [Article I, Section 8 of the Constitution] is explicit that the Congress shall have the responsibility for organizing, arming, and disciplining the Militia (now the National Guard), with certain responsibilities being reserved to the respective States. Congress has enacted appropriate legislation pursuant to Art. I, 8, cl. 16, and has also authorized the President -- as the Commander in Chief of the Armed Forces -- to prescribe regulations governing organization and discipline of the National Guard. The Guard is an essential reserve component of the Armed Forces of the United States, available with regular forces in time of war. The Guard also may be federalized in addition to its role under state governments, to assist in controlling civil disorders. The relief sought by respondents, requiring initial judicial review and continuing surveillance by a federal court over the training, weaponry, and orders of the Guard, would therefore embrace critical areas of responsibility vested by the Constitution in the Legislative and Executive Branches of the Government.
>
> * * *
>
> It would be difficult to think of a clearer example of the type of governmental action that was intended by the Constitution to be left to the political branches directly responsible -- as the Judicial Branch is not -- to the electoral process. Moreover, it is difficult to conceive of an area of governmental activity in which the courts have less competence. The complex, subtle, and professional decisions as to the composition, training, equipping, and control of a military force are essentially professional military judgments, subject always to civilian control of the Legislative and

> Executive Branches. The ultimate responsibility for these decisions is appropriately vested in branches of the government which are periodically subject to electoral accountability.

In *Gilligan*, the dispute revolved around matters that are unequivocally committed by the Constitution to the political branches, and it involved a subject with respect to which the courts have no competence. Thus, the first two political question characteristics set forth in *Baker v. Carr* were present, and the Court (albeit a divided one) determined that it should refrain from addressing the merits. Other cases, however, reveal that the commentators who have criticized the political question doctrine as unprincipled, or at least vague, have a point.

Powell v. McCormack

395 U.S. 486 (1969)[26]

> MR. CHIEF JUSTICE WARREN delivered the opinion of the Court.
>
> In November 1966, petitioner Adam Clayton Powell, Jr., was duly elected from the 18th Congressional District of New York to serve in the United States House of Representatives for the 90th Congress. However, pursuant to a House resolution, he was not permitted to take his seat. Powell (and some of the voters of his district) then filed suit in Federal District Court, claiming that the House could exclude him only if it found he failed to meet the standing requirements of age, citizenship, and residence contained in Art. I, 2, of the Constitution - requirements the House specifically found Powell met - and thus had excluded him unconstitutionally.
>
> [During the 89th Congress (1965-66), Congressman Powell was investigated for improprieties relating to the use of official funds. No formal action was taken during that Congress. However, after he won re-election and the 90th Congress convened in January of 1967, Powell was denied the opportunity to take the oath of office and a Select Committee was convened to determine his "eligibility" to take his seat. The committee concluded that Powell met the technical eligibility requirements, but recommended that he be censured and fined for certain violations of House ethics rules. The full House debated the committee's report and recommendation, rejected the recommended punishment, and instead voted 307 to 116 in favor of

[26] Footnotes and some citations found in the original decision have been omitted from this excerpted version.

excluding Powell from the House. Powell argues, among other things, that the House's decision to exclude him violated the Constitution, which sets forth at Article I, Section 2 the exclusive eligibility requirements for the seating of House members: age, citizenship and residency. In response, the House argues that its decision to exclude a member is not subject to judicial review because Article I, Section 5 mandates that "each house shall be the judge of the elections, returns and qualifications of its own members."]

The resolution excluding petitioner Powell was adopted by a vote in excess of two-thirds of the 434 Members of Congress - 307 to 116. 113 Cong. Rec. 5037-5038. Article I, 5, grants the House authority to expel a member "with the Concurrence of two thirds." Respondents assert that the House may expel a member for any reason whatsoever and that, since a two-thirds vote was obtained, the procedure by which Powell was denied his seat in the 90th Congress should be regarded as an expulsion, not an exclusion.

[Further, the House's own rules indicate that it will not expel a member for conduct that occurred prior to his membership in the current Congress. Powell had not been seated before the exclusion vote was taken; consequently, the House, by its own rules, could not have expelled him for any alleged conduct in which he engaged as a member.]

The Speaker ruled that House Resolution No. 278 contemplated an exclusion proceeding. We must reject respondents' suggestion that we overrule the Speaker and hold that, although the House manifested an intent to exclude Powell, its action should be tested by whatever standards may govern an expulsion.

* * *

[Now] we must determine whether the structure of the Federal Government renders the issue presented a "political question" - that is, a question which is not justiciable in federal court because of the separation of powers provided by the Constitution.

* * *

Respondents' first contention is that this case presents a political question because under Art. I, 5, there has been a "textually demonstrable constitutional commitment" to the House of the "adjudicatory power" to determine Powell's qualifications. Thus it is argued that the House, and the House alone, has power to determine who is qualified to be a member.

In order to determine whether there has been a textual commitment to a co-ordinate department of the Government, we must interpret the Constitution. In other words, we must first determine what power the Constitution confers upon the House through Art. I, 5, before we can determine to what extent, if any, the exercise of that power is subject to judicial review. Respondents maintain that the House has broad power under 5, and, they argue, the House may determine which are the qualifications necessary for membership. On the other hand, petitioners allege that the Constitution provides that an elected representative may be denied his seat only if the House finds he does not meet one of the standing qualifications expressly prescribed by the Constitution.

* * *

[The Court then undertook an extensive review of the English historical precedent relating to expulsion and exclusion, as well as the pertinent legislative history from the Constitutional Convention.]

Had the intent of the Framers emerged from these materials with less clarity, we would nevertheless have been compelled to resolve any ambiguity in favor of a narrow construction of the scope of Congress' power to exclude members-elect. A fundamental principle of our representative democracy is, in Hamilton's words, "that the people should choose whom they please to govern them." 2 Elliot's Debates 257. As Madison pointed out at the Convention, this principle is undermined as much by limiting whom the people can select as by limiting the franchise itself. In apparent agreement with this basic philosophy, the Convention adopted his suggestion limiting the power to expel. To allow essentially that same power to be exercised under the guise of judging qualifications, would be to ignore Madison's warning, borne out in the Wilkes case and some of Congress' own post-Civil War exclusion cases, against "vesting an improper & dangerous power in the Legislature." 2 Farrand 249. Moreover, it would effectively nullify the Convention's decision to require a two-thirds vote for expulsion. Unquestionably, Congress has an interest in preserving its institutional integrity, but in most cases that interest can be sufficiently safeguarded by the exercise of its power to punish its members for disorderly behavior and, in extreme cases, to expel a member with the concurrence of two-thirds. In short, both the intention of the Framers, to the extent it can be determined, and an examination of the basic principles of our democratic system persuade us that the Constitution does not vest in the Congress a discretionary power to deny membership by a majority vote.

For these reasons, we have concluded that Art. I, 5, is at most a "textually demonstrable commitment" to Congress to judge only the qualifications expressly set forth in the Constitution. Therefore, the "textual commitment" formulation of the political question doctrine does not bar federal courts from adjudicating petitioners' claims.

Respondents' alternate contention is that the case presents a political question because judicial resolution of petitioners' claim would produce a "potentially embarrassing confrontation between coordinate branches" of the Federal Government. But, as our interpretation of Art. I, 5, discloses, a determination of petitioner Powell's right to sit would require no more than an interpretation of the Constitution. Such a determination falls within the traditional role accorded courts to interpret the law, and does not involve a "lack of the respect due [a] co-ordinate [branch] of government," nor does it involve an "initial policy determination of a kind clearly for non-judicial discretion." Baker v. Carr, 369 U.S. 186, at 217. Our system of government requires that federal courts on occasion interpret the Constitution in a manner at variance with the construction given the document by another branch. The alleged conflict that such an adjudication may cause cannot justify the courts' avoiding their constitutional responsibility.

[JUSTICE DOUGLAS concurred and JUSTICE STEWART dissented on the basis that the case had been mooted by events subsequent to Congressman Powell's exclusion.]

The *Powell* Court was willing to involve itself in the House's decision to exclude a member even though, arguably at least, this decision was (to use the terminology of *Baker v. Carr*) the subject of "a textually demonstrable constitutional commitment of the issue to a coordinate political department." Contrast the Court's approach in *Powell* with its approach 24 years later in the following case, *Nixon v. United States*.

United States District Judge Walter Nixon was convicted of perjury in 1986 and sentenced to five years in prison. Because he refused to resign from the federal bench, he continued to draw his salary as a federal judge for the first three years of his prison sentence, until the Senate convicted him on impeachment charges in November 1989. Had he not been convicted in Senate impeachment proceedings, this convicted felon could have resumed his seat as a federal judge upon completing his sentence.

Nixon challenged the Senate's procedure for trying and convicting him. Senate Rule XI permitted a committee of senators to review the evidence and report their findings to the full Senate, which then voted to convict. Nixon asserts that this procedure violates the constitutional requirement that he be "tried" by the Senate.

(Interestingly, 30 years earlier, Judge Nixon had been counsel to *amici curiae* supporting the voters who challenged Tennessee's electoral mis-apportionment in *Baker v. Carr*. In *Baker*, Nixon was on the winning side in arguing against application of the political question doctrine. When his interests were more personal three decades later, he again argued against application of the doctrine -- this time unsuccessfully.)

Nixon v. United States

506 U.S. 224 (1993)[27]

CHIEF JUSTICE REHNQUIST delivered the opinion of the Court.

Petitioner Walter L. Nixon, Jr., asks this Court to decide whether Senate Rule XI, which allows a committee of Senators to hear evidence against an individual who has been impeached and to report that evidence to the full Senate, violates the Impeachment Trial Clause, Art. I, 3, cl. 6. That Clause provides that the "Senate shall have the sole Power to try all Impeachments." But before we reach the merits of such a claim, we must decide whether it is "justiciable," that is, whether it is a claim that may be resolved by the courts. We conclude that it is not.

* * *

A controversy is nonjusticiable - i.e., involves a political question - where there is "a textually demonstrable constitutional commitment of the issue to a coordinate political department; or a lack of judicially discoverable and manageable standards for resolving it. . . ." Baker v. Carr, 369 U.S. 186, 217 (1962). But the courts must, in the first instance, interpret the text in question and determine whether and to what extent the issue is textually committed. See ibid; Powell v. McCormack, 395 U.S. 486, 519, (1969). As the discussion that

[27] Footnotes and some citations found in the original decision have been omitted from this excerpted version.

follows makes clear, the concept of a textual commitment to a coordinate political department is not completely separate from the concept of a lack of judicially discoverable and manageable standards for resolving it; the lack of judicially manageable standards may strengthen the conclusion that there is a textually demonstrable commitment to a coordinate branch.

In this case, we must examine Art. I, 3, cl. 6, to determine the scope of authority conferred upon the Senate by the Framers regarding impeachment. It provides:

> The Senate shall have the sole Power to try all Impeachments. When sitting for that Purpose, they shall be on Oath or Affirmation. When the President of the United States is tried, the Chief Justice shall preside: And no Person shall be convicted without the Concurrence of two thirds of the Members present.

The language and structure of this Clause are revealing. The first sentence is a grant of authority to the Senate, and the word "sole" indicates that this authority is reposed in the Senate, and nowhere else. The next two sentences specify requirements to which the Senate proceedings shall conform: The Senate shall be on oath or affirmation, a two-thirds vote is required to convict, and when the President is tried the Chief Justice shall preside.

Petitioner argues that the word "try" in the first sentence imposes by implication an additional requirement on the Senate, in that the proceedings must be in the nature of a judicial trial. From there petitioner goes on to argue that this limitation precludes the Senate from delegating to a select committee the task of hearing the testimony of witnesses, as was done pursuant to Senate Rule XI. "[T]ry" means more than simply "vote on" or "review" or "judge." In 1787 and today, trying a case means hearing the evidence, not scanning a cold record. Brief for Petitioner 25. Petitioner concludes from this that courts may review whether or not the Senate "tried" him before convicting him.

There are several difficulties with this position which lead us ultimately to reject it. The word "try," both in 1787 and later, has considerably broader meanings than those to which petitioner would limit it.

* * *

The conclusion that the use of the word "try" in the first sentence of the Impeachment Trial Clause lacks sufficient precision to afford any judicially manageable standard of review of the Senate's actions is fortified by the existence of the three very specific requirements that the Constitution does impose on the Senate when trying impeachments: The Members must be under oath, a two-thirds vote is required to convict, and the Chief Justice presides when the President is tried. These limitations are quite precise, and their nature suggests that the Framers did not intend to impose additional limitations on the form of the Senate proceedings by the use of the word "try" in the first sentence.

Petitioner devotes only two pages in his brief to negating the significance of the word "sole" in the first sentence of Clause 6. As noted above, that sentence provides that "[t]he Senate shall have the sole Power to try all Impeachments." We think that the word "sole" is of considerable significance. Indeed, the word "sole" appears only one other time in the Constitution - with respect to the House of Representatives' "sole Power of Impeachment." Art. I, 2, cl. 5. The commonsense meaning of the word "sole" is that the Senate alone shall have authority to determine whether an individual should be acquitted or convicted. The dictionary definition bears this out. "Sole" is defined as "having no companion," "solitary," "being the only one," and "functioning . . . independently and without assistance or interference." Webster's Third New International Dictionary 2168 (1971). If the courts may review the actions of the Senate in order to determine whether that body "tried" an impeached official, it is difficult to see how the Senate would be "functioning . . . independently and without assistance or interference."

* * *

The history and contemporary understanding of the impeachment provisions support our reading of the constitutional language. The parties do not offer evidence of a single word in the history of the Constitutional Convention or in contemporary commentary that even alludes to the possibility of judicial review in the context of the impeachment powers.

* * *

[J]udicial review would be inconsistent with the Framers' insistence that our system be one of checks and balances. In our constitutional system, impeachment was designed to be the only check on the Judicial Branch by the Legislature . . . Judicial involvement in impeachment proceedings, even if only for purposes of judicial review, is counterintuitive, because it would eviscerate the "important constitutional check" placed on the Judiciary by the Framers. Nixon's argument would place final reviewing authority with respect to impeachments in the hands of the same body that the impeachment process is meant to regulate.

* * *

Petitioner finally contends that a holding of nonjusticiability cannot be reconciled with our opinion in Powell v. McCormack, 395 U.S. 486 (1969). The relevant issue in Powell was whether courts could review the House of Representatives' conclusion that Powell was "unqualified" to sit as a Member because he had been accused of misappropriating public funds and abusing the process of the New York courts. We stated that the question of justiciability turned on whether the Constitution committed authority to the House to judge its Members' qualifications, and if so, the extent of that commitment. Id., at 519, 521. Article I, 5, provides that "Each House shall be the Judge of the Elections, Returns and Qualifications of its own Members." In turn, Art. I, 2, specifies three requirements for membership in the House: the candidate must be at least 25 years of age, a citizen of the United States for no less than seven years, and an inhabitant of the State he is chosen to represent. We held that, in light of the three requirements specified in the Constitution, the word "qualifications" -- of which the House was to be the Judge -- was of a precise, limited nature. Id., at 522; see also The Federalist, No. 60, p. 409 (J. Cooke ed. 1961) ("The qualifications of the persons who may choose or be chosen, as has been remarked upon another occasion, are defined and fixed in the constitution; and are unalterable by the legislature") (quoted in Powell, supra, 395 U.S., at 539).

Our conclusion in Powell was based on the fixed meaning of "[q]ualifications" set forth in Art. I, 2. The claim by the House that its power to "be the Judge of the Elections, Returns and Qualifications of its own Members" was a textual commitment of unreviewable authority was defeated by the existence of this separate provision specifying the only qualifications which might be imposed for House membership. The decision as to whether a Member satisfied these qualifications was placed with the House, but the decision as to what these qualifications consisted of was not.

In the case before us, there is no separate provision of the Constitution that could be defeated by allowing the Senate final authority to determine the meaning of the word "try" in the Impeachment Trial

Clause. We agree with Nixon that courts possess power to review either legislative or executive action that transgresses identifiable textual limits. As we have made clear, "whether the action of [either the Legislative or Executive Branch] exceeds whatever authority has been committed is itself a delicate exercise in constitutional interpretation, and is a responsibility of this Court as ultimate interpreter of the Constitution." Baker v. Carr, supra, at 211; accord, Powell, supra, at 521. But we conclude, after exercising that delicate responsibility, that the word "try" in the Impeachment Trial Clause does not provide an identifiable textual limit on the authority which is committed to the Senate.

[JUSTICE STEVENS concurred.]

JUSTICE SOUTER concurred and explained that, at some outer limit of arbitrariness in Senate impeachment procedures -- for example, if a coin toss were used to determined guilt or innocence -- "judicial interference might well be appropriate."

JUSTICE WHITE concurred, but argued that the political question doctrine should not be applied to prevent the Court from evaluating whether the method used by the Senate met constitutional requirements. Justice White notes that the finding of "a clear textual commitment" of a matter to another branch cannot be sufficient to warrant judicial abstention from a dispute. The Constitution grants "*all* legislative power" to the House and Senate, "yet the Court has never thought it would unduly interfere with the operation of the Legislative Branch to entertain difficult and important questions as to the extent of the legislative power." Rather, the proper question is "whether the Constitution has given one of the political branches final responsibility for interpreting the scope and nature of such a power."]

Powell and *Nixon* both represent occasions on which the Court weighed whether it should intrude into matters that were confined exclusively within the Legislative Branch; these were not struggles between the two political branches. At least as often, political question analysis takes place when there is disagreement between the Legislative Branch and the Executive Branch. One such occasion is found in *Goldwater v. Carter,* which resulted in a fractured decision by the Supreme Court, thereby reflecting the indeterminate nature of the political question doctrine.

Goldwater stemmed from President Jimmy Carter's decision to terminate unilaterally a mutual defense treaty between the United States and Taiwan, in an effort to improve U.S. relations with the People's Republic of China. Senator Barry Goldwater (Republican representing Arizona) and other legislators challenged President Carter's authority to terminate the treaty, arguing that, because Senate approval is necessary to ratify a treaty, Senate permission is also necessary to terminate a treaty. The D.C. Circuit, sitting *en banc*, ruled that Senate approval is not necessary for presidential termination of an international treaty. The court's conclusion rested, among other things, on the President's primary role in the conduct of international relations and on the absence of an explicit constitutional requirement of Senate approval to terminate a treaty.

The Supreme Court issued a *per curiam* order vacating the D.C. Circuit's decision and remanding the case to the district court with instructions that the legislators' complaint be dismissed. In concurring opinions, the justices expressed differing views as to whether this dispute between the two political branches raised a non-justiciable political question.

Goldwater v. Carter

444 U.S. 996 (1979)[28]

The petition for a writ of certiorari is granted. The judgment of the Court of Appeals is vacated and the case is remanded to the District Court with directions to dismiss the complaint.

Mr. Justice POWELL, concurring.

Although I agree with the result reached by the Court, I would dismiss the complaint as not ripe for judicial review.

This Court has recognized that an issue should not be decided if it is not ripe for judicial review. Buckley v. Valeo, 424 U.S. 1, 113-114 (1976) (per curiam). Prudential considerations persuade me that a dispute between Congress and the President is not ready for judicial review unless and until each branch has taken action asserting its constitutional authority. Differences between the President and the Congress are commonplace under our system. The differences should, and almost invariably do, turn on political rather than legal considerations. The Judicial Branch should not decide issues affecting the allocation of power between the President and Congress until the political branches reach a constitutional impasse. Otherwise, we

[28] Footnotes and some citations found in the original decision have been omitted from this excerpted version.

would encourage small groups or even individual Members of Congress to seek judicial resolution of issues before the normal political process has the opportunity to resolve the conflict.

In this case, a few Members of Congress claim that the President's action in terminating the treaty with Taiwan has deprived them of their constitutional role with respect to a change in the supreme law of the land. Congress has taken no official action. In the present posture of this case, we do not know whether there ever will be an actual confrontation between the Legislative and Executive Branches . . . If the Congress chooses not to confront the President, it is not our task to do so. I therefore concur in the dismissal of this case.

Mr. Justice Rehnquist suggests, however, that the issue presented by this case is a nonjusticiable political question which can never be considered by this Court. I cannot agree. In my view, reliance upon the political-question doctrine is inconsistent with our precedents. As set forth in the seminal case of Baker v. Carr, 369 U.S. 186, 217 (1962), the doctrine incorporates three inquiries: (i) Does the issue involve resolution of questions committed by the text of the Constitution to a coordinate branch of Government? (ii) Would resolution of the question demand that a court move beyond areas of judicial expertise? (iii) Do prudential considerations counsel against judicial intervention? In my opinion the answer to each of these inquiries would require us to decide this case if it were ready for review.

First, the existence of "a textually demonstrable constitutional commitment of the issue to a coordinate political department," ibid., turns on an examination of the constitutional provisions governing the exercise of the power in question. Powell v. McCormack, 395 U.S. 486, 519 (1969). No constitutional provision explicitly confers upon the President the power to terminate treaties. Further, Art. II, 2, of the Constitution authorizes the President to make treaties with the advice and consent of the Senate. Article VI provides that treaties shall be a part of the supreme law of the land. These provisions add support to the view that the text of the Constitution does not unquestionably commit the power to terminate treaties to the President alone. Cf. Gilligan v. Morgan, 413 U.S. 1, 6 (1973); Luther v. Borden, 7 How. 1, 42 (1849).

Second, there is no "lack of judicially discoverable and manageable standards for resolving" this case; nor is a decision impossible "without an initial policy determination of a kind clearly for nonjudicial discretion." Baker v. Carr, supra, 369 U.S., at 217. We are asked to decide whether the President may terminate a treaty under the Constitution without congressional approval. Resolution of the question may not be easy, but it only requires us to apply normal principles of interpretation to the constitutional provisions at issue. See Powell v. McCormack, supra, 395 U.S., at 548-549. The present case involves neither review of the President's activities as Commander in Chief nor impermissible interference in the field of foreign affairs. Such a case would arise if we were asked to decide, for example, whether a treaty required the President to order troops into a foreign country. But "it is error to suppose that every case or controversy which touches foreign relations lies beyond judicial cognizance." Baker v. Carr, supra, 369 U.S., at 211. This case "touches" foreign relations, but the question presented to us concerns only the constitutional division of power between Congress and the President.

A simple hypothetical demonstrates the confusion that I find inherent in Mr. Justice Rehnquist's opinion concurring in the judgment. Assume that the President signed a mutual defense treaty with a foreign country and announced that it would go into effect despite its rejection by the Senate. Under Mr. Justice Rehnquist's analysis that situation would present a political question even though Art. II, 2, clearly would resolve the dispute. Although the answer to the hypothetical case seems self-evident because it demands textual rather than interstitial analysis, the nature of the legal issue presented is no different from the issue presented in the case before us. In both cases, the Court would interpret the Constitution to decide whether congressional approval is necessary to give a Presidential decision on the validity of a treaty the force of law. Such an inquiry demands no special competence or information beyond the reach of the Judiciary. Cf. Chicago & Southern Air Lines v. Waterman S.S. Corp., 333 U.S. 103, 111 (1948).

Finally, the political-question doctrine rests in part on prudential concerns calling for mutual respect among the three branches of Government. Thus, the Judicial Branch should avoid "the potentiality of embarrassment [that would result] from multifarious pronouncements by various departments on one question." Similarly, the doctrine restrains judicial action where there is an "unusual need for unquestioning adherence to a political decision already made." Baker v. Carr, supra, 369 U.S., at 217.

If this case were ripe for judicial review, none of these prudential considerations would be present. Interpretation of the Constitution does not imply lack of respect for a coordinate branch. Powell v.

McCormack, supra, 395 U.S., at 548. If the President and the Congress had reached irreconcilable positions, final disposition of the question presented by this case would eliminate, rather than create, multiple constitutional interpretations. The specter of the Federal Government brought to a halt because of the mutual intransigence of the President and the Congress would require this Court to provide a resolution pursuant to our duty "'to say what the law is.'" United States v. Nixon, 418 U.S. 683, 703 (1974), quoting Marbury v. Madison, 1 Cranch 137, 177 (1803).

In my view, the suggestion that this case presents a political question is incompatible with this Court's willingness on previous occasions to decide whether one branch of our Government has impinged upon the power of another. See Buckley v. Valeo, 424 U.S., at 138; United States v. Nixon, supra, 418 U.S., at 707; The Pocket Veto Case, 279 U.S. 655, 676-678 (1929); Myers v. United States, 272 U.S. 52 (1926). Under the criteria enunciated in Baker v. Carr, we have the responsibility to decide whether both the Executive and Legislative Branches have constitutional roles to play in termination of a treaty. If the Congress, by appropriate formal action, had challenged the President's authority to terminate the treaty with Taiwan, the resulting uncertainty could have serious consequences for our country. In that situation, it would be the duty of this Court to resolve the issue.

Mr. Justice REHNQUIST, with whom THE CHIEF JUSTICE, Mr. Justice STEWART, and Mr. Justice STEVENS join, concurring in the judgment.

I am of the view that the basic question presented by the petitioners in this case is "political" and therefore nonjusticiable because it involves the authority of the President in the conduct of our country's foreign relations and the extent to which the Senate or the Congress is authorized to negate the action of the President. In Coleman v. Miller, 307 U.S. 433 (1939), a case in which members of the Kansas Legislature brought an action attacking a vote of the State Senate in favor of the ratification of the Child Labor Amendment, Mr. Chief Justice Hughes wrote in what is referred to as the "Opinion of the Court":

> We think that . . . the question of the efficacy of ratifications by state legislatures, in the light of previous rejection or attempted withdrawal, should be regarded as a political question pertaining to the political departments, with the ultimate authority in the

> Congress in the exercise of its control over the promulgation of the adoption of the Amendment.
>
> The precise question as now raised is whether, when the legislature of the State, as we have found, has actually ratified the proposed amendment, the Court should restrain the state officers from certifying the ratification to the Secretary of State, because of an earlier rejection, and thus prevent the question from coming before the political departments. We find no basis in either Constitution or statute for such judicial action. Article V, speaking solely of ratification, contains no provision as to rejection. . . .

Id., at 450.

Thus, Mr. Chief Justice Hughes' opinion concluded that "Congress in controlling the promulgation of the adoption of a constitutional amendment has the final determination of the question whether by lapse of time its proposal of the amendment had lost its vitality prior to the required ratifications." Id., at 456.

I believe it follows *a fortiori* from Coleman that the controversy in the instant case is a nonjusticiable political dispute that should be left for resolution by the Executive and Legislative Branches of the Government. Here, while the Constitution is express as to the manner in which the Senate shall participate in the ratification of a treaty, it is silent as to that body's participation in the abrogation of a treaty. In this respect the case is directly analogous to Coleman, supra. As stated in Dyer v. Blair, 390 F.Supp. 1291, 1302 (N.D.Ill.1975) (three-judge court):

> A question that might be answered in different ways for different amendments must surely be controlled by political standards rather than standards easily characterized as judicially manageable.

In light of the absence of any constitutional provision governing the termination of a treaty, and the fact that different termination procedures may be appropriate for different treaties, the instant case in my view also "must surely be controlled by political standards."

I think that the justifications for concluding that the question here is political in nature are even more compelling than in Coleman because it involves foreign relations -- specifically a treaty commitment to use military force in the defense of a foreign government if attacked. In United States v. Curtiss-Wright Corp., 299 U.S. 304 (1936), this Court said:

> Whether, if the Joint Resolution had related solely to internal affairs it would be open to the challenge that it constituted an unlawful delegation of legislative power to the Executive, we find it unnecessary to determine. The whole aim of the resolution is to affect a situation entirely external to the United States, and falling within the category of foreign affairs. . . .

Id., at 315.

The present case differs in several important respects from Youngstown Sheet & Tube Co. v. Sawyer, 343 U.S. 579 (1952), cited by petitioners as authority both for reaching the merits of this dispute and for reversing the Court of Appeals. In Youngstown, private litigants brought a suit contesting the President's authority under his war powers to seize the Nation's steel industry, an action of profound and demonstrable domestic impact. Here, by contrast, we are asked to settle a dispute between coequal branches of our Government, each of which has resources available to protect and assert its interests, resources not available to private litigants outside the judicial forum. Moreover, as in Curtiss-Wright, the effect of this action, as far as we can tell, is "entirely external to the United States, and [falls] within the category of foreign affairs." Finally, as already noted, the situation presented here is closely akin to that presented in Coleman, where the Constitution spoke only to the procedure for ratification of an amendment, not to its rejection.

[Justices BLACKMUN and BRENNAN issued separate, brief dissenting opinions.]

DISCUSSION AND QUESTIONS

1. In *Powell*, the Court was willing to evaluate on the merits -- and to overturn -- the decision by a legislative chamber to exclude one of its own members. In *Nixon*, the Court was unwilling to intrude into the decision of one chamber to remove a federal judge. Is there inconsistency in how the Court handled these two situations? Chief Justice Rehnquist rationalized the contrasting outcomes by explaining that there was a fixed and judicially discernible meaning to the concept of

"qualifications" for membership in the House, while there was no such discernible meaning attached to the concept of a "trial" in impeachment proceedings. Stated differently, the Judicial Branch felt itself fully capable of determining the qualifications for membership in a separate branch, but incapable of determining what constitutes a trial. The Constitution sets the standard of conduct for federal judges as "good behaviour." Article III, Section 1. A judge who deviates from "good behaviour" is subject to removal by impeachment. Suppose that Walter Nixon had challenged his Senate conviction by arguing that the Senate had not properly applied the "good behaviour" standard. Should a federal court resolve the claim on the merits, or should the court apply the political question doctrine and decline to address the claim on the theory that federal judges lack judicially manageable standards to evaluate what is and is not "good behaviour" for federal judges?

2. In *Nixon*, Chief Justice Rehnquist concluded that a political question was presented because the Constitution expressly committed to the Senate the responsibility for trying impeachments ("the word 'sole' indicates that this authority is reposed in the Senate, and nowhere else"). But 14 years earlier, in *Goldwater*, then- Justice Rehnquist concluded that it was constitutional *silence* that mandated application of the doctrine (it is "the absence of any constitutional provision governing the termination of a treaty" that makes it a political question). Does Chief Justice Rehnquist's inconsistency on the "clear commitment" prong of the political question doctrine shed any light on the doctrine itself? While the "clear commitment" prong can sometimes be helpful in explaining the Court's decision to abstain from a particular dispute, it is the "judicially manageable standards" prong on which the doctrine truly turns. In practice, it is the lack of judicially manageable standards that determines whether there is (or is not) a clear commitment of the question to another branch. When the Court perceives that it lacks rules or standards that it can comfortably and competently utilize in resolving a given constitutional question about the role or authority of another branch, it realizes that the Framers intended for the Judicial Branch to play no role in the matter.

3. In most matters that come before the Senate, debate is unlimited, which means that a filibuster can be employed to delay a vote indefinitely. Under Senate Rule XXII, concurrence of "three fifths of the senators duly chosen and sworn" is required to invoke "cloture" and end debate. As a consequence, it is sometimes lamented that nothing of consequence can happen in the Senate without the approval of a 60-senator super-majority. However, as part of the Budget Act of 1974, a procedure called "reconciliation" was enacted, by which certain matters related strictly to taxing and spending can be subject to a limit of just 20 hours of debate. The reconciliation rules represent an unusual instance in which Senate procedural rules are codified as law. 2 U.S.C. §641. For a measure that proceeds

under "reconciliation," there can be no filibuster, cloture is unnecessary, and a simple majority vote is all that is needed to pass the measure. There are strict limitations as to the types of measures that can proceed under reconciliation. Such measures must effect a change in outlays or revenues. Other matters are considered "extraneous" and may be challenged under a point of order known as the "Byrd Rule" (named for Robert Byrd, the Democratic senator from West Virginia who sponsored the rule). 2 U.S.C. §644. When a point of order is raised during Senate debate, the Presiding Officer of the Senate rules on the question. If the senator raising the point of order is dissatisfied with the ruling, he may appeal the ruling to the full Senate.

Imagine these circumstances: The majority party in the Senate wishes to pass controversial legislation and, in order to avoid a filibuster by the minority, chooses to do so under the reconciliation procedures codified at 2 U.S.C. §§641-644. But the legislation would make substantive policy changes that go well beyond taxing and spending, and therefore contains "extraneous matter" that can be challenged under the Byrd Rule. During consideration of this legislation, a senator from the minority party raises a point of order that the legislation cannot properly be processed under reconciliation rules because it contains extraneous matter. The Presiding Officer (a member of the majority party) rules that the legislation does not contain extraneous matter and overrules the point of order. When the question is appealed to the full Senate, the majority party votes as a bloc to sustain the ruling. The bill passes the Senate with a simple majority vote along party lines, the same measure passes in the House, and it is signed into law by the President.

Should the federal courts entertain a challenge to this law on the basis that it was not validly passed in the Senate -- that it was passed under reconciliation procedures even though it was ineligible for these special procedures? Would this challenge present a non-justiciable political question? On one hand, as in *Nixon*, it seems unlikely that the courts would feel comfortable passing judgment on a matter of internal Senate procedures. Article I, Section 5 provides that "each house may determine the rules of its proceedings," which appears to be a clear commitment to the Senate of the authority for managing its internal deliberations and voting. Further, in *Field v. Clark*, 143 U.S. 649 (1892), the Supreme Court indicated that it was not the role of the judiciary to scrutinize the proceedings of the legislature to tease out details as to how -- or even whether -- legislation had been duly enacted:

> The signing by the Speaker of the House of Representatives and by the President of the Senate, in open session, of an enrolled bill is an official attestation by the two houses of such bill as one that has passed Congress. It is a declaration by the two houses, through their presiding officers, to the

> President that a bill, thus attested, has received, in due form, the sanction of the legislative branch of the government and that it is delivered to him in obedience to the constitutional requirement that all bills which pass Congress shall be presented to him. And when a bill thus attested receives his approval and is deposited in the public archives, its authentication as a bill that has passed Congress should be deemed complete and unimpeachable.

143 U.S. at 672. On the other hand, the particular Senate rules at issue have been given the force of law through formal codification. The United States Code explains the reconciliation process and the circumstances in which it can properly be utilized, provides a definition of "extraneous matter," and details how points of order are to be raised and resolved by the Senate. Does not this codification of Senate procedure provide the courts with judicially manageable standards by which to evaluate the propriety of the reconciliation process?

CHAPTER NINE: THE SHARED AND RESPECTIVE WAR POWERS OF THE POLITICAL BRANCHES

HISTORICAL PERSPECTIVE

At Article I, Section 8, the Constitution gives to Congress the "power . . . to declare war." Congress is also given the responsibility to "raise and support armies" and "provide and maintain a navy," and the authority "to make rules for the government and regulation of the land and naval forces." Article II, Section 2 makes the President "commander in chief of the army and navy of the United States." If this allocation of military authority were taken at face value, one might conclude that Congress is the institution that creates and funds the armed forces and decides when they should be used in war, while the President commands the armed forces as they prepare for and prosecute such war. However, the true scope of presidential authority, and the relative powers of the branches, in circumstances of armed conflict have been and continue to be hotly debated. No topic within the study of separation of powers is more important or more contentious.

In the more than two centuries since the War Powers Clause went into effect, Congress has formally declared war five times. These occasions were:

- The War of 1812
- The Mexican-American War (1846)
- The Spanish-American War (1898)
- World War I (1917)
- World War II (1941)

Notably, the costliest armed conflict in terms of American lives lost -- the Civil War -- was not a declared war.

Although there has been no formally declared war since the end of World War II in 1945, the United States has nevertheless been deeply involved in the armed conflicts known as the Korean War and the Vietnam War, two armed conflicts in the Persian Gulf, and an armed conflict in Afghanistan. Only one of these involvements in armed conflict abroad resulted directly from an attack against the United States (Afghanistan, which was a response to the terrorist attacks of September 11, 2001). How is it that the United States can send tens of thousands of its armed forces to engage in armed conflict abroad without a precipitating attack on the United States or a formal declaration of war? How can such undertakings be legal -- under either U.S. law or international law?

American involvement in Korea was based on international law in the form of a resolution by the United Nations. United Nations Security Council Resolution 83, issued on June 27, 1950, requested U.N. members to assist South Korea in resisting aggression by communist North Korea. Based on this resolution, President Harry Truman quickly committed U.S. troops to lead the U.N. effort to assist South Korea.

In the late 1950s during the Eisenhower Administration and in the early 1960s under the Kennedy Administration, a limited number of American military "advisors" were in South Vietnam assisting that government in resisting a communist insurgency that was supported by North Vietnam. However, the extensive and lasting commitment of U.S. forces that became the Vietnam War started with the Gulf of Tonkin resolution of 1964. This was a joint congressional resolution that was passed in response to reports of North Vietnamese attacks on American naval forces in the Tonkin Gulf, which is a branch of the South China Sea immediately to the east of the Vietnamese coast. The resolution authorized the President to use armed force as he deemed necessary to assist nations in Southeast Asia "in defense of their freedom" against incursions by North Vietnam.

The Persian Gulf War of 1990-91, the Afghanistan War that began in 2001, and the Iraq War that began in 2003 followed the model of Vietnam in the sense that they were authorized by congressional resolutions short of formal declarations of war. The modern preference in the Congress appears to be to avoid formal declarations of war even when a majority deems military action to be warranted.

There have also been occasions on which presidents have initiated military action internationally without any express legal authorization. Modern examples include Operation Urgent Fury, which was President Ronald Reagan's 1983 invasion of the Caribbean island of Grenada, and Operation Just Cause, which was President George H.W. Bush's 1989 invasion of Panama. President Reagan justified his invasion of Grenada based primarily on the need to protect U.S. citizens who were attending medical school there when civil unrest erupted, as well as the general need for the United States to restore order in a location so close to its shores. President Bush justified the invasion of Panama by arguing that increasing disorder and anti-American hostility threatened American troops and citizens living in Panama and that the United States was entitled to act to protect the neutrality of the Panama Canal under the terms of the 1977 treaty by which the U.S. gifted the canal to Panama.

As a result of public sentiment against, and perceived presidential mishandling of, the Vietnam War, Congress passed the War Powers Resolution in 1973. It overrode President Nixon's veto to do so. This act purports to limit the President's ability to commit troops to hostilities in the absence of either formal congressional approval or an attack on the United States. 50 U.S.C. §1541 *et seq.* Every President since its enactment has considered the act unconstitutional and the courts have not ruled in any meaningful way on its enforceability. It is effectively a non-law.

How far a President may go in "war-making" absent congressional approval remains a question that has not been -- and may never be -- fully answered. Some early light was shed as a result of President Lincoln's actions to preserve the Union during the Civil War.

In April 1861, in response to the secession of several southern states and the Confederate attack on Fort Sumter in the harbor of Charleston, South Carolina, President Lincoln ordered the blockade of southern ports as a war measure to prevent southern access to foreign markets. As a result of the blockade, several private trading vessels were captured and taken as "prizes" of war, as was customary and accepted under the international law of war. The owners of four ships captured in May, June and July 1861 challenged the captures on the basis that there was no legal war and, therefore, captures could not be justified under the law of war.

The Prize Cases

67 U.S. 635 (1863)[29]

Mr. Justice GRIER.

There are certain propositions of law which must necessarily affect the ultimate decision of these cases, and many others, which it will be proper to discuss and decide before we notice the special facts peculiar to each.

They are, 1st. Had the President a right to institute a blockade of ports in possession of persons in armed rebellion against the Government, on the principles of international law, as known and acknowledged among civilized States?

[29] Footnotes and some citations found in the original decision have been omitted from this excerpted version.

2d. Was the property of persons domiciled or residing within those States a proper subject of capture on the sea as 'enemies' property?'

Neutrals have a right to challenge the existence of a blockade de facto, and also the authority of the party exercising the right to institute it. They have a right to enter the ports of a friendly nation for the purposes of trade and commerce, but are bound to recognize the rights of a belligerent engaged in actual war, to use this mode of coercion, for the purpose of subduing the enemy.

That a blockade de facto actually existed, and was formally declared and notified by the President on the 27th and 30th of April, 1861, is an admitted fact in these cases.

That the President, as the Executive Chief of the Government and Commander-in-chief of the Army and Navy, was the proper person to make such notification, has not been, and cannot be disputed.

The right of prize and capture has its origin in the "jus belli," and is governed and adjudged under the law of nations. To legitimate the capture of a neutral vessel or property on the high seas, a war must exist de facto, and the neutral must have knowledge or notice of the intention of one of the parties belligerent to use this mode of coercion against a port, city, or territory, in possession of the other.

Let us enquire whether, at the time this blockade was instituted, a state of war existed which would justify a resort to these means of subduing the hostile force.

War has been well defined to be, "That state in which a nation prosecutes its right by force."

The parties belligerent in a public war are independent nations. But it is not necessary to constitute war, that both parties should be acknowledged as independent nations or sovereign States. A war may exist where one of the belligerents, claims sovereign rights as against the other.

Insurrection against a government may or may not culminate in an organized rebellion, but a civil war always begins by insurrection against the lawful authority of the Government. A civil war is never solemnly declared; it becomes such by its accidents -- the number, power, and organization of the persons who originate and carry it on. When the party in rebellion occupy and hold in a hostile manner a certain portion of territory; have declared their independence; have cast off their allegiance; have organized armies; have commenced hostilities against their former sovereign, the world acknowledges them as belligerents, and the contest a war. They claim to be in arms to establish their liberty and independence, in order to become a sovereign State, while the sovereign party treats them as insurgents and rebels who owe allegiance, and who should be punished with death for their treason.

The laws of war, as established among nations, have their foundation in reason, and all tend to mitigate the cruelties and misery produced by the scourge of war. Hence the parties to a civil war usually concede to each other belligerent rights. They exchange prisoners, and adopt the other courtesies and rules common to public or national wars.

* * *

By the Constitution, Congress alone has the power to declare a national or foreign war. It cannot declare war against a State, or any number of States, by virtue of any clause in the Constitution. The Constitution confers on the President the whole Executive power. He is bound to take care that the laws be faithfully executed. He is Commander- in-chief of the Army and Navy of the United States, and of the militia of the several States when called into the actual service of the United States. He has no power to initiate or declare a war either against a foreign nation or a domestic State. But by the Acts of Congress of February 28th, 1795, and 3d of March, 1807, he is authorized to called out the militia and use the military and naval forces of the United States in case of invasion by foreign nations, and to suppress insurrection against the government of a State or of the United States.

If a war be made by invasion of a foreign nation, the President is not only authorized but bound to resist force by force. He does not initiate the war, but is bound to accept the challenge without waiting for any special legislative authority. And whether the hostile party be a foreign invader, or States organized in rebellion, it is none the less a war, although the declaration of it be "unilateral." Lord Stowell (1 Dodson, 247) observes, "It is not the less a war on that account, for war may exist without a declaration on either side." It is so laid down by the best writers on the law of nations. A declaration of war by one country only, is not a mere challenge to be accepted or refused at pleasure by the other.

* * *

It is not the less a civil war, with belligerent parties in hostile array, because it may be called an "insurrection" by one side, and the insurgents be considered as rebels or traitors. It is not necessary that the independence of the revolted province or State be acknowledged in order to constitute it a party belligerent in a war according to the law of nations. Foreign nations acknowledge it as war by a declaration of neutrality. The condition of neutrality cannot exist unless there be two belligerent parties.

* * *

As soon as the news of the attack on Fort Sumter, and the organization of a government by the seceding States, assuming to act as belligerents, could become known in Europe, to wit, on the 13th of May, 1861, the Queen of England issued her proclamation of neutrality, "recognizing hostilities as existing between the Government of the United States of American and certain States styling themselves the Confederate States of America." This was immediately followed by similar declarations or silent acquiescence by other nations.

After such an official recognition by the sovereign, a citizen of a foreign State is estopped to deny the existence of a war with all its consequences as regards neutrals. They cannot ask a Court to affect a technical ignorance of the existence of a war, which all the world acknowledges to be the greatest civil war known in the history of the human race, and thus cripple the arm of the Government and paralyze its power by subtle definitions and ingenious sophisms.

The law of nations is also called the law of nature; it is founded on the common consent as well as the common sense of the world. It contains no such anomalous doctrine as that which this Court are now for the first time desired to pronounce, to wit: That insurgents who have risen in rebellion against their sovereign, expelled her Courts, established a revolutionary government, organized armies, and commenced hostilities, are not enemies because they are traitors; and a war levied on the Government by traitors, in order to dismember and destroy it, is not a war because it is an "insurrection."

Whether the President in fulfilling his duties, as Commander-in-chief, in suppressing an insurrection, has met with such armed hostile resistance, and a civil war of such alarming proportions as will compel him to accord to them the character of belligerents, is a question to be decided by him, and this Court must be governed by the decisions and acts of the political department of the Government to which this power was entrusted. "He must determine what degree of force the crisis demands." The proclamation of blockade is itself official and conclusive evidence to the Court that a state of war existed which demanded and authorized a recourse to such a measure, under the circumstances peculiar to the case.

[The Court concluded that the President possessed authority to impose the blockade and seize prizes of war. It then went on to make specific determinations about the specific circumstances and forfeited property relating to the individual seized ships and their cargoes.]

Mr. Justice NELSON, dissenting.

* * *

[One of the objections] to the seizure of this vessel and cargo is that there was no existing war between the United States and the States in insurrection within the meaning of the law of nations, which drew after it the consequences of a public or civil ar. A contest by force between independent sovereign States is called a public war; and, when duly commenced by proclamation or otherwise, it entitles both of the belligerent parties to all the rights of war against each other, and as respects neutral nations.

* * *

The legal consequences resulting from a state of war between two countries at this day are well understood, and will be found described in every approved work on the subject of international law. The people of the two countries become immediately the enemies of each other, all intercourse commercial or otherwise between them unlawful, all contracts existing at the commencement of the war suspended, and all made during its existence utterly void. The insurance of enemies' property, the drawing of bills of exchange or purchase on the enemies' country, the remission of bills or money to it are illegal and void. Existing partnerships between citizens or subjects of the two countries are dissolved, and, in fine, interdiction of trade and intercourse direct or indirect is absolute and complete by the mere force and effect of war itself. All the property of the people of the two countries on land or sea are subject to capture and confiscation by the adverse party as enemies' property, with certain qualifications as it respects property on land, (Brown vs. United States, 8 Cranch, 110,) all treaties between the belligerent parties are annulled, The ports of the respective countries may be blockaded, and letters of marque and reprisal granted as rights of war, and the law of prizes as defined by the law of nations comes into full and complete operation, resulting from maritime captures, jure belli. War also effects a change in the mutual relations of all States or countries, not directly, as in the case of the belligerents, but immediately and indirectly, though they take no part in the contest, but remain neutral.

This great and pervading change in the existing condition of a country, and in the relations of all her citizens or subjects, external and internal, from a state of peace, is the immediate effect and result of a state of war: and hence the same code which has annexed to the existence of a war all these disturbing consequences has declared that the right of making war belongs exclusively to the supreme or sovereign power of the State.
This power in all civilized nations is regulated by the fundamental laws or municipal constitution of the country.

By our constitution this power is lodged in Congress. Congress shall have power "to declare war, grant letters of marque and reprisal, and make rules concerning captures on land and water."

We have thus far been considering the status of the citizens or subjects of a country at the breaking out of a public war when recognized or declared by the competent power.

In the case of a rebellion or resistance of a portion of the people of a country against the established government, there is no doubt, if in its progress and enlargement the government thus sought to be overthrown sees fit, it may by the competent power recognize or declare the existence of a state of civil war, which will draw after it all the consequences and rights of war between the con ending parties as in the case of a public war. Mr. Wheaton observes, speaking of civil war, "But the general usage of nations regards such a war as entitling both the contending parties to all the rights of war as against each other, and even as respects neutral nations." It is not to be denied, therefore, that if a civil war existed between that portion of the people in organized insurrection to overthrow this Government at the time this vessel and cargo were seized, and if she was guilty of a violation of the blockade, she would be lawful prize of war. But before this insurrection against the established Government can be dealt with on the footing of a civil war, within the meaning of the law of nations and the Constitution of the United States, and which will draw after it belligerent rights, it must be recognized or declared by the war-making power of the Government. No power short of this can change the legal status of the Government or the relations of its citizens from that of peace to a state of war, or bring into existence all those duties and obligations of neutral third parties growing out of a state of war.

The war power of the Government must be exercised before this changed condition of the Government and people and of neutral third parties can be admitted. There is no difference in this respect between a civil or a public war.

*   *   *

Now, in one sense, no doubt this is war, and may be a war of the most extensive and threatening dimensions and effects, but it is a statement simply of its existence in a material sense, and has no relevancy or weight when the question is what constitutes war in a legal sense, in the sense of the law of nations, and of the Constitution of the United States? For it must be a war in this sense to attach to it all the consequences that belong to belligerent rights. Instead, therefore, of inquiring after armies and navies, and victories lost and won, or organized rebellion against the general Government, the inquiry should be into the law of nations and into the municipal fundamental laws of the Government. For we find there that to constitute a civil war in the sense in which we are speaking, before it can exist, in contemplation of law, it must be recognized or declared by the sovereign power of the State, and which sovereign power by our Constitution is lodged in the Congress of the United States -- civil war, therefore, under our system of government, can exist only by an act of Congress, which requires the assent of two of the great departments of the Government, the Executive and Legislative.

[Justice Nelson explains that the Constitution amply provides for an executive response to a violent insurrection, but such a response, whether it is large or small is not legally "war." He also notes that, in July of 1861, Congress assembled and passed legislation that essentially ratified President Lincoln's blockade of southern ports and otherwise "recognized a state of civil war."]

But this is a very different question from the one before us, which is whether the President can recognize or declare a civil war, under the Constitution, with all its belligerent rights, between his own Government and a portion of its citizens in a state of insurrection. That power, as we have seen, belongs to Congress. We agree when such a war is recognized or declared to exist by the war-making power, but not otherwise, it is the duty of the Courts to follow the decision of the political power of the Government.

*   *   *

> Upon the whole, after the most careful consideration of this case which the pressure of other duties has admitted, I am compelled to the conclusion that no civil war existed between this Government and the States in insurrection till recognized by the Act of Congress 13th of July, 1861; that the President does not possess the power under the Constitution to declare war or recognize its existence within the meaning of the law of nations, which carries with it belligerent rights, and thus change the country and all its citizens from a state of peace to a state of war; that this power belongs exclusively to the Congress of the United States, and, consequently, that the President had no power to set on foot a blockade under the law of nations . . .

DISCUSSION AND QUESTIONS

1. Are Justice Grier and Justice Nelson answering the same question? Can a given armed conflict constitute "war" under one legal regime but something other than war under a different legal regime? Was the Court tasked with applying international law or domestic U.S. law in this case? For purposes of this case, is there a difference?

2. President Lincoln called Congress into special session on July 4, 1861 to take steps to address the putative southern secession. Lincoln pointedly did not seek from Congress a declaration of war because he believed such action would tend to validate the Confederacy as a separate and independent nation under international law. In his message to the special session, Lincoln described southern belligerency as "rebellion," and therefore unlawful. Did the Supreme Court, by holding that a state of war existed between the Union and the Confederacy, undermine Lincoln's desire to characterize the secessionist states as a rebel faction?

3. If the Supreme Court were presented with *The Prize Cases* today, would it be likely to address the merits of the case, or would it conclude that the dispute presents a non-justiciable political question? As was explained in Chapter Eight, application of the political question doctrine turns most decisively on the judiciary's assessment of whether there are judicially manageable standards available that can be utilized to answer the question presented. A second important inquiry is whether the matter at issue is clearly committed by the Constitution to one (or both) of the political branches. Would the modern Court believe that there are judicially manageable standards for determining whether a legal state of war exists between belligerents engaged in armed conflict? Given the Constitution's grant of the war-making power to the two political branches, would the Court conclude that it has a

role to play in evaluating independently whether the United States is or is not at war? (See the *Campbell v. Clinton* and *Doe v. Bush* decisions later in this chapter.)

DECLARING WAR WITHOUT DECLARING WAR

The decision in *The Prize Cases* teaches that the United States can be at war even in the absence of the formal congressional declaration of war contemplated by Article I, Section 8. The decision also confirms what had been, and remains, the well-accepted principle that the President has inherent authority -- indeed, not only the authority but the obligation -- to respond to attacks against the security of the United States, even in the absence of any congressional action or other legal justification.

On some occasions, Congress has elected to authorize military action in a fashion short of formally declaring war. This first occurred in the circumstances of the Quasi-War with France, which took place from 1798 to 1800. Congress passed several acts that effectively authorized the President to engage in hostilities, for example, by protecting U.S. ships against French attack and by seizing ships bound for France. In a seizure case not unlike the *Prize Cases* of six decades later, the Supreme Court was called upon to determine whether France was a military "enemy" of the United States. Justice Washington explained that there can be "perfect" war, which is a declared, complete state of war between nations, and "imperfect" war, which is "confined in its nature and extent. . . because those who are authorized to commit hostilities, act under special authority, and can go no further than to the extent of their commission." Justice Washington concluded that Congress had not intended the "perfect" war that would attend a formal declaration of war; nevertheless, Congress had authorized hostilities against France -- an "imperfect" war, which made France an "enemy" nation for purposes of taking prizes on the high seas. *Bas v. Tingy*, 4 U.S. 37 (1800).

More recent events have confirmed that Congress can authorize what amounts to war without formally declaring war as such. Two examples are set forth below.

Authorization for the Use of Military Force
September 18, 2001
(Senate Joint Resolution 23)

[The joint resolution first recites various findings relating to the September 11, 2001 terrorist attacks on the United States and the need for the United States to take measures to respond to international terrorism and preserve its national security. It goes on to grant authority to the President as follows.]

[T]he President is authorized to use all necessary and appropriate force against those nations, organizations, or persons he determines planned, authorized, committed, or aided the terrorist attacks that occurred on September 11, 2001, or harbored such organizations or persons, in order to prevent any future acts of international terrorism against the United States by such nations, organizations or persons.

<u>Authorization for the Use of Military Force Against Iraq</u>

October 16, 2002
(House Joint Resolution 114)

[The joint resolution first makes lengthy findings about the government of Iraq's aggression in the Gulf Region, its continuing violation of various United Nation's resolutions, its brutal repression of its people, its pursuit of weapons of mass destruction, and its threat to U.S. national security and national interests. It then grants war-making authority to the President as follows.]

The President is authorized to use the Armed Forces of the United States as he determines to be necessary and appropriate in order to (1) defend the national security of the United States against the continuing threat posed by Iraq; and (2) enforce all relevant United Nations Security Council resolutions regarding Iraq.

<u>DISCUSSION AND QUESTIONS</u>

1. Under the two authorizations excerpted above, who determines what degree and what type of military force is to be used? The 2001 resolution states that "the President is authorized to use all necessary and appropriate force . . . ," and the 2002 resolution declares that "the President is authorized to use [the military] as he determines to be necessary and appropriate . . ." Do one or both of these resolutions grant unreviewable authority to the President? The 2002 resolution quite clearly indicates that decisions about the nature and scope of force to be used are committed entirely to the President's discretion ("as *he determines* to be necessary and

appropriate"). In comparison, does the 2001 resolution imply that there is some objective standard by which "necessary and appropriate" can be measured? If so, how and by whom would such a standard be enforced?

In *Gilligan v. Morgan* (see Chapter Eight, pages 221-23), Chief Justice Burger explained that, when it comes to questions about how military force is used:

> [I]t is difficult to conceive of an area of governmental activity in which the courts have less competence. The complex, subtle, and professional decisions as to the composition, training, equipping, and control of a military force are essentially professional military judgments, subject always to civilian control of the Legislative and Executive Branches. The ultimate responsibility for these decisions is appropriately vested in branches of the government which are periodically subject to electoral accountability.

It seems likely that the courts would be reluctant in the extreme to entertain questions about what level of military force is "necessary and appropriate" in any given circumstances. Would the result change if a congressional resolution authorizing military action expressly empowered the courts to take on such cases -- that is, if the resolution explicitly stated that the courts "shall have jurisdiction over, and shall resolve, claims brought by persons aggrieved by the use of excessive military force"?

2. The 2001 resolution authorizes the President to act against any person, organization or nation that "he determines" was involved in the terrorist attacks of September 11. This appears to be a congressional pronouncement that no one but the President may make such determinations. Does this mean that the President's assessment of who was involved in the attacks is entirely unreviewable and unchecked? Suppose faulty intelligence led President Bush to conclude that interests in Switzerland or Belgium or Mexico had somehow assisted in the attacks; would he have been authorized to send tens of thousands of U.S. troops into one of these nations to engage in combat operations against the perceived enemy interests?

3. Suppose the President determined that certain United States citizens residing within the U.S. had assisted the terrorists who perpetrated the September 11 attacks; would the President be authorized under the 2001 resolution to use "all necessary and appropriate force" against these citizens? If he did, would the President's classification of these citizens as enemies be subject to any sort of review? In theory, at least, could a President abuse the extraordinarily broad -- and

possibly unreviewable -- discretion bestowed by a congressional authorization like the 2001 resolution?

4. Rather than granting essentially unlimited discretion to the President to prosecute military action against the nation's enemies, could Congress place limits on the President's discretion or permissible scope of action when it enacts a use of force authorization? For example, could Congress authorize the President to pursue terrorists who attacked the United States, but not to the extent of invading a sovereign state? Or could Congress have authorized the President to invade Iraq but at the same time mandated that U.S. troops could only remain in Iraq for a maximum of three years? Could Congress authorize the President to use military force but limit it to air and naval power and exclude the use of ground forces? How would one argue in favor of and against the validity of such restrictions?

There is little precedent on the question of whether Congress can authorize the President to prosecute armed conflict while, at the same time, limiting his options for doing so. One case from more than two centuries ago suggests that Congress may, if it chooses, impose such limitations. The Quasi-War was a conflict between the United States and France fought entirely on the high seas between 1798 and 1800. The antagonism between the two nations, which had been allied against Britain just 20 years earlier during the American Revolutionary War, resulted primarily from America's newfound rapprochement with Britain, as well as lingering unpaid American war debt to France. Congress chose not to make a formal declaration of war, but it passed various laws aimed at suspending U.S. commerce with France and protecting U.S. commerce with other nations. Among other things, Congress authorized the President to use American naval vessels to seize U.S.-owned ships that were "bound or sailing *to* any port or place within the territory of the French Republic or her dependencies" (emphasis added). When the seizure of a vessel coming *from* a French port was challenged, Chief Justice Marshall, writing for a unanimous court, explained that the seizure was unauthorized by the pertinent legislation and therefore illegal -- in authorizing the President to conduct what amounted to a naval war with France, Congress could permit the President to seize vessels going to France but preclude him from seizing vessels coming from France. *Little v. Barreme*, 6 U.S. 170 (1804).

EARLY RECOGNITION THAT THE WAR POWER HAS LIMITS

Even when a President is exercising his commander-in-chief authority in a *de facto* or *de jure* war, there are limits to his discretion and power. The Judiciary Branch is sometimes called upon to delineate these limits, which -- history reveals --

become clearer and more constraining the further from the battlefield the President's actions occur. President Lincoln exercised extraordinary executive power during the crisis that was the Civil War; yet, even in those extreme circumstances, the courts occasionally found that the Executive Branch had gone too far. One of the best-known examples is the case of *Ex parte Milligan*, a habeas corpus case that is excerpted below.

Challenges to executive power during times of armed conflict have often come in the form of habeas corpus proceedings initiated by prisoners who are held by the Executive Branch. In Anglo-American jurisprudence, the writ of habeas corpus -- also known as the "Great Writ" -- is issued by judicial tribunals to the authorities who are detaining an individual and is the means by which the tribunal may investigate the legal basis for, and the propriety of, the detention. The fundamental principle underlying habeas corpus proceedings is that no person should be imprisoned by governmental authorities except for valid legal reasons and through proper legal process. It is a principle that has been recognized since at least eight centuries ago when it was enshrined in the Magna Carta. This "Great Charter" was negotiated in 1215 between King John of England and a group of rebellious nobles and became the basis for the enduring concept that those who govern should not be above the law. It guaranteed, among other things, that "no free man shall be seized or imprisoned . . . except by the lawful judgment of his peers or by the law of the land." The Framers of the Constitution perceived the availability of the Great Writ to be so necessary to the rule of law that they accorded it special and explicit protection. Article I, Section 9 provides that "the privilege of the writ of habeas corpus shall not be suspended, unless when in cases of rebellion or invasion the public safety may require it."

During the Civil War, President Lincoln suspended the writ of habeas corpus on several occasions in several areas. He directed military commanders to detain Confederate operatives and sympathizers, without charge and as they deemed necessary to the war effort. For example, in April 1861, Lincoln wrote to General Winfield Scott, who served as commanding general of the Union army in the first months of the war:

> You are engaged in repressing an insurrection against the laws of the United States. If at any point on or in the vicinity of the military line which is now used between the city of Philadelphia via Perryville, Annapolis City and Annapolis Junction you find resistance which renders it necessary to suspend the writ of habeas corpus for the public safety, you personally or through the officer in command at the

> point where resistance occurs are authorized to suspend that writ.

Similar authorizations were sent to other commanders during the course of the war. Lincoln's suspension of habeas corpus was challenged in the courts, usually to no avail. Although courts held that Lincoln's unilateral suspension of habeas corpus was unconstitutional, Lincoln ignored their orders that he release prisoners who were illegitimately detained -- most famously, when Chief Justice Roger Taney ordered the release of John Merryman. Merryman was a member of the Maryland militia and a Confederate sympathizer who was detained at Baltimore's Fort McHenry. Chief Justice Taney, who was riding circuit at the time, ruled that the President lacked authority under the Constitution to suspend habeas corpus; the power to do so was held by the Congress, not the President, as demonstrated by the placement of the power in Article I rather than Article II. *Ex parte Merryman*, 17 F. Cas. 144 (1861). Taney ordered the commander of Fort McHenry to release Merryman, but the order was ignored.

When Congress met in special session in July 1861 to assist the President in responding to the southern insurrection, President Lincoln requested that Congress ratify legislatively his suspension of habeas corpus. In his July 4, 1861 message to the special session, Lincoln acknowledged that he had suspended habeas corpus and that the propriety of this action had been questioned. He then asked the rhetorical question, "are all the laws but one to go unexecuted, and the government itself go to pieces, lest that one be violated?" The special session of Congress acceded to several of Lincoln's requests for legislative support of his war measures, but declined to suspend habeas corpus until two years later, when it passed the Habeas Corpus Act of 1863.

The case of Lambdin Milligan arose after Congress finally authorized what amounted to a partial suspension of habeas corpus. Milligan was a resident of Indiana (a state that had not seceded) who was arrested, tried by a military court, and sentenced to death for plotting to steal Union weapons and free prisoners of war from Union prison camps. Although Congress had acted in 1863 to suspend habeas corpus, it had placed on the suspension certain limits that enabled Milligan successfully to seek the writ. The Habeas Corpus Act of 1863 provided that civilians who were detained eventually had to be indicted by a grand jury or released. Although he was tried and convicted by a military tribunal, the allegations against Milligan had also been presented to a civilian grand jury, which had declined to indict him. Consequently, he was able to claim that, even under the limited habeas corpus regime then in place, he was entitled to be freed. Milligan's case turned on the legitimacy of the military tribunal that had condemned him.

Ex parte Milligan

71 U.S. 2 (1866)[30]

Mr. Justice DAVIS delivered the opinion of the court.

On the 10th day of May, 1865, Lambdin P. Milligan presented a petition to the Circuit Court of the United States for the District of Indiana to be discharged from an alleged unlawful imprisonment. The case made by the petition is this: Milligan is a citizen of the United States; has lived for twenty years in Indiana, and, at the time of the grievances complained of, was not, and never had been, in the military or naval service of the United States. On the 5th day of October, 1864, while at home, he was arrested by order of General Alvin P. Hovey, commanding the military district of Indiana, and has ever since been kept in close confinement.

On the 21st day of October, 1864, he was brought before a military commission, convened at Indianapolis by order of General Hovey, tried on certain charges and specifications, found guilty, and sentenced to be hanged, and the sentence ordered to be executed on Friday, the 19th day of May, 1865.

On the 2d day of January, 1865, after the proceedings of the military commission were at an end, the Circuit Court of the United States for Indiana met at Indianapolis and empaneled a grand jury, who were charged to inquire whether the laws of the United States had been violated, and, if so, to make presentments. The court adjourned on the 27th day of January, having, prior thereto, discharged from further service the grand jury, who did not find any bill of indictment or make any presentment against Milligan for any offence whatever, and, in fact, since his imprisonment, no bill of indictment has been found or presentment made against him by any grand jury of the United States.

Milligan insists that said military commission had no jurisdiction to try him upon the charges preferred, or upon any charges whatever, because he was a citizen of the United States and the State of Indiana, and had not been, since the commencement of the late Rebellion, a resident of any of the States whose citizens were arrayed against the government, and that the right of trial by jury was guaranteed to him by the Constitution of the United States.

---

[30] Footnotes and some citations found in the original decision have been omitted from this excerpted version.

The prayer of the petition was that, under the act of Congress approved March 3d, 1863, entitled, "An act relating to habeas corpus and regulating judicial proceedings in certain cases," he may be brought before the court and either turned over to the proper civil tribunal to be proceeded against according to the law of the land or discharged from custody altogether.

*   *   *

During the late wicked Rebellion, the temper of the times did not allow that calmness in deliberation and discussion so necessary to a correct conclusion of a purely judicial question. *Then,* considerations of safety were mingled with the exercise of power, and feelings and interests prevailed which are happily terminated. *Now* that the public safety is assured, this question, as well as all others, can be discussed and decided without passion or the admixture of any element not required to form a legal judgment. We approach the investigation of this case fully sensible of the magnitude of the inquiry and the necessity of full and cautious deliberation.

*   *   *

The controlling question in the case is this: upon the facts stated in Milligan's petition and the exhibits filed, had the military commission mentioned in it jurisdiction legally to try and sentence him? Milligan, not a resident of one of the rebellious states or a prisoner of war, but a citizen of Indiana for twenty years past and never in the military or naval service, is, while at his home, arrested by the military power of the United States, imprisoned, and, on certain criminal charges preferred against him, tried, convicted, and sentenced to be hanged by a military commission, organized under the direction of the military commander of the military district of Indiana. Had this tribunal the legal power and authority to try and punish this man?

*   *   *

The founders of our government were familiar with the history of that struggle, and secured in a written constitution every right which the people had wrested from power during a contest of ages. By that Constitution and the laws authorized by it, this question must be determined. The provisions of that instrument on the administration of criminal justice are too plain and direct to leave room for misconstruction or doubt of their true meaning. Those applicable to this case are found in that clause of the original Constitution which says "That the trial of all crimes, except in case of impeachment, shall be by jury," and in the fourth, fifth, and sixth articles of the amendments [which guarantee the right to be free from unreasonable search and seizure, grand jury indictment before criminal prosecution, due process, trial by jury, access to compulsory process and the right to confront witnesses].

Have any of the rights guaranteed by the Constitution been violated in the case of Milligan, and, if so, what are they?

Every trial involves the exercise of judicial power, and from what source did the military commission that tried him derive their authority? Certainly no part of judicial power of the country was conferred on them, because the Constitution expressly vests it "in one supreme court and such inferior courts as the Congress may from time to time ordain and establish," and it is not pretended that the commission was a court ordained and established by Congress. They cannot justify on the mandate of the President, because he is controlled by law, and has his appropriate sphere of duty, which is to execute, not to make, the laws, and there is "no unwritten criminal code to which resort can be had as a source of jurisdiction."

But it is said that the jurisdiction [of the military commission] is complete under the "laws and usages of war."

It can serve no useful purpose to inquire what those laws and usages are, whence they originated, where found, and on whom they operate; they can never be applied to citizens in states which have upheld the authority of the government, and where the courts are open and their process unobstructed. This court has judicial knowledge that, in Indiana, the Federal authority was always unopposed, and its courts always open to hear criminal accusations and redress grievances, and no usage of war could sanction a military trial there for any offence whatever of a citizen in civil life in nowise connected with the military service. Congress could grant no such power, and, to the honor of our national legislature be it said, it has never been provoked by the state of the country even to attempt its exercise. One of the plainest constitutional provisions was therefore infringed when Milligan was tried by a court not ordained and established by Congress and not composed of judges appointed during good behavior.

Why was he not delivered to the Circuit Court of Indiana to be proceeded against according to law? No reason of necessity could be urged against it, because Congress had declared penalties against the offences charged, provided for their punishment, and directed that court to hear and determine them. And soon after this military tribunal was ended, the Circuit Court met, peacefully transacted its business, and adjourned. It needed no bayonets to protect it, and required no military aid to execute its judgments. It was held in a state, eminently distinguished for patriotism, by judges commissioned during the Rebellion, who were provided with juries, upright, intelligent, and selected by a marshal appointed by the President. The government had no right to conclude that Milligan, if guilty, would not receive in that court merited punishment, for its records disclose that it was constantly engaged in the trial of similar offences, and was never interrupted in its administration of criminal justice. If it was dangerous, in the distracted condition of affairs, to leave Milligan unrestrained of his liberty because he "conspired against the government, afforded aid and comfort to rebels, and incited the people to insurrection," the law said arrest him, confine him closely, render him powerless to do further mischief, and then present his case to the grand jury of the district, with proofs of his guilt, and, if indicted, try him according to the course of the common law. If this had been done, the Constitution would have been vindicated, the law of 1863 enforced, and the securities for personal liberty preserved and defended.

* * *

It is claimed that martial law covers with its broad mantle the proceedings of this military commission. The proposition is this: that, in a time of war, the commander of an armed force (if, in his opinion, the exigencies of the country demand it, and of which he is to judge) has the power, within the lines of his military district, to suspend all civil rights and their remedies and subject citizens, as well as soldiers to the rule of *his will,* and, in the exercise of his lawful authority, cannot be restrained except by his superior officer or the President of the United States.

If this position is sound to the extent claimed, then, when war exists, foreign or domestic, and the country is subdivided into military departments for mere convenience, the commander of one of them can, if he chooses, within his limits, on the plea of necessity, with the approval of the Executive, substitute military force for and to the exclusion of the laws, and punish all persons as he thinks right and proper, without fixed or certain rules.

The statement of this proposition shows its importance, for, if true, republican government is a failure, and there is an end of liberty regulated by law. Martial law established on such a basis destroys every guarantee of the Constitution, and effectually renders the "military independent of and superior to the civil power" -- the attempt to do which by the King of Great Britain was deemed by our fathers such an offence that they assigned it to the world as one of the causes which impelled them to declare their independence. Civil liberty and this kind of martial law cannot endure together; the antagonism is irreconcilable, and, in the conflict, one or the other must perish.

* * *

[I]t is insisted that the safety of the country in time of war demands that this broad claim for martial law shall be sustained. If this were true, it could be well said that a country, preserved at the sacrifice of all the cardinal principles of liberty, is not worth the cost of preservation. Happily, it is not so.

It will be borne in mind that this is not a question of the power to proclaim martial law when war exists in a community and the courts and civil authorities are overthrown. Nor is it a question what rule a military commander, at the head of his army, can impose on states in rebellion to cripple their resources and quell the insurrection. The jurisdiction claimed is much more extensive. The necessities of the service during the late Rebellion required that the loyal states should be placed within the limits of certain military districts and commanders appointed in them, and it is urged that this, in a military sense, constituted them the theater of military operations, and as, in this case, Indiana had been and was again threatened with invasion by the enemy, the occasion was furnished to establish martial law. The conclusion does not follow from the premises. If armies were collected in Indiana, they were to be employed in another locality, where the laws were obstructed and the national authority disputed. On her soil there was no hostile foot; if once invaded, that invasion was at an end, and, with it, all pretext for martial law. Martial law cannot arise from a *threatened* invasion. The necessity must be actual and present, the invasion real, such as effectually closes the courts and deposes the civil administration.

It is difficult to see how the *safety* for the country required martial law in Indiana. If any of her citizens were plotting treason, the power of arrest could secure them until the government was prepared for their trial, when the courts were open and ready to try them. It was as easy to protect witnesses before a civil as a military tribunal, and as there could be no wish to convict except on sufficient legal evidence, surely an ordained and establish court was better able to judge of this than a military tribunal composed of gentlemen not trained to the profession of the law.

It follows from what has been said on this subject that there are occasions when martial rule can be properly applied. If, in foreign invasion or civil war, the courts are actually closed, and it is impossible to administer criminal justice according to law, *then,* on the theatre of active military operations, where war really prevails, there is a necessity to furnish a substitute for the civil authority, thus overthrown, to preserve the safety of the army and society, and as no power is left but the military, it is allowed to govern by martial rule until the laws can have their free course. As necessity creates the rule, so it limits its duration, for, if this government is continued *after* the courts are reinstated, it is a gross usurpation of power. Martial rule can never exist where the courts are open and in the proper and unobstructed exercise of their jurisdiction. It is also confined to the locality of actual war. Because, during the late Rebellion, it could have been enforced in Virginia, where the national authority was overturned and the courts driven out, it does not follow that it should obtain in Indiana, where that authority was never disputed and justice was always administered.

[Chief Justice CHASE, joined by three other justices, filed a separate opinion in which he found that Congress could have authorized military commissions such as the one that tried and convicted Milligan, but chose not to do so.]

DISCUSSION AND QUESTIONS

1. The gravamen of the *Milligan* decision is that martial law may not properly be declared (and, therefore, military commissions may not be utilized to try civilians) "where the courts are open and their process unobstructed . . . Martial rule can never exist where the courts are open and in the proper and unobstructed exercise of their jurisdiction. It is also confined to the locality of actual war." True martial law declarations have been rare in U.S. history. During the War of 1812, General Andrew Jackson declared martial in and around New Orleans during and after the battle for control of that city. The territory of Hawaii was placed under martial law for three years after the 1941 attack on Pearl Harbor. The military governor continued martial law long after the immediate danger of attack had passed suspended habeas corpus, and insisted that all criminal trials take place in military courts without juries, even though the civilian courts were open for business. Martia

law should not be confused with the domestic use of the military. That the military is called into action does not necessarily -- indeed, it does not usually -- mean that martial law is in place. For example, in 1894, when President Grover Cleveland sent federal troops to Chicago to quell the Pullman Strike, protect mail delivery and enforce a federal court injunction, it was not considered a declaration of martial law (although it was viewed by strikers as an incitement and increased tensions). When President Eisenhower used federal troops to enforce school desegregation efforts in Little Rock, Arkansas in 1957, when President Kennedy used federal troops in Mississippi in 1962, and when President Johnson used federal troops in Alabama in 1964, martial law was neither declared nor, as a practical matter, in effect. Troops were present and had a specific mission to perform, but these were not situations in which military authority had supplanted civil governmental authority.

2. Justice Davis suggests in *Milligan* that military tribunals can be used to try civilians only when martial law has properly been declared, which means only when the normal civilian courts are unavailable. Yet both President George W. Bush and President Barack Obama used military commissions to try suspected terrorists in the so-called "War on Terror" that began with the terrorist attacks of September 11, 2001. Civilian courts were consistently open and operating during the War on Terror. How then could military commissions be used to try suspected terrorists? (More on this question in Chapter Ten.)

3. The *Milligan* Court implicitly bases its analysis on the notion that Milligan must be categorized as either a member of the enemy military, and therefore a prisoner of war, or a civilian. Because he is a civilian, he is entitled to be tried in civilian courts under civilian law. Has the Court oversimplified the analysis and missed a category? Spies and saboteurs are civilians, yet they are players in the armed conflict and are acting on behalf of the enemy. How should such persons be categorized? (Hint: See Chapter Ten for discussion of unlawful combatants.)

WAR POWER ABUSED -- SEPARATION OF POWERS FAILS

World War II brought a different question about the government's power over civilians during war time. In February 1942, three months after the Empire of Japan attacked the United States at Pearl Harbor and the United States declared war in response, President Franklin Roosevelt issued Executive Order 9066. The stated purpose of the order was "protection against espionage and against sabotage." Invoking his commander-in-chief powers, the President authorized military commanders to "prescribe military areas . . . from which any or all persons may be excluded . . . subject to whatever restrictions . . . the appropriate military commander may impose in his discretion." The order further provided that the military should "provide for residents of any such area who are excluded therefrom, such transportation, food, shelter, and other accommodations as may be necessary." A month later, Congress expressed its approval of, and effectively ratified, the President's order by enacting legislation that criminalized violations of military exclusion orders that were issued pursuant to the President's executive order. As a result of the President's executive order, military commanders declared "exclusion zones," the largest of which covered the nation's entire West Coast. Tens of thousands of Americans of Japanese ancestry (and, to a much lesser extent, German and Italian Americans) were ordered by the military to leave the exclusion zones -- that is, to leave their homes, businesses and schools -- indefinitely. Most were American citizens. They were transferred by the War Relocation Authority to Relocation Centers, which were primitive internment camps located in remote areas with only the most spartan facilities.

Korematsu v. United States

323 U.S. 214 (1944)[31]

Mr. Justice BLACK delivered the opinion of the Court.

[Fred Korematsu was an American citizen of Japanese descent who was criminally prosecuted for remaining in San Leandro, California after it was declared to be within a "military area" that all persons of Japanese descent were directed to leave.]

It should be noted, to begin with, that all legal restrictions which curtail the civil rights of a single racial group are immediately suspect. That is not to say that all such restrictions are unconstitutional. It is to say that courts must subject them to the most rigid scrutiny. Pressing public necessity may sometimes justify the existence of such restrictions; racial antagonism never can.

* * *

One of the series of orders and proclamations, a curfew order, which like the exclusion order here was promulgated pursuant to Executive Order 9066, subjected all persons of Japanese ancestry in prescribed West Coast military areas to remain in their residences from 8 p.m. to 6 a.m. As is the case with the exclusion order here, that prior curfew order was designed as a "protection against espionage and against

[31] Footnotes and some citations found in the original decision have been omitted from this excerpted version.

sabotage." In Kiyoshi Hirabayashi v. United States, 320 U.S. 81, 63 S.Ct. 1375, we sustained a conviction obtained for violation of the curfew order. The Hirabayashi conviction and this one thus rest on the same 1942 Congressional Act and the same basic executive and military orders, all of which orders were aimed at the twin dangers of espionage and sabotage.

The 1942 Act was attacked in the Hirabayashi case as an unconstitutional delegation of power; it was contended that the curfew order and other orders on which it rested were beyond the war powers of the Congress, the military authorities and of the President, as Commander in Chief of the Army; and finally that to apply the curfew order against none but citizens of Japanese ancestry amounted to a constitutionally prohibited discrimination solely on account of race. To these questions, we gave the serious consideration which their importance justified. We upheld the curfew order as an exercise of the power of the government to take steps necessary to prevent espionage and sabotage in an area threatened by Japanese attack.

In the light of the principles we announced in the Hirabayashi case, we are unable to conclude that it was beyond the war power of Congress and the Executive to exclude those of Japanese ancestry from the West Coast war area at the time they did. True, exclusion from the area in which one's home is located is a far greater deprivation than constant confinement to the home from 8 p.m. to 6 a.m. Nothing short of apprehension by the proper military authorities of the gravest imminent danger to the public safety can constitutionally justify either. But exclusion from a threatened area, no less than curfew, has a definite and close relationship to the prevention of espionage and sabotage. The military authorities, charged with the primary responsibility of defending our shores, concluded that curfew provided inadequate protection and ordered exclusion. They did so, as pointed out in our Hirabayashi opinion, in accordance with Congressional authority to the military to say who should, and who should not, remain in the threatened areas.

* * *

Like curfew, exclusion of those of Japanese origin was deemed necessary because of the presence of an unascertained number of disloyal members of the group, most of whom we have no doubt were loyal to this country. It was because we could not reject the finding of the military authorities that it was impossible to bring about an immediate segregation of the disloyal from the loyal that we sustained the validity of the curfew order as applying to the whole group. In the instant case, temporary exclusion of the entire group was rested by the military on the same ground. The judgment that exclusion of the whole group was for the same reason a military imperative answers the contention that the exclusion was in the nature of group punishment based on antagonism to those of Japanese origin. That there were members of the group who retained loyalties to Japan has been confirmed by investigations made subsequent to the exclusion. Approximately five thousand American citizens of Japanese ancestry refused to swear unqualified allegiance to the United States and to renounce allegiance to the Japanese Emperor, and several thousand evacuees requested repatriation to Japan.

We uphold the exclusion order as of the time it was made and when the petitioner violated it . . . In doing so, we are not unmindful of the hardships imposed by it upon a large group of American citizens . . . But hardships are part of war, and war is an aggregation of hardships. All citizens alike, both in and out of uniform, feel the impact of war in greater or lesser measure. Citizenship has its responsibilities as well as its privileges, and in time of war the burden is always heavier. Compulsory exclusion of large groups of citizens from their homes, except under circumstances of direst emergency and peril, is inconsistent with our basic governmental institutions. But when under conditions of modern warfare our shores are threatened by hostile forces, the power to protect must be commensurate with the threatened danger.

* * *

It is now argued that the validity of the exclusion order cannot be considered apart from the orders requiring [petitioner Korematsu], after departure from the area, to report and to remain in an assembly or relocation center. The contention is that we must treat these separate orders as one and inseparable; that, for this reason, if detention in the assembly or relocation center would have illegally deprived the petitioner of his liberty, the exclusion order and his conviction under it cannot stand.

We are thus being asked to pass at this time upon the whole subsequent detention program in both assembly and relocation centers, although the only issues framed at the trial related to petitioner's remaining in the prohibited area in violation of the exclusion order. Had petitioner here left the prohibited area and gone to an assembly center we cannot say either as a matter of fact or law, that his presence in that center would have resulted in his detention in a relocation center. Some who did report to the assembly center were not sent to relocation centers but were released upon condition that they remain outside the prohibited zone until the military orders were modified or lifted. This illustrates that they pose different problems and may be governed by different principles. The lawfulness of one does not necessarily determine the lawfulness of the others.

* * *

Since the petitioner has not been convicted of failing to report or to remain in an assembly or relocation center, we cannot in this case determine the validity of those separate provisions of the order. It is sufficient here for us to pass upon the order which petitioner violated. To do more would be to go beyond the issues raised, and to decide momentous questions not contained within the framework of the pleadings or the evidence in this case. It will be time enough to decide the serious constitutional issues which petitioner seeks to raise when an assembly or relocation order is applied or is certain to be applied to him, and we have its terms before us.

* * *

It is said that we are dealing here with the case of imprisonment of a citizen in a concentration camp solely because of his ancestry, without evidence or inquiry concerning his loyalty and good disposition towards the United States. Our task would be simple, our duty clear, were this a case involving the imprisonment of a loyal citizen in a concentration camp because of racial prejudice. Regardless of the true nature of the assembly and relocation centers-and we deem it unjustifiable to call them concentration camps with all the ugly connotations that term implies-we are dealing specifically with nothing but an exclusion order. To cast this case into outlines of racial prejudice, without reference to the real military dangers which were presented, merely confuses the issue. Korematsu was not excluded from the Military Area because of hostility to him or his race. He was excluded because we are at war with the Japanese Empire, because the properly constituted military authorities feared an invasion of our West Coast and felt constrained to take proper security measures, because they decided that the military urgency of the situation demanded that all citizens of Japanese ancestry be segregated from the West Coast temporarily, and finally, because Congress, reposing its confidence in this time of war in our military leaders -- as inevitably it must -- determined that they should have the power to do just this. There was evidence of disloyalty on the part of some, the military authorities considered that the need for action was great, and time was short. We cannot -- by availing ourselves of the calm perspective of hindsight -- now say that at that time these actions were unjustified.

AFFIRMED.

Mr. Justice FRANKFURTER, concurring.

* * *

The provisions of the Constitution which confer on the Congress and the President powers to enable this country to wage war are as much part of the Constitution as provisions looking to a nation at peace. And we have had recent occasion to quote approvingly the statement of former Chief Justice Hughes that the war power of the Government is "the power to wage war successfully." Hirabayashi v. United States, supra, 320 U.S. at page 93, and see Home Bldg. & L. Ass'n v. Blaisdell, 290 U.S. 398, 426. Therefore, the validity of action under the war power must be judged wholly in the context of war. That action is not to be stigmatized as lawless because like action in times of peace would be lawless. To talk about a military order that expresses an allowable judgment of war needs by those entrusted with the duty of conducting war as "an unconstitutional order" is to suffuse a part of the Constitution with an atmosphere of unconstitutionality. The respective spheres of action of military authorities and of judges are of course very different. But within their sphere, military authorities are no more outside the bounds of obedience to the Constitution than are judges within theirs. 'The war power of the United States, like its other powers ... is subject to applicable constitutional limitations', Hamilton v. Kentucky Distilleries, Co., 251 U.S. 146, 156. To recognize that military orders are "reasonably expedient military precautions" in time of war and yet to deny them constitutional legitimacy makes of the Constitution an instrument for dialetic subtleties not reasonably to be attributed to the hard-headed Framers, of whom a majority had had actual participation in war. If a military order such as that under review does not transcend the means appropriate for conducting war, such action by the military is as constitutional as would be any authorized action by the Interstate Commerce Commission within the limits of the constitutional power to regulate commerce. And being an exercise of the war power explicitly granted by the Constitution for safeguarding the national life by prosecuting war effectively, I find nothing in the Constitution which denies to Congress the power to enforce such a valid military order by making its violation an offense triable in the civil courts . . . To find that the Constitution does not forbid the military measures now complained of does not carry with it approval of that which Congress and the Executive did. That is their business, not ours.

[Justice ROBERTS dissented, arguing that the petitioner was faced with the choice of either remaining in his home and violating the military exclusion order or leaving his home and complying with the order by submitting himself to what amounted to military imprisonment. This case is not like the Hirabayashi case on which the majority relies. This "is the case of convicting a citizen as a punishment for not submitting to imprisonment in a concentration camp, based on his ancestry, and solely because of his ancestry, without evidence or inquiry concerning his loyalty and good disposition towards the United States."]

Mr. Justice MURPHY, dissenting.

This exclusion of "all persons of Japanese ancestry, both alien and non-alien," from the Pacific Coast area on a plea of military necessity in the absence of martial law ought not to be approved. Such exclusion goes over "the very brink of constitutional power" and falls into the ugly abyss of racism.

In dealing with matters relating to the prosecution and progress of a war, we must accord great respect and consideration to the judgments of the military authorities who are on the scene and who have full knowledge of the military facts. The scope of their discretion must, as a matter of necessity and common sense, be wide. And their judgments ought not to be overruled lightly by those whose training and duties ill-equip them to deal intelligently with matters so vital to the physical security of the nation.

At the same time, however, it is essential that there be definite limits to military discretion, especially where martial law has not been declared. Individuals must not be left impoverished of their constitutional rights on a plea of military necessity that has neither substance nor support. Thus, like other claims conflicting with the asserted constitutional rights of the individual, the military claim must subject itself to the judicial process of having its reasonableness determined and its conflicts with other interests reconciled. "What are the allowable limits of military discretion, and whether or not they have been overstepped in a particular case, are judicial questions." Sterling v. Constantin, 287 U.S. 378, 401.

*　*　*

It must be conceded that the military and naval situation in the spring of 1942 was such as to generate a very real fear of invasion of the Pacific Coast, accompanied by fears of sabotage and espionage in that area. The military command was therefore justified in adopting all reasonable means necessary to combat these dangers. In adjudging the military action taken in light of the then apparent dangers, we must not erect too high or too meticulous standards; it is necessary only that the action have some reasonable relation to the removal of the dangers of invasion, sabotage and espionage. But the exclusion, either temporarily or permanently, of all persons with Japanese blood in their veins has no such reasonable relation. And that relation is lacking because the exclusion order necessarily must rely for its reasonableness upon the assumption that all persons of Japanese ancestry may have a dangerous tendency to commit sabotage and espionage and to aid our Japanese enemy in other ways. It is difficult to believe that reason, logic or experience could be marshalled in support of such an assumption.

That this forced exclusion was the result in good measure of this erroneous assumption of racial guilt rather than bona fide military necessity is evidenced by the Commanding General's Final Report on the evacuation from the Pacific Coast area. In it he refers to all individuals of Japanese descent as 'subversive,' as belonging to 'an enemy race' whose 'racial strains are undiluted,' and as constituting 'over 112,000 potential enemies ... at large today' along the Pacific Coast. In support of this blanket condemnation of all persons of Japanese descent, however, no reliable evidence is cited to show that such individuals were generally disloyal, or had generally so conducted themselves in this area as to constitute a special menace to defense installations or war industries, or had otherwise by their behavior furnished reasonable ground for their exclusion as a group.

Justification for the exclusion is sought, instead, mainly upon questionable racial and sociological grounds not ordinarily within the realm of expert military judgment, supplemented by certain semi-military conclusions drawn from an unwarranted use of circumstantial evidence. Individuals of Japanese ancestry are condemned because they are said to be "a large, unassimilated, tightly knit racial group, bound to an enemy nation by strong ties of race, culture, custom and religion." They are claimed to be given to "emperor worshipping ceremonies" and to "dual citizenship." Japanese language schools and allegedly pro-Japanese organizations are cited as evidence of possible group disloyalty, together with facts as to certain persons being educated and residing at length in Japan. It is intimated that many of these individuals deliberately resided "adjacent to strategic points," thus enabling them "to carry into execution a tremendous program of sabotage on a mass scale should any considerable number of them have been inclined to do so." The need for protective custody is also asserted. The report refers without identity to "numerous incidents of violence" as well as to other admittedly unverified or cumulative incidents.

* * *

The military necessity which is essential to the validity of the evacuation order thus resolves itself into a few intimations that certain individuals actively aided the enemy, from which it is inferred that the entire group of Japanese Americans could not be trusted to be or remain loyal to the United States. No one denies, of course, that there were some disloyal persons of Japanese descent on the Pacific Coast who did all in their power to aid their ancestral land. Similar disloyal activities have been engaged in by many persons of German, Italian and even more pioneer stock in our country. But to infer that examples of individual disloyalty prove group disloyalty and justify discriminatory action against the entire group is to deny that under our system of law individual guilt is the sole basis for deprivation of rights.

* * *

I dissent, therefore, from this legalization of racism. Racial discrimination in any form and in any degree has no justifiable part whatever in our democratic way of life. It is unattractive in any setting but it is utterly revolting among a free people who have embraced the principles set forth in the Constitution of the United States. All residents of this nation are kin in some way by blood or culture to a foreign land. Yet they are primarily and necessarily a part of the new and distinct civilization of the United States. They must accordingly be treated at all times as the heirs of the American experiment and as entitled to all the rights and freedoms guaranteed by the Constitution.

Mr. Justice JACKSON, dissenting.

Korematsu was born on our soil, of parents born in Japan. The Constitution makes him a citizen of the United States by nativity and a citizen of California by residence. No claim is made that he is not loyal to this country. There is no suggestion that apart from the matter involved here he is not law- abiding and well disposed. Korematsu, however, has been convicted of an act not commonly a crime. It consists merely of being present in the state whereof he is a citizen, near the place where he was born, and where all his life he has lived.

Even more unusual is the series of military orders which made this conduct a crime. They forbid such a one to remain, and they also forbid him to leave. They were so drawn that the only way Korematsu could avoid violation was to give himself up to the military authority. This meant submission to custody, examination, and transportation out of the territory, to be followed by indeterminate confinement in detention camps.

A citizen's presence in the locality, however, was made a crime only if his parents were of Japanese birth. Had Korematsu been one of four -- the others being, say, a German alien enemy, an Italian alien enemy, and a citizen of American-born ancestors, convicted of treason but out on parole -- only Korematsu's presence would have violated the order. The difference between their innocence and his crime would result, not from anything he did, said, or thought, different than they, but only in that he was born of different racial stock.

Now, if any fundamental assumption underlies our system, it is that guilt is personal and not inheritable. Even if all of one's antecedents had been convicted of treason, the Constitution forbids its penalties to be visited upon him, for it provides that "no Attainder of Treason shall work Corruption of Blood, or Forfeiture except during the Life of the Person attained." Article 3, 3, cl. 2. But here is an attempt to make an otherwise innocent act a crime merely because this prisoner is the son of parents as to whom he had no choice, and belongs to a race from which there is no way to resign. If Congress in peace-time legislation should enact such a criminal law, I should suppose this Court would refuse to enforce it.

* * *

It would be impracticable and dangerous idealism to expect or insist that each specific military command in an area of probable operations will conform to conventional tests of constitutionality. When an area is so beset that it must be put under military control at all, the paramount consideration is that its measures be successful, rather than legal. The armed services must protect a society, not merely its Constitution. The very essence of the military job is to marshal physical force, to remove every obstacle to its effectiveness, to give it every strategic advantage. Defense measures will not, and often should not, be held within the limits that bind civil authority in peace.

No court can require such a commander in such circumstances to act as a reasonable man; he may be unreasonably cautious and exacting. Perhaps he should be. But a commander in temporarily focusing the life of a community on defense is carrying out a military program; he is not making law in the sense the courts know the term. He issues orders, and they may have a certain authority as military commands, although they may be very bad as constitutional law.

But if we cannot confine military expedients by the Constitution, neither would I distort the Constitution to approve all that the military may deem expedient. This is what the Court appears to be doing, whether consciously or not. I cannot say, from any evidence before me, that the orders of General DeWitt were not reasonably expedient military precautions, nor could I say that they were. But even if they were permissible military procedures, I deny that it follows that they are constitutional. If, as the Court holds, it does follow, then we may as well say that any military order will be constitutional and have done with it.

The limitation under which courts always will labor in examining the necessity for a military order are illustrated by this case. How does the Court know that these orders have a reasonable basis in necessity? No evidence whatever on that subject has been taken by this or any other court. There is sharp controversy as to the credibility of the DeWitt report. So the Court, having no real evidence before it, has no choice but to accept General DeWitt's own unsworn, self-serving statement, untested by any cross-examination, that what he did was reasonable. And thus it will always be when courts try to look into the reasonableness of a military order.

In the very nature of things military decisions are not susceptible of intelligent judicial appraisal. They do not pretend to rest on evidence, but are made on information that often would not be admissible and on assumptions that could not be proved. Information in support of an order could not be disclosed to courts without danger that it would reach the enemy. Neither can courts act on communications made in confidence. Hence courts can never have any real alternative to accepting the mere declaration of the authority that issued the order that it was reasonably necessary from a military viewpoint.

* * *

I should hold that a civil court cannot be made to enforce an order which violates constitutional limitations even if it is a reasonable exercise of military authority. The courts can exercise only the judicial power, can apply only law, and must abide by the Constitution, or they cease to be civil courts and become instruments of military policy. Of course the existence of a military power resting on force, so vagrant, so centralized, so necessarily heedless of the individual, is an inherent threat to liberty. But I would not lead people to rely on this Court for a review that seems to me wholly delusive. The military reasonableness of these orders can only be determined by military superiors. If the people ever let command of the war power fall into irresponsible and unscrupulous hands, the courts wield no power equal to its restraint. The chief restraint upon those who command the physical forces of the country, in the future as in the past, must be their responsibility to the political judgments of their contemporaries and to the moral judgments of history.

My duties as a justice as I see them do not require me to make a military judgment as to whether General DeWitt's evacuation and detention program was a reasonable military necessity. I do not suggest that the courts should have attempted to interfere with the Army in carrying out its task. But I do not think they may be asked to execute a military expedient that has no place in law under the Constitution I would reverse the judgment and discharge the prisoner.

DISCUSSION AND QUESTIONS

1. The *Korematsu* decision has not been directly overturned by subsequent Supreme Court cases; however, Fred Korematsu's conviction and, more generally, the forced internment of tens of thousands of Americans for no reason other than their national heritage, have been discredited by history. Fred Korematsu's conviction was vacated in 1984 on a writ of coram nobis, an extraordinary procedure used at common law to correct judgments that are demonstrably based on fundamental errors. In vacating Korematsu's conviction more than 40 years later, U.S. District Judge Marilyn Patel concluded that the government had omitted material information and had provided misleading evidence in justifying the military exclusion order that was at issue in Korematsu's prosecution -- a finding that had been presaged by Justice Murphy's observation at the time that the exclusion order was based "mainly upon questionable racial and sociological grounds not ordinarily within the realm of expert military judgment, supplemented by certain semi-military conclusions drawn from an unwarranted use of circumstantial evidence." See *Korematsu v. United States*, 584 F. Supp. 1406 (N.D. Cal. 1984). In 1982, a Presidential Commission on Wartime Relocation and Internment of Civilians concluded that the forced internment of Japanese Americans

was based not on military necessity, but on "race prejudice, war hysteria, and a failure of political leadership." Based on the Commission's report, Congress passed the Civil Liberties Act of 1988, which offered a formal national apology for the "grave injustice" of internment and appropriated funds "to make restitution to those individuals of Japanese ancestry who were interned."

The forced relocation and internment of tens of thousands of American citizens based on nothing but their ancestry, and the absence of a judicial brake on such governmental action as is reflected in the *Korematsu* decision, represent an occasion in American history when the carefully crafted checks and balances among the branches failed. *Korematsu* illustrates why the constitutional separation of powers is not a wholly reliable system to deter overreaching government action: Because the three branches sometimes agree on governmental abuse of power. During World War II, the Executive Branch thought it appropriate to relocate Japanese Americans and ordered that such relocation occur; the Legislative Branch affirmatively facilitated such action through the passage of legislation; and the Judicial Branch -- rather than carefully scrutinize and question the actions of the political branches -- acquiesced.

2. The majority in *Korematsu* is careful to distinguish *exclusion* from *detention.* It makes clear that it is evaluating only the validity of the order excluding Japanese Americans from certain areas, not any supposedly separate questions that might arise from their detention at assembly centers or relocation centers. On the same day it issued the *Korematsu* decision, the Court also issued its decision in *Ex parte Endo*, which was a habeas corpus proceeding. Petitioner Endo had been held by the civilian War Relocation Authority and sought release through a habeas corpus petition. The government admitted that she was not disloyal to the United States and posed no threat of sabotage or espionage. The Court held that, even in a time of war, the government may not detain a loyal citizen who is charged with no crime and presents no threat:

> A citizen who is concededly loyal presents no problem of espionage or sabotage. Loyalty is a matter of the heart and mind, not of race, creed, or color. He who is loyal is, by definition, not a spy or a saboteur. When the power to detain is derived from the power to protect the war effort against espionage and sabotage, detention which has no relationship to that objective is unauthorized.

Ex parte Endo, 323 U.S. 283, 302 (1944). Is it possible to reconcile *Korematsu* with *Endo*? If detention of a loyal citizen cannot be justified even as a war measure, can the forcible exclusion of loyal citizens from their homes be justified -- particularly if the exclusion is accompanied by de facto detention in relocation camps? How would the courts have responded if the tens of thousands of other Japanese Americans placed in relocation camps had filed habeas corpus petitions? Undoubtedly, with respect to the vast majority of these individuals, the government would have been unable to produce evidence of disloyalty or threat. Under the reasoning of *Endo*, then, the detention of such individuals would be unrelated to the war effort and, therefore, unauthorized. Would the courts order the release of such individuals from relocation centers without further ordering that they must be permitted to return to their homes? If not, how would the courts (and the other branches, for that matter) legitimize the forcible exclusion of such individuals from their homes in the face of a judicial finding that there was no basis for detaining them?

3. Justice Jackson states he is unwilling to review the propriety of the exclusion order because that is a peculiarly military matter that is not within the purview of the courts. Yet, he would entertain Korematsu's appeal on the merits and would find that his conviction was unconstitutional. He explains that the military may enforce its own unconstitutional order (by excluding Japanese Americans from certain areas), but the courts should not enforce such an order (by imposing criminal penalties on those who violate the military's exclusion order). Justice Jackson seems to contemplate a republic where, during a time of war, the courts continue to enforce the Constitution and laws, yet exercise no oversight on the military, even when it engages in constitutionally suspect behavior. How would Justice Jackson have responded to a habeas corpus petition through which a civilian challenged as unlawful his detention by the military? Two years prior to the *Korematsu* decision, Justice Jackson participated in the unanimous decision in *Ex parte Quirin*, in which the Court held that the President, as commander in chief, was authorized to try spies and saboteurs in military commissions. (See Chapter 10, pages 292-99.) Is Justice Jackson's dissent in *Korematsu* consistent with the Court's approach in *Quirin*?

JUDICIAL RELUCTANCE TO INTERVENE

In the *Prize*, *Milligan*, *Korematsu* and *Endo* cases, the Judicial Branch was willing to address the claims on the merits, and in *Milligan* and *Endo*, to resolve the claims in favor of the individuals who were challenging the executive's asserted war power. Often, however, the Judicial Branch has been reluctant to place itself in the position of supervising the political branches' exercise of their constitutional war power. For example, in the matter of *Mitchell v. United States*, 386 U.S. 972 (1967), the petitioner was convicted of refusing to report for induction into the military; the Supreme Court declined to accept his appeal, which was based on the theory that U.S. "aggression" in Vietnam was illegal under international law. The same year, in

Mora v. McNamara, 389 U.S. 934 (1967), the Court refused to address the claim by members of the Army that they could not be ordered to Vietnam because the U.S. engagement there was not a properly declared war. Similarly, in yet another challenge to American military involvement in Vietnam, the D.C. Circuit characterized as a non-justiciable political question the debate about whether a "war" in the constitutional sense existed. *Mitchell v. Laird*, 488 F.2d 611 (1973).

More recently, courts have continued to find ways to avoid making pronouncements about the validity or invalidity of armed conflict abroad.

Campbell v. Clinton

203 F.3d 19 (D.C. Cir. 2000)[32]

SILBERMAN, Circuit Judge:

A number of congressmen, led by Tom Campbell of California, filed suit claiming that the President violated the War Powers Resolution and the War Powers Clause of the Constitution by directing U.S. forces' participation in the recent NATO campaign in Yugoslavia. The district court dismissed for lack of standing. We agree with the district court and therefore affirm.

On March 24, 1999, President Clinton announced the commencement of NATO air and cruise missile attacks on Yugoslav targets. Two days later he submitted to Congress a report, "consistent with the War Powers Resolution," detailing the circumstances necessitating the use of armed forces, the deployment's scope and expected duration, and asserting that he had "taken these actions pursuant to [his] authority ... as Commander in Chief and Chief Executive." On April 28, Congress voted on four resolutions related to the Yugoslav conflict: It voted down a declaration of war 427 to 2 and an "authorization" of the air strikes 213 to 213, but it also voted against requiring the President to immediately end U.S. participation in the NATO operation and voted to fund that involvement. The conflict between NATO and Yugoslavia continued for 79 days, ending on June 10 with Yugoslavia's agreement to withdraw its forces from Kosovo and allow deployment of a NATO-led peacekeeping force. Throughout this period Pentagon, State Department, and NATO spokesmen informed the public on a frequent basis of developments in the fighting.

---

[32] Footnotes and some citations found in the original decision have been omitted from this excerpted version.

Appellants, 31 congressmen opposed to U.S. involvement in the Kosovo intervention, filed suit prior to termination of that conflict seeking a declaratory judgment that the President's use of American forces against Yugoslavia was unlawful under both the War Powers Clause of the Constitution and the War Powers Resolution ("the WPR").

* * *

The government does not respond to appellants' claim on the merits. Instead the government challenges the jurisdiction of the federal courts to adjudicate this claim on three separate grounds: the case is moot; appellants lack standing, as the district court concluded; and the case is non-justiciable. Since we agree with the district court that the congressmen lack standing, it is not necessary to decide whether there are other jurisdictional defects.

The question whether congressmen have standing in federal court to challenge the lawfulness of actions of the executive was answered, at least in large part, in the Supreme Court's recent decision in *Raines v. Byrd*, 521 U.S. 811 (1997). *Raines* involved a constitutional challenge to the President's authority under the short-lived Line Item Veto Act. Individual congressmen claimed that under that Act a President could veto (unconstitutionally) only part of a law and thereby diminish the institutional power of Congress. Observing it had never held that congressmen have standing to assert an institutional injury as against the executive, *see id.* at 821, the Court held that petitioners in the case lacked "legislative standing" to challenge the Act. The Court observed that petitioners already possessed an adequate political remedy, since they could vote to have the Line Item Veto Act repealed, or to provide individual spending bills with a statutory exemption. *See id.* at 829.

Thereafter in *Chenoweth v. Clinton*, 181 F.3d 112, 115 (D.C. Cir. 1999), emphasizing the separation-of-powers problems inherent in legislative standing, we held that congressmen had no standing to challenge the President's introduction of a program through executive order rather than statute. As in *Raines*, appellants contended that the President's action inflicted an institutional injury upon Congress, in this case by circumventing its legislative authority, but, we said,

> it is uncontested that the Congress could terminate the [contested program] were a sufficient number in each House so inclined. Because the parties' dispute is

> therefore fully susceptible to political resolution, we would [under circuit precedent] dismiss the complaint to avoid "meddl[ing] in the internal affairs of the legislative branch." Applying *Raines* , we would reach the same conclusion.

Id . at 116 (citation omitted).

* * *

In this case, Congress certainly could have passed a law forbidding the use of U.S. forces in the Yugoslav campaign; indeed, there was a measure -- albeit only a concurrent resolution -- introduced to require the President to withdraw U.S. troops. Unfortunately, however, for those congressmen who, like appellants, desired an end to U.S. involvement in Yugoslavia, this measure was *defeated* by a 139 to 290 vote. Of course, Congress always retains appropriations authority and could have cut off funds for the American role in the conflict. Again there was an effort to do so but it failed; appropriations were authorized. And there always remains the possibility of impeachment should a President act in disregard of Congress' authority on these matters.

* * *

SILBERMAN, Circuit Judge, concurring:

Appellants argued that we should consider in our standing analysis that if congressmen lack standing only military personnel might be able to challenge a President's arguably unlawful use of force, and it would be undesirable to put the armed forces in such a position. Although that is not a consideration that bears on standing, *see Schlesinger v. Reservists Comm. to Stop the War*, 418 U.S. 208, 227 (1974), that argument leads me to observe that, in my view, no one is able to bring this challenge because the two claims are not justiciable. We lack "judicially discoverable and manageable standards" for addressing them, and the War Powers Clause claim implicates the political question doctrine. *See Baker v. Carr* , 369 U.S. 186, 217 (1962).

Prior litigation under the WPR has turned on the threshold test whether U.S. forces are engaged in hostilities or are in imminent danger of hostilities. But the question posed by appellants -- whether the President's refusal to discontinue American activities in Yugoslavia violates the WPR -- necessarily depends on the statute having been triggered in the first place. It has been held that the statutory threshold standard is not precise enough and too obviously calls for a political judgment to be one suitable for judicial determinations. *See, e.g.*, *Sanchez-Espinoza v. Reagan*, 770 F.2d 202, 209 (D.C. Cir. 1985) (aid to Contras); *Crockett v. Reagan*, 720 F.2d 1355, 1356-57 (D.C. Cir. 1983) (U.S. advisors in El Salvador); *see also Ange v. Bush*, 752 F. Supp. 509, 514 (D.D.C. 1990) (pre-Gulf War buildup); *Lowry v. Reagan*, 676 F. Supp. 333, 340 n.53 (D.D.C. 1987) (reflagging operations in the Persian Gulf). I think that is correct.

* * *

Nor is the constitutional claim justiciable. Appellants contend this case is governed by *Mitchell v. Laird* , 488 F.2d 611, 614 (D.C. Cir. 1973), where we said that "[t]here would be no insuperable difficulty in a court determining whether" the Vietnam conflict constituted a war in the Constitutional sense. *See also Dellums v. Bush* , 752 F. Supp. 1141, 1146 (D.D.C. 1990) ("[T]he Court has no hesitation in concluding that an offensive entry into Iraq by several hundred thousand United States servicemen ... could be described as a 'war' within the meaning ... of the Constitution."). But a careful reading of both cases reveals that the language upon which appellants rely is only dicta. (In *Laird* the Court ultimately held that the resolution of the issues was a political question. *See* 488 F.2d at 616.)

Appellants cannot point to any constitutional test for what is war. *See, e.g., Holtzman v. Schlesinger*, 414 U.S. 1316 (1973) (Justice Douglas, in chambers, vacating order of Court of Appeals granting stay of district court's injunction against bombing of Cambodia), 411 U.S. 1321 (1973) (Justice Marshall, in chambers, granting stay the same day with the concurrence of the other Justices); *Holtzman v. Schlesinger*, 484 F.2d 1307 (2d Cir. 1973) (holding legality of Cambodia bombing nonjusticiable because courts lack expertise to determine import of various military actions). Instead, appellants offer a rough definition of war provided in 1994 by an Assistant Attorney General to four Senators with respect to a planned intervention in Haiti, as well as a number of law review articles each containing its own definition of war. I do not think any of these sources, however, offers a coherent test for judges to apply to the question what constitutes war, a point only accentuated by the variances, for instance, between the numerous law review articles . . . Even if this court knows all there is to know about the Kosovo conflict, we still do not know what standards to apply to those facts.

* * *

Even assuming a court could determine what "war" is, it is important to remember that the Constitution grants Congress the power to declare war, which is not necessarily the same as the power to determine whether U.S. forces will fight in a war. This distinction was drawn in the *Prize Cases*, 67 U.S. 635 (1862). There, petitioners challenged the authority of the President to impose a blockade on the secessionist States, an act of war, where Congress had not declared war against the Confederacy. The Court, while recognizing that the President "has no power to initiate or declare a war," observed that "war may exist without a declaration on either side." *Id.* at 668. In instances where war is declared against the United States by the actions of another country, the President "does not initiate the war, but is bound to accept the challenge without waiting for any special legislative authority." *Id.* Importantly, the Court made clear that it would not dispute the President on measures necessary to repel foreign aggression. The President alone must determine what degree of force the crisis demands.

* * *

I read the *Prize Cases* to stand for the proposition that the President has independent authority to repel aggressive acts by third parties even without specific congressional authorization, and courts may not review the level of force selected. *See* Geoffrey Corn, *Presidential War Power: Do the Courts Offer Any Answers?*, 157 Mil. L. Rev. 180, 214 (1998); J. Gregory Sidak, *To Declare War*, 41 Duke L.J. 27, 54 (1991); Cyrus R. Vance, *Striking the Balance: Congress and the President Under the War Powers Resolution*, 133 U. Pa. L. Rev. 79, 85 (1984). Therefore, I assume, *arguendo*, that appellants are correct and only Congress has authority to *initiate* "war." If the President may direct U.S. forces in response to third-party initiated war, then the question any plaintiff who challenges the constitutionality of a war must answer is, who started it? The question of who is responsible for a conflict is, as history reveals, rather difficult to answer, and we lack judicial standards for resolving it.

* * *

In sum, there are no standards to determine either the statutory or constitutional questions raised in this case, and the question of whether the President has intruded on the war-declaring authority of Congress fits squarely within the political question doctrine. We therefore have another basis for our affirming the district court's dismissal of appellants' case.

[Judge RANDOLPH filed a concurring opinion in which he further discussed standing and mootness issues.]

TATEL, Circuit Judge, concurring:

I do not share [Judge Silberman's] view that the case poses a nonjusticiable political question. In my view, were this case brought by plaintiffs with standing, we could determine whether the President, in undertaking the air campaign in Yugoslavia, exceeded his authority under the Constitution or the War Powers Resolution.

To begin with, I do not agree that courts lack judicially discoverable and manageable standards for "determining the existence of a 'war.'" Brief of Appellee at 36. Whether the military activity in Yugoslavia amounted to "war" within the meaning of the Declare War Clause, U.S. Const. art. I, § 8, cl. 11, is no more standardless than any other question regarding the constitutionality of government action. Precisely what police conduct violates the Fourth Amendment guarantee "against unreasonable searches and seizures?" When does government action amount to "an establishment of religion" prohibited by the First Amendment? When is an election district so bizarrely shaped as to violate the Fourteenth Amendment guarantee of "equal protection of the laws?" Because such constitutional terms are not self-defining, standards for answering these questions have evolved, as legal standards always do, through years of judicial decisionmaking. Courts have proven no less capable of developing standards to resolve war powers challenges.

Since the earliest years of the nation, courts have not hesitated to determine when military action constitutes "war." In *Bas v. Tingy*, 4 U.S. 37 (1800), the Supreme Court had to decide whether hostilities between France and the United States amounted to a state of war in order to resolve disputes over captured ships. Because outright war had not been declared, the justices examined both the facts of the conflict ("the scene of bloodshed, depredation and confiscation, which has unhappily occurred," *id.* at 39) and the acts of Congress that had authorized limited military action: "In March 1799, congress had raised an army; stopped all intercourse with France; dissolved our treaty; built and equipt ships of war; and commissioned private armed ships; enjoining the former, and authorising the latter, to defend themselves against the armed ships of France, to attack them on the high seas, to subdue and take them as prize, and to re-capture armed vessels found in their possession." *Id.* at 41. Given these events, Justice Bushrod Washington concluded that France and the United States were at war both "[i]n fact and in law." *Id.* at 42. "If they were not our enemies," he said, "I know not what constitutes an enemy." *Id.* at 41. One year later, Chief Justice Marshall, focusing on the same conflict with France, said: "The whole powers of war being, by the constitution of the United States, vested in congress, the acts of that body can alone be resorted to as our guides in this enquiry.... To determine the real situation of America in regard to France, the acts of congress are to be inspected." *Talbot v. Seeman*, 5 U.S. 1, 28 (1801).

Half a century later, in *The Prize Cases*, 67 U.S. 635, 666 (1862), the Court had to determine whether a state of war, though undeclared, existed " *de facto*" between the United States and the confederacy, and if so, whether it justified the U.S. naval blockade of confederate ports. "As a civil war is never publicly proclaimed, ... its actual existence is a fact in our domestic history which the Court is bound to notice and to know." *Id.* at 667. There was no formal declaration of war, the Court explained, because the Constitution does not permit Congress to "declare war against a State, or any number of States." *Id.* at 668. Yet the Court, guided by the definition of war as "[t]hat state in which a nation prosecutes its right by force," *id.* at 666, determined that a state of war actually existed. "A civil war is never solemnly declared; it becomes such by its accidents -- the number, power, and organization of the persons who originate and carry it on. When the party in rebellion occupy and hold in a hostile manner a certain portion of territory; have declared their independence; have cast off their allegiance; have organized armies; have commenced hostilities against their former sovereign, the world acknowledges them as belligerents, and the contest *a war*." *Id.* at 666-67. In making this determination, the Court looked to the facts of the conflict, *id.*, to the acts of foreign governments recognizing the war and declaring their neutrality, *id.* at 669, and to congressional action authorizing the President's use of force, *id.* at 670-71. Given these facts, the Court refused "to affect a technical ignorance of the existence of a war, which all the world acknowledges to be the greatest civil war known in the history of the human race." *Id.* at 669.

*   *   *

The undisputed facts of this case are equally compelling with respect to plaintiffs' constitutional claim. If in 1799 the Supreme Court could recognize that sporadic battles between American and French vessels amounted to a state of war, and if in 1862 it could examine the record of hostilities and conclude that a state of war existed with the confederacy, then surely we, looking to similar evidence, could determine whether months of daily airstrikes involving 800 U.S. aircraft flying more than 20,000 sorties and causing thousands of enemy casualties amounted to "war" within the meaning of Article I, section 8, clause 11.

Determining whether a state of war exists would certainly be more difficult in situations involving more limited military force over a shorter period of time. But just as we never shrink from deciding a First Amendment case simply because we can imagine a more difficult one, the fact that a challenge to a different military action might present a closer question would not justify abdicating our responsibility to construe the law and apply it to the facts of this case.

Doe v. Bush

323 F.3d 133 (1st. Cir. 2003)[33]

LYNCH, Circuit Judge:

Plaintiffs are active-duty members of the military, parents of military personnel, and members of the U.S. House of Representatives. They filed a complaint in district court seeking a preliminary injunction to prevent the defendants, President George W. Bush and Secretary of Defense Donald Rumsfeld, from initiating a war against Iraq. They assert that such an action would violate the Constitution. The district court dismissed the suit, and plaintiffs appeal. We affirm the dismissal.

In October 2002, Congress passed the Authorization for Use of Military Force Against Iraq Resolution of 2002 (the "October Resolution"), Pub L. No. 107-243, 116 Stat. 1498. Plaintiffs argue that the October Resolution is constitutionally inadequate to authorize the military offensive that defendants are now planning against Iraq. *See* U.S. Const. art. I, § 8, cl. 11 (granting Congress the power "[t]o declare war"). They base this argument on two theories. They argue that Congress and the President are in collision -- that the President is about to act in violation of the October Resolution. They also argue that Congress and the President are in collusion -- that Congress has handed over to the President its exclusive power to declare war.

[33] Footnotes and some citations found in the original decision have been omitted from this excerpted version.

In either case, plaintiffs argue, judicial intervention is necessary to preserve the principle of separation of powers which undergirds our constitutional structure. Only the judiciary, they argue, has the constitutionally assigned role and the institutional competence to police the boundaries of the constitutional mandates given to the other branches: Congress alone has the authority to declare war and the President alone has the authority to make war.

The plaintiffs argue that important and increasingly vital interests are served by the requirement that it be Congress which decides whether to declare war. Quoting Thomas Jefferson, they argue that congressional involvement will slow the "dogs of war"; that Congress, the voice of the people, should make this momentous decision, one which will cost lives; and that congressional support is needed to ensure that the country is behind the war, a key element in any victory. They also argue that, absent an attack on this country or our allies, congressional involvement must come prior to war, because once war has started, Congress is in an uncomfortable default position where the use of its appropriations powers to cut short any war is an inadequate remedy.

The defendants are equally eloquent about the impropriety of judicial intrusion into the "extraordinarily delicate foreign affairs and military calculus, one that could be fatally upset by judicial interference." Such intervention would be all the worse here, defendants say, because Congress and the President are in accord as to the threat to the nation and the legitimacy of a military response to that threat.

The case before us is a somber and weighty one. We have considered these important concerns carefully, and we have concluded that the circumstances call for judicial restraint. The theory of collision between the legislative and executive branches is not suitable for judicial review, because there is not a ripe dispute concerning the President's acts and the requirements of the October Resolution passed by Congress. By contrast, the theory of collusion, by its nature, assumes no conflict between the political branches, but rather a willing abdication of congressional power to an emboldened and enlarged presidency. That theory is not fit for judicial review for a different, but related, reason: Plaintiffs' claim that Congress and the President have transgressed the boundaries of their shared war powers, as demarcated by the Constitution, is presently insufficient to present a justiciable issue. Common to both is our assessment that, before courts adjudicate a case involving the war powers allocated to the two political branches, they must be presented with a case or controversy that clearly raises the specter of undermining the constitutional structure.

* * *

The Constitution reserves the war powers to the legislative and executive branches. This court has declined the invitation to become involved in such matters once before. Over thirty years ago, the First Circuit addressed a war powers case challenging the constitutionality of the Vietnam War on the basis that Congress had not declared war. *Massachusetts v. Laird,* 451 F.2d 26 (1st Cir.1971). The court found that other actions by Congress, such as continued appropriations to fund the war over the course of six years, *id.* at 34, provided enough indication of congressional approval to put the question beyond the reach of judicial review:

> The war in Vietnam is a product of the jointly supportive actions of the two branches to whom the congeries of the war powers have been committed. Because the branches are not in opposition, there is no necessity of determining boundaries. Should either branch be opposed to the continuance of hostilities, however, and present the issue in clear terms, a court might well take a different view. This question we do not face.

Id.

* * *

The lack of a fully developed dispute between the two elected branches, and the consequent lack of a clearly defined issue, is exactly the type of concern which causes courts to find a case unripe. In his concurring opinion in *Goldwater v. Carter,* 444 U.S. 996 (1979), Justice Powell stated that courts should decline, on ripeness grounds, to decide "issues affecting the allocation of power between the President and Congress until the political branches reach a constitutional impasse." *Id.* at 997 (Powell, J., concurring). A number of courts have adopted Justice Powell's ripeness reasoning in cases involving military powers. *See Greenham Women Against Cruise Missiles v. Reagan,* 755 F.2d 34, 37 (2d Cir.1985) (per curiam); *Dellums v. Bush,* 752 F.Supp. 1141, 1150 & nn. 23-25 (D.D.C.1990); *see also Sanchez-Espinoza v. Reagan,* 770 F.2d 202, 210-11 (D.C.Cir.1985) (R. Ginsburg, J., concurring).

Ripeness doctrine involves more than simply the timing of the case. It mixes various mutually reinforcing constitutional and prudential considerations. *See Mangual v. Rotger-Sabat,* 317 F.3d 45, 59 (1st Cir.2003). One such consideration is the need "to prevent the courts, through avoidance of premature adjudication, from entangling themselves in abstract disagreements." *Abbott Labs. v. Gardner,* 387 U.S. 136, 148 (1967). Another is to avoid unnecessary constitutional decisions. *Reg'l Rail Reorganization Act Cases,* 419 U.S. 102, 138 (1974). A third is the recognition that, by waiting until a case is fully developed before deciding it, courts benefit from a focus sharpened by particular facts. *See Ohio Forestry Ass'n v. Sierra Club,* 523 U.S. 726, 736 (1998). The case before us raises all three of these concerns.

* * *

For various reasons, this issue is not fit now for judicial review. For example, should there be an attack, Congress may take some action immediately. The purported conflict between the political branches may disappear. "[T]hat the future event may never come to pass augurs against a finding of fitness." *McInnis-Misenor,* 319 F.3d at 72.

Many important questions remain unanswered about whether there will be a war, and, if so, under what conditions. Diplomatic negotiations, in particular, fluctuate daily. The President has emphasized repeatedly that hostilities still may be averted if Iraq takes certain actions. The Security Council is now debating the possibility of passing a new resolution that sets a final deadline for Iraqi compliance. United Nations weapons inspectors continue their investigations inside Iraq. Other countries ranging from Canada to Cameroon have reportedly pursued their own proposals to broker a compromise. As events unfold, it may become clear that diplomacy has either succeeded or failed decisively. The Security Council, now divided on the issue, may reach a consensus. To evaluate this claim now, the court would need to pile one hypothesis on top of another. We would need to assume that the Security Council will not authorize war, and that the President will proceed nonetheless. *See id.* at 72-73 (outlining chain of uncertain events necessary to make case ripe); *Ernst & Young,* 45 F.3d at 538 (same).

Thus, even assuming that plaintiffs correctly interpret the commands of the legislative branch, it is impossible to say yet whether or not those commands will be obeyed. As was the situation in *Goldwater,* "[i]n the present posture of this case, we do not know whether there will ever be an actual confrontation between the Legislative and Executive Branches." 444 U.S. at 998 (Powell, J., concurring).

DISCUSSION AND QUESTIONS

1. Cases like *Campbell v. Clinton*, *Doe v. Bush*, and the several Vietnam-era challenges to American military involvement in southeast Asia have arisen in large part because, although Congress implicitly or explicitly supported military action on those occasions, it chose not to declare war. Many important legal questions about the exercise of governmental power, particularly executive power, are answered when Congress formally declares war. Why is Congress unwilling to declare war even when a majority clearly favors an extensive deployment of American military power? Given Congress' unwillingness formally to declare war before the Persian Gulf War of 1990-91, before the Iraq War that began in 2003, or in response to the attacks of September 11, 2001, could one plausibly predict that Congress will never again declare war in any circumstances that can reasonably be foreseen?

2. In *Campbell v. Clinton*, the court relied on standing doctrine to avoid addressing the merits, but the more interesting aspect of the case is the debate between Judges Silberman and Tatel in their concurring opinions. Silberman believes that, in general, disputes about whether an armed conflict amounts to "war" for legal purposes and whether a particular military action is legal or illegal will always be non-justiciable political questions because there are no judicially manageable standards for determining what war is. In contrast, Tatel believes that such disputes may be difficult to decide on the merits, but no more difficult than many other types of constitutional disputes that courts resolve every day. Who is correct? Does not Judge Tatel have a valid point when he opines that a court "could determine whether months of daily airstrikes involving 800 U.S. aircraft flying more than 20,000 sorties and causing thousands of enemy casualties" amounts to war? On the other hand, if the courts are asked to determine whether a particular armed conflict is *legal* or *illegal*, is that a different question?

3. The court in *Doe v. Bush* uses ripeness doctrine to avoid the merits. Distilled to its essence, the court appears to be saying that a dispute about the exercise of governmental war power cannot be ripe until the nation's armed forces are actually embroiled in military conflict; until that moment arrives, the courts cannot know that armed conflict will actually take place and, if it does, under precisely what circumstances or for exactly what reasons. Does this approach reflect judicial prudence or imprudence? If there is non-frivolous argument to be made that a President is exceeding his war-making authority, is a court in a better position to

provide a remedy for such potential abuse of power if it waits until tens of thousands of troops are sent to foreign lands and actively engaged in armed conflict?

4. There are many cases that exemplify judicial reluctance to make binding pronouncements about the legitimacy or illegitimacy of military action; whether by reference to standing, ripeness, political question or other jurisprudential doctrines, courts generally find ways to avoid ruling on the merits of disputes about the nature and scope of the war power. Would it make a difference in how courts handle such cases if Congress were to include in an authorization for the use of military force an express provision favoring judicial review? Suppose that, in response to some future threat, Congress enacted a joint resolution that provided:

> The Congress hereby authorizes the President to use all necessary and appropriate military force [against certain enemies for certain purposes]. Any United States citizen who is materially and adversely affected by the President's decision to use military force may seek and obtain judicial review of the propriety of such use of military force in the courts of the United States.

Would the language providing for judicial review be enforceable? Would the courts provide such review, or -- despite the stated intentions of Congress -- would they find ways to avoid reviewing the President's decisions about the use of military force?

CHAPTER TEN:
WAR POWER -- EVOLUTION OF THE JUDICIARY'S ROLE AND DIMINUTION OF EXECUTIVE POWER

As is explained above in Chapter Nine, with a very few notable exceptions (*Ex parte Milligan*, for example), the Judicial Branch has historically declined to overturn decisions made by the political branches with respect to prosecuting war. The courts tend either to stay on the sidelines (as in *Campbell v. Clinton* and *Doe v. Bush*) or affirmatively to approve the actions taken (as in *Korematsu*). This pattern was followed in two habeas corpus cases brought by enemy combatants as a result of World War II: *Ex parte Quirin* and *Johnson v. Eisentrager*, which are excerpted below.

Largely as a result of the Supreme Court's hands-off approach in these World War II cases, the Administration of President George W. Bush believed it understood the scope of its authority -- that is, essentially unlimited -- to detain and prosecute unlawful enemy combatants captured in the "War on Terror" that followed the terrorist attacks of September 11, 2001. However, the Supreme Court of the early twenty-first century responded to bold exercises of the commander in chief power much differently from the Supreme Court of six decades earlier. The cases that arose as a result of the War on Terror reveal a court that is much more willing to engage in active supervision of the other branches, especially the executive, and even to reverse their decisions about managing armed conflict.

This chapter will review and compare the two World War II cases and the four War on Terror cases of 2004 through 2008, and will thereby highlight the relative expansion of judicial power and concomitant diminution of executive power that has resulted.

ENEMY COMBATANTS: WORLD WAR II

In 1942, Germany launched a covert operation to attack transportation and industrial facilities in the United States. The plan was dubbed "Operation Pastorius" after Franz Daniel Pastorius, who was one of the earliest German settlers in North America in the 17th century. The operation commenced with the successful insertion of eight saboteurs on the East Coast by U-boat; however, the mission was foiled and the would-be saboteurs captured when one of them, George Dasch, with the knowledge and support of team member Ernst Burger, decided to betray the plan and revealed it to the Federal Bureau of Investigation.

After their capture, at the direction of President Franklin Roosevelt, the eight saboteurs -- one of whom was a U.S. citizen -- were tried by military commission for violations of the laws of war. All eight were convicted and six were executed. The turncoats, Dasch and Burger, were given commuted sentences by President Roosevelt and later were given clemency by President Truman and sent back to Germany. The defendants filed habeas corpus petitions asserting that the President lacked authority to try them by military commission.

Ex parte Quirin

317 U.S. 1 (1942)[34]

Mr. Chief Justice STONE delivered the opinion of the Court.

These cases are brought here by petitioners' several applications for leave to file petitions for habeas corpus in this Court, and by their petitions for certiorari to review orders of the District Court for the District of Columbia, which denied their applications for leave to file petitions for habeas corpus in that court.

The question for decision is whether the detention of petitioners by respondent for trial by Military Commission, appointed by Order of the President of July 2, 1942, on charges preferred against them purporting to set out their violations of the law of war and of the Articles of War, is in conformity to the laws and Constitution of the United States.

[The Court summarizes the facts: The petitioners are agents of the German government who came secretly to the United States to engage in sabotage. They were captured by the FBI. One claims to be a naturalized U.S. citizen.]

The President, as President and Commander in Chief of the Army and Navy, by Order of July 2, 1942,2 appointed a Military Commission and directed it to try petitioners for offenses against the law of war and the Articles of War, and prescribed regulations for the procedure on the trial and for review of the record of the trial and of any judgment or sentence of the Commission. On the same day, by Proclamation,3 the President declared that

[34] Footnotes and some citations found in the original decision have been omitted from this excerpted version.

> all persons who are subjects, citizens or residents of any nation at war with the United States or who give obedience to or act under the direction of any such nation, and who during time of war enter or attempt to enter the United States ... through coastal or boundary defenses, and are charged with committing or attempting or preparing to commit sabotage, espionage, hostile or warlike acts, or violations of the law of war, shall be subject to the law of war and to the jurisdiction of military tribunals.

The Proclamation also stated in terms that all such persons were denied access to the courts.

* * *

On July 3, 1942, the Judge Advocate General's Department of the Army prepared and lodged with the Commission the following charges against petitioners, supported by specifications:

1. Violation of the law of war.

2. Violation of Article 81 of the Articles of War, defining the offense of relieving or attempting to relieve, or corresponding with or giving intelligence to, the enemy.

3. Violation of Article 82, defining the offense of spying.

4. Conspiracy to commit the offenses alleged in charges 1, 2 and 3.

The Commission met on July 8, 1942, and proceeded with the trial, which continued in progress while the causes were pending in this Court. On July 27th, before petitioners' applications to the District Court, all the evidence for the prosecution and the defense had been taken by the Commission and the case had been closed except for arguments of counsel. It is conceded that ever since petitioners' arrest the state and federal courts in Florida, New York, and the District of Columbia, and in the states in which each of the petitioners was arrested or detained, have been open and functioning normally.

* * *

Petitioners' main contention is that the President is without any statutory or constitutional authority to order the petitioners to be tried by military tribunal for offenses with which they are charged; that in consequence they are entitled to be tried in the civil courts with the safeguards, including trial by jury, which the Fifth and Sixth Amendments guarantee to all persons charged in such courts with criminal offenses. In any case it is urged that the President's Order, in prescribing the procedure of the Commission and the method for review of its findings and sentence, and the proceedings of the Commission under the Order, conflict with Articles of War adopted by Congress-particularly Articles 38, 43, 46, 50 1/2 and 70-and are illegal and void.

* * *

Congress and the President, like the courts, possess no power not derived from the Constitution. But one of the objects of the Constitution, as declared by its preamble, is to 'provide for the common defence'. As a means to that end the Constitution gives to Congress the power to 'provide for the common Defence', Art. I, 8, cl. 1; 'To raise and support Armies', 'To provide and maintain a Navy', Art. I, 8, cls. 12, 13; and 'To make Rules for the Government and Regulation of the land and naval Forces', Art. I, 8, cl. 14. Congress is given authority 'To declare War, grant Letters of Marque and Reprisal, and make Rules concerning Captures on Land and Water', Art. I, 8, cl. 11; and 'To define and punish Piracies and Felonies committed on the high Seas, and Offenses against the Law of Nations', Art. I, 8, cl. 10. And finally the Constitution authorizes Congress 'To make all Laws which shall be necessary and proper for carrying into Execution the foregoing Powers, and all other Powers vested by this Constitution in the Government of the United States, or in any Department or Officer thereof.' Art. I, 8, cl. 18.

The Constitution confers on the President the 'executive Power', Art II, 1, cl. 1, and imposes on him the duty to 'take Care that the Laws be faithfully executed'. Art. II, 3. It makes him the Commander in Chief of the Army and Navy, Art. II, 2, cl. 1, and empowers him to appoint and commission officers of the United States. Art. II, 3, cl. 1.

The Constitution thus invests the President as Commander in Chief with the power to wage war which Congress has declared, and to carry into effect all laws passed by Congress for the conduct of war and for the government and regulation of the Armed Forces, and all laws defining and punishing offences against the law of nations, including those which pertain to the conduct of war.

By the Articles of War, 10 U.S.C. 1471-1593, 10 U.S.C.A. 1471-1593, Congress has provided rules for the government of the Army. It has provided for the trial and punishment, by courts martial, of violations of the Articles by members of the armed forces and by specified classes of persons associated or serving with the Army. Arts. 1, 2. But the Articles also recognize the "military commission" appointed by military command as an appropriate tribunal for the trial and punishment of offenses against the law of war not ordinarily tried by court martial. See Arts. 12, 15. Articles 38 and 46 authorize the President, with certain limitations, to prescribe the procedure for military commissions. Articles 81 and 82 authorize trial, either by court martial or military commission, of those charged with relieving, harboring or corresponding with the enemy and those charged with spying. And Article 15 declares that 'the provisions of these articles conferring jurisdiction upon courts-martial shall not be construed as depriving military commissions ... or other military tribunals of concurrent jurisdiction in respect of offenders or offenses that by statute or by the law of war may be triable by such military commissions ... or other military tribunals'. Article 2 includes among those persons subject to military law the personnel of our own military establishment. But this, as Article 12 provides, does not exclude from that class 'any other person who by the law of war is subject to trial by military tribunals' and who under Article 12 may be tried by court martial or under Article 15 by military commission.

Similarly the Espionage Act of 1917, which authorizes trial in the district courts of certain offenses that tend to interfere with the prosecution of war, provides that nothing contained in the act 'shall be deemed to limit the jurisdiction of the general courts-martial, military commissions, or naval courts-martial'. 50 U.S.C. 38, 50 U.S.C.A. 38.

From the very beginning of its history this Court has recognized and applied the law of war as including that part of the law of nations which prescribes, for the conduct of war, the status, rights and duties of enemy nations as well as of enemy individuals. By the Articles of War, and especially Article 15, Congress has explicitly provided, so far as it may constitutionally do so, that military tribunals shall have jurisdiction to try offenders or offenses against the law of war in appropriate cases. Congress, in addition to making rules for the government of our Armed Forces, has thus exercised its authority to define and punish offenses against the law of nations by sanctioning, within constitutional limitations, the jurisdiction of military commissions to try persons for offenses which, according to the rules and precepts of the law of nations, and more particularly the law of war, are cognizable by such tribunals. And the President, as Commander in Chief, by his Proclamation in time of war his invoked that law. By his Order creating the present Commission he has undertaken to exercise the authority conferred upon him by Congress, and also such authority as the Constitution itself gives the Commander in Chief, to direct the performance of those functions which may constitutionally be performed by the military arm of the nation in time of war.

An important incident to the conduct of war is the adoption of measures by the military command not only to repel and defeat the enemy, but to seize and subject to disciplinary measures those enemies who in their attempt to thwart or impede our military effort have violated the law of war. It is unnecessary for present purposes to determine to what extent the President as Commander in Chief has constitutional power to create military commissions without the support of Congressional legislation. For here Congress has authorized trial of offenses against the law of war before such commissions. We are concerned only with the question whether it is within the constitutional power of the national government to place petitioners upon trial before a military commission for the offenses with which they are charged.

* * *

By universal agreement and practice the law of war draws a distinction between the armed forces and the peaceful populations of belligerent nations and also between those who are lawful and unlawful combatants. Lawful combatants are subject to capture and detention as prisoners of war by opposing military forces. Unlawful combatants are likewise subject to capture and detention, but in addition they are subject to trial and punishment by military tribunals for acts which render their belligerency unlawful. The spy who secretly and without uniform passes the military lines of a belligerent in time of war, seeking to gather military information and communicate it to the enemy, or an enemy combatant who without uniform comes secretly through the lines for the purpose of waging war by destruction of life or property, are familiar examples of belligerents who are generally deemed not to be entitled to the status of prisoners of war, but to be offenders against the law of war subject to trial and punishment by military tribunals. See Winthrop, Military Law, 2d Ed., pp. 1196-1197, 1219-1221; Instructions for the Government of Armies of the United States in the Field, approved by the President, General Order No. 100, April 24, 1863, sections IV and V.

[Through law and treaty, the United States has recognized that "lawful belligerents" are combatants who bear arms openly and display fixed insignia indicating their allegiance. Those who engage in hostilities without identification are punishable as war criminals.]

Our Government, by thus defining lawful belligerents entitled to be treated as prisoners of war, has recognized that there is a class of unlawful belligerents not entitled to that privilege, including those who though combatants do not wear "fixed and distinctive emblems." And by Article 15 of the Articles of War Congress has made provision for their trial and punishment by military commission, according to "the law of war."

By a long course of practical administrative construction by its military authorities, our Government has likewise recognized that those who during time of war pass surreptitiously from enemy territory into our own, discarding their uniforms upon entry, for the commission of hostile acts involving destruction of life or property, have the status of unlawful combatants punishable as such by military commission. This precept of the law of war has been so recognized in practice both here and abroad, and has so generally been accepted as valid by authorities on international law that we think it must be regarded as a rule or principle of the law of war recognized by this Government by its enactment of the Fifteenth Article of War.

[The offenses with which the petitioners are charged would, if proved, be violations of the law of war, and therefore triable by military commission.]

Citizenship in the United States of an enemy belligerent does not relieve him from the consequences of a belligerency which is unlawful because in violation of the law of war. Citizens who associate themselves with the military arm of the enemy government, and with its aid, guidance and direction enter this country bent on hostile acts are enemy belligerents within the meaning of the Hague Convention and the law of war. Cf. Gates v. Goodloe, 101 U.S. 612, 615, 617, 618 . . .

Nor are petitioners any the less belligerents if, as they argue, they have not actually committed or attempted to commit any act of depredation or entered the theatre or zone of active military operations. The argument leaves out of account the nature of the offense which the Government charges and which the Act of Congress, by incorporating the law of war, punishes. It is that each petitioner, in circumstances which gave him the status of an enemy belligerent, passed our military and naval lines and defenses or went behind those lines, in civilian dress and with hostile purpose. The offense was complete when with that purpose they entered -- or, having so entered, they remained upon -- our territory in time of war without uniform or other appropriate means of identification. For that reason, even when committed by a citizen, the offense is distinct from the crime of treason defined in Article III, 3 of the Constitution, since the absence of uniform essential to one is irrelevant to the other. Cf. Morgan v. Devine, 237 U.S. 632; Albrecht v. United States, 273 U.S. 1, 11.

[The Court explains that the protections afforded to criminal defendants by the Fifth and Sixth Amendments do not apply in the context of military commissions. These amendments were not intended to expand the rights set forth therein beyond their accepted application at the time the amendments were adopted. For example, the Sixth Amendment guarantee of a jury trial was not intended to apply to military commissions, because the trial of war criminals by military commission has never been deemed to require a jury of one's peers.]

Petitioners, and especially petitioner Haupt [the American citizen], stress the pronouncement of this Court in the Milligan case, 4 Wall. page 121, that the law of war "can never be applied to citizens in states which have upheld the authority of the government, and where the courts are open and their process unobstructed." Elsewhere in its opinion, 4 Wall. at pages 118, 121, 122, and 131, the Court was at pains to point out that Milligan, a citizen twenty years resident in Indiana, who had never been a resident of any of the states in rebellion, was not an enemy belligerent either entitled to the status of a prisoner of war or subject to the penalties imposed upon unlawful belligerents. We construe the Court's statement as to the inapplicability of the law of war to Milligan's case as having particular reference to the facts before it. From them the Court concluded that Milligan, not being a part of or associated with the armed forces of the enemy, was a non-belligerent, not subject to the law of war save as -- in circumstances found not there to be present and not involved here -- martial law might be constitutionally established.

The Court's opinion is inapplicable to the case presented by the present record. We have no occasion now to define with meticulous care the ultimate boundaries of the jurisdiction of military tribunals to try persons according to the law of war. It is enough that petitioners here, upon the conceded facts, were plainly within those boundaries, and were held in good faith for trial by military commission, charged with being enemies who, with the purpose of destroying war materials

> and utilities, entered or after entry remained in our territory without uniform-an offense against the law of war. We hold only that those particular acts constitute an offense against the law of war which the Constitution authorizes to be tried by military commission.

DISCUSSION AND QUESTIONS

1. Notably, the petitioners in *Quirin* did not challenge their classification as unlawful combatants; rather, they tacitly accepted their characterization as unlawful combatants but argued that, even so, the President lacked the power to try them before military commissions instead of the federal courts. How would the Court have reacted to the habeas corpus petition if the defendants had argued that they could not be tried before military commissions because they simply were not combatants at all? Would the Judicial Branch permit habeas corpus petitioners to challenge the commander in chief's designation of who is an unlawful combatant, or would the courts accord complete deference on such matters to the commander in chief, who is actually responsible for the war effort?

2. The principal teaching of *Quirin* is that the commander in chief may use military commissions to try unlawful combatants for violations of the law of war -- the power to do so is an inherent element of the general power to do that which is necessary effectively to prosecute war. Yet, there are many questions left unanswered by *Quirin*, such as: What are the rules for military commissions? What degree of due process is required (if any)? And, who decides these matters? The President? The Congress? The courts? The *Quirin* Court found that Congress had authorized the use of military commissions. Suppose that, in doing so, the Congress spelled out specific evidentiary and other procedural rules to govern the work of such commissions -- would the President be bound by such rules, or could he, as commander in chief, disregard such rules and substitute other rules that he believed to be more suitable to the particular circumstances?

3. According to the reasoning in *Quirin*, citizenship is no protection against being tried by military commission. Nor does geography offer any protection; even individuals found hundreds or thousands of miles away from the battlefield may be classified and tried as unlawful combatants. What safeguards would be in place, then, to prevent an unethical and unrestrained President from declaring certain political enemies as unlawful combatants and trying them by military commissions that, ultimately, are answerable only to him? In his 2004 documentary *Fahrenheit 9/11*, liberal filmmaker Michael Moore was extremely

critical of President George W. Bush's War on Terror and also critical of the President personally. Imagine that an angry President Bush had classified Moore as an unlawful combatant who had (in some unspecified or manufactured fashion) given aid to the al Qaeda terrorist network, and then directed Moore's trial by military commission. Would there be any judicial check on such presidential abuse of power?

Several years after the *Quirin* defendants were tried by military commission, similar tribunals were used again to try German nationals located in China who had violated the law of war by continuing to engage in hostile action after their nation unconditionally surrendered. After their transfer to Landsberg Prison in Germany, the defendants sought habeas corpus relief. Unlike *Quirin*, however, the case turned not on the legitimacy of military commission proceedings, but on the threshold question of whether aliens detained abroad could invoke the Great Writ in the courts of the United States.

Johnson v. Eisentrager

339 U.S. 763 (1950)[35]

MR. JUSTICE JACKSON delivered the opinion of the Court.

The ultimate question in this case is one of jurisdiction of civil courts of the United States vis-a-vis military authorities in dealing with enemy aliens overseas. The issues come here in this way:

Twenty-one German nationals petitioned the District Court of the District of Columbia for writs of habeas corpus. They alleged that, prior to May 8, 1945, they were in the service of German armed forces in China. They amended to allege that their employment there was by civilian agencies of the German Government. Their exact affiliation is disputed, and, for our purposes, immaterial. On May 8, 1945, the German High Command executed an act of unconditional surrender, expressly obligating all forces under German control at once to cease active hostilities. These prisoners have been convicted of violating laws of war, by engaging in, permitting or ordering continued military activity against the United States after surrender of Germany and before surrender of Japan. Their hostile operations consisted principally of collecting and furnishing intelligence

[35] Footnotes and some citations found in the original decision have been omitted from this excerpted version.

concerning American forces and their movements to the Japanese armed forces. They, with six others who were acquitted, were taken into custody by the United States Army after the Japanese surrender and were tried and convicted by a Military Commission constituted by our Commanding General at Nanking by delegation from the Commanding General, United States Forces, China Theater, pursuant to authority specifically granted by the Joint Chiefs of Staff of the United States. The Commission sat in China, with express consent of the Chinese Government. The proceeding was conducted wholly under American auspices and involved no international participation. After conviction, the sentences were duly reviewed and, with immaterial modification, approved by military reviewing authority.

The prisoners were repatriated to Germany to serve their sentences. Their immediate custodian is Commandant of Landsberg Prison, an American Army officer under the Commanding General, Third United States Army, and the Commanding General, European Command. He could not be reached by process from the District Court. Respondents named in the petition are Secretary of Defense, Secretary of the Army, Chief of Staff of the Army, and the Joint Chiefs of Staff of the United States.

The petition alleges, and respondents denied, that the jailer is subject to their direction. The Court of Appeals assumed, and we do likewise, that, while prisoners are in immediate physical custody of an officer or officers not parties to the proceeding, respondents named in the petition have lawful authority to effect their release.

The petition prays an order that the prisoners be produced before the District Court, that it may inquire into their confinement and order them discharged from such offenses and confinement. It is claimed that their trial, conviction and imprisonment violate Articles I and III of the Constitution, and the Fifth Amendment thereto, and other provisions of the Constitution and laws of the United States and provisions of the Geneva Convention governing treatment of prisoners of war.

* * *

We are cited to no instance where a court, in this or any other country where the writ is known, has issued it on behalf of an alien enemy who, at no relevant time and in no stage of his captivity, has been within its territorial jurisdiction. Nothing in the text of the Constitution extends such a right, nor does anything in our statutes. Absence of support from legislative or juridical sources is implicit in the statement of the court below that "The answers stem directly from fundamentals. They cannot be found by casual reference to statutes or cases." The breadth of the court's premises and solution requires us to consider questions basic to alien enemy and kindred litigation which for some years have been beating upon our doors.

Modern American law has come a long way since the time when outbreak of war made every enemy national an outlaw, subject to both public and private slaughter, cruelty and plunder. But even by the most magnanimous view, our law does not abolish inherent distinctions recognized throughout the civilized world between citizens and aliens, nor between aliens of friendly and of enemy allegiance, nor between resident enemy aliens who have submitted themselves to our laws and non-resident enemy aliens who at all times have remained with, and adhered to, enemy governments.

With the citizen we are now little concerned, except to set his case apart as untouched by this decision and to take measure of the difference between his status and that of all categories of aliens. Citizenship as a head of jurisdiction and a ground of protection was old when Paul invoked it in his appeal to Caesar. The years have not destroyed nor diminished the importance of citizenship nor have they sapped the vitality of a citizen's claims upon his government for protection. If a person's claim to United States citizenship is denied by any official, Congress has directed our courts to entertain his action to declare him to be a citizen "regardless of whether he is within the United States or abroad." 54 Stat. 1171, 8 U.S.C. 903. This Court long ago extended habeas corpus to one seeking admission to the country to assure fair hearing of his claims to citizenship, Chin Yow v. United States, 208 U.S. 8, and has secured citizenship against forfeiture by involuntary formal acts, Perkins v. Elg, 307 U.S. 325. Because the Government's obligation of protection is correlative with the duty of loyal support inherent in the citizen's allegiance, Congress has directed the President to exert the full diplomatic and political power of the United States on behalf of any citizen, but of no other, in jeopardy abroad. When any citizen is deprived of his liberty by any foreign government, it is made the duty of the President to demand the reasons and, if the detention appears wrongful, to use means not amounting to acts of war to effectuate his release. It is neither sentimentality nor chauvinism to repeat that "Citizenship is a high privilege." United States v. Manzi, 276 U.S. 463, 467.

The alien, to whom the United States has been traditionally hospitable, has been accorded a generous and ascending scale of rights as he increases his identity with our society. Mere lawful presence in the country creates an implied assurance of safe conduct and gives him certain rights; they become more extensive and secure when he makes preliminary declaration of intention to become a citizen, and they expand to those of full citizenship upon naturalization. During his probationary residence, this Court has steadily enlarged his right against Executive deportation except upon full and fair hearing. The Japanese Immigrant Case, 189 U.S. 86; Low Wah Suey v. Backus, 225 U.S. 460; Tisi v. Tod, 264 U.S. 131; United States ex rel. Vajtauer v. Comm'r, 273 U.S. 103; Bridges v. Wixon, 326 U.S. 135; Wong Yang Sung v. McGrath, 339 U.S. 33. And, at least since 1886, we have extended to the person and property of resident aliens important constitutional guaranties - such as the due process of law of the Fourteenth Amendment. Yick Wo v. Hopkins, 118 U.S. 356 .

But, in extending constitutional protections beyond the citizenry, the Court has been at pains to point out that it was the alien's presence within its territorial jurisdiction that gave the Judiciary power to act.

* * *

It is war that exposes the relative vulnerability of the alien's status. The security and protection enjoyed while the nation of his allegiance remains in amity with the United States are greatly impaired when his nation takes up arms against us.

* * *

The resident enemy alien is constitutionally subject to summary arrest, internment and deportation whenever a "declared war" exists. Courts will entertain his plea for freedom from Executive custody only to ascertain the existence of a state of war and whether he is an alien enemy and so subject to the Alien Enemy Act. Once these jurisdictional elements have been determined, courts will not inquire into any other issue as to his internment. Ludecke v. Watkins, 335 U.S. 160

* * *

The foregoing demonstrates how much further we must go if we are to invest these enemy aliens, resident, captured and imprisoned abroad, with standing to demand access to our courts.

We are here confronted with a decision whose basic premise is that these prisoners are entitled, as a constitutional right, to sue in some court of the United States for a writ of habeas corpus. To support that assumption we must hold that a prisoner of our military authorities is constitutionally entitled to the writ, even though he (a) is an enemy alien; (b) has never been or resided in the United States; (c) was captured outside of our territory and there held in military custody as a prisoner of war; (d) was tried and convicted by a Military Commission sitting outside the United States; (e) for offenses against laws of war committed outside the United States; (f) and is at all times imprisoned outside the United States.

We have pointed out that the privilege of litigation has been extended to aliens, whether friendly or enemy, only because permitting their presence in the country implied protection. No such basis can be invoked here, for these prisoners at no relevant time were within any territory over which the United States is sovereign, and the scenes of their offense, their capture, their trial and their punishment were all beyond the territorial jurisdiction of any court of the United States.

* * *

A basic consideration in habeas corpus practice is that the prisoner will be produced before the court. This is the crux of the statutory scheme established by the Congress; indeed, it is inherent in the very term "habeas corpus." And though production of the prisoner may be dispensed with where it appears on the face of the application that no cause for granting the writ exists, Walker v. Johnston, 312 U.S. 275, 284, we have consistently adhered to and recognized the general rule. Ahrens v. Clark, 335 U.S. 188, 190 - 191. To grant the writ to these prisoners might mean that our army must transport them across the seas for hearing. This would require allocation of shipping space, guarding personnel, billeting and rations. It might also require transportation for whatever witnesses the prisoners desired to call as well as transportation for those necessary to defend legality of the sentence. The writ, since it is held to be a matter of right, would be equally available to enemies during active hostilities as in the present twilight between war and peace. Such trials would hamper the war effort and bring aid and comfort to the enemy. They would diminish the prestige of our commanders, not only with enemies but with wavering neutrals. It would be difficult to devise more effective fettering of a field commander than to allow the very enemies he is ordered to reduce to submission to call him to account in his own civil courts and divert his efforts and attention from the military offensive abroad to the legal defensive at home. Nor is it unlikely that the result of such enemy litigiousness would be a conflict between judicial and military opinion highly comforting to enemies of the United States.

* * *

The prisoners rely, however, upon two decisions of this Court to get them over the threshold - Ex parte Quirin, 317 U.S. 1, and In re Yamashita, 327 U.S. 1. Reliance on the Quirin case is clearly mistaken. Those prisoners were in custody in the District of Columbia. One was, or claimed to be, a citizen. They were tried by a Military Commission sitting in the District of Columbia at a time when civil courts were open and functioning normally. They were arrested by civil authorities and the prosecution was personally directed by the Attorney General, a civilian prosecutor, for acts committed in the United States. They waived arraignment before a civil court and it was contended that the civil courts thereby acquired jurisdiction and could not be ousted by the Military. None of the places where they were acting, arrested, tried or imprisoned were, it was contended, in a zone of active military operations or under martial law or any other military control, and no circumstances justified transferring them from civil to military jurisdiction. None of these grave grounds for challenging military jurisdiction can be urged in the case now before us.

Nor can the Court's decision in the Yamashita case aid the prisoners. This Court refused to receive Yamashita's petition for a writ of habeas corpus. For hearing and opinion, it was consolidated with another application for a writ of certiorari to review the refusal of habeas corpus by the Supreme Court of the Philippines over whose decisions the statute then gave this Court a right of review. 28 U.S.C. 349, repealed by Act of June 25, 1948, c. 646, 39, 62 Stat. 992, 1000. By reason of our sovereignty at that time over these insular possessions, Yamashita stood much as did Quirin before American courts. Yamashita's offenses were committed on our territory, he was tried within the jurisdiction of our insular courts and he was imprisoned within territory of the United States. None of these heads of jurisdiction can be invoked by these prisoners.

[Responding to other arguments made by the petitioners, Justice Jackson explains that the Fifth and Sixth Amendments do not apply to aliens abroad and that military commissions are appropriate tribunals for the trial of alleged war crimes.]

MR. JUSTICE BLACK, with whom MR. JUSTICE DOUGLAS and MR. JUSTICE BURTON concur, dissenting.

Not only is United States citizenship a "high privilege," it is a priceless treasure. For that citizenship is enriched beyond price by our goal of equal justice under law - equal justice not for citizens alone, but for all persons coming within the ambit of our power. This ideal gave birth to the constitutional provision for an independent judiciary with authority to check abuses of executive power and to issue writs of habeas corpus liberating persons illegally imprisoned.

This case tests the power of courts to exercise habeas corpus jurisdiction on behalf of aliens, imprisoned in Germany, under sentences imposed by the executive through military tribunals.

* * *

Since the Court expressly disavows conflict with the Quirin or Yamashita decisions, it must be relying not on the status of these petitioners as alien enemy belligerents but rather on the fact that they were captured, tried and imprisoned outside our territory. The Court cannot, and despite its rhetoric on the point does not, deny that if they were imprisoned in the United States our courts would clearly have jurisdiction to hear their habeas corpus complaints. Does a prisoner's right to test legality of a sentence then depend on where the Government chooses to imprison him? Certainly the Quirin and Yamashita opinions lend no support to that conclusion, for in upholding jurisdiction they place no reliance whatever on territorial location. The Court is fashioning wholly indefensible doctrine if it permits the executive branch, by deciding where its prisoners will be tried and imprisoned, to deprive all federal courts of their power to protect against a federal executive's illegal incarcerations.

* * *

[The narrow question here] is whether the judiciary has power in habeas corpus proceedings to test the legality of criminal sentences imposed by the executive through military tribunals in a country which we have occupied for years. The extent of such a judicial test of legality under charges like these, as we have already held in the Yamashita case, is of most limited scope. We ask only whether the military tribunal was legally constituted and whether it had jurisdiction to impose punishment for the conduct charged. Such a limited habeas corpus review is the right of every citizen of the United States, civilian or soldier (unless the Court adopts the Government's argument that Americans imprisoned abroad have lost their right to habeas corpus). Any contention that a similarly limited use of habeas corpus for these prisoners would somehow give them a preferred position in the law cannot be taken seriously.

Though the scope of habeas corpus review of military tribunal sentences is narrow, I think it should not be denied to these petitioners and others like them. We control that part of Germany we occupy. These prisoners were convicted by our own military tribunals under our own Articles of War, years after hostilities had ceased. However illegal their sentences might be, they can expect no relief from German courts or any other branch of the German Government we permit to function. Only our own courts can inquire into the legality of their imprisonment. Perhaps, as some nations believe, there is merit in leaving the administration of criminal laws to executive and military agencies completely free from judicial scrutiny. Our Constitution has emphatically expressed a contrary policy.

*   *   *

Our constitutional principles are such that their mandate of equal justice under law should be applied as well when we occupy lands across the sea as when our flag flew only over thirteen colonies. Our nation proclaims a belief in the dignity of human beings as such, no matter what their nationality or where they happen to live. Habeas corpus, as an instrument to protect against illegal imprisonment, is written into the Constitution. Its use by courts cannot in my judgment be constitutionally abridged by Executive or by Congress. I would hold that our courts can exercise it whenever any United States official illegally imprisons any person in any land we govern. Courts should not for any reason abdicate this, the loftiest power with which the Constitution has endowed them.

DISCUSSION AND QUESTIONS

1. The gravamen of *Eisentrager* is that aliens held captive outside the sovereign territory of the United States have no recourse in the courts of the United States. Why should the location of the prisoner matter? What real difference is there between the U.S. military detaining an individual in a prison in Germany and the U.S. military detaining an individual in a brig in South Carolina? Does the location of captivity make a difference to the military? Does it make a difference to the prisoner? Are not the players and the operative circumstances -- the U.S. military is

imprisoning the individual -- the same in each scenario? And do not the courts of the United States have jurisdiction over the United States military?

2. The majority in *Eisentrager* views the writ of habeas corpus as a privilege that is enjoyed by certain persons in certain circumstances and not enjoyed by other persons in other circumstances; the analysis is very fact-specific and individualized. Justice Black, dissenting, seems to view the writ of habeas corpus as something more universal -- as a tool by which the courts may check abuses of executive power wherever they occur and regardless of whom they target. As a general proposition, the majority's view results in more judicial deference to the executive, and the dissenting view results in less deference. Which approach is more consistent with the Framers' intent when they created a co-equal and independent judiciary? Keep these two approaches in mind when reviewing the War on Terror cases later in this chapter (especially *Rasul* and *Boumediene*), and consider which approach best describes the results in those cases.

3. Suppose that an alleged unlawful combatant were captured on U.S. soil and then transported to Germany, Kuwait or Afghanistan for trial by military commission. Would this situation be more like *Quirin* because the defendant was captured in the U.S., or more like *Eisentrager* because the defendant is held and tried outside the U.S.? Under the teachings of the two World War II cases on unlawful combatants, should a civilian court of the United States entertain the defendant's petition for a writ of habeas corpus?

4. In both the *Quirin* and *Eisentrager* cases, the unlawful combatants were indisputably affiliated with, and acting on behalf of, an enemy nation in a declared war. The fact that war had been officially declared left little question about the status of the defendants as enemy combatants subject to the law of war. But how would the legal dynamics change if aliens are captured while engaged in hostile acts against the United States when no war has been declared? May the commander in chief treat such individuals as unlawful combatants and try them before military commissions for violations of the law of war? If the President were to do so, would the courts offer the same high degree of deference to the actions of the executive that they offered in *Quirin* and *Eisentrager*? Suppose that one of the terrorist hijackers who perpetrated the attacks of September 11, 2001 had survived. At the time of the attacks, there was no declaration of war nor, even a congressional authorization for the use of force. In such circumstances, could the President properly have classified the surviving hijacker as an unlawful enemy combatant and directed that he be tried for war crimes by a military commission? (In 2000, Al Qaeda terrorists bombed a U.S. Navy ship, the U.S.S. Cole, while it was berthed in Aden Harbor in the nation of Yemen. The attack killed 17 American sailors. The individuals identified as

being responsible for the attack were indicted in civilian court proceedings. In 1993, Middle Eastern terrorists exploded a truck bomb in the underground parking garage of the World Trade Center in Manhattan. Six people were killed and hundreds more were injured. The perpetrators were indicted and tried in civilian courts.)

ENEMY COMBATANTS: THE TWENTY-FIRST CENTURY WAR ON TERROR

Taken together, the essential results of the World War II cases, *Quirin* and *Eisentrager*, are that (1) the commander in chief may use military commissions to try unlawful enemy combatants for alleged violations of the law of war, and (2) alien enemies detained outside of the United States will have no recourse to the civilian courts of the United States. The Administration of George W. Bush sought to utilize these principles in prosecuting the War on Terror that resulted from the terrorist attacks of September 11, 2001. On November 13, 2001, President Bush issued a military order relating to the detention, treatment and prosecution of non-citizen international terrorists. Among other things, the military order provided that such persons would be "tried by military commission for any and all offenses triable by military commission that such individual is alleged to have committed." Military Order: Detention, Treatment, and Trial of Certain Non-Citizens in the War Against Terrorism, § 4(a). The order directed that such trials be "full and fair," but also stated that such trials would not be subject to "the principles of law and the rules of evidence generally recognized in the trial of criminal cases in the United States district courts." Id., §§ 4(c)(2), 1(f). The order also provided that the only review of a military commission judgment would be by the President or the Secretary of Defense. Id., § 4(c)(8).

In October of 2001, the U.S. military began Operation Enduring Freedom, which was the effort to disrupt the Al Qaeda terrorist organization based in Afghanistan and to oust the Taliban regime that had supported and given safe haven to Al Qaeda. The Global War on Terror that began at the same time was also pursued in places such as the Philippines and various African nations. Members of Al Qaeda and others who were captured in Afghanistan and elsewhere and classified as terrorists were transferred to the U.S. naval base at Guantanamo Bay, Cuba. The Administration classified these detainees as "unlawful enemy combatants" and indicated that at least some of them would be tried by military commissions. Based largely on *Eisentrager*, the Administration also argued that the courts had no jurisdiction over either the detention or trial of such individuals because Guantanamo Bay is part of Cuba and not territory over which the United States exercises sovereignty.

The Bush Administration's position that it could both detain individuals and try them by military commission without any judicial supervision whatsoever led to a series of decisions in which the Judicial Branch took a much more vigorous role in supervising the commander in chief than was foretold by the World War II cases.

Rasul v. Bush

542 U.S. 466 (2004)[36]

JUSTICE STEVENS delivered the opinion of the Court.

These two cases present the narrow but important question whether United States courts lack jurisdiction to consider challenges to the legality of the detention of foreign nationals captured abroad in connection with hostilities and incarcerated at the Guantanamo Bay Naval Base, Cuba.

On September 11, 2001, agents of the al Qaeda terrorist network hijacked four commercial airliners and used them as missiles to attack American targets. While one of the four attacks was foiled by the heroism of the plane's passengers, the other three killed approximately 3,000 innocent civilians, destroyed hundreds of millions of dollars of property, and severely damaged the U. S. economy. In response to the attacks, Congress passed a joint resolution authorizing the President to use "all necessary and appropriate force against those nations, organizations, or persons he determines planned, authorized, committed, or aided the terrorist attacks ... or harbored such organizations or persons." Authorization for Use of Military Force, Pub. L. 107-40, §§1-2, 115 Stat. 224. Acting pursuant to that authorization, the President sent U. S. Armed Forces into Afghanistan to wage a military campaign against al Qaeda and the Taliban regime that had supported it.

Petitioners in these cases are 2 Australian citizens and 12 Kuwaiti citizens who were captured abroad during hostilities between the United States and the Taliban. Since early 2002, the U. S. military has held them -- along with, according to the Government's estimate, approximately 640 other non-Americans captured abroad -- at the Naval Base at Guantanamo Bay. Brief for United States. The United States occupies the Base, which comprises 45 square miles of land and water along the southeast coast of Cuba, pursuant to a 1903 Lease

[36] Footnotes and some citations found in the original decision have been omitted from this excerpted version.

Agreement executed with the newly independent Republic of Cuba in the aftermath of the Spanish-American War. Under the Agreement, "the United States recognizes the continuance of the ultimate sovereignty of the Republic of Cuba over the [leased areas]," while "the Republic of Cuba consents that during the period of the occupation by the United States ... the United States shall exercise complete jurisdiction and control over and within said areas." In 1934, the parties entered into a treaty providing that, absent an agreement to modify or abrogate the lease, the lease would remain in effect "[s]o long as the United States of America shall not abandon the ... naval station of Guantanamo."

In 2002, petitioners, through relatives acting as their next friends, filed various actions in the U. S. District Court for the District of Columbia challenging the legality of their detention at the Base. All alleged that none of the petitioners has ever been a combatant against the United States or has ever engaged in any terrorist acts. They also alleged that none has been charged with any wrongdoing, permitted to consult with counsel, or provided access to the courts or any other tribunal.

[The district court, relying on *Johnson v. Eisentrager*, concluded that it had no jurisdiction to entertain a habeas corpus petition submitted by aliens held abroad. The circuit court affirmed.]

Congress has granted federal district courts, "within their respective jurisdictions," the authority to hear applications for habeas corpus by any person who claims to be held "in custody in violation of the Constitution or laws or treaties of the United States." 28 U. S. C. §§2241(a), (c)(3). The statute traces its ancestry to the first grant of federal court jurisdiction: Section 14 of the Judiciary Act of 1789 authorized federal courts to issue the writ of habeas corpus to prisoners "in custody, under or by colour of the authority of the United States, or committed for trial before some court of the same." Act of Sept. 24, 1789, ch. 20, §14, 1 Stat. 82. In 1867, Congress extended the protections of the writ to "all cases where any person may be restrained of his or her liberty in violation of the constitution, or of any treaty or law of the United States." Act of Feb. 5, 1867, ch. 28, 14 Stat. 385. See *Felker* v. *Turpin,* 518 U. S. 651, 659-660 (1996).

* * *

As it has evolved over the past two centuries, the habeas statute clearly has expanded habeas corpus "beyond the limits that obtained during the 17th and 18th centuries." *Swain* v. *Pressley,* 430 U. S. 372,

380, n. 13 (1977). But "[a]t its historical core, the writ of habeas corpus has served as a means of reviewing the legality of Executive detention, and it is in that context that its protections have been strongest." *INS* v. *St. Cyr,* 533 U. S. 289, 301 (2001). See also *Brown* v. *Allen,* 344 U. S. 443, 533 (1953) (Jackson, J., concurring in result) ("The historic purpose of the writ has been to relieve detention by executive authorities without judicial trial"). As Justice Jackson wrote in an opinion respecting the availability of habeas corpus to aliens held in U. S. custody:

> Executive imprisonment has been considered oppressive and lawless since John, at Runnymede, pledged that no free man should be imprisoned, dispossessed, outlawed, or exiled save by the judgment of his peers or by the law of the land. The judges of England developed the writ of habeas corpus largely to preserve these immunities from executive restraint.

Shaughnessy v. *United States ex rel. Mezei,* 345 U. S. 206, 218-219 (1953) (dissenting opinion).

Consistent with the historic purpose of the writ, this Court has recognized the federal courts' power to review applications for habeas relief in a wide variety of cases involving Executive detention, in wartime as well as in times of peace. The Court has, for example, entertained the habeas petitions of an American citizen who plotted an attack on military installations during the Civil War, *Ex parte Milligan,* 4 Wall. 2 (1866), and of admitted enemy aliens convicted of war crimes during a declared war and held in the United States, *Ex parte Quirin,* 317 U. S. 1 (1942), and its insular possessions, *In re Yamashita,* 327 U. S. 1 (1946).

The question now before us is whether the habeas statute confers a right to judicial review of the legality of Executive detention of aliens in a territory over which the United States exercises plenary and exclusive jurisdiction, but not "ultimate sovereignty."

* * *

Petitioners in these cases differ from the *Eisentrager* detainees in important respects: They are not nationals of countries at war with the United States, and they deny that they have engaged in or plotted acts of aggression against the United States; they have never been afforded access to any tribunal, much less charged with and convicted of wrongdoing; and for more than two years they have been imprisoned in territory over which the United States exercises exclusive jurisdiction and control.

[Justice White next explains that the landscape of the law on habeas corpus jurisdiction has changed in the more than 50 years since *Eisentrager* was decided. Due to statutory changes to habeas corpus law, it is now no longer necessary that the courts have jurisdictions over the person of the petitioner; rather, the courts may act if they have jurisdiction over the official who has custody of the petitioner.]

* * *

Respondents themselves concede that the habeas statute would create federal-court jurisdiction over the claims of an American citizen held at the base. Considering that the statute draws no distinction between Americans and aliens held in federal custody, there is little reason to think that Congress intended the geographical coverage of the statute to vary depending on the detainee's citizenship. Aliens held at the base, no less than American citizens, are entitled to invoke the federal courts' authority under [the habeas statute].

* * *

In the end, the answer to the question presented is clear. Petitioners contend that they are being held in federal custody in violation of the laws of the United States. No party questions the District Court's jurisdiction over petitioners' custodians. Cf. *Braden,* 410 U. S., at 495. [The habeas statute], by its terms, requires nothing more. We therefore hold that [the habeas statute] confers on the District Court jurisdiction to hear petitioners' habeas corpus challenges to the legality of their detention at the Guantanamo Bay Naval Base.

* * *

Whether and what further proceedings may become necessary after respondents make their response to the merits of petitioners' claims are matters that we need not address now. What is presently at stake is only whether the federal courts have jurisdiction to determine the legality of the Executive's potentially indefinite detention of individuals who claim to be wholly innocent of wrongdoing. Answering that question in the affirmative, we reverse the judgment of the Court of Appeals and remand for the District Court to consider in the first instance the merits of petitioners' claims.

JUSTICE KENNEDY, concurring in the judgment.

*   *   *

The decision in *Eisentrager* indicates that there is a realm of political authority over military affairs where the judicial power may not enter. The existence of this realm acknowledges the power of the President as Commander in Chief, and the joint role of the President and the Congress, in the conduct of military affairs. A faithful application of *Eisentrager*, then, requires an initial inquiry into the general circumstances of the detention to determine whether the Court has the authority to entertain the petition and to grant relief after considering all of the facts presented. A necessary corollary of *Eisentrager* is that there are circumstances in which the courts maintain the power and the responsibility to protect persons from unlawful detention even where military affairs are implicated. See also *Ex parte Milligan,* 4 Wall. 2 (1866).

The facts here are distinguishable from those in *Eisentrager* in two critical ways, leading to the conclusion that a federal court may entertain the petitions. First, Guantanamo Bay is in every practical respect a United States territory, and it is one far removed from any hostilities. The opinion of the Court well explains the history of its possession by the United States. In a formal sense, the United States leases the Bay; the 1903 lease agreement states that Cuba retains "ultimate sovereignty" over it. Lease of Lands for Coaling and Naval Stations, Feb. 23, 1903, U. S.-Cuba, Art. III, T. S. No. 418. At the same time, this lease is no ordinary lease. Its term is indefinite and at the discretion of the United States. What matters is the unchallenged and indefinite control that the United States has long exercised over Guantanamo Bay. From a practical perspective, the indefinite lease of Guantanamo Bay has produced a place that belongs to the United States, extending the "implied protection" of the United States to it. *Eisentrager, supra,* at 777-778.

The second critical set of facts is that the detainees at Guantanamo Bay are being held indefinitely, and without benefit of any legal proceeding to determine their status. In *Eisentrager*, the prisoners were tried and convicted by a military commission of violating the laws of war and were sentenced to prison terms. Having already been subject to procedures establishing their status, they could not justify "a limited opening of our courts" to show that they were "of friendly personal disposition" and not enemy aliens. 339 U. S., at 778. Indefinite detention without trial or other proceeding presents altogether different considerations. It allows friends and foes alike to remain in detention. It suggests a weaker case of military necessity and much greater alignment with the traditional function of habeas corpus. Perhaps, where detainees are taken from a zone of hostilities, detention without proceedings or trial would be justified by military necessity for a matter of weeks; but as the period of detention stretches from months to years, the case for continued detention to meet military exigencies becomes weaker.

In light of the status of Guantanamo Bay and the indefinite pretrial detention of the detainees, I would hold that federal-court jurisdiction is permitted in these cases. This approach would avoid creating automatic statutory authority to adjudicate the claims of persons located outside the United States, and remains true to the reasoning of *Eisentrager*. For these reasons, I concur in the judgment of the Court.

JUSTICE SCALIA, with whom THE CHIEF JUSTICE and JUSTICE THOMAS join, dissenting.

[Justice Scalia offers an extensive rebuttal of the majority's assertion that the habeas corpus jurisdiction of U.S. courts has been statutorily extended since *Eisentrager*.]

The Court gives only two reasons why the presumption against extraterritorial effect does not apply to Guantanamo Bay. First, the Court says (without any further elaboration) that "the United States exercises 'complete jurisdiction and control' over the Guantanamo Bay Naval Base [under the terms of a 1903 lease agreement], and may continue to exercise such control permanently if it so chooses [under the terms of a 1934 Treaty]." But that lease agreement explicitly recognized "the continuance of the ultimate sovereignty of the Republic of Cuba over the [leased areas]," Lease of Lands for Coaling and Naval Stations, Feb. 23, 1903, U. S.-Cuba, Art. III, T. S. No. 418, and the Executive Branch -- whose head is "exclusively responsible" for the "conduct of diplomatic and foreign affairs," *Eisentrager*, *supra*, at 789 -- affirms that the lease and treaty do not render Guantanamo Bay the sovereign territory of the United States, see Brief for Respondents 21.

The Court does not explain how "complete jurisdiction and control" without sovereignty causes an enclave to be part of the United States for purposes of its domestic laws. Since "jurisdiction and control" obtained through a lease is no different in effect from "jurisdiction and control" acquired by lawful force of arms, parts of Afghanistan and Iraq should logically be regarded as subject to our domestic laws. Indeed, if "jurisdiction and control" rather than sovereignty were the test, so should the Landsberg Prison in Germany, where the United States held the *Eisentrager* detainees.

The second and last reason the Court gives for the proposition that domestic law applies to Guantanamo Bay is the Solicitor General's concession that there would be habeas jurisdiction over a United States citizen in Guantanamo Bay. "Considering that the statute draws no distinction between Americans and aliens held in federal custody, there is little reason to think that Congress intended the geographical coverage of the statute to vary depending on the detainee's citizenship." But the reason the Solicitor General conceded there would be jurisdiction over a detainee who was a United States citizen had *nothing to do* with the special status of Guantanamo Bay: "Our answer to that question, Justice Souter, is that citizens of the United States, because of their constitutional circumstances, may have greater rights with respect to the scope and reach of the Habeas Statute as the Court has or would interpret it." Tr. of Oral Arg. 40. See also *id.*, at 27-28. And *that* position -- the position that United States citizens throughout the world may be entitled to habeas corpus rights -- is precisely the position that this Court adopted in *Eisentrager*, see 339 U. S., at 769-770, even while holding that aliens abroad *did not have* habeas corpus rights. Quite obviously, the Court's second reason has no force whatever.

* * *

Departure from our rule of *stare decisis* in statutory cases is always extraordinary; it ought to be unthinkable when the departure has a potentially harmful effect upon the Nation's conduct of a war. The Commander in Chief and his subordinates had every reason to expect that the internment of combatants at Guantanamo Bay would not have the consequence of bringing the cumbersome machinery of our domestic courts into military affairs. Congress is in session. If it wished to change federal judges' habeas jurisdiction from what this Court had previously held that to be, it could have done so. And it could have done so by intelligent revision of the statute, instead of by today's clumsy, countertextual reinterpretation that confers upon wartime prisoners greater habeas rights than domestic detainees. The latter must challenge their present physical confinement in the district of their confinement, see *Rumsfeld* v. *Padilla*, whereas under today's strange holding Guantanamo Bay detainees can petition in any of the 94 federal judicial districts. The fact that extraterritorially located detainees lack the district of detention that the statute requires has been converted from a factor that precludes their ability to bring a petition at all into a factor that frees them to petition wherever they wish--and, as a result, to forum shop. For this Court to create such a monstrous scheme in time of war, and in frustration of our military commanders' reliance upon clearly stated prior law, is judicial adventurism of the worst sort. I dissent.

DISCUSSION AND QUESTIONS

1. Justice Stevens explains that the law on habeas corpus has evolved such that the courts may act so long as they have jurisdiction over the *jailer*, regardless of where the petitioner happens to be located. Isn't this principle sufficient to decide the case? Why does Justice Stevens also point out that "the United States exercises plenary and exclusive jurisdiction" over Guantanamo Bay? What is really the crux of this decision? Is it that the courts have jurisdiction over the jailer (which, as Justice Stevens observes, no party denies), or is it that the United States exercises total control over the location where the petitioners are imprisoned? Justice Kennedy concurring, says it is a critical factor in the decision that "Guantanamo Bay is in every practical respect a United States territory."

2. Justice Stevens considers it important that the petitioners "are not nationals of countries at war with the United States." Is this a fact that matters in determining whether alleged enemy combatants should be granted access to United States courts? Is there a meaningful legal distinction between the status of the *Eisentrager* petitioners, who were nationals of a country at war with the United States, and the *Rasul* petitioners, who were classified as enemy belligerents under the Authorization for the Use of Military Force? The lengthy armed conflict between the United States and North Vietnam in the 1960s and early 1970s was not a declared war. Under Justice Stevens' reasoning, would a North Vietnamese soldier captured in 1968 by U.S. forces and held in South Vietnam be entitled to have U.S. courts consider his habeas corpus petition?

Hamdi v. Rumsfeld

542 U.S. 507 (2004)[37]

JUSTICE O'CONNOR announced the judgment of the Court and delivered an opinion, in which THE CHIEF JUSTICE, JUSTICE KENNEDY, and JUSTICE BREYER join.

At this difficult time in our Nation's history, we are called upon to consider the legality of the Government's detention of a United States citizen on United States soil as an "enemy combatant" and to address the process that is constitutionally owed to one who seeks to challenge his classification as such. The United States Court of Appeals for the Fourth Circuit held that petitioner's detention was legally authorized and that he was entitled to no further opportunity to challenge his enemy-combatant label. We now vacate and remand. We hold that although Congress authorized the detention of combatants in the narrow circumstances alleged here, due process demands that a citizen held in the United States as an enemy combatant be given a meaningful opportunity to contest the factual basis for that detention before a neutral decisionmaker.

On September 11, 2001, the al Qaeda terrorist network used hijacked commercial airliners to attack prominent targets in the United States. Approximately 3,000 people were killed in those attacks. One week later, in response to these "acts of treacherous violence," Congress passed a resolution authorizing the President to "use all necessary and appropriate force against those nations, organizations, or persons he determines planned, authorized, committed, or aided the terrorist attacks" or "harbored such organizations or persons, in order to prevent any future acts of international terrorism against the United States by such nations, organizations or persons." Authorization for Use of Military Force ("the AUMF"), 115 Stat. 224. Soon thereafter, the President ordered United States Armed Forces to Afghanistan, with a mission to subdue al Qaeda and quell the Taliban regime that was known to support it.

This case arises out of the detention of a man whom the Government alleges took up arms with the Taliban during this conflict. His name is Yaser Esam Hamdi. Born an American citizen in Louisiana in 1980, Hamdi moved with his family to Saudi Arabia as a child. By 2001, the parties agree, he resided in Afghanistan. At some point that year, he was seized by members of the Northern Alliance, a coalition of

---

[37] Footnotes and some citations found in the original decision have been omitted from this excerpted version.

military groups opposed to the Taliban government, and eventually was turned over to the United States military. The Government asserts that it initially detained and interrogated Hamdi in Afghanistan before transferring him to the United States Naval Base in Guantanamo Bay in January 2002. In April 2002, upon learning that Hamdi is an American citizen, authorities transferred him to a naval brig in Norfolk, Virginia, where he remained until a recent transfer to a brig in Charleston, South Carolina. The Government contends that Hamdi is an "enemy combatant," and that this status justifies holding him in the United States indefinitely -- without formal charges or proceedings -- unless and until it makes the determination that access to counsel or further process is warranted.

[Justice O'Connor reviews the procedural history of the case and notes that the only evidence introduced by the government in support of its classification of the petitioner as an enemy combatant is a declaration submitted by a Department of Defense official named Mobbs.]

[The Mobbs Declaration] states that Hamdi "traveled to Afghanistan" in July or August 2001, and that he thereafter "affiliated with a Taliban military unit and received weapons training." *Ibid.* It asserts that Hamdi "remained with his Taliban unit following the attacks of September 11" and that, during the time when Northern Alliance forces were "engaged in battle with the Taliban," "Hamdi's Taliban unit surrendered" to those forces, after which he "surrender[ed] his Kalishnikov assault rifle" to them. *Id.*, at 148-149. The Mobbs Declaration also states that, because al Qaeda and the Taliban "were and are hostile forces engaged in armed conflict with the armed forces of the United States," "individuals associated with" those groups "were and continue to be enemy combatants." *Id.*, at 149. Mobbs states that Hamdi was labeled an enemy combatant "[b]ased upon his interviews and in light of his association with the Taliban." *Ibid.* According to the declaration, a series of "U. S. military screening team[s]" determined that Hamdi met "the criteria for enemy combatants," and "a subsequent interview of Hamdi has confirmed that he surrendered and gave his firearm to Northern Alliance forces, which supports his classification as an enemy combatant." *Id.*, at 149-150.

* * *

The threshold question before us is whether the Executive has the authority to detain citizens who qualify as "enemy combatants."

* * *

The Government maintains that no explicit congressional authorization is required, because the Executive possesses plenary authority to detain pursuant to Article II of the Constitution. We do not reach the question whether Article II provides such authority, however, because we agree with the Government's alternative position, that Congress has in fact authorized Hamdi's detention, through the AUMF.

Our analysis on that point, set forth below, substantially overlaps with our analysis of Hamdi's principal argument for the illegality of his detention. He posits that his detention is forbidden by 18 U. S. C. §4001(a). Section 4001(a) states that "[n]o citizen shall be imprisoned or otherwise detained by the United States except pursuant to an Act of Congress." Congress passed §4001(a) in 1971 as part of a bill to repeal the Emergency Detention Act of 1950, 50 U. S. C. §811 *et seq.*, which provided procedures for executive detention, during times of emergency, of individuals deemed likely to engage in espionage or sabotage. Congress was particularly concerned about the possibility that the Act could be used to reprise the Japanese internment camps of World War II. H. R. Rep. No. 92-116 (1971); *id.*, at 4 ("The concentration camp implications of the legislation render it abhorrent").

* * *

The AUMF authorizes the President to use "all necessary and appropriate force" against "nations, organizations, or persons" associated with the September 11, 2001, terrorist attacks. 115 Stat. 224. There can be no doubt that individuals who fought against the United States in Afghanistan as part of the Taliban, an organization known to have supported the al Qaeda terrorist network responsible for those attacks, are individuals Congress sought to target in passing the AUMF. We conclude that detention of individuals falling into the limited category we are considering, for the duration of the particular conflict in which they were captured, is so fundamental and accepted an incident to war as to be an exercise of the "necessary and appropriate force" Congress has authorized the President to use.

* * *

There is no bar to this Nation's holding one of its own citizens as an enemy combatant. In *Quirin*, one of the detainees, Haupt, alleged that he was a naturalized United States citizen. 317 U. S., at 20. We held that "[c]itizens who associate themselves with the military arm of the enemy government, and with its aid, guidance and direction enter this country bent on hostile acts, are enemy belligerents within the meaning of ... the law of war." *Id.,* at 37-38. While Haupt was tried for violations of the law of war, nothing in *Quirin* suggests that his citizenship would have precluded his mere detention for the duration of the relevant hostilities. See *id.,* at 30-31.

* * *

Hamdi contends that the AUMF does not authorize indefinite or perpetual detention. Certainly, we agree that indefinite detention for the purpose of interrogation is not authorized. Further, we understand Congress' grant of authority for the use of "necessary and appropriate force" to include the authority to detain for the duration of the relevant conflict, and our understanding is based on longstanding law-of-war principles. If the practical circumstances of a given conflict are entirely unlike those of the conflicts that informed the development of the law of war, that understanding may unravel. But that is not the situation we face as of this date. Active combat operations against Taliban fighters apparently are ongoing in Afghanistan . . . The United States may detain, for the duration of these hostilities, individuals legitimately determined to be Taliban combatants who "engaged in an armed conflict against the United States." If the record establishes that United States troops are still involved in active combat in Afghanistan, those detentions are part of the exercise of "necessary and appropriate force," and therefore are authorized by the AUMF.

[Justice O'Connor reviews the *Milligan* and *Quirin* cases and explains that *Milligan* is distinguishable from the current case because Milligan was not captured on the battlefield and was not a prisoner of war. Notwithstanding *Milligan*, *Quirin* instructs that a citizen can be treated as an enemy combatant.]

Even in cases in which the detention of enemy combatants is legally authorized, there remains the question of what process is constitutionally due to a citizen who disputes his enemy-combatant status. Hamdi argues that he is owed a meaningful and timely hearing and that "extra-judicial detention [that] begins and ends with the submission of an affidavit based on third-hand hearsay" does not comport with the Fifth and Fourteenth Amendments. The Government counters that any more process than was provided below would be both unworkable and "constitutionally intolerable." Our resolution of this dispute requires a careful examination both of the writ of habeas corpus, which Hamdi now seeks to employ as a mechanism of judicial review, and of the Due Process Clause, which informs the procedural contours of that mechanism in this instance.

[The government argues that the Mobbs Declaration should be sufficient to meet due process requirements for justifying Hamdi's detention as an enemy combatant and] that further factual exploration is unwarranted and inappropriate in light of the extraordinary constitutional interests at stake. Under the Government's most extreme rendition of this argument, "[r]espect for separation of powers and the limited institutional capabilities of courts in matters of military decision-making in connection with an ongoing conflict" ought to eliminate entirely any individual process, restricting the courts to investigating only whether legal authorization exists for the broader detention scheme. Brief for Respondents 26. At most, the Government argues, courts should review its determination that a citizen is an enemy combatant under a very deferential "some evidence" standard. *Id.*, at 34 ("Under the some evidence standard, the focus is exclusively on the factual basis supplied by the Executive to support its own determination" (citing *Superintendent, Mass. Correctional Institution at Walpole* v. *Hill,* 472 U. S. 445, 455-457 (1985) (explaining that the some evidence standard "does not require" a "weighing of the evidence," but rather calls for assessing "whether there is any evidence in the record that could support the conclusion")). Under this review, a court would assume the accuracy of the Government's articulated basis for Hamdi's detention, as set forth in the Mobbs Declaration, and assess only whether that articulated basis was a legitimate one.

* * *

In response, Hamdi emphasizes that this Court consistently has recognized that an individual challenging his detention may not be held at the will of the Executive without recourse to some proceeding before a neutral tribunal to determine whether the Executive's asserted justifications for that detention have basis in fact and warrant in law. See, *e.g., Zadvydas* v. *Davis,* 533 U. S. 678, 690 (2001); *Addington* v. *Texas,* 441 U. S. 418, 425-427 (1979).

* * *

Striking the proper constitutional balance here is of great importance to the Nation during this period of ongoing combat. But it is equally vital that our calculus not give short shrift to the values that this country holds dear or to the privilege that is American citizenship. It is during our most challenging and uncertain moments that our

Nation's commitment to due process is most severely tested; and it is in those times that we must preserve our commitment at home to the principles for which we fight abroad. See *Kennedy* v. *Mendoza-Martinez,* 372 U. S. 144, 164-165 (1963) ("The imperative necessity for safeguarding these rights to procedural due process under the gravest of emergencies has existed throughout our constitutional history, for it is then, under the pressing exigencies of crisis, that there is the greatest temptation to dispense with guarantees which, it is feared, will inhibit government action"); see also *United States* v. *Robel,* 389 U. S. 258, 264 (1967) ("It would indeed be ironic if, in the name of national defense, we would sanction the subversion of one of those liberties ... which makes the defense of the Nation worthwhile").

* * *

We therefore hold that a citizen-detainee seeking to challenge his classification as an enemy combatant must receive notice of the factual basis for his classification, and a fair opportunity to rebut the Government's factual assertions before a neutral decisionmaker. See *Cleveland Bd. of Ed.* v. *Loudermill,* 470 U. S. 532, 542 (1985) ("An essential principle of due process is that a deprivation of life, liberty, or property 'be preceded by notice and opportunity for hearing appropriate to the nature of the case' " (quoting *Mullane* v. *Central Hanover Bank & Trust Co.,* 339 U. S. 306, 313 (1950)); *Concrete Pipe & Products of Cal., Inc.* v. *Construction Laborers Pension Trust for Southern Cal.,* 508 U. S. 602, 617 (1993) ("due process requires a 'neutral and detached judge in the first instance' " (quoting *Ward* v. *Monroeville,* 409 U. S. 57, 61-62 (1972)). "For more than a century the central meaning of procedural due process has been clear: 'Parties whose rights are to be affected are entitled to be heard; and in order that they may enjoy that right they must first be notified.' It is equally fundamental that the right to notice and an opportunity to be heard 'must be granted at a meaningful time and in a meaningful manner.' " *Fuentes* v. *Shevin,* 407 U. S. 67, 80 (1972) (quoting *Baldwin* v. *Hale,* 1 Wall. 223, 233 (1864); *Armstrong* v. *Manzo,* 380 U. S. 545, 552 (1965) (other citations omitted)). These essential constitutional promises may not be eroded.

At the same time, the exigencies of the circumstances may demand that, aside from these core elements, enemy combatant proceedings may be tailored to alleviate their uncommon potential to burden the Executive at a time of ongoing military conflict. Hearsay, for example, may need to be accepted as the most reliable available evidence from the Government in such a proceeding. Likewise, the Constitution would not be offended by a presumption in favor of the

Government's evidence, so long as that presumption remained a rebuttable one and fair opportunity for rebuttal were provided. Thus, once the Government puts forth credible evidence that the habeas petitioner meets the enemy-combatant criteria, the onus could shift to the petitioner to rebut that evidence with more persuasive evidence that he falls outside the criteria. A burden-shifting scheme of this sort would meet the goal of ensuring that the errant tourist, embedded journalist, or local aid worker has a chance to prove military error while giving due regard to the Executive once it has put forth meaningful support for its conclusion that the detainee is in fact an enemy combatant. In the words of *Mathews*, process of this sort would sufficiently address the "risk of erroneous deprivation" of a detainee's liberty interest while eliminating certain procedures that have questionable additional value in light of the burden on the Government. 424 U. S., at 335.

* * *

In so holding, we necessarily reject the Government's assertion that separation of powers principles mandate a heavily circumscribed role for the courts in such circumstances. Indeed, the position that the courts must forgo any examination of the individual case and focus exclusively on the legality of the broader detention scheme cannot be mandated by any reasonable view of separation of powers, as this approach serves only to *condense* power into a single branch of government. We have long since made clear that a state of war is not a blank check for the President when it comes to the rights of the Nation's citizens. *Youngstown Sheet & Tube*, 343 U. S., at 587. Whatever power the United States Constitution envisions for the Executive in its exchanges with other nations or with enemy organizations in times of conflict, it most assuredly envisions a role for all three branches when individual liberties are at stake. *Mistretta* v. *United States,* 488 U. S. 361, 380 (1989) (it was "the central judgment of the Framers of the Constitution that, within our political scheme, the separation of governmental powers into three coordinate Branches is essential to the preservation of liberty"); *Home Building & Loan Assn.* v. *Blaisdell,* 290 U. S. 398, 426 (1934) (The war power "is a power to wage war successfully, and thus it permits the harnessing of the entire energies of the people in a supreme cooperative effort to preserve the nation. But even the war power does not remove constitutional limitations safeguarding essential liberties"). Likewise, we have made clear that, unless Congress acts to suspend it, the Great Writ of habeas corpus allows the Judicial Branch to play a necessary role in maintaining this delicate balance of governance, serving as an important judicial check on the Executive's discretion in the realm of detentions. See *St. Cyr*, 533 U. S., at 301 ("At its historical core, the writ of habeas corpus has served as a means of reviewing the legality of Executive detention, and it is in that context that its protections have been strongest"). Thus, while we do not question that our due process assessment must pay keen attention to the particular burdens faced by the Executive in the context of military action, it would turn our system of checks and balances on its head to suggest that a citizen could not make his way to court with a challenge to the factual basis for his detention by his government, simply because the Executive opposes making available such a challenge. Absent suspension of the writ by Congress, a citizen detained as an enemy combatant is entitled to this process.

JUSTICE SCALIA, with whom JUSTICE STEVENS joins, dissenting.

Petitioner, a presumed American citizen, has been imprisoned without charge or hearing in the Norfolk and Charleston Naval Brigs for more than two years, on the allegation that he is an enemy combatant who bore arms against his country for the Taliban. His father claims to the contrary, that he is an inexperienced aid worker caught in the wrong place at the wrong time. This case brings into conflict the competing demands of national security and our citizens' constitutional right to personal liberty. Although I share the Court's evident unease as it seeks to reconcile the two, I do not agree with its resolution.

Where the Government accuses a citizen of waging war against it, our constitutional tradition has been to prosecute him in federal court for treason or some other crime. Where the exigencies of war prevent that, the Constitution's Suspension Clause, Art. I, §9, cl. 2, allows Congress to relax the usual protections temporarily. Absent suspension, however, the Executive's assertion of military exigency has not been thought sufficient to permit detention without charge. No one contends that the congressional Authorization for Use of Military Force, on which the Government relies to justify its actions here, is an implementation of the Suspension Clause.

* * *

The proposition that the Executive lacks indefinite wartime detention authority over citizens is consistent with the Founders' general mistrust of military power permanently at the Executive's disposal. In the Founders' view, the "blessings of liberty" were threatened by "those military establishments which must gradually poison its very fountain." The Federalist No. 45, p. 238 (J. Madison).

[Justice Scalia reviews the history and purpose of the writ of habeas corpus, distinguishes the *Quirin* decision, which permitted the trial by military commission of an American citizen, and concludes that an American citizen on American soil who is viewed as an enemy combatant should be charged and tried in civilian courts for treason or similar crimes. A citizen in these circumstances may be held indefinitely only if Congress has suspended the writ.]

JUSTICE THOMAS, dissenting.

The Executive Branch, acting pursuant to the powers vested in the President by the Constitution and with explicit congressional approval, has determined that Yaser Hamdi is an enemy combatant and should be detained. This detention falls squarely within the Federal Government's war powers, and we lack the expertise and capacity to second-guess that decision. As such, petitioners' habeas challenge should fail, and there is no reason to remand the case. The plurality reaches a contrary conclusion by failing adequately to consider basic principles of the constitutional structure as it relates to national security and foreign affairs and by using the balancing scheme of *Mathews* v. *Eldridge,* 424 U. S. 319 (1976). I do not think that the Federal Government's war powers can be balanced away by this Court. Arguably, Congress could provide for additional procedural protections, but until it does, we have no right to insist upon them. But even if I were to agree with the general approach the plurality takes, I could not accept the particulars. The plurality utterly fails to account for the Government's compelling interests and for our own institutional inability to weigh competing concerns correctly. I respectfully dissent.

* * *

I acknowledge that the question whether Hamdi's executive detention is lawful is a question properly resolved by the Judicial Branch, though the question comes to the Court with the strongest presumptions in favor of the Government. The plurality agrees that Hamdi's detention is lawful if he is an enemy combatant. But the question whether Hamdi is actually an enemy combatant is "of a kind for which the Judiciary has neither aptitude, facilities nor responsibility and which has long been held to belong in the domain of political power not subject to judicial intrusion or inquiry." *Chicago & Southern Air Lines*, 333 U. S., at 111. That is, although it is appropriate for the Court to determine the judicial question whether the President has the asserted authority, see, *e.g., Ex parte Endo*, *supra*, we lack the information and expertise to question whether

Hamdi is actually an enemy combatant, a question the resolution of which is committed to other branches.

* * *

I agree with the plurality that the Federal Government has power to detain those that the Executive Branch determines to be enemy combatants. But I do not think that the plurality has adequately explained the breadth of the President's authority to detain enemy combatants, an authority that includes making virtually conclusive factual findings. In my view, the structural considerations discussed above, as recognized in our precedent, demonstrate that we lack the capacity and responsibility to second-guess this determination.

[JUSTICE SOUTER dissents in part, asserting that the AUMF is not the sort of "Act of Congress" that may support the detention of a citizen under the Anti-Detention Act, 18 U.S.C. § 4001(a).]

DISCUSSION AND QUESTIONS

1. The plurality opinion holds that, even when detention is authorized (as it was here by the AUMF), due process still demands that "a *citizen*-detainee seeking to challenge his classification as an enemy combatant must receive notice of the factual basis for his classification, and a fair opportunity to rebut the Government's factual assertions before a neutral decisionmaker" (emphasis added). The Court later reiterates, "Absent suspension of the writ by Congress, a *citizen* detained as an enemy combatant is entitled to this process" (emphasis added). The Court emphasizes that its ruling is limited only to citizens, but on what basis does it implicitly distinguish citizens from non-citizens? The Fifth Amendment's mandate of basic due process is not limited to citizens; rather, the Fifth Amendment provides that no "person" may be deprived of liberty "without due process of law." As the *Eisentrager* Court observed, aliens within the United States are entitled to due process of law. *See also, e.g., United States v. Verdugo-Urquidez*, 494 U.S. 259, 265, 269 (1990) (noting that the term "person" in the Fifth Amendment has "relatively universal" application in contrast to the less inclusive "the people" used in the First, Second, Fourth, Ninth and Tenth Amendments, which refers to "a class of persons who are part of a national community"). If a citizen challenging his classification as an enemy combatant is entitled to the basic elements of due process -- notice and a hearing before a neutral tribunal -- would not an alien held by the U.S. government on U.S. soil enjoy the same protection? Suppose that a member of Al

Qaeda who is a Yemeni national were captured in New York while attempting to explode a truck bomb in Times Square. Suppose further that the U.S. government classified him as an unlawful enemy combatant and announced its intention to detain him for the duration of hostilities between the U.S. and Al Qaeda. Would this detainee be legally entitled to challenge his classification before a neutral tribunal? If not, why not?

Hamdan v. Rumsfeld

548 U.S. 557 (2006)[38]

JUSTICE STEVENS announced the judgment of the Court.

Petitioner Salim Ahmed Hamdan, a Yemeni national, is in custody at an American prison in Guantanamo Bay, Cuba. In November 2001, during hostilities between the United States and the Taliban (which then governed Afghanistan), Hamdan was captured by militia forces and turned over to the U. S. military. In June 2002, he was transported to Guantanamo Bay. Over a year later, the President deemed him eligible for trial by military commission for then-unspecified crimes. After another year had passed, Hamdan was charged with one count of conspiracy "to commit ... offenses triable by military commission." App. to Pet. for Cert. 65a.

Hamdan filed petitions for writs of habeas corpus and mandamus to challenge the Executive Branch's intended means of prosecuting this charge. He concedes that a court-martial constituted in accordance with the Uniform Code of Military Justice (UCMJ), 10 U. S. C. §801 *et seq.* (2000 ed. and Supp. III), would have authority to try him. His objection is that the military commission the President has convened lacks such authority, for two principal reasons: First, neither congressional Act nor the common law of war supports trial by this commission for the crime of conspiracy--an offense that, Hamdan says, is not a violation of the law of war. Second, Hamdan contends, the procedures that the President has adopted to try him violate the most basic tenets of military and international law, including the principle that a defendant must be permitted to see and hear the evidence against him.

[The United States was attacked by the Al Qaeda terrorist organization on September 11, 2001. In response, Congress enacted

---

[38] Footnotes and some citations found in the original decision have been omitted from this excerpted version.

the Authorization for the Use of Military Force (AUMF) that authorized the President to use necessary and appropriate force against the attackers and their supporters. President Bush issued his November 13 Order directing that certain non-citizens would be detained as enemy combatants and potentially subject to trial by military commission. In July 2003, President Bush determined that Hamdan, among others, would be tried by military commission.]

[In the charging document] only the final two paragraphs, entitled "Charge: Conspiracy," contain allegations against Hamdan. Paragraph 12 charges that "from on or about February 1996 to on or about November 24, 2001," Hamdan "willfully and knowingly joined an enterprise of persons who shared a common criminal purpose and conspired and agreed with [named members of al Qaeda] to commit the following offenses triable by military commission: attacking civilians; attacking civilian objects; murder by an unprivileged belligerent; and terrorism." App. to Pet. for Cert. 65a. There is no allegation that Hamdan had any command responsibilities, played a leadership role, or participated in the planning of any activity.

Paragraph 13 lists four "overt acts" that Hamdan is alleged to have committed sometime between 1996 and November 2001 in furtherance of the "enterprise and conspiracy": (1) he acted as Osama bin Laden's "bodyguard and personal driver," "believ[ing]" all the while that bin Laden "and his associates were involved in" terrorist acts prior to and including the attacks of September 11, 2001; (2) he arranged for transportation of, and actually transported, weapons used by al Qaeda members and by bin Laden's bodyguards (Hamdan among them); (3) he "drove or accompanied [O]sama bin Laden to various al Qaida-sponsored training camps, press conferences, or lectures," at which bin Laden encouraged attacks against Americans; and (4) he received weapons training at al Qaeda-sponsored camps. *Id.*, at 65a-67a.

[Justice Stevens addresses the government's arguments that the Detainee Treatment Act of 2005 strips the courts of jurisdiction to consider habeas corpus petitions filed by Guantanamo Bay detainees. He applies canons of statutory construction and refers to legislative history and concludes that the Act was not intended to apply retroactively to petitions -- such as Hamdan's -- that were pending at the time of its enactment. He also rejects the government's argument that courts should abstain from reviewing the proceedings of military tribunals, such as courts martial, until the work of such tribunals has been completed. Justice Stevens observes that the military commissions at issue here are unlike courts martial. Here, the proper approach for the judiciary is to review the matter promptly, as the *Quirin* court did, prior to the final outcome of the military proceedings.]

The military commission, a tribunal neither mentioned in the Constitution nor created by statute, was born of military necessity. See W. Winthrop, Military Law and Precedents 831 (rev. 2d ed. 1920) (hereinafter Winthrop). Though foreshadowed in some respects by earlier tribunals like the Board of General Officers that General Washington convened to try British Major John André for spying during the Revolutionary War, the commission "as such" was inaugurated in 1847. *Id.*, at 832; G. Davis, A Treatise on the Military Law of the United States 308 (2d ed. 1909) (hereinafter Davis). As commander of occupied Mexican territory, and having available to him no other tribunal, General Winfield Scott that year ordered the establishment of both " '*military commissions*' " to try ordinary crimes committed in the occupied territory and a "*council of war*" to try offenses against the law of war. Winthrop 832 (emphases in original).

When the exigencies of war next gave rise to a need for use of military commissions, during the Civil War, the dual system favored by General Scott was not adopted. Instead, a single tribunal often took jurisdiction over ordinary crimes, war crimes, and breaches of military orders alike. As further discussed below, each aspect of that seemingly broad jurisdiction was in fact supported by a separate military exigency. Generally, though, the need for military commissions during this period—as during the Mexican War—was driven largely by the then very limited jurisdiction of courts-martial: "The *occasion* for the military commission arises principally from the fact that the jurisdiction of the court-martial proper, in our law, is restricted by statute almost exclusively to members of the military force and to certain specific offences defined in a written code." *Id.*, at 831 (emphasis in original).

[In *Quirin*, the Court upheld the use of military commissions, in part, because Congress had authorized them in Article of War 15. The language of that old Article 15 is now found at Article 21 of the Uniform Code of Military Justice (UCMJ). Nothing in the more recent Authorization for the Use of Military Force (AUMF) or Detainee Treatment Act (DTA) adds to the authority granted to the President to use military commissions beyond that which is granted by UCMJ Article 21. Article 21 is a general statement that military commissions may be used according to "the law of war."]

The common law governing military commissions may be gleaned from past practice and what sparse legal precedent exists. Commissions historically have been used in three situations. See Bradley & Goldsmith, Congressional Authorization and the War on Terrorism, 118 Harv. L. Rev. 2048, 2132–2133 (2005); Winthrop 831–846; Hearings on H. R. 2498 before the Subcommittee of the House Committee on Armed Services, 81st Cong., 1st Sess., 975 (1949). First, they have substituted for civilian courts at times and in places where martial law has been declared. Their use in these circumstances has raised constitutional questions, see *Duncan* v. *Kahanamoku,* 327 U. S. 304 (1946); *Milligan*, 4 Wall., at 121–122, but is well recognized. See Winthrop 822, 836–839. Second, commissions have been established to try civilians "as part of a temporary military government over occupied enemy territory or territory regained from an enemy where civilian government cannot and does not function." *Duncan*, 327 U. S., at 314; see *Milligan*, 4 Wall., at 141–142 (Chase, C. J., concurring in judgment) (distinguishing "martial law proper" from "military government" in occupied territory). Illustrative of this second kind of commission is the one that was established, with jurisdiction to apply the German Criminal Code, in occupied Germany following the end of World War II. See *Madsen* v. *Kinsella,* 343 U. S. 341, 356 (1952).

The third type of commission, convened as an "incident to the conduct of war" when there is a need "to seize and subject to disciplinary measures those enemies who in their attempt to thwart or impede our military effort have violated the law of war," *Quirin*, 317 U. S., at 28–29, has been described as "utterly different" from the other two. Bickers, Military Commissions are Constitutionally Sound: A Response to Professors Katyal and Tribe, 34 Tex. Tech. L. Rev. 899, 902 (2002–2003). Not only is its jurisdiction limited to offenses cognizable during time of war, but its role is primarily a factfinding one — to determine, typically on the battlefield itself, whether the defendant has violated the law of war. The last time the U. S. Armed Forces used the law-of-war military commission was during World War II.

* * *

The classic treatise penned by Colonel William Winthrop, whom we have called "the 'Blackstone of Military Law,' " *Reid* v. *Covert,* 354 U. S. 1, 19, n. 38 (1957) (plurality opinion), describes at least four preconditions for exercise of jurisdiction by a tribunal of the type convened to try Hamdan. First, "[a] military commission, (except where otherwise authorized by statute), can legally assume jurisdiction only of offenses committed within the field of the command of the convening commander." Winthrop 836. The "field of command" in these circumstances means the "theatre of war." *Ibid.* Second, the offense charged "must have been committed within the period of the war." *Id.*, at 837. No jurisdiction exists to try offenses "committed either before or after the war." *Ibid.* Third, a military commission not established pursuant to martial law or an occupation may try only "[i]ndividuals of the enemy's army who have been guilty of illegitimate warfare or other offences in violation of the laws of war" and members of one's own army "who, in time of war, become chargeable with crimes or offences not cognizable, or triable, by the criminal courts or under the Articles of war." *Id.*, at 838. Finally, a law-of-war commission has jurisdiction to try only two kinds of offense: "Violations of the laws and usages of war cognizable by military tribunals only," and "[b]reaches of military orders or regulations for which offenders are not legally triable by court-martial under the Articles of war." *Id.*, at 839.

All parties agree that Colonel Winthrop's treatise accurately describes the common law governing military commissions, and that the jurisdictional limitations he identifies were incorporated in Article of War 15 and, later, Article 21 of the UCMJ. It also is undisputed that Hamdan's commission lacks jurisdiction to try him unless the charge "properly set[s] forth, not only the details of the act charged, but the circumstances conferring *jurisdiction*." *Id.*, at 842 (emphasis in original). The question is whether the preconditions designed to ensure that a military necessity exists to justify the use of this extraordinary tribunal have been satisfied here.

The charge against Hamdan alleges a conspiracy extending over a number of years, from 1996 to November 2001. All but two months of that more than 5-year-long period preceded the attacks of September 11, 2001, and the enactment of the AUMF — the Act of Congress on which the Government relies for exercise of its war powers and thus for its authority to convene military commissions. Neither the purported agreement with Osama bin Laden and others to commit war crimes, nor a single overt act, is alleged to have occurred in a theater of war or on any specified date after September 11, 2001. None of the overt acts that Hamdan is alleged to have committed violates the law of war.

These facts alone cast doubt on the legality of the charge and, hence, the commission; as Winthrop makes plain, the offense alleged must have been committed both in a theater of war and *during*, not before, the relevant conflict. But the deficiencies in the time and place allegations also underscore — indeed are symptomatic of — the most serious defect of this charge: The offense it alleges is not triable by law-of-war military commission. See *Yamashita*, 327 U. S., at 13 ("Neither congressional action nor the military orders constituting the commission authorized it to place petitioner on trial unless the charge proffered against him is of a violation of the law of war").

* * *

At a minimum, the Government must make a substantial showing that the crime for which it seeks to try a defendant by military commission is acknowledged to be an offense against the law of war. That burden is far from satisfied here. The crime of "conspiracy" has rarely if ever been tried as such in this country by any law-of-war military commission not exercising some other form of jurisdiction, and does not appear in either the Geneva Conventions or the Hague Conventions — the major treaties on the law of war. Winthrop explains that under the common law governing military commissions, it is not enough to intend to violate the law of war and commit overt acts in furtherance of that intention unless the overt acts either are themselves offenses against the law of war or constitute steps sufficiently substantial to qualify as an attempt. See Winthrop 841 ("[T]he jurisdiction of the military commission should be restricted to cases of offence consisting in *overt acts*, *i.e.*, in unlawful commissions or actual attempts to commit, and not in intentions merely" (emphasis in original)).

[Justice Stevens explains that neither the *Quirin* decision nor two other authorities cited by the government establish that "conspiracy" can be considered a violation of the law of war. Conspiracy charges were occasionally prosecuted before military commissions during the Civil War, but that was because those tribunals were sitting in the dual role of war crime tribunals and martial law tribunals; in the latter capacity, military commissions were called upon to consider ordinary crimes.]

Finally, international sources confirm that the crime charged here is not a recognized violation of the law of war. As observed above, see *supra*, at 40, none of the major treaties governing the law of war identifies conspiracy as a violation thereof. And the only "conspiracy" crimes that have been recognized by international war crimes tribunals (whose jurisdiction often extends beyond war crimes proper to crimes against humanity and crimes against the peace) are conspiracy to commit genocide and common plan to wage aggressive war, which is a crime against the peace and requires for its commission actual participation in a "concrete plan to wage war." 1 Trial of the Major War Criminals Before the International Military Tribunal: Nuremberg, 14 November 1945–1 October 1946, p. 225 (1947). The International Military Tribunal at Nuremberg, over the prosecution's objections, pointedly refused to recognize as a violation of the law of war conspiracy to commit war crimes, see, *e.g.*, 22 *id.*, at 469, and convicted only Hitler's most senior associates of conspiracy to wage aggressive war, see S. Pomorski, Conspiracy and Criminal Organization, in the Nuremberg Trial and International Law 213, 233–235 (G. Ginsburgs & V. Kudriavtsev eds. 1990).

*   *   *

The charge's shortcomings are not merely formal, but are indicative of a broader inability on the Executive's part here to satisfy the most basic precondition — at least in the absence of specific congressional authorization — for establishment of military commissions: military necessity. Hamdan's tribunal was appointed not by a military commander in the field of battle, but by a retired major general stationed away from any active hostilities. Cf. *Rasul* v. *Bush,* 542 U. S., at 487 (Kennedy, J., concurring in judgment) (observing that "Guantanamo Bay is … far removed from any hostilities"). Hamdan is charged not with an overt act for which he was caught redhanded in a theater of war and which military efficiency demands be tried expeditiously, but with an *agreement* the inception of which long predated the attacks of September 11, 2001 and the AUMF. That may well be a crime, but it is not an offense that "by the law of war may be tried by military commissio[n]." 10 U. S. C. §821. None of the overt acts alleged to have been committed in furtherance of the agreement is itself a war crime, or even necessarily occurred during time of, or in a theater of, war. Any urgent need for imposition or execution of judgment is utterly belied by the record; Hamdan was arrested in November 2001 and he was not charged until mid-2004. These simply are not the circumstances in which, by any stretch of the historical evidence or this Court's precedents, a military commission established by Executive Order under the authority of Article 21 of the UCMJ may lawfully try a person and subject him to punishment.

Whether or not the Government has charged Hamdan with an offense against the law of war cognizable by military commission, the commission lacks power to proceed. The UCMJ conditions the President's use of military commissions on compliance not only with the American common law of war, but also with the rest of the UCMJ itself, insofar as applicable, and with the "rules and precepts of the law of nations," *Quirin*, 317 U. S., at 28 — including, *inter alia*, the four Geneva Conventions signed in 1949. See *Yamashita*, 327 U. S., at 20–21, 23–24. The procedures that the Government has decreed will govern Hamdan's trial by commission violate these laws.

[The commission procedures offer certain basic procedural rights to the accused, such as the right to be informed of the charges against him, the right to counsel, and the presumption of innocence.] These rights are subject, however, to one glaring condition: The accused and his civilian counsel may be excluded from, and precluded from ever learning what evidence was presented during, any part of the proceeding that either the Appointing Authority or the presiding officer decides to "close." Grounds for such closure "include the protection of information classified or classifiable … ; information protected by law or rule from unauthorized disclosure; the physical safety of participants in Commission proceedings, including prospective witnesses; intelligence and law enforcement sources, methods, or activities; and other national security interests." [Commission Order] §6(B)(3). Appointed military defense counsel must be privy to these closed sessions, but may, at the presiding officer's discretion, be forbidden to reveal to his or her client what took place therein. *Ibid.*

Another striking feature of the rules governing Hamdan's commission is that they permit the admission of *any* evidence that, in the opinion of the presiding officer, "would have probative value to a reasonable person." §6(D)(1). Under this test, not only is testimonial hearsay and evidence obtained through coercion fully admissible, but neither live testimony nor witnesses' written statements need be sworn. See §§6(D)(2)(b), (3). Moreover, the accused and his civilian counsel may be denied access to evidence in the form of "protected information" (which includes classified information as well as "information protected by law or rule from unauthorized disclosure" and "information concerning other national security interests," §§6(B)(3), 6(D)(5)(a)(v)), so long as the presiding officer concludes that the evidence is "probative" under §6(D)(1) and that its admission without the accused's knowledge would not "result in the denial of a full and fair trial." §6(D)(5)(b). Finally, a presiding officer's determination that evidence "would not have probative value to a reasonable person" may be overridden by a majority of the other commission members. §6(D)(1).

Once all the evidence is in, the commission members (not including the presiding officer) must vote on the accused's guilt. A two-thirds vote will suffice for both a verdict of guilty and for imposition of any sentence not including death (the imposition of which requires a unanimous vote). §6(F). Any appeal is taken to a three-member review panel composed of military officers and designated by the Secretary of Defense, only one member of which need have experience as a judge. §6(H)(4). The review panel is directed to "disregard any variance from procedures specified in this Order or elsewhere that would not materially have affected the outcome of the trial before the Commission." *Ibid.* Once the panel makes its recommendation to the Secretary of Defense, the Secretary can either remand for further proceedings or forward the record to the President with his recommendation as to final disposition. §6(H)(5). The President then, unless he has delegated the task to the Secretary, makes the "final decision." §6(H)(6). He may change the commission's findings or sentence only in a manner favorable to the accused. *Ibid.*

* * *

In part because the difference between military commissions and courts-martial originally was a difference of jurisdiction alone, and in part to protect against abuse and ensure evenhandedness under the pressures of war, the procedures governing trials by military commission historically have been the same as those governing courts-martial . . . As recently as the Korean and Vietnam wars, during which use of military commissions was contemplated but never made, the principle of procedural parity was espoused as a background assumption.

[The requirements of the UCMJ extend to a detainee in Hamdan's position, and the Geneva Convention Relative to the Treatment of Prisoners of War extends its protections to "prisoners of war prosecuted under the laws of the Detaining Power for acts committed prior to capture."]

Article 36 [of the UCMJ] places two restrictions on the President's power to promulgate rules of procedure for courts-martial and military commissions alike. First, no procedural rule he adopts may be "contrary to or inconsistent with" the UCMJ — however practical it may seem. Second, the rules adopted must be "uniform insofar as practicable." That is, the rules applied to military commissions must be the same as those applied to courts-martial unless such uniformity proves impracticable.

* * *

Without reaching the question whether any provision of Commission Order No. 1 is strictly "contrary to or inconsistent with" other provisions of the UCMJ, we conclude that the "practicability" determination the President has made is insufficient to justify variances from the procedures governing courts-martial. Subsection (b) of Article 36 was added after World War II, and requires a different showing of impracticability from the one required by subsection (a). Subsection (a) requires that the rules the President promulgates for courts-martial, provost courts, and military commissions alike conform to those that govern procedures in *Article III courts*, "so far as *he considers* practicable." 10 U. S. C. §836(a) (emphasis added). Subsection (b), by contrast, demands that the rules applied in courts-martial, provost courts, and military commissions — whether or not they conform with the Federal Rules of Evidence — be "uniform *insofar as practicable*." §836(b) (emphasis added). Under the latter provision, then, the rules set forth in the Manual for Courts-Martial must apply to military commissions unless impracticable.

* * *

Nothing in the record before us demonstrates that it would be impracticable to apply court-martial rules in this case. There is no suggestion, for example, of any logistical difficulty in securing properly sworn and authenticated evidence or in applying the usual principles of relevance and admissibility. Assuming *arguendo* that the reasons articulated in the President's Article 36(a) determination ought to be considered in evaluating the impracticability of applying court-martial rules, the only reason offered in support of that determination is the danger posed by international terrorism. Without for one moment underestimating that danger, it is not evident to us why it should require, in the case of Hamdan's trial, any variance from the rules that govern courts-martial.

* * *

Under the circumstances, then, the rules applicable in courts-martial must apply. Since it is undisputed that Commission Order No. 1 deviates in many significant respects from those rules, it necessarily violates Article 36(b).

* * *

The procedures adopted to try Hamdan also violate the Geneva Conventions.

*   *   *

[Common Article 3 of the Geneva Conventions applies certain protections to combatants detained in a "conflict not of an international character occurring in the territory of one of the High Contracting Parties" (even those persons who do not qualify as prisoners of war). Because the conflict with Al Qaeda is not a conflict between *nations*, it is "not of an international character." Thus, combatants detained in the conflict are entitled to the protections of Common Article 3. In pertinent part, it prohibits "the passing of sentences and the carrying out of executions without previous judgment pronounced by a regularly constituted court affording all the judicial guarantees which are recognized as indispensable by civilized peoples."]

Common Article 3, then, is applicable here and, as indicated above, requires that Hamdan be tried by a "regularly constituted court affording all the judicial guarantees which are recognized as indispensable by civilized peoples." 6 U. S. T., at 3320 (Art. 3, ¶1(d)). While the term "regularly constituted court" is not specifically defined in either Common Article 3 or its accompanying commentary, other sources disclose its core meaning. The commentary accompanying a provision of the Fourth Geneva Convention, for example, defines "'regularly constituted'" tribunals to include "ordinary military courts" and "definitely exclud[e] all special tribunals." GCIV Commentary 340 (defining the term "properly constituted" in Article 66, which the commentary treats as identical to "regularly constituted"); see also *Yamashita*, 327 U. S., at 44 (Rutledge, J., dissenting) (describing military commission as a court "specially constituted for a particular trial"). And one of the Red Cross' own treatises defines "regularly constituted court" as used in Common Article 3 to mean "established and organized in accordance with the laws and procedures already in force in a country." Int'l Comm. of Red Cross, 1 Customary International Humanitarian Law 355 (2005); see also GCIV Commentary 340 (observing that "ordinary military courts" will "be set up in accordance with the recognized principles governing the administration of justice").

*   *   *

At a minimum, a military commission "can be 'regularly constituted' by the standards of our military justice system only if some practical need explains deviations from court-martial practice." *Post*, at 10. As we have explained, *supra*, no such need has been demonstrated here.

[JUSTICE BREYER issued a short concurring opinion noting that military commissions of the type invalidated by this decision could be legitimized by express congressional authorization. It is the absence of such express congressional authorization that led to the Court's conclusion here.

JUSTICE KENNEDY issued a concurring opinion noting that the use of military tribunals raises important separation of powers concerns because such tribunals effectively concentrate the prosecutorial and adjudicative functions within the Executive Branch. In this case, through the UCMJ, Congress has exercised its authority to provide for a certain type of military commission in certain circumstances. Because the President's Military Commission Order No. 1 creates military tribunals that deviate from what Congress has authorized, this is a situation that falls into the third category in Justice Jackson's taxonomy of executive action -- one in which the Executive Branch is acting inconsistently with the intentions of the Legislative Branch, and so executive power is at its lowest ebb.

JUSTICE SCALIA dissented, arguing against the Court's conclusion that the Detainee Treatment Act did not divest the Court of jurisdiction to consider Hamdan's appeal.

JUSTICE THOMAS dissented, arguing that the AUMF itself constituted an authorization of military commissions independent of the UCMJ. The President's use of military commissions should be viewed as executive action taken with express support from Congress and, therefore, entitled to the utmost judicial deference. The Court should be much more deferential to the determinations of the President on questions of what is chargeable as a war crime and what is required by "military necessity."

JUSTICE ALITO dissented, arguing that the plurality was incorrect in concluding that Hamdan's military commission is not a "regularly constituted court" within the meaning of Common Article 3 of the Geneva Convention. All that is required for a tribunal to be "regularly constituted" is that it be authorized by law. Military commissions are authorized under U.S. law, and therefore meet the requirements of Common Article 3.]

DISCUSSION AND QUESTIONS

1. The practical effect of Justice Stevens' opinion in *Hamdan* is that, in theory, military commissions may be used to try unlawful combatants for war crimes, but such military commissions must look very much like the courts martial that are used to try members of the United States military under the Uniform Code of Military Justice. Did Congress intend these sorts of constraints on the commander in chief when it authorized him to "use all necessary and appropriate force" against the September 11 attackers and those who aided them? Is it likely that, when Congress enacted such a broad and sweeping authorization, it intended the sort of searching review of the commander in chief's prosecution of the war that is represented by *Hamdan*? In relying so heavily upon its interpretation of Common Article 3 of the Geneva Convention, was the Court hewing to the notion that the President is the "sole organ of the federal government in the field of international relations," as was stated by the Court in *Curtiss-Wright*. Plainly, President Bush did not believe that Common Article 3 prohibited his use of military commissions; indeed, he took the position that Common Article 3 had no applicability to Hamdan whatsoever because Al Qaeda is not a signatory to the treaty. *Hamdan v. Rumsfeld*, No. 05-184, Brief for Respondents, at 37-39 (U.S. 2006). Was the Court assuming its proper role in the Framers' carefully constructed constitutional separation of powers when it substituted its own interpretation of a treaty -- particularly one that deals with the conduct of armed conflict -- for the President's interpretation?

2. Justice Stevens concludes that Hamdan cannot be tried by military commission because "conspiracy" is not a recognized war crime. Yet, as Justice Stevens notes, the substantive allegation against Hamdan is that he

> willfully and knowingly joined an enterprise of persons who shared a common criminal purpose and conspired and agreed with [named members of al Qaeda] to commit the following offenses triable by military commission: attacking civilians; attacking civilian objects; murder by an unprivileged belligerent; and terrorism.

And, in furtherance of this enterprise,

> (1) he acted as Osama bin Laden's "bodyguard and personal driver," "believ[ing]" all the while that bin Laden "and his associates were involved in" terrorist acts prior to and including the attacks of September 11, 2001;

> (2) he arranged for transportation of, and actually transported, weapons used by al Qaeda members and by bin Laden's bodyguards (Hamdan among them);
>
> (3) he "drove or accompanied [O]sama bin Laden to various al Qaida-sponsored training camps, press conferences, or lectures," at which bin Laden encouraged attacks against Americans; and
>
> (4) he received weapons training at al Qaeda-sponsored camps.

As is succinctly stated by Principle VII of the Principles of International Law Recognized in the Charter of the Nüremberg Tribunal and in the Judgment of the Tribunal (1950), "complicity in the commission of . . . a war crime . . . is a crime under international law." If the government had charged Hamdan with "complicity" in war crimes rather than "conspiracy," would Justice Stevens have been able to find that the allegations against Hamdan could not be tried before a military commission? When the commander in chief is exercising his authority to try alleged unlawful combatants before military commissions, should the Judicial Branch parse the charges so closely that a few dictional choices by prosecutors can entirely undo the President's fundamental decision?

3. Justice Stevens explains that "the most basic precondition . . . for establishment of military commissions" is "military necessity." Apparently, the commander in chief believed that such military necessity was present, because he elected to create military commissions for use in the War on Terror. Do separation of powers principles, properly applied, permit the judiciary to substitute its judgment for that of the commander in chief on the question of whether there is a "military necessity" of one sort or another? Drawing on the political question doctrine (see, generally, Chapter Eight), are there judicially manageable standards for assessing the presence, absence, or degree of "military necessity"? In *Gilligan v. Morgan*, 413 U.S. 1 (1973), Chief Justice Burger opined that the Judicial Branch was not competent to second-guess the political branches when it comes to the "complex, subtle, and professional decisions as to the composition, training, equipping, and control of a military force." Was Justice Stevens' willingness to evaluate "military necessity" consistent with the historical approach of the courts when asked to intervene in Executive Branch decisions relating to armed conflict?

4. Justice Stevens asserts that military commissions may only be used when they are required by "military necessity," and he suggests that such "military necessity" exists only when the trial must occur on or near a field of battle and when

circumstances create a genuine sense of urgency. If Justice Stevens is correct, can military commissions ever be utilized in the War on Terror? If the ongoing armed conflict between the United States and Al Qaeda (and other terrorist organizations) can truly be considered a "war," it is certainly a limited, asymmetrical war, one that is fought almost entirely outside of the United States, and one that cannot be said to interfere with the availability and regular operation of the civilian courts. Among the hundreds of alleged unlawful combatants who were held at Guantanamo Bay, the vast majority were detained for several years before they were brought before any sort of tribunal to review their status or to consider war crimes allegations. Given the availability of the civilian courts, and given the apparent lack of urgency in prosecuting alleged unlawful combatants in the War on Terror, could anyone credibly argue in favor of "military necessity" as Justice Stevens defines it?

Boumediene v. Bush

553 U.S. 723 (2008)[39]

JUSTICE KENNEDY delivered the opinion of the Court.

Petitioners are aliens designated as enemy combatants and detained at the United States Naval Station at Guantanamo Bay, Cuba. There are others detained there, also aliens, who are not parties to this suit.

Petitioners present a question not resolved by our earlier cases relating to the detention of aliens at Guantanamo: whether they have the constitutional privilege of habeas corpus, a privilege not to be withdrawn except in conformance with the Suspension Clause, Art. I, §9, cl. 2. We hold these petitioners do have the habeas corpus privilege. Congress has enacted a statute, the Detainee Treatment Act of 2005 (DTA), 119 Stat. 2739, that provides certain procedures for review of the detainees' status. We hold that those procedures are not an adequate and effective substitute for habeas corpus. Therefore §7 of the Military Commissions Act of 2006 (MCA), 28 U. S. C. A. §2241(e) (Supp. 2007), operates as an unconstitutional suspension of the writ.

* * *

Under the Authorization for Use of Military Force (AUMF), §2(a), 115 Stat. 224, note following 50 U. S. C. §1541 (2000 ed., Supp. V),

[39] Footnotes and some citations found in the original decision have been omitted from this excerpted version.

the President is authorized "to use all necessary and appropriate force against those nations, organizations, or persons he determines planned, authorized, committed, or aided the terrorist attacks that occurred on September 11, 2001, or harbored such organizations or persons, in order to prevent any future acts of international terrorism against the United States by such nations, organizations or persons."

In *Hamdi* v. *Rumsfeld*, 542 U. S. 507 (2004), five Members of the Court recognized that detention of individuals who fought against the United States in Afghanistan "for the duration of the particular conflict in which they were captured, is so fundamental and accepted an incident to war as to be an exercise of the 'necessary and appropriate force' Congress has authorized the President to use." *Id.*, at 518 (plurality opinion of O'Connor, J.), *id.*, at 588–589 (Thomas, J., dissenting). After *Hamdi*, the Deputy Secretary of Defense established Combatant Status Review Tribunals (CSRTs) to determine whether individuals detained at Guantanamo were "enemy combatants," as the Department defines that term. See App. to Pet. for Cert. in No. 06–1195, p. 81a. A later memorandum established procedures to implement the CSRTs. See App. to Pet. for Cert. in No. 06–1196, p. 147. The Government maintains these procedures were designed to comply with the due process requirements identified by the plurality in *Hamdi*. See Brief for Respondents 10.

Interpreting the AUMF, the Department of Defense ordered the detention of these petitioners, and they were transferred to Guantanamo. Some of these individuals were apprehended on the battlefield in Afghanistan, others in places as far away from there as Bosnia and Gambia. All are foreign nationals, but none is a citizen of a nation now at war with the United States. Each denies he is a member of the al Qaeda terrorist network that carried out the September 11 attacks or of the Taliban regime that provided sanctuary for al Qaeda. Each petitioner appeared before a separate CSRT; was determined to be an enemy combatant; and has sought a writ of habeas corpus in the United States District Court for the District of Columbia.

The first actions commenced in February 2002. The District Court ordered the cases dismissed for lack of jurisdiction because the naval station is outside the sovereign territory of the United States. See *Rasul* v. *Bush*, 215 F. Supp. 2d 55 (2002). The Court of Appeals for the District of Columbia Circuit affirmed. See *Al Odah* v. *United States*, 321 F. 3d 1134, 1145 (2003). We granted certiorari and reversed, holding that 28 U. S. C. §2241 extended statutory habeas corpus jurisdiction to Guantanamo. See *Rasul* v. *Bush*, 542 U. S. 466,

473 (2004). The constitutional issue presented in the instant cases was not reached in *Rasul*. *Id.*, at 476.

[In direct response to the *Hamdan* decision, Congress enacted the Military Commissions Act of 2007 (MCA), which purported to strip the federal courts of jurisdiction to consider habeas corpus petitions filed by persons detained as enemy combatants, even petitions pending before the MCA's enactment.]

As a threshold matter, we must decide whether MCA §7 denies the federal courts jurisdiction to hear habeas corpus actions pending at the time of its enactment. We hold the statute does deny that jurisdiction, so that, if the statute is valid, petitioners' cases must be dismissed.

As amended by the terms of the MCA, 28 U. S. C. A. §2241(e) (Supp. 2007) now provides:

> (1) No court, justice, or judge shall have jurisdiction to hear or consider an application for a writ of habeas corpus filed by or on behalf of an alien detained by the United States who has been determined by the United States to have been properly detained as an enemy combatant or is awaiting such determination.
>
> (2) Except as provided in [§§1005(e)(2) and (e)(3) of the DTA] no court, justice, or judge shall have jurisdiction to hear or consider any other action against the United States or its agents relating to any aspect of the detention, transfer, treatment, trial, or conditions of confinement of an alien who is or was detained by the United States and has been determined by the United States to have been properly detained as an enemy combatant or is awaiting such determination.

* * *

[W]e agree with [the Court of Appeals'] conclusion that the MCA deprives the federal courts of jurisdiction to entertain the habeas corpus actions now before us.

In deciding the constitutional questions now presented we must determine whether petitioners are barred from seeking the writ or invoking the protections of the Suspension Clause either because of their status, *i.e.*, petitioners' designation by the Executive Branch as enemy combatants, or their physical location, *i.e.*, their presence at

Guantanamo Bay. The Government contends that noncitizens designated as enemy combatants and detained in territory located outside our Nation's borders have no constitutional rights and no privilege of habeas corpus. Petitioners contend they do have cognizable constitutional rights and that Congress, in seeking to eliminate recourse to habeas corpus as a means to assert those rights, acted in violation of the Suspension Clause.

[Justice Kennedy engages in an extended review of the Anglo-American history and evolution of the writ of habeas corpus, its availability to aliens, and its territorial application.]

We . . . do not question the Government's position that Cuba, not the United States, maintains sovereignty, in the legal and technical sense of the term, over Guantanamo Bay. But this does not end the analysis. Our cases do not hold it is improper for us to inquire into the objective degree of control the Nation asserts over foreign territory. As commentators have noted, " '[s]overeignty' is a term used in many senses and is much abused. " See 1 Restatement (Third) of Foreign Relations Law of the United States §206, Comment *b,* p. 94 (1986). When we have stated that sovereignty is a political question, we have referred not to sovereignty in the general, colloquial sense, meaning the exercise of dominion or power, see Webster's New International Dictionary 2406 (2d ed. 1934) ("sovereignty," definition 3), but sovereignty in the narrow, legal sense of the term, meaning a claim of right, see 1 Restatement (Third) of Foreign Relations, *supra,* §206, Comment *b,* at 94 (noting that sovereignty "implies a state's lawful control over its territory generally to the exclusion of other states, authority to govern in that territory, and authority to apply law there"). Indeed, it is not altogether uncommon for a territory to be under the *de jure* sovereignty of one nation, while under the plenary control, or practical sovereignty, of another. This condition can occur when the territory is seized during war, as Guantanamo was during the Spanish-American War. See, *e.g.*, *Fleming* v. *Page*, 9 How. 603, 614 (1850) (noting that the port of Tampico, conquered by the United States during the war with Mexico, was "undoubtedly ... subject to the sovereignty and dominion of the United States," but that it "does not follow that it was a part of the United States, or that it ceased to be a foreign country"); *King* v. *Earl of Crewe ex parte Sekgome*, [1910] 2 K. B. 576, 603–604 (C. A.) (opinion of Williams, L. J.) (arguing that the Bechuanaland Protectorate in South Africa was "under His Majesty's dominion in the sense of power and jurisdiction, but is not under his dominion in the sense of territorial dominion"). Accordingly, for purposes of our analysis, we accept the Government's position that Cuba, and not the United States, retains *de jure* sovereignty over Guantanamo Bay. As we did in *Rasul*, however, we take notice of the obvious and uncontested fact that the United States, by virtue of its complete jurisdiction and control over the base, maintains *de facto* sovereignty over this territory. See 542 U. S., at 480; *id.*, at 487 (Kennedy, J., concurring in judgment).

Were we to hold that the present cases turn on the political question doctrine, we would be required first to accept the Government's premise that *de jure* sovereignty is the touchstone of habeas corpus jurisdiction. This premise, however, is unfounded. For the reasons indicated above, the history of common-law habeas corpus provides scant support for this proposition; and, for the reasons indicated below, that position would be inconsistent with our precedents and contrary to fundamental separation-of-powers principles.

* * *

The United States has maintained complete and uninterrupted control of the bay for over 100 years. At the close of the Spanish-American War, Spain ceded control over the entire island of Cuba to the United States and specifically "relinquishe[d] all claim[s] of sovereignty ... and title." See Treaty of Paris, Dec. 10, 1898, U. S.-Spain, Art. I, 30 Stat. 1755, T. S. No. 343. From the date the treaty with Spain was signed until the Cuban Republic was established on May 20, 1902, the United States governed the territory "in trust" for the benefit of the Cuban people. *Neely* v. *Henkel*, 180 U. S. 109, 120 (1901); H. Thomas, Cuba or The Pursuit of Freedom 436, 460 (1998). And although it recognized, by entering into the 1903 Lease Agreement, that Cuba retained "ultimate sovereignty" over Guantanamo, the United States continued to maintain the same plenary control it had enjoyed since 1898. Yet the Government's view is that the Constitution had no effect there, at least as to noncitizens, because the United States disclaimed sovereignty in the formal sense of the term. The necessary implication of the argument is that by surrendering formal sovereignty over any unincorporated territory to a third party, while at the same time entering into a lease that grants total control over the territory back to the United States, it would be possible for the political branches to govern without legal constraint.

Our basic charter cannot be contracted away like this. The Constitution grants Congress and the President the power to acquire, dispose of, and govern territory, not the power to decide when and where its terms apply. Even when the United States acts outside its borders, its powers are not "absolute and unlimited" but are subject "to such restrictions as are expressed in the Constitution." *Murphy* v.

Ramsey, 114 U. S. 15, 44 (1885). Abstaining from questions involving formal sovereignty and territorial governance is one thing. To hold the political branches have the power to switch the Constitution on or off at will is quite another. The former position reflects this Court's recognition that certain matters requiring political judgments are best left to the political branches. The latter would permit a striking anomaly in our tripartite system of government, leading to a regime in which Congress and the President, not this Court, say "what the law is." *Marbury* v. *Madison*, 1 Cranch 137, 177 (1803).

These concerns have particular bearing upon the Suspension Clause question in the cases now before us, for the writ of habeas corpus is itself an indispensable mechanism for monitoring the separation of powers. The test for determining the scope of this provision must not be subject to manipulation by those whose power it is designed to restrain.

As we recognized in *Rasul*, 542 U. S., at 476; *id.*, at 487 (Kennedy, J., concurring in judgment), the outlines of a framework for determining the reach of the Suspension Clause are suggested by the factors the Court relied upon in *Eisentrager* . . . the *Eisentrager* Court found relevant that each petitioner:

> (a) is an enemy alien; (b) has never been or resided in the United States; (c) was captured outside of our territory and there held in military custody as a prisoner of war; (d) was tried and convicted by a Military Commission sitting outside the United States; (e) for offenses against laws of war committed outside the United States; (f) and is at all times imprisoned outside the United States.

339 U. S., at 777. Based on this language from *Eisentrager*, and the reasoning in our other extraterritoriality opinions, we conclude that at least three factors are relevant in determining the reach of the Suspension Clause: (1) the citizenship and status of the detainee and the adequacy of the process through which that status determination was made; (2) the nature of the sites where apprehension and then detention took place; and (3) the practical obstacles inherent in resolving the prisoner's entitlement to the writ.

Applying this framework, we note at the onset that the status of these detainees is a matter of dispute. The petitioners, like those in *Eisentrager*, are not American citizens. But the petitioners in

Eisentrager did not contest, it seems, the Court's assertion that they were "enemy alien[s]." *Ibid.* In the instant cases, by contrast, the detainees deny they are enemy combatants. They have been afforded some process in CSRT proceedings to determine their status; but, unlike in *Eisentrager, supra*, at 766, there has been no trial by military commission for violations of the laws of war. The difference is not trivial. The records from the *Eisentrager* trials suggest that, well before the petitioners brought their case to this Court, there had been a rigorous adversarial process to test the legality of their detention. The *Eisentrager* petitioners were charged by a bill of particulars that made detailed factual allegations against them. See 14 United Nations War Crimes Commission, Law Reports of Trials of War Criminals 8–10 (1949) (reprint 1997). To rebut the accusations, they were entitled to representation by counsel, allowed to introduce evidence on their own behalf, and permitted to cross-examine the prosecution's witnesses. See Memorandum by Command of Lt. Gen. Wedemeyer, Jan. 21, 1946 (establishing "Regulations Governing the Trial of War Criminals" in the China Theater), in Tr. of Record in *Johnson* v. *Eisentrager,* O. T. 1949, No. 306, pp. 34–40.

In comparison the procedural protections afforded to the detainees in the CSRT hearings are far more limited, and, we conclude, fall well short of the procedures and adversarial mechanisms that would eliminate the need for habeas corpus review. Although the detainee is assigned a "Personal Representative" to assist him during CSRT proceedings, the Secretary of the Navy's memorandum makes clear that person is not the detainee's lawyer or even his "advocate." See App. to Pet. for Cert. in No. 06–1196, at 155, 172. The Government's evidence is accorded a presumption of validity. *Id.*, at 159. The detainee is allowed to present "reasonably available" evidence, *id.*, at 155, but his ability to rebut the Government's evidence against him is limited by the circumstances of his confinement and his lack of counsel at this stage. And although the detainee can seek review of his status determination in the Court of Appeals, that review process cannot cure all defects in the earlier proceedings. See Part V, *infra*.

As to the second factor relevant to this analysis, the detainees here are similarly situated to the *Eisentrager* petitioners in that the sites of their apprehension and detention are technically outside the sovereign territory of the United States. As noted earlier, this is a factor that weighs against finding they have rights under the Suspension Clause. But there are critical differences between Landsberg Prison, circa 1950, and the United States Naval Station at Guantanamo Bay in 2008. Unlike its present control over the naval station, the United States' control over the prison in Germany was neither absolute nor indefinite. Like all parts of occupied Germany, the prison was under the jurisdiction of the combined Allied Forces. See Declaration Regarding the Defeat of Germany and the Assumption of Supreme Authority with Respect to Germany, June 5, 1945, U. S.-U. S. S. R.-U. K.-Fr., 60 Stat. 1649, T. I. A. S. No. 1520. The United States was therefore answerable to its Allies for all activities occurring there. Cf. *Hirota* v. *MacArthur*, 338 U. S. 197, 198 (1948) *(per curiam)* (military tribunal set up by Gen. Douglas MacArthur, acting as "the agent of the Allied Powers," was not a "tribunal of the United States"). The Allies had not planned a long-term occupation of Germany, nor did they intend to displace all German institutions even during the period of occupation. See Agreements Respecting Basic Principles for Merger of the Three Western German Zones of Occupation, and Other Matters, Apr. 8, 1949, U. S.-U. K.-Fr., Art. 1, 63 Stat. 2819, T. I. A. S. No. 2066 (establishing a governing framework "[d]uring the period in which it is necessary that the occupation continue" and expressing the desire "that the German people shall enjoy self-government to the maximum possible degree consistent with such occupation"). The Court's holding in *Eisentrager* was thus consistent with the Insular Cases, where it had held there was no need to extend full constitutional protections to territories the United States did not intend to govern indefinitely. Guantanamo Bay, on the other hand, is no transient possession. In every practical sense Guantanamo is not abroad; it is within the constant jurisdiction of the United States. See *Rasul*, 542 U. S., at 480; *id.*, at 487 (Kennedy, J., concurring in judgment).

As to the third factor, we recognize, as the Court did in *Eisentrager*, that there are costs to holding the Suspension Clause applicable in a case of military detention abroad. Habeas corpus proceedings may require expenditure of funds by the Government and may divert the attention of military personnel from other pressing tasks. While we are sensitive to these concerns, we do not find them dispositive. Compliance with any judicial process requires some incremental expenditure of resources. Yet civilian courts and the Armed Forces have functioned alongside each other at various points in our history. See, *e.g., Duncan* v. *Kahanamoku*, 327 U. S. 304 (1946); *Ex parte Milligan*, 4 Wall. 2 (1866). The Government presents no credible arguments that the military mission at Guantanamo would be compromised if habeas corpus courts had jurisdiction to hear the detainees' claims. And in light of the plenary control the United States asserts over the base, none are apparent to us.

*   *   *

It is true that before today the Court has never held that noncitizens detained by our Government in territory over which another country maintains *de jure* sovereignty have any rights under our Constitution. But the cases before us lack any precise historical parallel. They involve individuals detained by executive order for the duration of a conflict that, if measured from September 11, 2001, to the present, is already among the longest wars in American history. See Oxford Companion to American Military History 849 (1999). The detainees, moreover, are held in a territory that, while technically not part of the United States, is under the complete and total control of our Government. Under these circumstances the lack of a precedent on point is no barrier to our holding.

We hold that Art. I, §9, cl. 2, of the Constitution has full effect at Guantanamo Bay. If the privilege of habeas corpus is to be denied to the detainees now before us, Congress must act in accordance with the requirements of the Suspension Clause. Cf. *Hamdi,* 542 U. S., at 564 (Scalia, J., dissenting) ("[I]ndefinite imprisonment on reasonable suspicion is not an available option of treatment for those accused of aiding the enemy, absent a suspension of the writ"). This Court may not impose a *de facto* suspension by abstaining from these controversies. See *Hamdan*, 548 U. S., at 585, n. 16 ("[A]bstention is not appropriate in cases … in which the legal challenge 'turn[s] on the status of the persons as to whom the military asserted its power' " (quoting *Schlesinger* v. *Councilman*, 420 U. S. 738, 759 (1975))). The MCA does not purport to be a formal suspension of the writ; and the Government, in its submissions to us, has not argued that it is. Petitioners, therefore, are entitled to the privilege of habeas corpus to challenge the legality of their detention.

[The government asserts that, even if Guantanamo detainees are entitled to the writ of habeas corpus, the Combatant Status Review Tribunals (CSRTs) created by the Detainee Treatment Act (DTA), along with the limited judicial review permitted under that Act, are an adequate substitute for the traditional judicial review that occurs as a result of a habeas corpus petition. These tribunals permit detainees to challenge their status as enemy combatants.]

We do not endeavor to offer a comprehensive summary of the requisites for an adequate substitute for habeas corpus. We do consider it uncontroversial, however, that the privilege of habeas corpus entitles the prisoner to a meaningful opportunity to demonstrate that he is being held pursuant to "the erroneous application or interpretation" of relevant law. *St. Cyr*, 533 U. S., at 302. And the habeas court must have the power to order the conditional release of an individual unlawfully detained—though release need not be the exclusive remedy and is not the appropriate one in every case in which the writ is granted.

* * *

Where a person is detained by executive order, rather than, say, after being tried and convicted in a court, the need for collateral review is most pressing. A criminal conviction in the usual course occurs after a judicial hearing before a tribunal disinterested in the outcome and committed to procedures designed to ensure its own independence. These dynamics are not inherent in executive detention orders or executive review procedures. In this context the need for habeas corpus is more urgent. The intended duration of the detention and the reasons for it bear upon the precise scope of the inquiry. Habeas corpus proceedings need not resemble a criminal trial, even when the detention is by executive order. But the writ must be effective. The habeas court must have sufficient authority to conduct a meaningful review of both the cause for detention and the Executive's power to detain.

To determine the necessary scope of habeas corpus review, therefore, we must assess the CSRT process, the mechanism through which petitioners' designation as enemy combatants became final. Whether one characterizes the CSRT process as direct review of the Executive's battlefield determination that the detainee is an enemy combatant — as the parties have and as we do — or as the first step in the collateral review of a battlefield determination makes no difference in a proper analysis of whether the procedures Congress put in place are an adequate substitute for habeas corpus. What matters is the sum total of procedural protections afforded to the detainee at all stages, direct and collateral.

Petitioners identify what they see as myriad deficiencies in the CSRTs. The most relevant for our purposes are the constraints upon the detainee's ability to rebut the factual basis for the Government's assertion that he is an enemy combatant. [A]t the CSRT stage the detainee has limited means to find or present evidence to challenge the Government's case against him. He does not have the assistance of counsel and may not be aware of the most critical allegations that the Government relied upon to order his detention. See App. to Pet. for Cert. in No. 06–1196, at 156, ¶F(8) (noting that the detainee can access only the "unclassified portion of the Government Information"). The detainee can confront witnesses that testify during the CSRT proceedings. *Id.*, at 144, ¶g(8). But given that there are in effect no limits on the admission of hearsay evidence — the only requirement is that the tribunal deem the evidence "relevant and helpful," *ibid.*, ¶g(9) — the detainee's opportunity to question witnesses is likely to be more theoretical than real.

* * *

For the writ of habeas corpus, or its substitute, to function as an effective and proper remedy in this context, the court that conducts the habeas proceeding must have the means to correct errors that occurred during the CSRT proceedings. This includes some authority to assess the sufficiency of the Government's evidence against the detainee. It also must have the authority to admit and consider relevant exculpatory evidence that was not introduced during the earlier proceeding. Federal habeas petitioners long have had the means to supplement the record on review, even in the postconviction habeas setting. See *Townsend* v. *Sain*, 372 U. S. 293, 313 (1963), overruled in part by *Keeney* v. *Tamayo-Reyes*, 504 U. S. 1, 5 (1992). Here that opportunity is constitutionally required.

* * *

Assuming the DTA can be construed to allow the Court of Appeals to review or correct the CSRT's factual determinations, as opposed to merely certifying that the tribunal applied the correct standard of proof, we see no way to construe the statute to allow what is also constitutionally required in this context: an opportunity for the detainee to present relevant exculpatory evidence that was not made part of the record in the earlier proceedings.

* * *

Under the DTA the Court of Appeals has the power to review CSRT determinations by assessing the legality of standards and procedures. This implies the power to inquire into what happened at the CSRT hearing and, perhaps, to remedy certain deficiencies in that proceeding. But should the Court of Appeals determine that the CSRT followed appropriate and lawful standards and procedures, it will have reached the limits of its jurisdiction. There is no language in the DTA that can be construed to allow the Court of Appeals to admit and consider newly discovered evidence that could not have been made part of the CSRT record because it was unavailable to either the Government or the detainee when the CSRT made its findings. This evidence, however, may be critical to the detainee's argument that he is not an enemy combatant and there is no cause to detain him.

*   *   *

By foreclosing consideration of evidence not presented or reasonably available to the detainee at the CSRT proceedings, the DTA disadvantages the detainee by limiting the scope of collateral review to a record that may not be accurate or complete. In other contexts, *e.g.*, in post-trial habeas cases where the prisoner already has had a full and fair opportunity to develop the factual predicate of his claims, similar limitations on the scope of habeas review may be appropriate. See *Williams* v. *Taylor*, 529 U. S. 420, 436–437 (2000) (noting that §2254 "does not equate prisoners who exercise diligence in pursuing their claims with those who do not"). In this context, however, where the underlying detention proceedings lack the necessary adversarial character, the detainee cannot be held responsible for all deficiencies in the record.

*   *   *

We do not imply DTA review would be a constitutionally sufficient replacement for habeas corpus but for these limitations on the detainee's ability to present exculpatory evidence. For even if it were possible, as a textual matter, to read into the statute each of the necessary procedures we have identified, we could not overlook the cumulative effect of our doing so. To hold that the detainees at Guantanamo may, under the DTA, challenge the President's legal authority to detain them, contest the CSRT's findings of fact, supplement the record on review with exculpatory evidence, and request an order of release would come close to reinstating the §2241 habeas corpus process Congress sought to deny them. The language of the statute, read in light of Congress' reasons for enacting it, cannot bear this interpretation. Petitioners have met their burden of establishing that the DTA review process is, on its face, an inadequate substitute for habeas corpus.

*   *   *

Our decision today holds only that the petitioners before us are entitled to seek the writ; that the DTA review procedures are an inadequate substitute for habeas corpus; and that the petitioners in these cases need not exhaust the review procedures in the Court of Appeals before proceeding with their habeas actions in the District Court. The only law we identify as unconstitutional is MCA §7, 28 U. S. C. A. §2241(e) (Supp. 2007). Accordingly, both the DTA and the CSRT process remain intact. Our holding with regard to exhaustion should not be read to imply that a habeas court should intervene the moment an enemy combatant steps foot in a territory where the writ runs. The Executive is entitled to a reasonable period of time to determine a detainee's status before a court entertains that detainee's habeas corpus petition. The CSRT process is the mechanism Congress and the President set up to deal with these issues. Except in cases of undue delay, federal courts should refrain from entertaining an enemy combatant's habeas corpus petition at least until after the Department, acting via the CSRT, has had a chance to review his status.

* * *

Our opinion does not undermine the Executive's powers as Commander in Chief. On the contrary, the exercise of those powers is vindicated, not eroded, when confirmed by the Judicial Branch. Within the Constitution's separation-of-powers structure, few exercises of judicial power are as legitimate or as necessary as the responsibility to hear challenges to the authority of the Executive to imprison a person. Some of these petitioners have been in custody for six years with no definitive judicial determination as to the legality of their detention. Their access to the writ is a necessity to determine the lawfulness of their status, even if, in the end, they do not obtain the relief they seek.

[JUSTICE SOUTER concurred and noted that, in light of the *Rasul* decision four years earlier, no one should be surprised by the outcome in *Hamdan.* He also opined that this decision can hardly be viewed as "a judicial victory in a contest for power between the Court and the political branches," given that the Executive Branch has managed to avoid effective habeas corpus review for Guantanamo detainees for as much as six years.

CHIEF JUSTICE ROBERTS dissented. He disagreed with the majority that aliens held at Guantanamo Bay enjoy constitutional habeas corpus protections; however, his principal complaint with the majority's approach is that it did not first permit the process set forth in the Detainee Treatment Act to play out before concluding that the process was inadequate. He argues that "the Court should have required petitioners to exhaust their remedies under the statute" before considering their claims.

JUSTICE SCALIA dissented and criticized the Court's extension of habeas corpus rights to aliens held outside of the United States. He argues that *Eisentrager* is the controlling precedent, and the consequence of departing from that precedent is that "Henceforth, as today's opinion makes unnervingly clear, how to handle enemy prisoners in this war will ultimately lie with the branch that knows least about the national security concerns that the subject entails."]

DISCUSSION AND QUESTIONS

1. Simply stated, Justice Kennedy's position is that the circumstances of the *Boumediene* petitioners are materially different from the circumstances of the *Eisentrager* petitioners in two ways: (1) The United States exercises total control over Guantanamo Bay and will continue to do so indefinitely, and (2) those held in Guantanamo Bay have already been detained for several years and, given the nature of the armed conflict that led to their capture, may be detained for many years to come. Are these appropriate bases for distinguishing among habeas corpus petitioners? If the writ of habeas corpus exists as a protection against wrongful detention by the government of the United States, why does it matter where the detention occurs or what degree of control the U.S. exercises over the geography? Is not the salient consideration -- from the perspective of both the detainee and the custodian -- that the United States government is the jailer, regardless of where the jail is located? Suppose that the nation of Jordan lent one of its prisons to the United States government and permitted the U.S. to imprison there any individuals it wished, for whatever reasons it wished, for as long as it wished. For purposes of protecting the rights of the detainees and checking potential abuses by the government, does it matter that the prison is located in a sovereign nation over which the United States does not exercise control?

In the case of *Maqaleh v. Gates*, 605 F.3d 390 (D.C. Cir. 2010), alien detainees at Bagram Airfield Military Base in Afghanistan sought habeas corpus relief, basing their arguments largely on the *Boumediene* decision. They contended that, like the *Boumediene* petitioners, they were detained by the U.S. military at a facility that, while outside the United States, was effectively under the control of the U.S. government. The U.S. military occupies the Bagram base pursuant to a lease with the government of Afghanistan that permits the U.S. to occupy the facility "until the United States or its successors determine that the premises are no longer required for its use." Id. at 87-88. Applying the three-factor test set forth in *Boumediene*, the D.C. Circuit concluded that the courts lacked jurisdiction to consider the petitions. While the factor relating to citizenship and status was comparable to that of the *Boumediene* detainees, the circumstances of the *Maqaleh* petitioners were distinguishable in that (1) the degree and duration of U.S. control over the Bagram base did not amount to de facto sovereignty, and (2) the Bagram base was located in an active theater of war, which made the practical obstacles associated with resolving the petitions insuperable.

2. The *Boumediene* decision is notable not only because it broke new ground in extending constitutional protections to alien enemy combatants, but also because it involved an effort by Congress to strip the courts of jurisdictions to consider certain types of cases. At Article III, § 1, the Constitution grants to Congress the power to "ordain and establish" the "inferior courts," which refers to all courts other than the Supreme Court. Further, Congress is not required to establish such lower courts at all; the Constitution suggests that Congress "may" establish such courts "from time to time." Because the Constitution makes the very existence of the lower courts entirely subject to the discretion of Congress, it seems highly likely that the Framers also intended that Congress could endow such courts with as little or as much jurisdiction as Congress deemed appropriate. Article III, § 2 sets forth the very limited original jurisdiction of the Supreme Court (which does not even arguably include habeas petitions filed by alien enemy combatants), and makes the Court's appellate jurisdiction entirely subject to "such exceptions . . . as the Congress shall make." Through the Military Commissions Act, Congress responded directly to the *Hamdan* decision by moving to strip the courts of jurisdiction to entertain any habeas corpus petitions filed by enemy combatants. The MCA was unequivocal in stating that "no court, justice, or judge shall have jurisdiction to hear or consider an application for a writ of habeas corpus filed by or on behalf of an alien [enemy combatant]." And Justice Kennedy agreed that "the MCA deprives the federal courts of jurisdiction to entertain the habeas corpus actions now before us." Yet, the Court proceeded to consider the petitions on the merits. How can the Court's willingness to disregard Congress' explicit limit on the courts' jurisdiction be squared with the Constitution's allocation to the Legislative Branch of the power to determine all federal court jurisdiction except the original jurisdiction of the Supreme Court?

In *Ex parte McCardle*, 74 U.S. 506 (1868), the Supreme Court concluded that it lacked jurisdiction to address the habeas corpus petition filed by a newspaper editor who had been jailed by the military for publishing anti-Reconstruction articles in Mississippi. The lower court found that McCardle's detention was lawful and denied his petition. While his appeal was pending before the Supreme Court, Congress passed a law that stripped the Court of its appellate jurisdiction over habeas corpus matters. Noting that Article III, § 2 makes the Court's appellate jurisdiction subject to "exceptions" determined by Congress, the Court concluded that it lacked jurisdiction and dismissed the appeal. The *McCardle* Court conceded that Congress could limit its jurisdiction, but the *Boumediene* Court (without explaining exactly why) rejected Congress' effort to restrict its jurisdiction. Is the implicit basis for the

Court's approach in *Boumediene* a newfound theory that the courts cannot be stripped of jurisdiction to hear *constitutional* claims? Although it did not say so explicitly, the majority in *Boumediene* appeared to believe that the Constitution's safeguards against abuses by the two political branches -- specifically as set forth in the Suspension Clause -- trump the power of Congress to determine the jurisdiction of the federal courts. The unstated rationale is that the Constitution's limitations on government action are rendered meaningless if the political branches can prevent the courts from acting as a check on the abuses of those branches.

3. As it commenced the post-September 11 War on Terror, the Administration of President George W. Bush understood -- based largely on the *Eisentrager* and *Quirin* decisions from more than a half century earlier -- that it could detain enemy combatants at Guantanamo Bay with no oversight by the Judicial Branch. *See, e.g.,* Office of Legal Counsel Memorandum for William J. Haines, II, "Re: Possible Habeas Jurisdiction Over Aliens Held In Guantanamo Bay, Cuba," December 28, 2001 ("the great weight of legal authority indicates that a federal district court could not properly exercise habeas jurisdiction over an alien detained at [Guantanamo Bay] . . . the analysis from *Eisentrager* should apply to bar any habeas application filed by an alien held at [Guantanamo Bay]"). The Administration also understood that the President, as commander in chief, enjoyed broad latitude to prosecute unlawful enemy combatants before military commissions of his creation. *See, e.g.,* Office of Legal Counsel Memorandum for Alberto R. Gonzales, "Re: Legality Of The Use Of Military Commissions To Try Terrorists," November 6, 2001 (concluding that the President possesses inherent authority to establish military commissions; citing *Quirin* for the proposition that, "if § 821 [of the UCMJ] were read as restricting the use of military commissions and prohibiting practices traditionally followed, it would infringe on the President's express constitutional powers as Commander in Chief"; and noting *Quirin's* teaching that "offenses triable by military commission under the laws of war were not within the commands of constitutional provisions guaranteeing certain procedures for criminal trials"). However, once the Executive Branch began taking action based on these understandings, the Judicial Branch intervened in unexpected ways. Through the *Rasul*, *Hamdi*, *Hamdan*, and *Boumediene* decisions, the Supreme Court ruled that alien combatants held at Guantanamo Bay do have access to the courts; that they may challenge their classification as enemy combatants and are entitled to fairly robust due process protections in doing so; and that, while military commissions may be used to try unlawful enemy combatants, such tribunals must offer essentially the same procedural and substantive protections to defendants as are present in courts martial under the UCMJ.

As these disagreements between that Executive Branch and the Judicial Branch played out, many observers vigorously criticized the executive for abuses of power in how it conducted the War on Terror. At the same time, many others vehemently accused the judiciary of intruding improperly into matters of armed conflict that should be left to the judgment of the commander in chief. The Executive Branch wanted to treat suspected terrorists and their accomplices much like the petitioners in *Quirin* and *Eisentrager* -- that is, like unlawful enemy combatants captured during armed conflict, who could be dealt with by the commander in chief with virtually no judicial oversight. In contrast, the Supreme Court of the early 21st century seemed to believe that such detainees are more like typical criminal defendants -- they should have access to civilian courts that would ensure they receive due process protections much like those found in criminal trials.

Why was there such a profound disconnect between the branches as to the scope of the executive's war power and the judiciary's appetite for supervising the exercise of that power? Was one branch entirely wrong in its understanding and the other entirely correct? Or might it be more accurate to say that both assessed the situation incorrectly, even if one might be considered "more wrong" than the other? Was the Executive Branch more wrong for treating suspected terrorists as if they were enemy combatants in a traditional war, or was the Judicial Branch more wrong for intruding into matters of national security with respect to which it lacks information, institutional expertise, and constitutional authority?

APPENDIX

CONSTITUTION OF THE UNITED STATES[40]

We the People of the United States, in Order to form a more perfect Union, establish Justice, insure domestic Tranquility, provide for the common defence, promote the general Welfare, and secure the Blessings of Liberty to ourselves and our Posterity, do ordain and establish this Constitution for the United States of America.

Article. I.

Section. 1.

All legislative Powers herein granted shall be vested in a Congress of the United States, which shall consist of a Senate and House of Representatives.

Section. 2.

The House of Representatives shall be composed of Members chosen every second Year by the People of the several States, and the Electors in each State shall have the Qualifications requisite for Electors of the most numerous Branch of the State Legislature.

No Person shall be a Representative who shall not have attained to the Age of twenty five Years, and been seven Years a Citizen of the United States, and who shall not, when elected, be an Inhabitant of that State in which he shall be chosen.

Representatives and direct Taxes shall be apportioned among the several States which may be included within this Union, according to their respective Numbers, which shall be determined by adding to the whole Number of free Persons, including those bound to Service for a Term of Years, and excluding Indians not taxed, three fifths of all other Persons. The actual Enumeration shall be made within three Years after the first Meeting of the Congress of the United States, and within every subsequent Term of ten Years, in such Manner as they shall by Law direct. The Number of Representatives shall not exceed one for every thirty Thousand, but each State shall have at Least one Representative; and until such enumeration shall be made, the State of New Hampshire shall be entitled to chuse three, Massachusetts eight, Rhode-Island and Providence Plantations one, Connecticut five, New-York six, New Jersey four, Pennsylvania eight, Delaware one, Maryland six, Virginia ten, North Carolina five, South Carolina five, and Georgia three.

---

[40] Text that is italicized here has been superseded or altered by amendment.

When vacancies happen in the Representation from any State, the Executive Authority thereof shall issue Writs of Election to fill such Vacancies.

The House of Representatives shall chuse their Speaker and other Officers; and shall have the sole Power of Impeachment.

Section. 3.

The Senate of the United States shall be composed of two Senators from each State, *chosen by the Legislature* thereof for six Years; and each Senator shall have one Vote.

Immediately after they shall be assembled in Consequence of the first Election, they shall be divided as equally as may be into three Classes. The Seats of the Senators of the first Class shall be vacated at the Expiration of the second Year, of the second Class at the Expiration of the fourth Year, and of the third Class at the Expiration of the sixth Year, so that one third may be chosen every second Year; *and if Vacancies happen by Resignation, or otherwise, during the Recess of the Legislature of any State, the Executive thereof may make temporary Appointments until the next Meeting of the Legislature, which shall then fill such Vacancies.*

No Person shall be a Senator who shall not have attained to the Age of thirty Years, and been nine Years a Citizen of the United States, and who shall not, when elected, be an Inhabitant of that State for which he shall be chosen.

The Vice President of the United States shall be President of the Senate, but shall have no Vote, unless they be equally divided.

The Senate shall chuse their other Officers, and also a President pro tempore, in the Absence of the Vice President, or when he shall exercise the Office of President of the United States.

The Senate shall have the sole Power to try all Impeachments. When sitting for that Purpose, they shall be on Oath or Affirmation. When the President of the United States is tried, the Chief Justice shall preside: And no Person shall be convicted without the Concurrence of two thirds of the Members present.

Judgment in Cases of Impeachment shall not extend further than to removal from Office, and disqualification to hold and enjoy any Office of honor, Trust or Profit under the United States: but the Party convicted shall nevertheless be liable and subject to Indictment, Trial, Judgment and Punishment, according to Law.

Section. 4.

The Times, Places and Manner of holding Elections for Senators and Representatives, shall be prescribed in each State by the Legislature thereof; but the Congress may at any time by Law make or alter such Regulations, except as to the Places of chusing Senators.

The Congress shall assemble at least once in every Year, and such Meeting shall *be on the first Monday in December*, unless they shall by Law appoint a different Day.

Section. 5.

Each House shall be the Judge of the Elections, Returns and Qualifications of its own Members, and a Majority of each shall constitute a Quorum to do Business; but a smaller Number may adjourn from day to day, and may be authorized to compel the Attendance of absent Members, in such Manner, and under such Penalties as each House may provide.

Each House may determine the Rules of its Proceedings, punish its Members for disorderly Behaviour, and, with the Concurrence of two thirds, expel a Member.

Each House shall keep a Journal of its Proceedings, and from time to time publish the same, excepting such Parts as may in their Judgment require Secrecy; and the Yeas and Nays of the Members of either House on any question shall, at the Desire of one fifth of those Present, be entered on the Journal.

Neither House, during the Session of Congress, shall, without the Consent of the other, adjourn for more than three days, nor to any other Place than that in which the two Houses shall be sitting.

Section. 6.

The Senators and Representatives shall receive a Compensation for their Services, to be ascertained by Law, and paid out of the Treasury of the United States. They shall in all Cases, except Treason, Felony and Breach of the Peace, be privileged from Arrest during their Attendance at the Session of their respective Houses, and in going to and returning from the same; and for any Speech or Debate in either House, they shall not be questioned in any other Place.

No Senator or Representative shall, during the Time for which he was elected, be appointed to any civil Office under the Authority of the United States, which shall have been created, or the Emoluments whereof shall have been encreased during such time; and no Person holding any Office under the United States, shall be a Member of either House during his Continuance in Office.

Section. 7.

All Bills for raising Revenue shall originate in the House of Representatives; but the Senate may propose or concur with Amendments as on other Bills.

Every Bill which shall have passed the House of Representatives and the Senate, shall, before it become a Law, be presented to the President of the United States: If he approve he shall sign it, but if not he shall return it, with his Objections to that House in which it shall have originated, who shall enter the Objections at large on their Journal, and proceed to reconsider it. If after such Reconsideration two thirds of that House shall agree to pass the Bill, it shall be sent, together with the Objections, to the other House, by which it shall likewise be reconsidered, and if approved by two thirds of that House, it shall become a Law. But in all such Cases the Votes of both Houses shall be determined by yeas and Nays, and the Names of the Persons voting for and against the Bill shall be entered on the Journal of each House respectively. If any Bill shall not be returned by the President within ten Days (Sundays excepted) after it shall have been presented to him, the Same shall be a Law, in like Manner as if he had signed it, unless the Congress by their Adjournment prevent its Return, in which Case it shall not be a Law.

Every Order, Resolution, or Vote to which the Concurrence of the Senate and House of Representatives may be necessary (except on a question of Adjournment) shall be presented to the President of the United States; and before the Same shall take Effect, shall be approved by him, or being disapproved by him, shall be repassed by two thirds of the Senate and House of Representatives, according to the Rules and Limitations prescribed in the Case of a Bill.

Section. 8.

The Congress shall have Power To lay and collect Taxes, Duties, Imposts and Excises, to pay the Debts and provide for the common Defence and general Welfare of the United States; but all Duties, Imposts and Excises shall be uniform throughout the United States;

To borrow Money on the credit of the United States;

To regulate Commerce with foreign Nations, and among the several States, and with the Indian Tribes;

To establish an uniform Rule of Naturalization, and uniform Laws on the subject of Bankruptcies throughout the United States;

To coin Money, regulate the Value thereof, and of foreign Coin, and fix the Standard of Weights and Measures;

To provide for the Punishment of counterfeiting the Securities and current Coin of the United States;

To establish Post Offices and post Roads;

To promote the Progress of Science and useful Arts, by securing for limited Times to Authors and Inventors the exclusive Right to their respective Writings and Discoveries;

To constitute Tribunals inferior to the supreme Court;

To define and punish Piracies and Felonies committed on the high Seas, and Offences against the Law of Nations;

To declare War, grant Letters of Marque and Reprisal, and make Rules concerning Captures on Land and Water;

To raise and support Armies, but no Appropriation of Money to that Use shall be for a longer Term than two Years;

To provide and maintain a Navy;

To make Rules for the Government and Regulation of the land and naval Forces;

To provide for calling forth the Militia to execute the Laws of the Union, suppress Insurrections and repel Invasions;

To provide for organizing, arming, and disciplining, the Militia, and for governing such Part of them as may be employed in the Service of the United States, reserving to the States respectively, the Appointment of the Officers, and the Authority of training the Militia according to the discipline prescribed by Congress;

To exercise exclusive Legislation in all Cases whatsoever, over such District (not exceeding ten Miles square) as may, by Cession of particular States, and the Acceptance of Congress, become the Seat of the Government of the United States, and to exercise like Authority over all Places purchased by the Consent of the Legislature of the State in which the Same shall be, for the Erection of Forts, Magazines, Arsenals, dock-Yards, and other needful Buildings;--And

To make all Laws which shall be necessary and proper for carrying into Execution the foregoing Powers, and all other Powers vested by this Constitution in the Government of the United States, or in any Department or Officer thereof.

Section. 9.

The Migration or Importation of such Persons as any of the States now existing shall think proper to admit, shall not be prohibited by the Congress prior to the Year one thousand eight hundred and eight, but a Tax or duty may be imposed on such Importation, not exceeding ten dollars for each Person.

The Privilege of the Writ of Habeas Corpus shall not be suspended, unless when in Cases of Rebellion or Invasion the public Safety may require it.

No Bill of Attainder or ex post facto Law shall be passed.

No Capitation, or other direct, Tax shall be laid, *unless in Proportion to the Census or enumeration herein before directed to be taken.*

No Tax or Duty shall be laid on Articles exported from any State.

No Preference shall be given by any Regulation of Commerce or Revenue to the Ports of one State over those of another; nor shall Vessels bound to, or from, one State, be obliged to enter, clear, or pay Duties in another.

No Money shall be drawn from the Treasury, but in Consequence of Appropriations made by Law; and a regular Statement and Account of the Receipts and Expenditures of all public Money shall be published from time to time.

No Title of Nobility shall be granted by the United States: And no Person holding any Office of Profit or Trust under them, shall, without the Consent of the Congress, accept of any present, Emolument, Office, or Title, of any kind whatever, from any King, Prince, or foreign State.

Section. 10.

No State shall enter into any Treaty, Alliance, or Confederation; grant Letters of Marque and Reprisal; coin Money; emit Bills of Credit; make any Thing but gold and silver Coin a Tender in Payment of Debts; pass any Bill of Attainder, ex post facto Law, or Law impairing the Obligation of Contracts, or grant any Title of Nobility.

No State shall, without the Consent of the Congress, lay any Imposts or Duties on Imports or Exports, except what may be absolutely necessary for executing it's inspection Laws: and the net Produce of all Duties and Imposts, laid by any State on Imports or Exports, shall be for the Use of the Treasury of the United States; and all such Laws shall be subject to the Revision and Controul of the Congress.

No State shall, without the Consent of Congress, lay any Duty of Tonnage, keep Troops, or Ships of War in time of Peace, enter into any Agreement or Compact with another State, or with a foreign Power, or engage in War, unless actually invaded, or in such imminent Danger as will not admit of delay.

Article. II.

Section. 1.

The executive Power shall be vested in a President of the United States of America. He shall hold his Office during the Term of four Years, and, together with the Vice President, chosen for the same Term, be elected, as follows:

Each State shall appoint, in such Manner as the Legislature thereof may direct, a Number of Electors, equal to the whole Number of Senators and Representatives to which the State may be entitled in the Congress: but no Senator or Representative, or Person holding an Office of Trust or Profit under the United States, shall be appointed an Elector.

The Electors shall meet in their respective States, and vote by Ballot for two Persons, of whom one at least shall not be an Inhabitant of the same State with themselves. And they shall make a List of all the Persons voted for, and of the Number of Votes for each; which List they shall sign and certify, and transmit sealed to the Seat of the Government of the United States, directed to the President of the Senate. The President of the Senate shall, in the Presence of the Senate and House of Representatives, open all the Certificates, and the Votes shall then be counted. The Person having the greatest Number of Votes shall be the President, if such Number be a Majority of the whole Number of Electors appointed; and if there be more than one who have such Majority, and have an equal Number of Votes, then the House of Representatives shall immediately chuse by Ballot one of them for President; and if no Person have a Majority, then from the five highest on the List the said House shall in like Manner chuse the President. But in chusing the President, the Votes shall be taken by States, the Representation from each State having one Vote; A quorum for this purpose shall consist of a Member or Members from two thirds of the States, and a Majority of all the States shall be necessary to a Choice. In every Case, after the Choice of the President, the Person having the greatest Number of Votes of the Electors shall be the Vice President. But if there should remain two or more who have equal Votes, the Senate shall chuse from them by Ballot the Vice President.

The Congress may determine the Time of chusing the Electors, and the Day on which they shall give their Votes; which Day shall be the same throughout the United States.

No Person except a natural born Citizen, or a Citizen of the United States, at the time of the Adoption of this Constitution, shall be eligible to the Office of President; neither shall any Person be eligible to that Office who shall not have attained to the Age of thirty five Years, and been fourteen Years a Resident within the United States.

In Case of the Removal of the President from Office, or of his Death, Resignation, or Inability to discharge the Powers and Duties of the said Office, the Same shall devolve on the Vice President, and the Congress may by Law provide for the Case of Removal, Death, Resignation or Inability, both of the President and Vice President, declaring what Officer shall then act as President, and such Officer shall act accordingly, until the Disability be removed, or a President shall be elected.

The President shall, at stated Times, receive for his Services, a Compensation, which shall neither be increased nor diminished during the Period for which he shall have been elected, and he shall not receive within that Period any other Emolument from the United States, or any of them.

Before he enter on the Execution of his Office, he shall take the following Oath or Affirmation:--"I do solemnly swear (or affirm) that I will faithfully execute the Office of President of the United States, and will to the best of my Ability, preserve, protect and defend the Constitution of the United States."

Section. 2.

The President shall be Commander in Chief of the Army and Navy of the United States, and of the Militia of the several States, when called into the actual Service of the United States; he may require the Opinion, in writing, of the principal Officer in each of the executive Departments, upon any Subject relating to the Duties of their respective Offices, and he shall have Power to grant Reprieves and Pardons for Offences against the United States, except in Cases of Impeachment.

He shall have Power, by and with the Advice and Consent of the Senate, to make Treaties, provided two thirds of the Senators present concur; and he shall nominate, and by and with the Advice and Consent of the Senate, shall appoint Ambassadors, other public Ministers and Consuls, Judges of the supreme Court, and all other Officers of the United States, whose Appointments are not herein otherwise provided for, and which shall be established by Law: but the Congress may by Law vest the Appointment of such inferior Officers, as they think proper, in the President alone, in the Courts of Law, or in the Heads of Departments.

The President shall have Power to fill up all Vacancies that may happen during the Recess of the Senate, by granting Commissions which shall expire at the End of their next Session.

Section. 3.

He shall from time to time give to the Congress Information of the State of the Union, and recommend to their Consideration such Measures as he shall judge necessary and expedient; he may, on extraordinary Occasions, convene both Houses, or either of them, and in Case of Disagreement between them, with Respect to the Time of Adjournment, he may adjourn them to such Time as he shall think proper; he shall receive Ambassadors and other public Ministers; he shall take Care that the Laws be faithfully executed, and shall Commission all the Officers of the United States.

Section. 4.

The President, Vice President and all civil Officers of the United States, shall be removed from Office on Impeachment for, and Conviction of, Treason, Bribery, or other high Crimes and Misdemeanors.

Article III.

Section. 1.

The judicial Power of the United States shall be vested in one supreme Court, and in such inferior Courts as the Congress may from time to time ordain and establish. The Judges, both of the supreme and inferior Courts, shall hold their Offices during good Behaviour, and shall, at stated Times, receive for their Services a Compensation, which shall not be diminished during their Continuance in Office.

Section. 2.

The judicial Power shall extend to all Cases, in Law and Equity, arising under this Constitution, the Laws of the United States, and Treaties made, or which shall be made, under their Authority;--to all Cases affecting Ambassadors, other public Ministers and Consuls;--to all Cases of admiralty and maritime Jurisdiction;--to Controversies to which the United States shall be a Party;--to Controversies between two or more States;-- *between a State and Citizens of another State*,--between Citizens of different States,--between Citizens of the same State claiming Lands under Grants of different States, and between a State, or the Citizens thereof, and foreign States, Citizens or Subjects.

In all Cases affecting Ambassadors, other public Ministers and Consuls, and those in which a State shall be Party, the supreme Court shall have original Jurisdiction. In all the other Cases before mentioned, the supreme Court shall have appellate

Jurisdiction, both as to Law and Fact, with such Exceptions, and under such Regulations as the Congress shall make.

The Trial of all Crimes, except in Cases of Impeachment, shall be by Jury; and such Trial shall be held in the State where the said Crimes shall have been committed; but when not committed within any State, the Trial shall be at such Place or Places as the Congress may by Law have directed.

Section. 3.

Treason against the United States, shall consist only in levying War against them, or in adhering to their Enemies, giving them Aid and Comfort. No Person shall be convicted of Treason unless on the Testimony of two Witnesses to the same overt Act, or on Confession in open Court.

The Congress shall have Power to declare the Punishment of Treason, but no Attainder of Treason shall work Corruption of Blood, or Forfeiture except during the Life of the Person attainted.

Article. IV.

Section. 1.

Full Faith and Credit shall be given in each State to the public Acts, Records, and judicial Proceedings of every other State. And the Congress may by general Laws prescribe the Manner in which such Acts, Records and Proceedings shall be proved, and the Effect thereof.

Section. 2.

The Citizens of each State shall be entitled to all Privileges and Immunities of Citizens in the several States.

A Person charged in any State with Treason, Felony, or other Crime, who shall flee from Justice, and be found in another State, shall on Demand of the executive Authority of the State from which he fled, be delivered up, to be removed to the State having Jurisdiction of the Crime.

No Person held to Service or Labour in one State, under the Laws thereof, escaping into another, shall, in Consequence of any Law or Regulation therein, be discharged from such Service or Labour, but shall be delivered up on Claim of the Party to whom such Service or Labour may be due.

Section. 3.

New States may be admitted by the Congress into this Union; but no new State shall be formed or erected within the Jurisdiction of any other State; nor any State be formed by the Junction of two or more States, or Parts of States, without the Consent of the Legislatures of the States concerned as well as of the Congress.

The Congress shall have Power to dispose of and make all needful Rules and Regulations respecting the Territory or other Property belonging to the United States; and nothing in this Constitution shall be so construed as to Prejudice any Claims of the United States, or of any particular State.

Section. 4.

The United States shall guarantee to every State in this Union a Republican Form of Government, and shall protect each of them against Invasion; and on Application of the Legislature, or of the Executive (when the Legislature cannot be convened), against domestic Violence.

Article. V.

The Congress, whenever two thirds of both Houses shall deem it necessary, shall propose Amendments to this Constitution, or, on the Application of the Legislatures of two thirds of the several States, shall call a Convention for proposing Amendments, which, in either Case, shall be valid to all Intents and Purposes, as Part of this Constitution, when ratified by the Legislatures of three fourths of the several States, or by Conventions in three fourths thereof, as the one or the other Mode of Ratification may be proposed by the Congress; Provided that no Amendment which may be made prior to the Year One thousand eight hundred and eight shall in any Manner affect the first and fourth Clauses in the Ninth Section of the first Article; and that no State, without its Consent, shall be deprived of its equal Suffrage in the Senate.

Article. VI.

All Debts contracted and Engagements entered into, before the Adoption of this Constitution, shall be as valid against the United States under this Constitution, as under the Confederation.

This Constitution, and the Laws of the United States which shall be made in Pursuance thereof; and all Treaties made, or which shall be made, under the Authority of the United States, shall be the supreme Law of the Land; and the Judges in every State shall be bound thereby, any Thing in the Constitution or Laws of any State to the Contrary notwithstanding.

The Senators and Representatives before mentioned, and the Members of the several State Legislatures, and all executive and judicial Officers, both of the United States and of the several States, shall be bound by Oath or Affirmation, to support this Constitution; but no religious Test shall ever be required as a Qualification to any Office or public Trust under the United States.

Article. VII.

The Ratification of the Conventions of nine States, shall be sufficient for the Establishment of this Constitution between the States so ratifying the Same.

[Signed on September 17, 1787. The names of the signing delegates to the Constitutional Convention have been omitted.]

THE AMENDMENTS

Amendment I

Congress shall make no law respecting an establishment of religion, or prohibiting the free exercise thereof; or abridging the freedom of speech, or of the press; or the right of the people peaceably to assemble, and to petition the government for a redress of grievances.

Amendment II

A well regulated militia, being necessary to the security of a free state, the right of the people to keep and bear arms, shall not be infringed.

Amendment III

No soldier shall, in time of peace be quartered in any house, without the consent of the owner, nor in time of war, but in a manner to be prescribed by law.

Amendment IV

The right of the people to be secure in their persons, houses, papers, and effects, against unreasonable searches and seizures, shall not be violated, and no warrants shall issue, but upon probable cause, supported by oath or affirmation, and particularly describing the place to be searched, and the persons or things to be seized.

Amendment V

No person shall be held to answer for a capital, or otherwise infamous crime, unless on a presentment or indictment of a grand jury, except in cases arising in the land or naval forces, or in the militia, when in actual service in time of war or public danger; nor shall any person be subject for the same offense to be twice put in jeopardy of life or limb; nor shall be compelled in any criminal case to be a witness against himself, nor be deprived of life, liberty, or property, without due process of law; nor shall private property be taken for public use, without just compensation.

Amendment VI

In all criminal prosecutions, the accused shall enjoy the right to a speedy and public trial, by an impartial jury of the state and district wherein the crime shall have been committed, which district shall have been previously ascertained by law, and to be informed of the nature and cause of the accusation; to be confronted with the witnesses against him; to have compulsory process for obtaining witnesses in his favor, and to have the assistance of counsel for his defense.

Amendment VII

In suits at common law, where the value in controversy shall exceed twenty dollars, the right of trial by jury shall be preserved, and no fact tried by a jury, shall be otherwise reexamined in any court of the United States, than according to the rules of the common law.

Amendment VIII

Excessive bail shall not be required, nor excessive fines imposed, nor cruel and unusual punishments inflicted.

Amendment IX

The enumeration in the Constitution, of certain rights, shall not be construed to deny or disparage others retained by the people.

Amendment X

The powers not delegated to the United States by the Constitution, nor prohibited by it to the states, are reserved to the states respectively, or to the people.

Amendment XI

The judicial power of the United States shall not be construed to extend to any suit in law or equity, commenced or prosecuted against one of the United States by citizens of another state, or by citizens or subjects of any foreign state.

Amendment XII

The electors shall meet in their respective states and vote by ballot for President and Vice-President, one of whom, at least, shall not be an inhabitant of the same state with themselves; they shall name in their ballots the person voted for as President, and in distinct ballots the person voted for as Vice-President, and they shall make distinct lists of all persons voted for as President, and of all persons voted for as Vice-President, and of the number of votes for each, which lists they shall sign and certify, and transmit sealed to the seat of the government of the United States, directed to the President of the Senate;--The President of the Senate shall, in the presence of the Senate and House of Representatives, open all the certificates and the votes shall then be counted;--the person having the greatest number of votes for President, shall be the President, if such number be a majority of the whole number of electors appointed; and if no person have such majority, then from the persons having the highest numbers not exceeding three on the list of those voted for as President, the House of Representatives shall choose immediately, by ballot, the President. But in choosing the President, the votes shall be taken by states, the representation from each state having one vote; a quorum for this purpose shall consist of a member or members from two-thirds of the states, and a majority of all the states shall be necessary to a choice. *And if the House of Representatives shall not choose a President whenever the right of choice shall devolve upon them, before the fourth day of March next following, then the Vice-President shall act as President, as in the case of the death or other constitutional disability of the President.* The person having the greatest number of votes as Vice-President, shall be the Vice-President, if such number be a majority of the whole number of electors appointed, and if no person have a majority, then from the two highest numbers on the list, the Senate shall choose the Vice-President; a quorum for the purpose shall consist of two-thirds of the whole number of Senators, and a majority of the whole number shall be necessary to a choice. But no person constitutionally ineligible to the office of President shall be eligible to that of Vice-President of the United States.

Amendment XIII

Section 1.
Neither slavery nor involuntary servitude, except as a punishment for crime whereof the party shall have been duly convicted, shall exist within the United States, or any place subject to their jurisdiction.

Section 2.
Congress shall have power to enforce this article by appropriate legislation.

Amendment XIV

Section 1.
All persons born or naturalized in the United States, and subject to the jurisdiction thereof, are citizens of the United States and of the state wherein they reside. No state shall make or enforce any law which shall abridge the privileges or immunities of citizens of the United States; nor shall any state deprive any person of life, liberty, or property, without due process of law; nor deny to any person within its jurisdiction the equal protection of the laws.

Section 2.
Representatives shall be apportioned among the several states according to their respective numbers, counting the whole number of persons in each state, excluding Indians not taxed. But when the right to vote at any election for the choice of electors for President and Vice President of the United States, Representatives in Congress, the executive and judicial officers of a state, or the members of the legislature thereof, is denied to any of the *male* inhabitants of such state, *being twenty-one years of age*, and citizens of the United States, or in any way abridged, except for participation in rebellion, or other crime, the basis of representation therein shall be reduced in the proportion which the number of such male citizens shall bear to the whole number of male citizens twenty-one years of age in such state.

Section 3.
No person shall be a Senator or Representative in Congress, or elector of President and Vice President, or hold any office, civil or military, under the United States, or under any state, who, having previously taken an oath, as a member of Congress, or as an officer of the United States, or as a member of any state legislature, or as an executive or judicial officer of any state, to support the Constitution of the United States, shall have engaged in insurrection or rebellion against the same, or given aid or comfort to the enemies thereof. But Congress may by a vote of two-thirds of each House, remove such disability.

Section 4.
The validity of the public debt of the United States, authorized by law, including debts incurred for payment of pensions and bounties for services in suppressing

insurrection or rebellion, shall not be questioned. But neither the United States nor any state shall assume or pay any debt or obligation incurred in aid of insurrection or rebellion against the United States, or any claim for the loss or emancipation of any slave; but all such debts, obligations and claims shall be held illegal and void.

Section 5.
The Congress shall have power to enforce, by appropriate legislation, the provisions of this article.

Amendment XV

Section 1.
The right of citizens of the United States to vote shall not be denied or abridged by the United States or by any state on account of race, color, or previous condition of servitude.

Section 2.
The Congress shall have power to enforce this article by appropriate legislation.

Amendment XVI

The Congress shall have power to lay and collect taxes on incomes, from whatever source derived, without apportionment among the several states, and without regard to any census or enumeration.

Amendment XVII

The Senate of the United States shall be composed of two Senators from each state, elected by the people thereof, for six years; and each Senator shall have one vote. The electors in each state shall have the qualifications requisite for electors of the most numerous branch of the state legislatures.

When vacancies happen in the representation of any state in the Senate, the executive authority of such state shall issue writs of election to fill such vacancies: Provided, that the legislature of any state may empower the executive thereof to make temporary appointments until the people fill the vacancies by election as the legislature may direct.

This amendment shall not be so construed as to affect the election or term of any Senator chosen before it becomes valid as part of the Constitution.

Amendment XVIII

Section 1.
After one year from the ratification of this article the manufacture, sale, or transportation of intoxicating liquors within, the importation thereof into, or the exportation thereof from the United States and all territory subject to the jurisdiction thereof for beverage purposes is hereby prohibited.

Section 2.
The Congress and the several states shall have concurrent power to enforce this article by appropriate legislation.

Section 3.
This article shall be inoperative unless it shall have been ratified as an amendment to the Constitution by the legislatures of the several states, as provided in the Constitution, within seven years from the date of the submission hereof to the states by the Congress.

Amendment XIX

The right of citizens of the United States to vote shall not be denied or abridged by the United States or by any state on account of sex.

Congress shall have power to enforce this article by appropriate legislation.

Amendment XX

Section 1.
The terms of the President and Vice President shall end at noon on the 20th day of January, and the terms of Senators and Representatives at noon on the 3d day of January, of the years in which such terms would have ended if this article had not been ratified; and the terms of their successors shall then begin.

Section 2.
The Congress shall assemble at least once in every year, and such meeting shall begin at noon on the 3d day of January, unless they shall by law appoint a different day.

Section 3.
If, at the time fixed for the beginning of the term of the President, the President elect shall have died, the Vice President elect shall become President. If a President shall not have been chosen before the time fixed for the beginning of his term, or if the President elect shall have failed to qualify, then the Vice President elect shall act as President until a President shall have qualified; and the Congress may by law provide for the case wherein neither a President elect nor a Vice President elect

shall have qualified, declaring who shall then act as President, or the manner in which one who is to act shall be selected, and such person shall act accordingly until a President or Vice President shall have qualified.

Section 4.
The Congress may by law provide for the case of the death of any of the persons from whom the House of Representatives may choose a President whenever the right of choice shall have devolved upon them, and for the case of the death of any of the persons from whom the Senate may choose a Vice President whenever the right of choice shall have devolved upon them.

Section 5.
Sections 1 and 2 shall take effect on the 15th day of October following the ratification of this article.

Section 6.
This article shall be inoperative unless it shall have been ratified as an amendment to the Constitution by the legislatures of three-fourths of the several states within seven years from the date of its submission.

Amendment XXI

Section 1.
The eighteenth article of amendment to the Constitution of the United States is hereby repealed.

Section 2.
The transportation or importation into any state, territory, or possession of the United States for delivery or use therein of intoxicating liquors, in violation of the laws thereof, is hereby prohibited.

Section 3.
This article shall be inoperative unless it shall have been ratified as an amendment to the Constitution by conventions in the several states, as provided in the Constitution, within seven years from the date of the submission hereof to the states by the Congress.

Amendment XXII

Section 1.
No person shall be elected to the office of the President more than twice, and no person who has held the office of President, or acted as President, for more than two years of a term to which some other person was elected President shall be elected to the office of the President more than once. But this article shall not apply to any person holding the office of President when this article was proposed by the Congress, and shall not prevent any person who may be holding the office of

President, or acting as President, during the term within which this article becomes operative from holding the office of President or acting as President during the remainder of such term.

Section 2.
This article shall be inoperative unless it shall have been ratified as an amendment to the Constitution by the legislatures of three-fourths of the several states within seven years from the date of its submission to the states by the Congress.

Amendment XXIII

Section 1.
The District constituting the seat of government of the United States shall appoint in such manner as the Congress may direct:

A number of electors of President and Vice President equal to the whole number of Senators and Representatives in Congress to which the District would be entitled if it were a state, but in no event more than the least populous state; they shall be in addition to those appointed by the states, but they shall be considered, for the purposes of the election of President and Vice President, to be electors appointed by a state; and they shall meet in the District and perform such duties as provided by the twelfth article of amendment.

Section 2.
The Congress shall have power to enforce this article by appropriate legislation.

Amendment XXIV

Section 1.
The right of citizens of the United States to vote in any primary or other election for President or Vice President, for electors for President or Vice President, or for Senator or Representative in Congress, shall not be denied or abridged by the United States or any state by reason of failure to pay any poll tax or other tax.

Section 2.
The Congress shall have power to enforce this article by appropriate legislation.

Amendment XXV

Section 1.
In case of the removal of the President from office or of his death or resignation, the Vice President shall become President.

Section 2.
Whenever there is a vacancy in the office of the Vice President, the President shall nominate a Vice President who shall take office upon confirmation by a majority vote of both Houses of Congress.

Section 3.
Whenever the President transmits to the President pro tempore of the Senate and the Speaker of the House of Representatives his written declaration that he is unable to discharge the powers and duties of his office, and until he transmits to them a written declaration to the contrary, such powers and duties shall be discharged by the Vice President as Acting President.

Section 4.
Whenever the Vice President and a majority of either the principal officers of the executive departments or of such other body as Congress may by law provide, transmit to the President pro tempore of the Senate and the Speaker of the House of Representatives their written declaration that the President is unable to discharge the powers and duties of his office, the Vice President shall immediately assume the powers and duties of the office as Acting President.

Thereafter, when the President transmits to the President pro tempore of the Senate and the Speaker of the House of Representatives his written declaration that no inability exists, he shall resume the powers and duties of his office unless the Vice President and a majority of either the principal officers of the executive department or of such other body as Congress may by law provide, transmit within four days to the President pro tempore of the Senate and the Speaker of the House of Representatives their written declaration that the President is unable to discharge the powers and duties of his office. Thereupon Congress shall decide the issue, assembling within forty-eight hours for that purpose if not in session. If the Congress, within twenty-one days after receipt of the latter written declaration, or, if Congress is not in session, within twenty-one days after Congress is required to assemble, determines by two-thirds vote of both Houses that the President is unable to discharge the powers and duties of his office, the Vice President shall continue to discharge the same as Acting President; otherwise, the President shall resume the powers and duties of his office.

Amendment XXVI

Section 1.
The right of citizens of the United States, who are 18 years of age or older, to vote, shall not be denied or abridged by the United States or any state on account of age.

Section 2.
The Congress shall have the power to enforce this article by appropriate legislation.

Amendment XXVII

No law, varying the compensation for the services of the Senators and Representatives, shall take effect, until an election of Representatives shall have intervened.

TABLE OF CASES

INDEX

D

F

G

H

I

J

K

L

M

N

O

P

Q

R

S

T

U

V

W

Y

www.ingramcontent.com/pod-product-compliance
Lightning Source LLC
LaVergne TN
LVHW062110200926
848484LV00007B/1628
* 9 7 8 1 6 0 0 4 2 1 3 2 7 *